Debating Unemployment Policy

In 2008 the world experienced the Great Recession, a financial and economic crisis of enormous proportions and the greatest economic downturn since the 1930s. In its wake, unemployment became a key preoccupation of West European publics and politicians. This comparative study considers the policy debates surrounding unemployment in the United Kingdom, Germany, France, Italy, Denmark and Switzerland since 2008. With an over-arching focus on drawing out cross-national commonalities and differences, the authors ask whether patterns of political communication vary across countries. Their analysis draws on interviews with labour market policy-makers in the six selected countries, and paints a revealing picture. Appealing to researchers in comparative politics, political communication and welfare state research, this book will also interest practitioners involved in labour market policy.

Laurent Bernhard is a senior researcher at the Swiss Centre for Expertise in the Social Sciences (FORS), which is based at the University of Lausanne.

Flavia Fossati is Assistant Professor for Social Policy at the University of Vienna. Her research interests include social, labour market and migration policy, labour market integration and discrimination research.

Regula Hänggli is a full professor specialized in political communication at the University of Fribourg (Switzerland). She is also a member of a federal expert group addressing the digital transformation of our society.

Hanspeter Kriesi holds the Stein Rokkan Chair in Comparative Politics at the European University Institute in Florence. In 2017, he received the Mattei-Dogan Prize. Currently he is working on an ERC project on the political consequences of the Great Recession in Europe.

Debating Unemployment Policy

Political Communication and the Labour Market in Western Europe

Edited by

Laurent Bernhard
University of Lausanne

Flavia Fossati
University of Vienna

Regula Hänggli
University of Fribourg

Hanspeter Kriesi
European University Institute, Florence

CAMBRIDGE
UNIVERSITY PRESS

CAMBRIDGE
UNIVERSITY PRESS

University Printing House, Cambridge CB2 8BS, United Kingdom

One Liberty Plaza, 20th Floor, New York, NY 10006, USA

477 Williamstown Road, Port Melbourne, VIC 3207, Australia

314–321, 3rd Floor, Plot 3, Splendor Forum, Jasola District Centre, New Delhi – 110025, India

79 Anson Road, #06–04/06, Singapore 079906

Cambridge University Press is part of the University of Cambridge.

It furthers the University's mission by disseminating knowledge in the pursuit of education, learning, and research at the highest international levels of excellence.

www.cambridge.org
Information on this title: www.cambridge.org/9781108497510
DOI: 10.1017/9781108609340

First published 2019

Printed and bound in Great Britain by Clays Ltd, Elcograf S.p.A.

A catalogue record for this publication is available from the British Library.

Library of Congress Cataloging-in-Publication Data
Names: Bernhard, Laurent, editor.
Title: Debating unemployment policy : political communication and the labour market in Western Europe / edited by Laurent Bernhard, Flavia Fossati, Regula Hanggli, Hanspeter Kriesi.
Description: Cambridge, United Kingdom ; New York, NY : Cambridge UniversityPress, 2019. | Includes bibliographical references and index.
Identifiers: LCCN 2019008382 | ISBN 9781108497510 (hardback)
Subjects: LCSH: Unemployment – Government policy – European Union countries. | Labor supply – European Union countries. | Communication in politics – European Union countries. | European Union countries – Economic conditions – 21st century. | BISAC: POLITICAL SCIENCE / Government / General.
Classification: LCC HD5764.A6 D4195 2019 | DDC 331.13/77094–dc23
LC record available at https://lccn.loc.gov/2019008382

ISBN 978-1-108-49751-0 Hardback

Contents

Contents

Contributors

LAURENT BERNHARD is a senior researcher at the Swiss Centre for Expertise in the Social Sciences (FORS), University of Lausanne.

CHRISTIAN ELMELUND-PRÆSTEKÆR (PhD) is Head of the Department of Political Science and Public Management at the University of Southern Denmark.

FLAVIA FOSSATI is Assistant Professor in Social Policy at the Political Science Department at the University of Vienna.

REGULA HÄNGGLI is specialized in Political Communication and full professor at the University of Fribourg (Switzerland). She is also a member of the Center for Politics and Communication (Amsterdam).

HANSPETER KRIESI holds the Stein Rokkan Chair in Comparative Politics at the European University Institute in Florence.

RICHARD VAN DER WURFF is Director of the College of Social Sciences (CSS) at the University of Amsterdam.

Part I

The Context Structures and the Policy-specific Debates

1 Introduction

Shaping the Debate on Unemployment and the Labor Market

Hanspeter Kriesi, Laurent Bernhard, Flavia Fossati and Regula Hänggli

In fall 2008, the world has experienced a financial and economic crisis of enormous proportions: the Great Recession. This has been the greatest economic downturn since the Great Depression in the 1930s. In its wake, unemployment became the most important preoccupation of Western European publics and politicians. Even before the crisis hit Western Europe, unemployment had been a chronic problem in the region's countries for many years. As a chronic problem, unemployment did not display the characteristic life-cycles of political issues as suggested by Downs (1972). Contrary to suddenly imposed real or symbolic crises, a chronic problem does not give rise to a cycle of media attention (Neuman 1990). Even if unemployment heavily preoccupied public opinion, it has not normally led to corresponding attention in the media: typically, it was 'a story without a story line'. Under the exceptional circumstances of the Great Recession, however, unemployment not only increased considerably in most countries, it also became exceptionally salient in the media and in the general public. Thus, in May 2010, at a time, when the overall economic situation was already considerably improving, the two most important issues for the European publics according to a Eurobarometer survey were 'unemployment' and 'the economic situation,' mentioned respectively by 48 percent and 40 percent of the populations in the 27 member states of the European Union (EU).[1]

In this volume, we propose to study comparatively the debate on unemployment-related policies in the shadow of this great economic crisis. Comparative studies in political communication are no longer as rare as they used to be (Gurevitch and Blumler 2004); the field has matured. Most comparative studies focus, however, on electoral

---

[1] Eurobarometer 73.4 (Fieldwork: May 2010; Publication: August 2010).

3

campaigns (e.g., Swanson and Mancini 1996, Esser and Strömbäck 2012a), news production (e.g., Esser 2008, Esser and Strömbäck 2012b), or media systems (e.g., Hallin and Mancini 2004, Esser et al. 2012). The analytical framework guiding comparison, in turn, tends to home in on country characteristics, most importantly on a country's political culture and communication culture (Hallin and Mancini 2004, Pfetsch 2003, 2004, Gurevitch and Blumler 2004, Couldry and Hepp 2012). It is very unusual for a comparative study to focus on a specific policy domain. We actually know of only two comparative studies that take as their focus the political communication in a given policy domain, the comparative study of the abortion discourse by Ferree et al. (2002) and the comparative study of globalization-related policies by Helbling et al. (2012).

As a study of political communication in unemployment-related policies, our investigation is situated at the crossroads of political communication and policy analysis: it compares the political debates on labor-market policy in the shadow of the Great Recession, and the way the most important political actors of this policy domain tried to shape and influence it. Our study takes a *supply side perspective* by examining the ways in which political actors try to shape the public debates on the issue of unemployment (Baglioni et al. 2008). It is devoted to the politicization of the problem of unemployment through communicative action by collective actors in the public space. We explore two key facets about the public debates on unemployment-related issues. On the one hand, we focus on the political actors and ask how they shape the debate on unemployment, i.e., we study the role played by different types of actors, by the configuration of power among the actors participating in the debate, by their action repertoires, their belief systems and their framing strategies – assuming that all these aspects are conditioned by the arena, in which the actors intervene. On the other hand, we ask about the policy-specific characteristics which are relevant for the debate. What makes an issue salient and what kind of issue characteristics contribute to its politicization in a given country context?

Against this background, this book is concerned with commonalities and differences at the contextual level. By looking at policy-specific debates in Western Europe, we ask whether patterns of political communication vary across countries. This in turn begs the question about the increased uniformity of communication practices throughout the Western world. Indeed, this topic has attracted a lot of scholarly attention among comparativists in recent years (Esser and Hanitzsch 2013, Pfetsch 2014). According to the convergence thesis, global trends such as technological advances, the commercialization and the professionalization of the media should result in homogeneous outcomes. However, diverging patterns of cross-national variations may still be available due to cultural and political peculiarities. To date, empirical evidence has not provided any conclusive findings (Boczkowski et al. 2011). In the framework of the present empirical analysis, we strive for contributing to this topical academic debate. Although both contents and methodological approaches vary considerably throughout this book, all chapters are bound together by their overarching interest in systematically considering the question of cross-national similarities and dissimilarities.

To that end, we shall compare the unemployment debates in six Western European countries – Denmark, France, Germany, Italy, Switzerland, and the United Kingdom (UK). As far as we know, this is the first time that politicians' communication strategies for such a large number of public debates are compared. Our country selection has been guided, on the one hand, by the existing differences in economic regimes in Western Europe in general and in labor-market regimes in particular, and, on the other hand, by the differences between media systems. In terms of the 'varieties of capitalism' literature (Hall and Soskice 2001, Schmidt 2009), our analysis includes a liberal market economy (LME) – the UK; two continental coordinated market economies (CME) – Switzerland and Germany; a Nordic coordinated market economy – Denmark; and two state-influenced market economies (SME) – France and Italy. In terms of the trajectories of labor-market regimes (Thelen 2012), we have selected three dualization countries – Germany, France and Italy; two flexicurity countries – Switzerland and Denmark; and a deregulation case – the UK. As far as the media systems distinguished by Hallin and Mancini (2004) are concerned, we have in our selection two Mediterranean or polarized pluralist models – France and Italy; a North Atlantic or liberal model – the UK; and three North/Central European or democratic corporatist models – Denmark, Germany, and Switzerland.

As we sought to understand the communication strategies of the actors involved in these debates, we came to realize that we needed to know quite a bit about the country-specific labor-market policies in order to make sense of what was going on in these debates – a seeming disorder of country-specific debates, a *Babylonian confusion*. If someone had picked up a local newspaper or watched national news broadcasts in any one of the countries covered by our study in fall 2010, chances would have been great that the reader would have come across a story about the problems of the national labor market and the government's attempt to deal with it. But, chances would also have been very great that the way the problems were presented in the media, the way the government tried to deal with them, and the arguments exchanged between political actors in the debate would have been quite country-specific. In Italy, for example, people were talking about the 'precari' – outsiders to the labor market, a concept which has been unknown to a foreign audience. In the UK, the debate in fall 2010 was focused on 'spending reviews' and 'universal credits,' terms which would have left foreigners perplexed. Similarly in Germany, 'Hartz IV' had become a household term but would have surely been a complete mystery to other Europeans. The same no doubt applies to the details of Danish activation policies debated in the Denmark's daily news at the time, or to a measure such as the French 'revenu de solidarité active,' which played an important role in French debates on labor-market policy in 2010.

Accordingly, a key lesson we learnt early on in our study is that policy-specific contexts matter a great deal. If we wanted to understand not only what political actors were talking about, but also why they talked about these policies in the way they did, we had to dig deeper into the substance of the labor-market policies. More generally, if we turn to specific policies, comparative studies of political communication cannot replace detailed knowledge of the substantive policies into which political communications are embedded. The context of political communication in this particular case not only includes the overall context of the economic crisis and the national political and communication cultures, but also policy-domain specific institutions and configurations of power as well as policy legacies that, together, decisively shape what is being communicated and how it is communicated.

A second key lesson gleaned during the early part of our study is that salient issues do not automatically translate into intensive public debates. The latter occur only in instances of politicization by political or media actors. This may partly be attributable to the less spectacular increase of unemployment rates as compared to previous major economic down-turns of the 30s and the 70s of the twentieth century. Another explanation may relate to the fact that the Great Recession came in various guises. Hence, related crisis topics such as real estate bubbles, undercapitalized banks, anemic growth rates, and a lack of financial discipline competed for the attention of both political and media actors. In any case, the fact that in 2010 unemployment was a very salient issue does not mean that these actors felt impelled to mobilize the citizen public on this topic. Newspapers may report on unemployment trends every day, they may point to factories closing and individual cases of people who have lost their jobs, or they may discuss the structural origins of unemployment without, however, necessarily discussing policies that would solve the unemployment problem. The politicization of a problem like unemployment presupposes that the problem is not only salient to the general public, but that it will also become part of the political agenda. This means that politicians start to address the problem, that it becomes the object of political conflict, and that the proposed political measures resonate with the general public, i.e., that the general public, as expressed by Schattschneider (1975), is 'socialized' into the conflict and gets actively involved in the debate among the political actors. Without politicization, the problem of unemployment remains an individual predicament for which the unemployed only have to blame themselves.

Policy-related Public Debates on Unemployment

A public debate refers to all public-oriented communication related to a particular issue in a given time frame (Helbling et al. 2012). This definition is close to what Ferree et al. (2002: 9) call "public discourse": "public communication about topics and actors related to either some particular policy domain or to the broader interests and values that are engaged". Following Helbling et al. (2012), we prefer to speak of 'public debate,' as the term better reflects the ongoing confrontation between political actors taking different positions and mobilizing different arguments. Even though public debates are rather open in nature, they are typically focused on a specific problem – such as unemployment.

Public debates about a specific problem extend far beyond the narrow confines of political arenas. They are held in the media and in the public at large and include communications about aspects of the problem which are not directly policy-related. In the case of unemployment, such aspects may include (among others) its overall level and development (e.g., the number of unemployed and trends in the unemployment figures), or individual cases that serve to illustrate its seriousness, discussions of its causes and consequences, or moral evaluations of the situation concerning the problem. In our study, we focus on the policy-related public debate on unemployment, which originates in the political arenas, from where they spill over into the media arenas and the public arena at large. Political arenas correspond to the institutionalized sites of political structuration where policy positions and their justifications are introduced and debated by political actors (Hilgartner and Bosk 1988: 55). Such sites include the electoral arena, the parliamentary arena, the administrative arena, and (in some countries) the direct-democratic arena. These arenas may be national in scope, or they may reach beyond the boundaries of the nation state and include debates in other nation-states or at the

8 *Hanspeter Kriesi, Laurent Bernhard, Flavia Fossati and Regula Hänggli*

Table 1.1 *Distribution of articles: Percentage shares of articles referring to policy measures, referring to policy measures from home country, and involving any kind of political actors or involving political actors from our list*

Articles	Referring to policy measures	From home country	Involving political actors	Involving political actors from list
Germany	37.3	30.4	18.8	14.3
France	25.3	17.6	9.3	4.4
Italy	22.9	15.6	8.5	5.4
Switzerland	26.4	16.4	9.0	3.0
Denmark	22.8	9.4	5.2	2.4
UK	20.8	17.0	7.5	3.6
Total	26.2	18.6	10.2	5.9

Source: Content analysis of a selection of major newspapers and TV news programs during fall 2010.

supranational level. Whatever their nature, political arenas are all focused on policy-related issues.

Unemployment is a topic of great concern to the general public that is widely debated by the public at large. In this debate, policy-related communications about unemployment make up only a relatively minor part. This is shown by the content analysis of the press and TV news coverage of the unemployment debate in the six selected countries during the fall period 2010.[2] *Table 1.1* presents some key results. Only about a quarter of the articles/news items we identified with our search in the press and TV news programs as dealing with problems of unemployment or jobs were actually referring to policy measures. The corresponding share was highest in Germany, where it amounted to more than a third (37.3 percent) of all press articles and TV news items, and it was lowest in the UK, where it corresponded to only roughly one quarter (20.8 percent) of all articles dealing with unemployment and jobs in one way or another. Once we consider that the media not only refer to national policy measures, but also to policies debated in other countries, the share of relevant articles/news items for national policy debates diminishes to less than one quarter

[2] The results reported are based on the content analysis of a large number of newspapers and TV news programs that has been conducted in the framework of the Module 4 of the NCCR-Democracy at the University of Zurich (see Vorläufiger Abschlussbericht Inhaltsanalyse NCCR II Modul 4, Version 7.2.2012. In addition to some country-specific terms, the keyword search for the identification of contributions to the public debate on unemployment in the press and TV news programs of the six countries studied was designed to take up any article with a reference to "unemploy*" or "job*".

overall, and to a range of 30.4 (Germany) to 9.4 (Denmark) percent per country.

In policy-related communications, some actors advocate policy change while some others defend the status quo. The political actors involved in a given debate attempt to control their fellow politicians, the media, and the public in order to impose their specific policy preferences. But political actors are not the only contributors to the policy debate. Indeed, a large part of the contributions to national policy-specific debates is not attributable to political actors at all, but to journalists. In fact, taking journalists' contributions to policy-specific debates into account reduces the share of the overall debate that can be attributed to political actors to no more than 10.2 percent overall, or to 18.8 percent of all unemployment or job-related articles and news items in Germany, and to as little as 5.2 percent in Denmark. Finally, only about half of the contributions by political actors or 5.9 percent of all contributions (varying from 14.3 percent in Germany to 2.4 percent in Denmark) are attributable to actors whom we covered in our project (see next section).

This is to say that the policy-specific debate on unemployment and jobs in times of crisis occupies only a rather limited part of the overall issue-specific debate and that the key political actors controlled an even smaller part of this debate during the period of our study. The large number of articles and news items that talk about unemployment without men-tioning policy measures report above all on factual trends about rising/ declining numbers of unemployed at home and abroad, or they report on estimates about the future trends of unemployment. Other articles and news items that include both information on policy measures and other aspects of unemployment also have a positive or negative tone (see *Figure 1.1*). During our period of observation in fall 2010, these reports were predominantly negative, although there were also some reports on positive trends. Given the extent of the crisis, this overall negative tone is of course not at all surprising. Indeed, the predominantly downbeat tone of reporting applies to all six countries. Even in Switzerland, where the unemployment rate was still very low by interna-tional standards, the great majority of the media reports on the develop-ment of unemployment were pessimistic, which goes a long way toward explaining why the Swiss were much preoccupied about unemployment in general. By contrast, the prognosis reported in the Swiss media was clearly more optimistic (44 percent exclusively positive prognosis) than in all other countries with the (surprising) exception of Italy (with 51 percent exclusively positive prognosis). Particularly bleak was the outlook in the media in the UK, with only 12.6 exclusively positive prognoses.

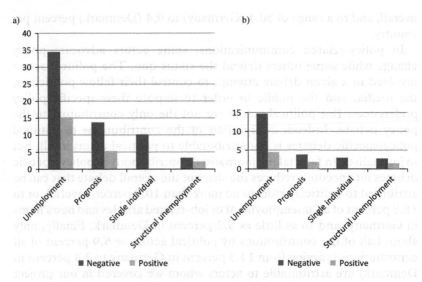

Figure 1.1 Topics covered by the public debate on unemployment and jobs other than policy measures
a) Articles/news items without references to policy measures
b) Articles/news items also including references to policy measures

In addition to reports about the state of unemployment and prognosis of future unemployment trends, the media also reported on the fate of single individuals (almost exclusively pointing out cases of individuals who lost their job). This happened most frequently in France (in 7.5 percent of all articles/news items). Some reports also discussed the two structural problems related to unemployment – youth and long-term unemployment.

Having identified the limits of the contributions of politicians to the public debate on unemployment, we want to point out two advantages of studying public debates from the perspective of political communication strategies. Most empirical analyses to date about the communication strategies of political actors have actually focused on electoral campaigns. As a consequence, the state of the art in this field is mainly restricted to political parties (and the affiliated individual candidates) operating in settings of extraordinarily intense communication. Examining public policy debates has two key advantages over the study of electoral debates: first of all, it presents the advantage of allowing for an analysis of the *full range of political actors*, including not only political parties, but also state actors, business organizations, public interest groups, social movements, think tanks, and research institutes. These actors may contribute to the debates by making verbal claims or by various forms of action enabling them to cross the threshold of public attention and gain access to the media – or the public sphere, which is of crucial importance in the context of public debates. Second, while electoral campaigns constitute moments of extraordinary intensification of political communication, public debates tend to represent much more *'ordinary politics,'* which is characterized by a high degree of routine-based behavior. In other words, the examination of public debates may be better able than electoral campaigns to reflect the political actors' standard communication practice of everyday politics.

The type of political actors who dominated the policy-specific public unemployment debates during our period of observation varies between the six countries. To get an initial idea about the leading players, we have divided the political actors into four broad categories: governments (national and regional) and parties; social partners (employers' associations and unions) and firms; public interest groups/NGOs, academic experts, and think tanks; and international organizations. *Table 1.2* presents the country-specific distributions of the articles and TV news items on these four categories. First of all, this table shows that the weight of the political actors in the policy-specific debate varies from a high of almost two-thirds of the contributions (in Germany and Denmark) to a low of roughly two-fifths (in the UK). Next the table shows that the (national) government and political parties largely dominate all other actors in Germany, and make up more than half

Table 1.2 *Political actors (organizations) involved in the debate on policy measures in home country, by country: Overall percentage share of political actors and percentage distribution of political actors*

	D	UK	DK	F	I	CH	Total
Share of political actors (%)	63.7	41.5	63.3	54.3	56.3	58.4	56.7
N (total)	1618	797	218	514	208	392	3747
Of which:							
Governments/parties	77.0	50.0	52.2	45.9	46.8	41.6	60.4
Social partners/firms	9.0	22.9	21.5	33.2	35.3	42.6	21.3
Public interest/experts/TT	13.4	24.0	25.3	19.1	16.6	12.8	16.8
International organizations	0.7	3.1	1.1	1.9	1.4	3.0	1.6
Total (%)	100.0	100.0	100.0	100.0	100.0	100.0	100.0
N	1030	331	138	279	117	229	2124

of all contributions of political actors in the UK and in Denmark. The dominance of the parties (in government and in opposition) in the German case has already been documented by the analysis of the abortion discourse (Ferree et al. 2002). By contrast, the (national) government and parties are less important in France and Italy, and much less important in Switzerland (where a share of no less than 21.0 percent is attributable to regional governments and cities). In these three countries, the social partners (and firms) played an important role in the public debate during the period under study.

The Crisis as a Common Context Condition of the Debate

We have chosen to study the debate in all six countries during a fixed period – in fall 2010 – in order to hold the overall context of the crisis and the related policy debates constant. As it turns out, not only the initial government responses, but also the economic decline and recovery developed in a strikingly uniform way across Western European countries.

As was the case in all European OECD countries, GDP decline set in at the beginning of 2008 in the six selected countries, accelerated by the end of 2008 and, as illustrated by *Figure 1.2*, reached its nadir in the second and third quarters of 2009. Growth figures improved thereafter, not least because of the effective short-term Keynesian policy

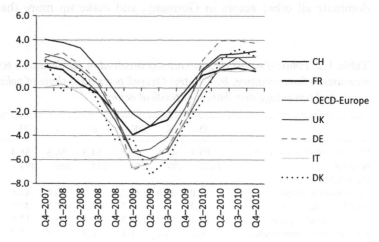

Figure 1.2 GDP growth rates compared to the same quarter of previous year, seasonally adjusted, by country
Source: OECD, quarterly national accounts.

response employed by national governments. By the fourth quarter of 2010, when we observed the public debates, the European OECD countries in general, and our six countries in particular, had all returned to positive growth rates. While the development was largely parallel in all six countries, there was some variation nevertheless: the decline was most pronounced in Denmark, where GDP contraction reached a maximum of −7.3 percent in the second quarter of 2009. It was almost as severe in Germany (−6.9 percent), Italy (−6.7 percent) and the UK (−5.9 percent). By contrast, Switzerland and France were less affected. The recovery was also somewhat uneven. While all six countries were growing again by the first quarter of 2010, Germany, Denmark, and Switzerland had recovered significantly more rapidly than France, Italy, and the UK.

Against this general background, the initial policy responses to the Great Recession by Western European governments went through two stages (see Clasen et al. 2012). First, these governments adopted a moderate, expansionary macroeconomic response. Pontusson and Raess (2012) characterize this response as "liberal Keynesianism" – a (short-term, limited) fiscal stimulus combined with monetary easing. They see a convergence among the five countries they studied (US, UK, France, Sweden, and Germany) on the American model of crisis management, buttressed by the expert consensus on Keynesian demand stimulus (see Farrell and Quiggin 2012). Armingeon (2012), who looks at a larger sample of countries, identified the same response pattern among most of the countries, although he also finds two alternative patterns (absence of response, and contractionary fiscal response). In addition, initial policy responses to the Great Recession were also distinguished by the absence of other kinds of crisis responses that were common, though not uniformly adopted, during the Long Recession of 1974–92. Thus, strikingly, Pontusson and Raess (2012) found hardly any substantial policy responses in the domains of trade, industrial, or labor-market policy.

The first stage of moderate Keynesian responses was short lived, however. Soon it was replaced by a growing focus on public finance concerns, which placed the debate on unemployment in an entirely different context. This second stage was initiated by the Greek crisis which burst onto the international scene in early 2010 (Farrell and Quiggin 2012: 37). Austerity rapidly became the only game in town, and the policy debates we have observed taking place during fall 2010 were generally inspired by the overarching theme of austerity. One might have thought that a crisis of the proportions of the Great Recession constituted a critical juncture ('a window of opportunity'), at which it would become possible to introduce substantial policy reforms in the policy-domains concerned with economic policy in general and labor-market policies in particular. But, surprisingly, at the time of our study, profound policy change was not typically on the agenda of the public debates of labor-market policies in Western Europe. Rather, politicians were muddling through or deepening structural reform attempts that they had been implementing already before the crisis struck. We shall see them mostly debating rather limited modifications of existing legislation. Only in one country, the UK, were they attempting reforms on a larger scale, but even there, these reforms did not deviate from the path labor-market policies had been following already before the crisis.

The lack of fundamental reforms may be less surprising, if we keep in mind that major reforms are highly contingent events. Thus, for the 'window of opportunity' of the crisis to produce major policy reforms, at least three additional conditions need to be fulfilled: first, there have to be major new policy ideas that promise to provide a solution to the problem at hand. Second, these ideas have to be adopted by key political actors, and, third, these actors need to have the capacity to impose themselves. Under extreme conditions such as the Great Recession, politicians face great uncertainty about possible solutions to the problems at hand. With Hall (1997, 2005), we may understand politics as a struggle for the interpretation of interests, a struggle which takes the form of communicative action, and which is particularly intense under conditions of great uncertainty. Major change occurs, when actors rethink the ways they think about their preferences (Blyth 2002: 33). While such rethinking is accelerated under conditions of crisis, political actors are probably hard to persuade of major new ideas. Moreover, new ideas impose themselves only when key actors can forge coalitions that are capable of imposing the new ideas about how to solve the problem at hand – either party-based coalitions (e.g., Hall (1993) or those based on interest associations (e.g., Gourevitch 1984, 1986).

Variation in the Public Debates Across the Six Countries

This *Babylonian confusion* to which we referred above, and which is characteristic not only for European debates on labor-market policies but also for such debates on social policy more generally, may to some extent be more imagined than real. In this study, we try to find out to what extent the national debates on labor-market policies are nationally specific and to what extent they are similarly structured by the classic left-right divide and/or by a policy consensus that, according to some experts, has been shaping up among the policy experts for some years. On the one hand, labor-market policy has been a traditional battle field between the left (including political parties, unions, and associated forces) and the right (including parties, business interest associations, employers, and associated forces). On the other hand, Ferrera (2012) has identified the formation of a "post-neoliberal ideological community" around *welfare state 'recalibration'* since the late 1990s. In his view, this emerging community has been formulating a synthesis on the welfare state that tries to pool the values of liberal democracy and social democracy. He sees three bridge concepts allowing to bring together these two sets of values: productivist or flexible solidarity (the idea that the collective guarantee of social benefits and services can contribute to economic performance, provided it is based on reciprocity); active inclusion (the idea that welfare recipients engage in activities allowing them to become economically self-sufficient again); and social promotion (i.e., the promotion of social investments preparing individuals to face the various risks they face in the course of their life). Similarly, for the domain of labor-market policy, Clasen et al. (2012) spotted the emergence of a new consensus around a more nuanced *'recalibration' agenda* that preceded the intervention of the Great Recession. According to their assessment, the overriding concern of 'recalibration' is to reduce labor-market segmentation and its central aim is to "reconcile economic competitiveness and social solidarity and to share the risks and opportunities of modern labor markets more equitably than in the past"(p. 5).

In many ways, the six countries we chose for this study are quite similar. In particular, in all six countries, unemployment was very salient in the general public at the time of our study. In our own survey that was put into the field at the beginning of the period covered by our study, unemployment was considered to be a very important problem *for the country* in all six countries. On a scale ranging from 1 (not important) to 10 (very important), the publics in all six countries averaged a value of more than eight. More specifically, the structural side of the problem for one's own country was considered more important than its personal implications: if asked about the personal importance of unemployment, respondents felt on average that it was less important than for the country as a whole.

However, although unemployment was very high on the public agenda everywhere and although there may be signs of policy convergence, the six countries still differ systematically in two respects which are of key importance for its politicization – the seriousness of the problem of unemployment and the heritage of the country-specific labor-market regimes. We shall only briefly address the question of policy heritage here, because we shall have much more to say about it in the next chapter. But let us just briefly introduce a few words on this issue here before we turn in some more detail to the seriousness of the problem of unemployment: When the Great Recession occurred, the approach to deal with the problem of unemployment was largely pre-structured by the national legacy of past attempts to solve this problem. This legacy shaped the way the problem was perceived, interpreted, and framed in the public debates. While we do not see interests as givens, especially not in a time of crisis, when they are difficult to interpret, the national policy legacy and the configuration of actors in a particular policy subsystem still largely predetermine how given actors are interpreting their interests. As a result of these nationally specific preconditions, the public debates on unemployment risk to be very different from one another.

As far as the seriousness of the problem is concerned, it is, of course, true that "some people are more unemployed than others" (Therborn 1986). This means that the unemployment debate may not take on the same urgency in all the countries. As is illustrated in *Figure 1.3*, three of our countries – France, Germany, and Italy – had chronically high unemployment rates even before the Great Recession, while the remaining three countries – Denmark, the UK, and Switzerland – have had structurally rather low unemployment rates since the late 1990s. Unemployment has always been comparatively low in Switzerland, and the unemployment rate fell rapidly in Denmark and the UK throughout the 1990s. Even in the high-unemployment countries, however, the rate had started to decline by the late 1990s (in Italy and France) or by the mid-2000s (in Germany). Then, as a reaction to the Great Recession, the unemployment rates shot up precipitously in four of our six countries, but not in Germany and Switzerland. In Germany, the declining trend continued throughout the crisis, while the Swiss situation remained rather stable at a low level up to and including the period covered by our study.

Two aspects of unemployment have proved to be particularly intractable for labor-market policies – youth unemployment and long-term unemployment. Western Europe has been increasingly struck by high and persistent levels of youth unemployment. As it turns out, the countries with chronically high unemployment rates also tend to have the most serious structural problems (*Table 1.3*). France and Italy are the two countries among our selection with the most serious problems of this kind: both their youth unemployment and their long-term unemployment have been high and continue to rise. Germany also has a very high long-term unemployment rate, but its youth unemployment is comparatively low. Moreover, both rates have decreased during the Great

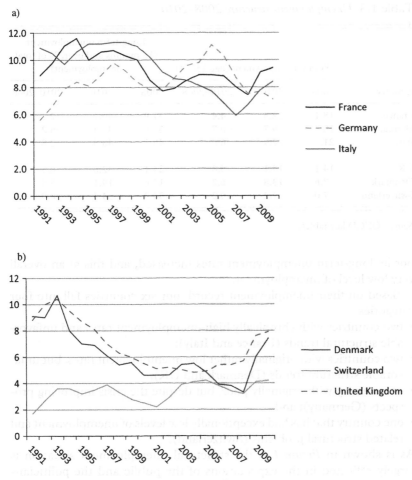

Figure 1.3 Unemployment rates in the six countries, 1991–2010
a) High unemployment countries
b) Low unemployment countries
Source: OECD.

Recession. By contrast, in two of the low-unemployment countries, the structural trends have been worsening: in both Denmark and the UK, youth unemployment and long-term unemployment have increased significantly since the beginning of the crisis. Switzerland is the only one among the originally low-unemployment countries that has not felt the impact of the crisis: up to the fall 2010, neither its youth unemployment

Table 1.3 *Unemployment structure 2008–2010*

Country	Youth unemployment (age 15–24)			Long-term unemployment (12 months and over, % of total unemployment)		
	2008	2010	2010–2008	2008	2010	2010–2008
France	18.1	22.5	4.4	37.9	40.1	2.2
Germany	10.4	9.7	−0.7	52.6	47.4	−5.2
Italy	21.3	27.9	6.6	45.7	48.5	2.8
UK	14.1	19.1	5.0	24.1	32.6	8.5
Denmark	7.6	13.8	6.2	13.6	19.1	5.5
Switzerland	7.0	7.2	0.2	34.3	34.3	0.0

Source: OECD key tables.

nor its long-term unemployment rates increased, and this at an overall very low level of unemployment.

Based on their unemployment record, our six countries fall into four categories:

• two countries with chronically high unemployment rates and unfavorable structural trends (France and Italy);
• two countries with originally rather low unemployment rates, but unfavorable structure trends (Denmark and UK);
• one country with originally poor, but despite the crisis improving prospects (Germany); and
• one country that has had exceptionally low levels of unemployment and related structural problems (Switzerland).

As is shown in *Figure 1.4*, the structural unemployment situation is largely reflected in the expectations of the public and the politicians about the temporal dynamics of the national labor markets at the time of our study. This figure is based on our own public survey and on our interviews with policy-makers, which we shall introduce below. The left-hand side of the figure refers to the public, the right-hand side to the policy-makers. The left-hand side shows that large majorities of the populations in three of the four countries with unfavorable structural trends evaluated the current situation on the labor market as bad/very bad, and getting worse. In Denmark, where unemployment shot up because of the crisis, the public was quite pessimistic about the situation on the labor market, too, but the trend was viewed more optimistically. The Germans were generally less pessimistic, and the Swiss were least pessimistic of all, but tended to view the future

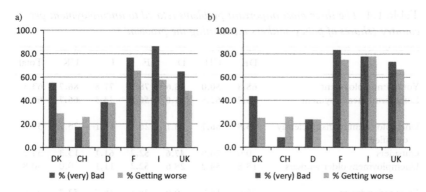

Figure 1.4 The perception of the situation on the labor market by the public and by policy-makers – current situation and likely development, by country (percentages)
a) Public
b) Policy-makers
Source: Our own study.

somewhat more pessimistically than the present. The policy-makers' assessments closely corresponded to the evaluations of their respective general publics. The pessimistic French, Italian, and British policy-makers contrasted with their more optimistic German, Danish, and Swiss colleagues. The relationship between the assessment of the current situation and the trend also turned out to be similar in the general publics and among the elites. If anything, the differences between the policy-makers from different countries were even more pronounced than those among the respective general populations: thus, the French, Italian, and British policy-makers tended to be more pessimistic than their general publics, while the Danish, Swiss, and German policy-makers are rather more optimistic than theirs.

In addition, we wanted to know from the policy-makers in somewhat more detail where they spotted the major problems in the labor market. We provided them with a list of ten problems related to unemployment and asked them to point out the three problems which they considered most important at the time of the interview. As it turns out, the two key structural problems of European labor markets indicated in *Table 1.4* – youth unemployment and long-term unemployment – were similarly perceived as crucial across the six countries. As is shown in *Table 1.4*, these two problems were mentioned as one of the three most important problems by no less than two-thirds of the policy-makers from the different countries. Only the Germans worried less about youth unemployment

Table 1.4 *The three most important problems related to unemployment per country (shares of policy-makers mentioning the problem[1])*

	DK	CH	D	F	I	UK	Total
Youth unemployment	68.8	50.0	28.6	78.3	77.8	86.7	63.3
Long term unemployment	86.7	62.5	81.0	56.5	33.3	66.7	63.8
Unemployment of insufficiently qualified	43.8	66.7	38.1	26.1	11.1	26.7	36.8
Outsiders	0.0	20.8	47.6	52.2	61.1	13.3	34.2
Unemployment older workers	18.8	54.2	28.6	52.2	11.1	0.0	30.8
Mass redundancy	25.0	16.7	0.0	26.1	16.7	53.3	21.4
Black labor	12.5	4.2	4.8	0.0	66.7	6.7	14.5
Unemployment single parents	12.5	16.7	33.3	4.4	5.6	13.3	14.5
Unemployment foreign workers	6.3	20.8	23.8	0.0	5.6	0.0	10.3

[1] *Source:* Our own study; up to three answers possible.

than their colleagues from other countries (which reflects the low level of German youth unemployment (see *Table 1.3*)), while, together with Danish policy-makers they worried more than the others about long-term unemployment (which, in turn, reflects the very high level of German long-term unemployment). Surprisingly, however, Italian policy-makers did not worry to the same extent about long-term unemployment, although it was actually even higher than the corresponding German level.

Apart from these two structural problems, there is considerable variation between the countries with respect to the labor-market problems mentioned by the policy-makers. Thus, the Italians were much concerned about the shadow labor market, a problem barely mentioned by policy-makers from the other countries. The French policy-makers, in turn, worried a good deal about the situation of unemployed older workers, a concern they shared with their Swiss colleagues. As we shall see, at the time of our study, France was shaken by a conflict over pension reform, which apparently had repercussions for the debate about labor-market policies as well. British policy-makers set themselves apart by the fact that, in addition to the two most frequently mentioned structural problems, they were particularly concerned about mass redundancies.

There are, however, some patterns which suggest that some countries may be more similar among themselves than others. Thus, German, Italian, and French policy-shared a concern for the precarious situation of outsiders, which distinguished them from the policy-makers in the other three countries. As we shall see in the next chapter, this specific concern of the policy-makers in the three countries is by no means accidental: the labor markets of these three countries are characterized by what we shall call 'increasing dualization,' which is why we have grouped these nations together for the rest of our study. Similarly, we have paired up Denmark and Switzerland, since they share many features with respect to their labor markets. In regard to the problems perceived by their policy-makers, the two countries distinguished themselves from the other four by the fact that the Danish and Swiss policy-makers perceived the unemployment of insufficiently qualified persons as a particularly significant problem.

Design of the Study

As noted above, our choice of a specific period of time to across which to study the parallel debates in all six countries was motivated by the idea of holding the overall context of the crisis constant. In addition, our choice was the result of pragmatic considerations: our study has been part of a larger study of unemployment debates, which also includes an in-depth content analysis of the news media, and an online panel survey of the public in the six countries. The content analysis, of which we have just reported some key background figures, covers the period from September 10, 2010 to December 10, 2010. For the UK and Italy, this period was extended to February 10, 2011. The first wave of the panel survey was held in October 2010 (between October 7 and 25), the second wave in December 2010 (between December 2 and 20). In the UK and Italy, a third wave was added in February 2011 (between February 14 and 28). Both the content analysis and the panel survey were greatly facilitated by the choice of an identical, relatively brief period in all six countries. Although we shall rely to some extent on these other sources, the largest part of our analysis builds on interviews with labor-market policy-makers in the six countries. This is due to the fact that we adopt a political supply-side perspective throughout this book.

The choice of an identical period in all six countries has, however, at least one considerable drawback: the period selected coincides with different stages of the national policy cycles. This means that, in some of our six countries, we may have had only minor public debates to study in the first place. As we shall see in Chapter 4, the policy-specific unemployment debates were, indeed, of relatively minor importance in some of our countries during the period covered. While our data deal with the specific debates that took place in the six countries in fall 2010, they do not just cover the issue-specific debates that took place during the period of our study. They also cover configurations of power, action repertoires, and political strategies in the national domain of labor-market policy more generally. Therefore, we believe that, in spite of the limits of the period-specific debates, our data still provide a plausible representation of how national debates on unemployment policy are shaped.

Our study primarily relies on interviews with key policy-makers in the domain of national labor-market policies. The interviews with these policy-makers consisted of two waves: one at the beginning of our period of observation, and one after this period had come to an end. This design was motivated by the fact that questions relating to strategic expectations are ideally asked in the run-up to the debates, whereas evaluative and debate-specific questions only make sense once they have taken place. The interviews were held over the phone and relied on semi-structured questionnaires which contained both closed and open-ended questions. The questionnaires included general questions which were the same for all the countries, as well as questions tailored specifically to the country-specific debates. Most interviews lasted from 30 to 45 minutes. The first wave took place in fall 2010, while the period for the second wave lasted from January to April 2011.

The policy-makers were selected as representatives of relevant organizations in the labor-market policy domain. The organizations, in turn, were chosen based on media analyses as well as on assessments made by country-specific labor-market experts. Among the participating organizations, we decided to interview the main person in charge of labor-market policy. We considered these experts most suited to answer our questions. In the first wave, we succeeded in interviewing 125 different respondents: 25 in France, 24 in Switzerland, 22 in Germany and Italy respectively, as well as 16 each in the United Kingdom and in Denmark. As expected, we faced no major problems in scheduling interview dates in Germany and Switzerland, and had no refusals in these two countries. In France and Denmark, by contrast, it proved difficult to secure interviews from representatives of public administrations, right-wing parties, and employers' associations. Nevertheless, we were able to speak to most of our targets in the end: only two French and four Danish organizations were not willing to participate. Our task turned out to be most difficult in Italy and the United Kingdom, where we had fourteen and thirteen refusals, respectively, to begin with. In the second wave, we lost seven interviewees (four Italians, one German, one Danish, and one British). *Table 1.5* presents the response rates for the two waves of interviews per country.

Table 1.5 *Response rates in the two waves of interviews with policy-makers per country (percentages)*

Response rates	First interview			Second interview	
	Contacted	Cooperated	%	Cooperated	%
DK	20	16	80.0	15	75.0
CH	24	24	100.0	24	100.0
D	25	22	88.0	21	84.0
F	27	25	92.6	25	92.6
I	36	22	61.1	18	50.0
UK	29	16	55.2	15	51.7
Total	161	125	77.6	118	73.3

In Switzerland, there were no problems at all with the interviews. In France, interviews were difficult to obtain, but once we had our respondents on the phone, everything went smoothly. In the other countries, not all of our respondents were able or willing to answer all the questions we asked them. Some (e.g., those working for think tanks or in public administration) refused to answer certain questions such as those concerning the policy-specific arguments, maintaining that they were politically neutral or that they could give us only a personal view. Some parties maintained that they could not answer certain questions without an official decision of the party. Critique of our questions was frequent: some questions were said to be too detailed (e.g., the list of the action repertoire), others not precise enough (e.g., our questions about policy measures), and the respondents tried to make them more specific. Our Italian interlocutors, in particular, insisted on more precise formulations regarding policy measures. The attempt on the part of the Italian respondents to adjust and (in their view) rectify every question distinguishes them from the policy-makers in the other countries. In Italy, social desirability also played a role, especially with respect to the questions about relations with journalists – thus, the responses are likely to underestimate the closeness of personal relationships between journalists and politicians.

We shall not go into the details of the ways we operationalized our theoretical concepts here. Instead, we shall introduce the operationalizations in the chapters where we introduce the respective concepts for the first time.

An Overview of the Study's Contents

Policy debates are embedded in national policy-specific contexts. The variability of these contexts goes a long way to explain why we find such great differences in the substance of the national debates between the countries. The next three chapters of Part I introduce the theoretical framework, the context structures and the policy-specific debates in the six countries. Chapter 2 presents our general approach for the analysis of political communication in times of 'ordinary' politics. As this chapter will clarify, our framework focuses on political actors and how their endowment with resources influences their coalition-formation, their action repertoire, and the way they craft their messages. It is important to recognize, however, that these actors are situated in a given context that affects their decisions. In Chapter 3, we present the key context characteristics that are likely to influence the actors' choices, i.e., political communication systems and relevant political arenas, as well as the labor-market regimes of the six countries in more detail. In Chapter 4, we introduce the variety of the country-specific policy debates which have taken place during the period covered by our study. As we shall see, these debates are decisively shaped by the legacy of the regime types: depending on the labor-market regimes, different aspects of unemployment related policies come into focus in the shadow of the crisis. Moreover, depending on the stage of the policy cycle, the debate turns out to be more or less salient and intensive.

The four chapters of Part II (Chapters 5 to 8) introduce the actors who shape the debate on how to fight unemployment in each country. Chapter 5 discusses the sources of power the different actors wield in this debate. Chapters 6 and 7 introduce the positions the actors' take with regard to labor-market policies more generally. The chapters do so by applying two quite different, but complementary, approaches. Chapter 6 starts out with the substantive content of the policy domain. Based on an analysis of the actors' positioning on key policy measures combined with the salience these measures have for the actors, it begins by drawing a two-dimensional policy space and shows that this space varies according to regime type. In a second step, it shows for each regime type the actors' configurations within the policy space. As the reader shall see, the resulting configurations are not simply opposing left and right, but are more complicated, allowing for cross-class coalitions and coalitions between state actors and actors representing societal interests. Chapter 7 changes perspective and looks at the cooperative relationships between the actors in question. While the actor configurations in Chapter 6 indicate which actors cluster together 'objectively,' i.e., on the basis of their positions taken with respect to the most important measures in the policy domain (positions weighted by their salience for the actors), the coalitions that are identified in Chapter 7 correspond to the actual patterns of cooperation that we found during the period covered by our study.

Chapter 8 presents the action repertoire the actors rely on for influencing the debate. It distinguishes between 'inside' and 'outside' activities. In other words, in this chapter we are interested in the extent to which political actors restrict the scope of their activities to the political decision-making arenas, and the extent to which they 'go public,' i.e., attempt to address the public in the media arena. For outside activities, we shall distinguish between 'information politics' and 'protest politics' as well as focus on the use of new social media. While the former refer to conventional activities to inform the public, the latter deal with the organization of collective action in general and the staging of protest in particular.

Part III closes in on the substantive content of the debates. Chapter 9 focuses on the factors which render a message important in a given debate. Over all debates, the salience of a message for the actors providing it, its resonance with other actors, and the sponsorship by powerful actors turn out to be the key factors behind the importance a given message assumes in a specific debate. Chapter 10 looks at the core policy beliefs of the actors and the arguments they provide in the debates. It attempts to show that although the actors in the different countries discuss different policies and use seemingly different terminologies, they essentially defend similar ideological positions and general arguments across Europe. Behind the smokescreen of highly idiosyncratic country-specific debates on unemployment we find a lot of similarity across countries. In all the countries, the debates turn out to be intimately linked to the classic left–right divide, which suggests that they lack new ideas and are led in ways which are less than promising for novel solutions to the pressing problem of unemployment.

Chapter 11 considers the strategic interaction between the actors involved in the debates. This chapter confirms that the conflict between left and right is prevalent in these debates, but actors from the left are generally shown to be more active in the public sphere. This can be attributed to the fact that the left enjoys 'issue ownership' in the labor-market domain. Alternatively, the prevalence of the left might be attributable to the fact that the right dominated the national governments in all country cases under study. Thus, the left had an incentive to go public in order to mobilize public opinion against the government. This chapter also highlights the crucial role played by debate characteristics – the interaction pattern can only be understood when considering the specific setting in which it takes place – as well as the specificities of the country-specific debates.

Chapter 12 assesses the quality of the different debates. This quality can be assessed on at least two dimensions – diversity and style.

The results suggest that public policy debates tend to be moderately diverse and media-oriented, which points to competitive debates as the most prevalent type (as compared to insider, scandalous, or deliberative debates). This finding fits a long tradition of news media research, which suggests that news media (at best) present two opposing views and that news media coverage is increasingly shaped by media logic. The chapter also suggests that actor perceptions of debate characteristics vary in line with actors' power and extremity of thought. More powerful actors perceive the debate as more diverse, arguably because they are able to get their message across and are therefore not confronted with debates in which their view is missing. More extreme actors, by contrast, perceive the debate to be more media-oriented, arguably because they are treated as outsiders and adopt a media-oriented communication style themselves. The results also suggest that another factor is also important for the actors' perception of the debate's quality – the extent to which they are satisfied with the outcome of the debates.

Chapter 13 provides the reader with a conclusion. In addition to summarizing the findings, it interprets them in terms of four distinct stages of conflict mobilization which involve four different types of politics: 'quiet politics'; 'committee politics'; 'plenum politics'; and 'forum politics'.

Overall Findings

Let us briefly summarize the overall findings right at the beginning of this study in order to delineate the contributions of this book. The first overall key insight of our study is that the arena in which actors communicate is very important for the structuration of a public debate. Regarding arenas, we shall distinguish between the parliamentary and the administrative arena (Chapter 2). In various chapters, we find that the mechanisms at work depend on the arena in which a debate takes place, and thus we illustrate the importance of the arena with the topic of conflict expansion (see also Chapter 13). In parliamentary debates (such as those in the UK, Germany, and Denmark), conflict expansion is predictable. It is proportional to problem pressure or relevance of the conflict, and it involves political parties as the main actors. In corporatist debates (see Chapter 9), which take place in the administrative arena, the process proves to be more variable. Thus, despite similar levels of problem pressure, the corporatist debates we studied are characterized by different levels of conflict expansion, ranging from no conflict expansion at all (the French debate) to the involvement of a wide variety of actors (the Italian debate). In such debates, unions can play an important role in addition to political parties. In the French case, no conflict expansion occurred, because the actors involved did not disagree (valence issue) and because the issue was highly complex. In the Italian case, by contrast, one union (the CGIL section of FIOM) offered resistance in response to the threat of delocalization, which triggered conflict expansion and ultimately led most employees to accept deteriorating working conditions. The arena is not only relevant for the mechanisms regarding the expansion of conflict, it is also relevant for the choice of the action repertoire (Chapter 8), for mechanisms regarding message importance (Chapter 9), the interaction between political actors (Chapter 11), as well as debate quality (Chapter 12; all parliamentary debates are competitive in nature).

The second overall key insight of our study is that the configuration of power and the type of actors involved are relevant factors for structuring a debate. This statement is well in line with an actor-centered approach. Power is relevant for the action repertoire (Chapter 8), message importance (Chapter 9), interaction between political actors (Chapter 11), and debate quality (Chapter 12). The actor type is relevant for explaining power (Chapter 5), positions in the labor-market policy space (Chapter 6), coalition formation (Chapter 7), action repertoire (Chapter 8), interactions (Chapter 11), and debate quality (Chapter 12). The combination of these factors offers a framework to analyze and explain various political debates. This is, for instance, illustrated by the role that unions play in setting the problem agenda and in offering politically feasible options for solution. While unions play a minor important role in parliamentary debates, they may be more influential in the administrative arena, as in the Italian debate. By contrast, in the Swiss case, unions were not successful: their message (the Swiss National Bank should prevent the appreciation of the Swiss Franc) was not heard because it was incongruent with dominant values (prevalence of a free market ethos and the value that the Swiss National Bank should be independent to steer the country's monetary policy) and not enhanced by increasing problem pressure.

The third overall finding enhances the lesson we learnt early on – that studies in political communication need to include policy-specific knowledge (see Chapters 6 and 10). First, the debate on unemployment is structured by the actors' left–right ideology and policy-specific preferences. We find that the new conflict dimension associated with the last decades' activation reforms is detectable in ordinary politics in times of crises. We go beyond the qualitative evidence in the field and show *empirically* that the political contest at the policy level is two-dimensional (Chapter 6). While the traditional axis of political competition in this domain, i.e., the left–right conflict, is similar in all countries, the second and more recent activation axis turns out to be regime-specific. Third, our study shows how conflicts at the general ideological or policy-specific level are translated into ordinary politics (Chapter 10). Thus, when looking at the *country-specific* arguments (the arguments discussed in the parliament or in the newspapers), we find more similarities in these debates than first meets the eye. We can clarify the *Babylonian confusion* and see that it is mainly the left–right divide that is expressed in the country-specific debates. Fourth and related to the last point, the institutional context contributes to explain why and when particular messages prevail in a public debate. For instance, the success of an argument demanding an increase in the level of unemployment expenditures depends on whether the labor-market regime's institutions are more or less generous. Or, in some countries (Italy and France), labor-market specialists use frames which are generally more in favor of solidarity with the unemployed than their colleagues in other countries. Since in Italy and France activation is a most needed but still underdeveloped reform strategy, political actors waste leverage by not discussing activation measures and relying instead on solidarity.

2 Theoretical Framework
Production of Policy-specific Political Communication

Regula Hänggli and Flavia Fossati

General Approach

Given the key role political communication plays in citizens' information processing, surprisingly little attention has been paid to the strategies employed by political actors in *ordinary politics*. In fact, political communication has been studied primarily in the contexts of elections and/or popular votes. Although, for a considerable time, researchers had found that campaigns had only "minimal effects," it is nowadays accepted that election campaigns can be pivotal (Iyengar and Simon 2000, Schmitt-Beck and Farrell 2002, Arcenaux 2006, Claassen 2011, van der Meer et al. 2016) because voters learn about the issue positions and the personalities of the candidates through campaign events and media coverage of those events. Campaign information provides them with the information necessary to make a choice consistent with their preexisting preferences (e.g., Finkel 1993, Gelman and King 1993, Gelman et al. 2008, Arceneaux 2006, Stimson 2015) and campaigns have been shown to influence voting behavior more generally (e.g., Fournier et al. 2004, Nadeau et al. 2008, Hillygus 2010).

More recent studies look at political communication from a different angle. They focus on the framing of issues and test the effects of media framing on citizens' understanding of politics. Mostly based on experimental data, these studies report significant framing effects of different issues, and have established an empirical basis for the existence of such effects (e.g., Nelson et al. 1997, Valkenburg et al. 1999, Druckman 2001, Berinsky and Kinder 2006, Slothuus 2008, Druckman et al. 2013). The magnitude and mechanisms of all these effects is hotly debated but researchers no longer claim that political campaigns have no effect whatsoever.

Political strategists and pundits have always believed in the power of political communication, as demonstrated by the enormous effort they invest into political communication. Therefore, in the present study of political communication in labor-market politics we take a closer look at these strategists. We define strategic action as a variant of instrumental (teleological) action that includes in the actor's calculation of success the expectations about the decisions of at least one other goal-oriented actor (Habermas 1981: 127) and that involves "few rules [...] but many choices" (Jasper 2006: 171). In other words, we focus on the actors' strategic choices in communicating to the public. More specifically, as noted in the Introduction, we shall focus on the communication strategies of political actors in 'ordinary politics' which belong to times of non-storm news coverage (Boydstun et al. 2014).

The approach we present in this chapter complements previous research on political communication because it provides a theoretical framework which is *supply-oriented* and *actor-centered*, and well suited to investigate *ordinary politics* in a specific policy field. In detail, it is designed to investigate political actors and their choices, and how these choices are constrained by macro- or system-, issue-, and debate-level elements. In the present study, we apply this approach and study the political communication in the field of unemployment policy, but our approach is applicable in other fields too. This chapter provides an overview of the concepts we shall use in the present study. For illustrative purposes, we shall also introduce some hypotheses here that will be elaborated in more detail in the individual chapters.

We argue that the production of political communication depends, first, on the *political actors' attributes*. We shall identify three key elements: i) the actors' beliefs and preferences; ii) their power; and iii) the coalition opportunities they face. Second, political actors need to make several *strategic choices* about how to intervene in a public debate. We distinguish between two types of strategic decisions: i) strategies to mobilize support in general; and ii) strategies related to the crafting of their messages in particular. Both mobilizing support and crafting of messages can be directed toward other political actors or to the general public. In other words, similar to what Bevan and Krewel (2015) propose for election campaigns, political actors do not only react to public preferences but more importantly also to their direct opponents. Mobilizing support deals with the choice of communication methods, interaction among political actors, and event management. Crafting the message is about the content and form of the message.

Actor configuration and the strategies regarding mobilization of support and the crafting of messages are embedded in specific contexts (Sabatier 1988: 134). In this respect, we first distinguish very general institutional settings that influence the debate. These settings are nationally specific and refer, on the one hand, to the media system in a given country and, on the other hand, to the political system in that location. These systems influence, in turn, the extent to which the strategies of political actors follow the media logic or the political logic (Strömbäck 2008). Second, there are issue-specific elements that affect the production of policy-specific communication, in our case, the labor market and unemployment policy regimes. Finally, at the most basic level, we have debate-specific factors that influence actors' strategies. These are the arenas in which these debates take place, in our case the parliamentary, and the administrative (or corporatist) arena. These contextual elements influence the production of political communication (see *Figure 2.1*). We shall now discuss the various elements of our framework inturn. The discussion of these

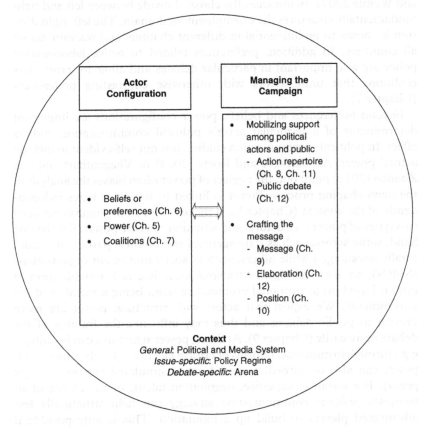

Figure 2.1 Framework of policy-specific production of news media content

aspects of the overall framework will allow us to situate the different chapters conceptually.

Model of Political Communication Production

As *Figure 2.1* shows, we understand political communication mainly as a product of *choices about how to manage the communication* made by political actors acting within a certain *actor configuration* and within a given *context*. This configuration is characterized by actors' beliefs and preferences (Chapter 6), their coalitions (Chapter 7), and their power (Chapter 5). Regarding beliefs, we argue that policy preferences are the manifestation of core beliefs, which are derived from actors' basic ideologies and from the demands and needs of their constituencies (Sabatier and Weible 2007). In our case, the classical divide between left and right fundamentally structures the unemployment domain. The left–right division is shown to be influential in different chapters and relevant across all countries. In addition, preferences related to active labor-market policy are also important in particular debates and allow for cross-class coalitions that unite actors with otherwise contrasting preferences (Chapter 7).

Beyond preferences and beliefs, power configurations are important determinants of a particular actor's political communication and its effect. In political communication studies, it is not self-evident to include actors' power. As Carragee and Roefs (2004) or Vliegenthart and van Zoonen (2011) point out, the neglect of power often biases the analysis of the news-shaping process. Power is linked to the actor types independently of the context (Chapter 5). It makes sense to distinguish between two types of power – structural and situation-specific power. On the one hand, some actors, such as state agencies and political parties, are structurally advantaged while others, such as social movement organizations (SMOs), are disadvantaged. *Structural power* is a rather stable form of power, based on institutional prominence (e.g., being a member of the government). We expect that actors with structural power are more present in public debates and thus may influence the framing of the debate more easily (Chapter 9). At times, power structures can be shifted, e.g., through institutional reforms or critical elections. On the other hand, power can also be earned, acquired, or accumulated (*situation-specific power*). For instance, expertise, negotiation talent, or the choice of an adequate political communication strategy can help structurally less advantaged players to build up a reputation. This is only possible if political communication is a long-term process and a debate rather than a monologue.

The coalition pattern also characterizes actor configuration. Common values or preferences can lay the ground for the coalition-formation process and can be expected to ease collaboration. In fact, a common understanding is a "natural way" of forming coalitions (Chapter 7) but it is by no means the only one. Merely strategic considerations can also lead to successful coalitions. Strategic or power-based coalitions aim at effectively reaching specific goals. Such coalitions mostly focus on short-term interest maximization rather than stable long-term cooperative relationships. The danger might be that they are detrimental for an actor's reputation.

Political Actors' Strategies: Mobilizing Support and Crafting the Message

There are many different strategic choices of political actors in political communication. In election campaigns, such choices involve a decision about whether to run for office, which issues to emphasize, which specific issues and messages to discuss, which kinds of media to use, and which citizens to target (Sides et al. 2015). In communicating everyday politics, the emphasis is on mobilizing support and crafting the message on specific issues. In order to mobilize support among political actors and the public, political actors use different action repertoires (Chapter 8 and Chapter 11) and adapt their behavior to the type of debate (Chapter 12).

Action Repertoire

When analyzing political communication strategies in times of ordinary politics, the distinction between inside and outside orientation is important (Kriesi et al. 2007). Inside-oriented activities are designed to influence decision-making in the parliamentary and administrative arenas directly. For instance, political actors can provide information to politicians and members of the administration, or they can participate in commission meetings and negotiations. The inside-oriented action repertoire includes sending information material to decision-makers, contacting other political actors, participating in internal or official meetings, negotiating, or taking legal action. In general, inside-oriented activities are unmediated forms of communication. By contrast, outside-oriented strategies aim at influencing political decisions indirectly by appealing to members or to the public – either by means of media-related activities or as a result of direct (=unmediated) mobilization efforts (see also Kriesi et al. 2009: 351).

Outside-oriented strategies include reactions to institutional events (see Chapter 11).

We can distinguish between two outside-oriented strategies: i) member-oriented and ii) mediated and unmediated public oriented strategies. First, member-oriented strategies are unmediated forms of communication which include contributions to blogs and newsletters. Second, mediated communication directed towards citizens or the general public seeks to obtain news coverage "for free" with actions like media conferences, press releases, mobilization of prominent figures, Twitter messages, and letters to the editor. Unmediated and costly forms of communication directed toward citizens include advertisements, posters, homepages, direct mailing, fliers, telephone marketing, door-to-door canvassing, and demonstrations. *Table 2.1* presents this action-repertoire typology.

Type of Public Debate

To characterize the way issue-specific information is presented in the news, we distinguish between types of debates. Debates in the media can be distinguished based on the degree of diversity and on the communication style (see Chapter 12). Diversity depends on whether different types of actors are involved, whether one or more viewpoints are presented, and whether these viewpoints are justified. The second dimension, communication style, can be described as media-oriented or policy-oriented based on the extent to which the debate is civilized, the extent to which actors respect other views, and the extent to which the focus in the debate is on the substance rather than on attacks and emotions. As we shall see in Chapter 12, by combining these two dimensions, we arrive at a four-fold typology of debates: scandalous, insider-oriented, competitive, and deliberative debates.

The arena is expected to influence the debate type. The debate quality, however, is also affected by the level of commercialization, which tends to reduces diversity in the news (Benson 2014). The debate type and debate quality strongly affects political actors, in particular the support an actor finds among the public. Thus, insider debates (policy debates of low diversity) can be expected to one-sidedly favor the government's position. In these campaigns, the public basically has no other choice than to support the position presented by the authorities because of a lack of alternative information. Conversely, in competitive and deliberative debates (debates of high diversity), the public can resort to differentiated information which reflects different viewpoints. Consequently, in such debates public support is based on stronger and better arguments as well as content-based political leanings (e.g., Sniderman and Theriault 2004,

Table 2.1 *Typology for action repertoire*

Orientation	Inside-oriented	Outside-oriented
Arena	Parliament Administration	Public Sphere (in the news media)
Target	Political actors, people involved in decision making	Members (like-minded citizens) Citizens or general public
Mediation	Unmediated	Unmediated — Mediated (Earned Media / Paid media)
Action Repertoire	Information provision to decision-makers Contacting politicians, the administration or associations directly Carry out internal consultations Participation in consultations (parliamentary) commissions (initiated by government) Negotiations with politicians, other parties, administration, associations Taking legal action	Blogs Newsletters Press releases Mobilization of prominent figures Twitter Letters to the editor Media conference Advertisements Posters Homepage Direct mailing Fliers Telephone marketing Door-to-door canvassing Demonstrations

Chong and Druckman 2007b, Slothuus 2010). Political actors can be expected to adapt their behavior to the debate type.

Crafting the Message

The message makes a difference. Morris (1999) advises that message is more important than money in election campaigns. He suggests that the key to winning any race is to come up with an affirmative message that outdistances the opponent's message. We distinguish between two kinds of strategies to bring the actors' message across: emphasis strategies (which message, Chapter 9) and evaluation strategies (Chapters 10 and 12). Emphasis strategies attempt to modify the weights (salience) of a message, while evaluation strategies attempt to modify the evaluative beliefs that characterize a debate. This distinction between influencing the weight (salience) of one's beliefs (its emphasis) and influencing its evaluative content (position) builds on the expectancy-value conception of attitudes (for more details, see Eagly and Chaiken 1993: 106–114, Chong and Druckman 2007c).

Emphasis Appeals: Which Message(s)? Political actors' struggle for public attention constitutes a key element of campaigning and of democratic politics more generally (Burstein 1998: vi). In this struggle, attention shifts (Jones 1994, Baumgartner and Jones 2002) become a crucial mechanism. As Schattschneider (1975: 66) famously suggested, "the definition of the alternatives is the supreme instrument of power." He thought that the actor who can define the agenda runs the country, "because the definition of the alternatives is the choice of conflicts, and the choice of conflict allocates power." In fact, most decision-makers, and the general public in particular, consider only a limited number of aspects. People are "cognitive misers" (Fiske and Tailor 1991): when asked to make a political decision, they suffer from availability bias, i.e., they do not make their decision based on everything they know, but rather based upon what is most accessible in their memory, what is "on top of the head" (Zaller 1992). Thus, political actors are expected to emphasize messages that have a high likelihood to stay at the forefront of citizens' minds and which are likely to influence the debate (Chapter 9). This means that strategically minded political actors can have a dramatic impact on public debates by shifting the point of reference of the debate from one aspect to the other.

Messages can be linked to three different content categories: they can be pragmatic (=utilitarian), identity-related (=ethical/cultural), or moral universalist (Habermas 1991: 100–118, 1992: 196ff., Helbling et al. 2010). Pragmatic arguments justify an actor's position regarding the expected output. They refer to the standard of efficiency. In an identity-related argument, justification relies on a specific conception of the collective identity. We would expect identity-related arguments to reso-nate more with the public because they concern individuals more directly than the more abstract moral messages. The moral arguments rely on standards of justice, the common good and mutually recognized rights.

Furthermore, empirical research has shown that news coverage is limited to a certain number of frames. Thus, a maximum of three to four main frames were found to shape political communication in both direct-democratic campaigns (Hänggli 2018) and in public policy debates about immigration (Benson 2014). We do not investigate the three Habermasian categories in the present study because the debates were dominated by the left–right dimension of politics which refers mainly to pragmatic arguments. In other debates of ordinary politics, however, there might be more variation or other categories used.

Evaluative Appeals: Which Degree of Elaboration and Which Position? There are at least two aspects which become important with regard to the evaluative aspect of messages. The first one is the type of appeal. We distinguish three types of appeals: substantive arguments; emotional appeals; and actor-centered appeals (Kriesi et al. 2009: 357, Bernhard 2015: 149). The second aspect refers to the direction of the message, whether it is positive (pro) or negative (contra).

Let us start by looking at the first aspect, the degree of elaboration. Strategies attempting to influence the evaluative component can either appeal to arguments or to emotions or actors' characteristics. Hänggli and Kriesi (2010) use this classification and distinguish between substantive and contest frames. Substantive frames are about the substance of an issue whereas contest frames concern non-substantive (i.e., actor- or process-centered) aspects of communication. In direct -democratic campaigns, the debate was found to be highly focused on substantive issues. A similar focus can be expected for debates on ordinary politics because the substantive information need of politicians and citizens is predominant (Hänggli 2018).

It has been argued that the societal modernization that goes along with individualization and technological revolutions drive the personalization of politics. More attention is paid to "persons" rather than "parties" in the political process (Swanson and Mancini 1996). Scholars such as Karvonen (2010) propose that an increasing personalization is an answer to catch-all parties that converge to indistinguishable positions and thus no longer offer enough choice to the voters. A second approach refers to the spread of new technologies that make it easier to personalize contents (pictures, tweets, etc.). In addition, commercialization and the diffusion of tabloids, which demand personalization, may affect the way in which political content is delivered. Finally, personalization caters to the need to simplify complex arguments and issues by using readily available short-cuts (Bohl 2016). The demand for simpler decision-making strategies is understandable especially in an increasingly complex world, where debates about specialized topics such as genetic engineering, stimulus packages, and rescue fund negotiations are no rarity. Looking at the development over time, even with increasing commercialization pres-sures, the share of actor-centered media coverage has not increased in elections (Kriesi 2011). Bohl (2016) introduces the distinction between an individualized and a privatized form of actor-centered appeal (instead of referring to "actor-centered" appeals, he speaks of "personalization"). An individualized form of actor-centered appeal focuses on candidates and leaders instead of institutions, parties, and policies. Conversely, a privatized form of appeal concentrates on candidates' and leaders' *traits* (like politician's hobbies or characteristics). In his comparative study of electoral campaigns, he confirms previous studies (Karvonen 2010, Kriesi 2011) that actor-centered appeals per se have *not* increased system-atically. Finally, there are emotional appeals intended to elicit an emo-tional response from the public. Emotional appeals have been found to be relatively successful because of their enduring effect (e.g., Jerit 2004). Oftentimes, campaigners try to weave together a cognitive and an emo-tional package of appeals (Goodwin et al. 2001: 16). In ordinary politics, we expect emotions and the characteristics of politicians and leaders to still be rather unimportant (in contrast to elections). We expect that in ordinary politics, arguments are most important because political actors do not (yet) need to reach the same level of mobilization required during electoral campaigns. The degree of elaboration becomes relevant in Chapter 12, which analyzes it in terms of communication style, where it plays an important role in how people process information. Social psychologists distinguish between a systematic and a peripheral route of information processing. Systematic processing is activated by arguments whereas peripheral processing is used in the case of endorsements (Stroebe 2007).

With regard to the direction of an argument, we can distinguish between positive (in support of the proposal) and negative (opposing the proposal) arguments. In his analysis of the ratification campaign for the American Constitution in 1787/88, Riker (1996: 66ff.) observed that many arguments were negative. He explained that speakers emphasize dangers rather than advantages because they believe that voters are generally risk averse. Typically, the camp defending the status quo (SQ) relies on negative arguments. Their rhetoric of reaction typically consists of three types of negative arguments against reform: pointing out the danger ("jeopardy"), futility, or even perversity of the reform (Hirschman 1991). By contrast, the reformers offer an alternative to the SQ. Their arguments typically contain the rhetoric of change (Gamson and Meyer 1996) which points out the urgency of reform, the opportunity for "agency," and the "new possibilities." We investigate positioning of actors in Chapter 10 and link the position back to core beliefs of actors.

The Influence of General, Issue-specific, and Debate-specific Contexts

Actors' production of political communication is embedded in a general, an issue-specific, and a debate-specific context. These contexts all influence the configuration of actors who participate in the campaign and their communication strategies. In other words, political communication in ordinary politics is pre-structured at the macro level by the institutional setting, i.e., the political and the media system. In terms of political systems, we distinguish between power-concentrating majoritarian and power-sharing consensual political systems (Lijphart 1999). In addition, we distinguish between different political arenas in which the debate can take place. Political arenas are the institutionalized sites where policy-related issues are processed, and where policy positions and their justifications are introduced and debated by political actors (Hilgartner and Bosk 1988: 55). In this study, we distinguish between the administrative or corporatist arena (the focus of interest group actors), and the parliamentary arena (the focus of partisan actors). When dealing with elections and direct democratic decisions, the electoral arena, and the direct-democratic arena become important, as well. The type of media/political communication system is defined by the degree of professionalization and of commercialization (Chapter 3). As we will show, the political communication system was found to be largely irrelevant in explaining political communication about unemployment in times of ordinary politics. It contributes only to explaining the differences in terms of communication *style*, as we document in Chapter 12. By contrast, Benson's work (2014) supports the idea that media system factors play a role in ordinary politics. By analyzing the production of immigration news, he shows that commercialization is decisive for the shape of news. In election or direct-democratic campaigns, "mood" (Marcus et al. 2000), and short-term events (exogenous shocks) intervening during the campaign also play a key role at this contextual level. However, they play a less influential role in ordinary politics because citizens do not have a final say in this type of politics.

At the issue-specific level, we find that the type of labor-market regime, and in particular the specific unemployment policies, play a role in shaping political communication. The labor-market regime is characterized by the degree of employment and unemployment protection. We distinguish a dualized type (Italy, Germany, and France), a deregulated type (UK), and a flexicurity type (Denmark and Switzerland) (Chapter 3). The labor-market regime type played a role for the positioning of the actors in Chapter 6 and Chapter 10.

If we zoom to the lowest level of aggregation, i.e., the debate-specific level, we find that the arena in which a debate takes place shapes political communication, as well. In various chapters, we find that the mechanisms at work depend on the arena in which a debate takes place. The arena is relevant for the mechanisms regarding the expansion of conflict (Chapter 4), for the choice of the action repertoire (Chapter 8), for mechanisms regarding message importance (Chapter 9), the interaction between political actors (Chapter 11), as well as debate quality (Chapter 12). The debates also vary in terms of intensity. Thereby, intensity can be linked to the arena – debates that take place in the parliamentary arena normally are more intense than those in the administrative arena – but the intensity can also vary within the same arena. For instance, some policy reforms discussed in parliament are highly visible in the news, whilst others are not. Intensively debated policy proposals are likely to be more important for (specific) political actors and thus trigger different strategic behavior as compared to low saliency issues. Thus, when thinking about the arena, one should also keep an eye on debate intensity.

Conclusion

In this chapter, we have offered a theoretical framework to analyze the production of political communication in times of ordinary politics. Thereby, we highlighted the key elements that we will analyze in more detail throughout the book. First, we focused on political actors and how their endowment with resources, such as power and beliefs/ preferences – i.e., the positioning in the political space in particular with regard to the left–right continuum – influences coalition-formation, their (strategic) decisions about their action repertoire, and the way they craft their messages.

Second, we also discussed context factors that affect the decisions of actors more or less heavily. Overall, the power configuration of the actors, policy-specific preferences, and the arena decisively shape political communication about unemployment.

Finally, throughout the book, we will point out and pay attention to whether particular strategies or processes *diverge* or *converge* across countries. In this sense this contribution can also be embedded in the debate about whether, under the liberalizing and mediatizing pressures of contemporary economies, countries are rather converging on a common path or whether they keep diverging. We find support for both trends and suggest that modern political communication is subject to contrasting forces that push the actors in different directions.

As we will demonstrate, *actor-based decisions* tend to be responsible for convergent developments across states. Thus, independent of country, state actors turn out to be among the most powerful actors. Moreover, we show that powerful actors tend to be more visible in the communication process, because they use outside communication strategies. We also find that positioning of actors can be traced back to their core beliefs. Finally, we show that, regardless of context, the most prevalent coalition formation rationale relates to the antagonism between left and right.

By contrast, we also find tendencies of divergence linked to the various *institutional* intervening factors, i.e., the arena, the labor-market regime type, and the media system. Thus, we found significant differences in the content of the debate. These differences originate from the regime-specific challenges a country faces and from the different stages in the policy process. In Italy, public debates focused on manufacturing plant closures and mass dismissals, which are consequences of the country's low level of international competitiveness. In Germany, political communication was centered on amending some details of a previous reform. Finally, in Switzerland, the country that was least affected by the global financial crisis and which had the lowest level of problem-pressure, unemployment was hardly an issue. In other words, political debates clearly vary depending on context, and by consequence give rise to divergent political communication outcomes.

The analytic approach adopted in this study is intended to be used to analyze political communication processes in other policy domains and in other countries. Of course, depending on the policy field some elements of our framework will need to be adapted. The number and diversity of actors who intervene in a specific debate is likely to depend on the policy field in question. When studying health policy, actors from the private sector, such as the pharmaceutical industry and medical lobby, will figure prominently in the political communication process because they provide expertise that other actors lack and because they are better organized than many other lobbies (theories of professional power, criticized by Immergut 1990). In highly technical debates, such as the that on climate change, the number of experts and the role they play in the decision-making process is likely to become more important (Rietig 2014). Finally, in areas such as trade and migration policy, we should expect supra- and international organizations, as well as foreign countries, to intervene in and influence national debates. Actor composition is, in turn, likely to influence and/or pre-structure the national actors' strategies. For instance, it is plausible to assume that in specialized debates, the nature of the crafted messages is more substantive and the quality of the debate is higher.

In sum, we suggest that to analyze a political communication process it is useful to conceptualize it as a product of *choices* taken by political actors and of *constraints* introduced by those actors' interactions with the institutional settings and their competitors. Our framework proposes several aspects that are relevant in the production of political communication and that will allow developing a deeper understanding of the variables that influence ordinary politics. This, in turn, will foster our knowledge about what actors' do to prepare for the "big races," i.e., winning elections and achieving desired policy reforms, where news coverage has become an essential tool for the general public and other political actors alike.

3 The Political Contexts of National Policy Debates

Hanspeter Kriesi, Flavia Fossati and Laurent Bernhard

Introduction

Public debates are embedded in a specific political context, which determines to a large extent the configuration of the actors involved, their communication repertoire, and the opportunities and constraints of their respective communication strategies, i.e. the chances of their success. Public debates and their possible outcomes are highly pre-structured by the institutional setting (including the media system), by the 'discursive opportunity structure' (Koopmans and Statham 1999), by the characteristics of the issues at stake, and by the short-term events (exogenous shocks) intervening during the debate.

Most immediately, the context determines the configuration of actors who become involved in the debate, their goals, and the distribution of resources among them. In an electoral campaign, for example, political parties are the key actors, which is not necessarily the case in a direct-democratic campaign, where the field of participants is much larger and where interest associations and NGOs may play the key part. In unconventional campaigns, such as those organized by social move-ment organizations, the protagonists are likely to be different again. In addition to these organizations, their allies in the political system, and the media, they may also include the police, counter-movements, and bystanders. In the 'ordinary politics' of public debates, which are our focus here, the set of actors involved may be very extensive, but it may also vary according to the arena in which the debate takes place. The configuration of actors is not just an assembly of individual or organizational actors. The actors involved in a campaign or public debate form coalitions, and it is typically these coalitions that craft and commu-nicate the relevant messages (frames) with the purpose of activating, mobilizing, and persuading the public. The ultimate goal of these coali-tions is not only to gain the attention of the media and the general public, but to mobilize the public's support for their cause.

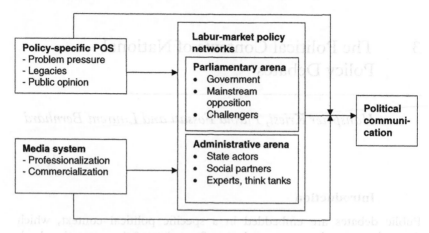

Figure 3.1 Heuristic framework for studying communication strategies in policy-specific public debates

This chapter is devoted to the comparative discussion of the political context of the political communication by key actors in the labor-market policy domain. For our purposes, it is important to keep in mind that the public debate we study is an *issue-specific debate*. This means that the relevant context is an issue-specific one and that the actors involved in the debate constitute an issue-specific subsystem which is not coextensive with the national political system of which it constitutes a part. *Figure 3.1* provides a rough summary of the way we conceive of the policy-specific context of a public debate.

As we have already pointed out in the previous chapter, policy-specific public debates in general and public debates in the domain of unemployment policy in particular are heavily influenced by a set of opportunities and constraints which refer to the policy-specific problem pressures, policy-legacies, and public opinions. According to our heuristic framework, in the final analysis, policy debates are driven by *problem pressures*. These challenges may be exogenous shocks such as the Great Recession, but they may also be shaped by the results of past policies (e.g. the widespread use of early retirement schemes to solve the unemployment problem in the past decades) that constrain the maneuvering space of political actors at any given moment. *Policy legacies*, in turn, not only contribute to problem pressures, but they also shape politicians' opportunities to deal with them. From the point of view of political communication, these legacies are particularly important, because they also influence the frames that politicians are likely to use in crafting their messages. The policy-specific *public opinion* refers to the salience of the issue in the general public, as well as to the preferences of the public with respect to the various aspects of the debate. For political actors, the preferences of the public are difficult to modify. If they do change, it is largely as a result of some economic downturn rather than as a result of the communication strategies of any individual actor. What political actors may influence, however, is the salience of a particular issue or issue attribute. Given that issues always have many different aspects, politicians may draw the public's attention to specific aspects of an issue in order to improve their chances of success in the public debate.

In addition to these exogenous opportunities and constraints, the political context, as we conceptualize it, also includes the actor-configurations in the relevant political arenas. As noted in the Introduction, there are several such arenas which might be relevant for a given policy-domain in each country featured in our study. In this study, we consider only two arenas, however: the parliamentary arena and the administrative (or corporatist) arena. Had we chosen another period for our study, the direct-democratic arena might have been relevant in the Swiss case. During the period in question, however, no direct-democratic vote took place with regard to Swiss unemployment policy, which is why we did not take this arena into systematic consideration here. The protest arena was important in several countries during the time of our study – especially in France and Italy, but we decided not to include it in the present analysis.

The political communications of the political actors who intervene in the different political arenas are mediated by the media, i.e. they reach the public in the media arena, where journalists are the key actors who select, interpret, and comment on the political communications of the political actors. In order to reach their audience, political communicators are forced to respond to the media's rules, aims, production logics, and constraints (Altheide and Snow 1979). What makes this dependence on the media particularly challenging for political actors is that the media now are increasingly independent of politics and operate according to a specific 'media logic', which refers to the media-specific rules of selecting, interpreting, and constructing political news messages (Esser 2013).

This logic is driven by processes of professionalization, commercialization, and technological change, which are exogenous to politics. As a result of their professionalization, journalists are ever more autonomous, follow their own set of professional norms, have a public service orientation, and frame and interpret the flow of political communication themselves. This growing media autonomy has been reinforced by economic imperatives that increasingly impose commercial rules on the media in order to maximize audience share, and by technological imperatives that make some formats more popular than others among the news-makers – television formats, for instance, are more linear, more visual, more affective, and less cognitively complex than print formats. Hallin and Mancini (2004: 290) call the 'media logic' a 'hybrid logic,' because, from the point of view of the media's autonomy, it has contradictory implications: while both professionalization and commercialization lead to a greater differentiation between the political system and the media system, commercialization leads to a greater dependence of the media system on the economic system.

While politicians need the media, the media also depend on the political actors for their reporting. Journalists need the thematic and interpretative propositions by the political actors (Jarren 2000: 38; Jarren and Donges 2002: 229–230). And even if politicians, parties and governments have to adapt to the imperatives of the 'media logic', they are not only the passive victims of a process they do not control. They devote more attention to what Esser (2013) calls the 'self-mediatization of politics,' i.e. the self-initiated stage-management of politics by means of strategic communication in an effort to master the new rules that govern access to the public sphere. Politicians, political parties, and governments professionalize their internal and external communication and devote more of their resources to communication (Esser and Matthes 2013).

As a result of these interdependent processes, journalists and politicians are involved in a competition for the control of the public sphere (Wolfsfeld 1997). In the American literature, the opinion seems to dominate that the media more heavily depend on the political actors than the other way around, as is illustrated by the famous quote from Gans (1979: 116): 'the relationship between sources and journalists resemble a dance, for sources seek access to journalists, and journalists seek access to sources. Although it takes two to tango, either sources or journalists can lead, but more often than not, sources do the leading.' Strömbäck and Nord (2006: 161), who have analyzed Swedish election campaigns, are not so sure about this: ultimately, they suggest, 'it is the journalists who choose who they are going to dance with.' We would like to suggest that the relationship in question depends a lot on two factors – the national system of political communication and the type of actors involved.

This chapter is divided into three sections. First, we introduce the political communication systems in the different countries covered in the study. Next, we turn to the two relevant political arenas.

Finally, we present the details of the country-specific labor-market policy legacies.

Political Communication Systems

The intrusion of the media logic as an institutional rule into politics very much depends on the type of media system in a given democracy. Adopting the well-known classification of media systems by Hallin and Mancini (2004), it can be observed that, in general, liberal media systems (such as those in the US and UK) have moved farthest in the direction of the imperatives of the media logic, while democratic-corporatist systems (Germany, Switzerland) have moved much less along this path, and polarized pluralist systems (Italy, France) have probably been least subject to its impact (Esser 2013, Esser and Matthes 2013). For our specific purposes, we shall propose a typology of *political communication systems*.

We propose to combine the typology of Hallin and Mancini (2004), which characterizes the media systems, with that of Pfetsch (2003), which characterizes political communication cultures. There is a striking parallelism between these two typologies, with the exception that Hallin and Mancini introduce only three types, while Pfetsch's scheme proposes four. Hallin and Mancini build their typology by combining the dimensions of professionalization and commercialization, while Pfetsch combines the distance between political actors and journalists with the dominating logic (media logic versus political logic) in political communication. *Table 3.1* presents the resulting typology, and suggests how our six countries are to be classified based on the conventional wisdom.

The first type is the *'democratic corporatist system'*, characterized by a strong elite orientation of political communication and a pronounced professionalism of the journalists. In this setting, newspapers cover the issues in a neutral, professional (Blumler and Gurevitch 1995) and quasi-scientific manner, and treat political actors respectfully. Journalists see their professional role as providing the citizens with quality information. They cover the different political positions in a balanced way and provide internal and external diversity in the media. The leitmotiv is to consider all politically relevant positions to allow the reader to form an educated opinion about a specific problem. In this type of media system, the *policies* are at the center of the interest and not individual personalities or specific reporting styles.

In the second type, called *'polarized pluralist system,'* newsmakers prominently address the elites in a *self-referential* manner (Mancini

Table 3.1 *Typology of media systems and of political communication cultures*

Professionalization/ *distance between political actors and journalists*	Commercialization (consumer-orientation)/*orientation of political communication*	
	Weak consumer-orientation/ *dominant political logic*	Strong consumer-orientation/ *dominant media logic*
Strong/*great distance*	**Democratic corporatist system/*strategic political communication culture*:** political actors attempt to outmaneuver media CH, D, DK (traditionally)	**Liberal system/** *media-oriented political communication culture*: media logic imposed on political actors UK (traditionally)
Weak/*small distance*	**Polarized pluralist system/** *party-political communication culture*: power calculation dominated I, F (traditionally)	**Populist system/** *PR-oriented political communication culture*: 'complicity' between political actors and journalists I (under Berlusconi), parts of the media in all countries (tabloids, free press)

Adapted from: Hallin and Mancini (2004) and Pfetsch (2003).

1997: 102). Generally, this style is not characterized by a professional journalistic ethos; rather, it is more a kind of entertainment for the elite provided by a cultivated advocacy journalism that, on occasions, resembles political or philosophical essays more than classical journalism. Journalists are mostly highly partisan (Blumler and Gurevitch 1995) and provide the reader with a more biased basis for developing an opinion on political issues. In this type of media system newspapers neither address the broad public nor give particular attention to research journalism. In fact, *style* largely prevails over issue. The media focus on politics, on political processes (judicial) scandals, and personalization. As a result of its self-referential character, this kind of journalism is accessible to the politically initiated only, the 'insiders'.

The third type is the *liberal system* or, as Blumler and Gurevitch (1995) call it, the '*Sacerdotal*' type, which aims to provide qualitatively good information to a broad public. As far as this concerns the journalistic professionalism, it is similar to the orientation taken in the 'democratic corporatist' media setting. Journalists are neutral observers of politics and pursue accurate research-based journalism. The difference to the more elite-oriented approach lies in the 'leading' role taken by the journalist. They select the important messages and political positions and sum them up to give a careful but structured report of the events. They aim at informing citizens by making the news accessible to the general public. This results in what could be called a 'telegraphic' and summary style, whereby articles are kept short, focused, and straightforward. Journalists assume an 'instructor's' attitude. Ultimately the interest still lies with the content and the transmission of specific issues to the general public and not with the political spectacle itself.

The fourth type, which we propose calling *'populist'*, is characterized by a low level of journalistic professionalism. It is characterized by what Mazzoleni (2008: 50) calls 'complicity' between journalists and politicians – he suggests that populist leaders can rely on some sort of 'media complicity'. The media target the broader public, but unlike the media of the 'sacerdotal' type, they do not focus on policies or issues but on political conflict and human interest stories. The policy discussed is more of a pretext to highlight the positions or acts of individual personalities and not a tool to initiate a discussion on policy alternatives. The populist type applies not only to Italy under Berlusconi, but also to the tabloid media in diverse countries (Mazzoleni 2008).

We have tried to operationalize empirically the country-specific political communication systems in our study. For this purpose, we rely on the two dimensions proposed by Pfetsch (2003): the predominant logic (media logic versus political logic) and the distance between journalists and politicians, both as perceived by the political actors we have interviewed. To get at the predominant logic, we asked the respondents, whose organizations had written one or more press releases during the debate, about the criteria which could be of importance in writing such a press release. Some of the criteria presented to them were clearly more media-centerd, while others were clearly more politics-centerd. For the operationalization of the distance between politicians and journalists, we submitted a set of statements about the relationship between the two types of actors to our respondents. These statements indicated either professional or personal relationships. Analyzing the responses of our respondents to these items,[1] we find that in Denmark, Italy, and the UK, media logic predominates and at the same time, journalists and policy-makers are rather close to each other. In other words, the political communication system in these three countries tends towards the

---

[1] Without going into details, suffice it to say that we analyzed the responses to both the list of 30 criteria as well as the 7 statements with factor analytical tools (see Tables A3.1-A3.3).

populist system. By contrast, in France, Germany, and Switzerland, political logic predominates and journalists and policy-makers are less close to each other. Their political communication systems correspond more closely to the democratic corporatist type. While the classification of Switzerland, Germany, and Italy is in line with received wisdom, this is not the case for France, Denmark, and the UK. Thus, in France, we expected a smaller distance between journalists and politicians than we found, and in Denmark and the UK a larger one. France's political communication system is still dominated by political logic, but it seems to have professionalized and the traditional political alignments between media and politicians seem to have been reduced. Indeed France's political communication system now seems closer to the systems of Switzerland and Germany than to Italy's, where journalists and policy-makers are rather close in personal terms. Britain, by contrast, has begun to follow the Italian model, given its warm professional and personal relationships between journalists and policy-makers. And so has Denmark, where we found not only less (professional, but not personal) distance, but also much more influence of the media logic than we expected. According to the present results, Denmark's political communication system is relatively populist, too.

The Relevant Political Arenas

The Parliamentary Arena

The parliamentary arena is characterized by the institutions of the country-specific regime of representative democracy and the current configuration of the party system. With respect to the former, following Lijphart (1999), we introduce the distinction between consensus and majoritarian democracies. As is well known, *consensus democracies* tend to divide power among a large number of actors, while *majoritarian democracies* tend to concentrate it in the hands of a few actors. In institutional terms, consensus democracies are typically characterized by a combination of parliamentary regimes with PR electoral systems. By contrast, majoritarian democracies can be either parliamentary regimes with majoritarian electoral systems, or (semi-)presidential regimes. Three of our countries are rather typical consensus democracies – Denmark, Switzerland, and (unique among large countries) Germany – while the other three countries represent rather more majoritarian democracies – UK, France, and Italy. The Italian case, it may be argued, is somewhat mixed, but more recently the Italian system has taken on some strong majoritarian characteristics (Bartolini et al. 2004, Bardi 2007, Kriesi and Bochsler 2013).

In terms of the classic distinction of democratic regime types, it is important to keep in mind that France has a semi-presidential system that focuses public attention on the president; Denmark, Germany, Italy, and the UK are parliamentary systems that focus attention on the cabinet and the Prime Minister (or Chancellor), while Switzerland's hybrid directorial system is least likely to personalize the public debate (Kriesi 2011).

With respect to the *configuration of the party system* during the period covered by our study, it is important to note that all countries, except Switzerland, were governed by a center-right coalition government, while the left was in the opposition everywhere. One could argue that even in Switzerland, where the left has been part of a grand coalition since 1959, the left has always been in a minority position in social policy in general and in labor-market policy in particular, which has always induced it to take an oppositional stance in these policy domains.

As pointed out by Häusermann et al. (2013), traditional partisan political literature on the welfare state has seen political parties as the key actors in socio-economic policy-making. Studies in the tradition of power resource theory have shown that left-wing parties were a driving force of welfare state expansion. Many studies indeed do still find such an effect, but the explanatory power of the 'left party variable' has become weaker (Bradley et al. 2003, Huber and Stephens 2001). This weakening is seen as evidence that parties matter less, and that their programmatic differences are increasingly constrained by exogenous forces, such as demographic pressures and policy legacies. According to Häusermann et al. (2013: 234), traditional partisan theory applies under three conditions: programmatic electoral linkages; an industrial social structure; and bipolar party systems. Given the deindustrialization and tertiarization of society's structure, the related changes in the electoral constituencies, as well as the changing dynamics of the party systems, the second and third conditions at least are no longer fulfilled as a matter of course. They are still most likely to apply to majoritarian party systems such as the British one, which offer clear choices for social and economic policies and whose electoral constituencies are still primarily divided by the traditional class cleavage. By contrast, in countries with a divided left (between socialists and communists), such as France or Italy (and to some extent Germany), the ideological polarization that goes along with it has to be taken into account as well. And in countries where a new cultural cleavage has come to divide the right (between the mainstream center-right and the new radical populist right), as has been the case in Denmark and Switzerland, we also need to consider the possibility that non-economic, cultural motivations (e.g. concerning immigrants) are introduced into labor-market policies.

The Administrative Arena

The *administrative arena* is characterized by the configuration which obtains between the social partners – business and labor unions – and the state actors (government and public administration). Experts and think tanks should be taken into account as well. In the labor-market policy domain, the *labor unions* are of particular interest, because their organizational structure and strength have traditionally been considered to be of key importance for understanding the coordination capacity of policy-making. As the literature on corporatism has consistently argued, the structure of the union movement is a precondition for its capacity to deliver in cooperative policy arrangements ('corporatist policy networks') between the social partners and the state (see Schmitter and Lehmbruch 1979, Katzenstein 1985). The more centralized the union movement, the better it could contribute to successful corporatist concertation. Highly centralized and concentrated union movements such as those in Scandinavia have traditionally been best prepared for stable corporatist policy-making, while more fragmented union movements in countries of continental and Southern Europe tended to be at best able to participate in sector-specific or temporary corporatist agreements. The pluralist union movements in Anglo-Saxon countries have not succeeded in participating in concerted actions at all. For our six countries, *Table 3.2* presents the development of the labor unions' strength over time, measured by their organizational density.

Table 3.2 *Strength of labor unions – organizational density*

Country	1985	1995	2000	2006
Denmark	78.3	77.0	87.5	69.4
Italy	47.6	38.5	35.4	33.4
UK	45.5	32.2	29.0	29.0
Germany	35.3	29.1	28.7	20.7
Switzerland	28.8	23.6	23.0	19.0
France	14.5	10.3	9.1	8.0

Source: Kriesi, Hanspeter 2007. Vergleichende Politikwissenschaft, Teil I: Grundlagen, Baden-Baden: Nomos, p. 277, 2006: OECD.

Political economists have come to replace the traditional distinction between pluralist and corporatist policy arrangements by the influential framework proposed by Hall and Soskice (2001). Compared to the traditional distinction between corporatist and pluralist countries, the 'varieties of capitalism' (VoC) approach is more focused on business corporations and concentrates on the question of how business corporations coordinate themselves strategically under the given institutional conditions. This framework distinguishes between *liberal market economies* (LMEs) and *coordinated market economies* (CMEs), which differ not only with respect to their production systems (corporate governance), but also with respect to their institutional regulation structures (regulation of the labor market, of vocational training ('skill regulation'), and of the financial markets). The relevant institutional structures allow the economic actors to coordinate themselves in such a way that a stable equilibrium develops, which guarantees all participants important benefits. The key difference between the two systems is whether employers are capable of strategic coordination among themselves and with labor in order to achieve joint gains through cooperation (CMEs) or not (LMEs) (Hall and Soskice 2001: 8). In LMEs, coordination takes place through the market, and not through political negotiations between the social partners (and the state). According to Hall and Soskice's functionalist argument, none of these systems is better than the other. Both seem to develop a stable equilibrium capable of governing the economy in a satisfactory way. The UK represents the typical liberal market economy, while Denmark, Germany and Switzerland represent the typical coordinated market economies.

As Schmidt (2009) argues, there is a third variety, *state-led market economies* (SMEs), which includes France and Italy. In these countries, the state, for better or worse, plays a much more active and directive role in the political economy than in the ideal-typical LMEs or CMEs. While France is the ideal-type of an SME, Italy (and Spain) represent more compound cases, where the state stepped in to help ensure greater business-labor coordination in a kind of macro-concertation between employers, unions and the governments.

Against the background of the past two decades of economic turmoil, the distinction between these varieties of capitalism has been called into question. A strong, structuralist argument has been made in favor of a convergence towards the LME model (Glyn 2006, Howell 2006, and Streeck 2009). According to this argument, under the onslaught of liberalization, the arrangements that used to distinguish the CMEs have eroded over the last twenty years in an imperceptible way. In line with convergence arguments, Hassel's (2013) review of the literature suggests that both labor-market institutions and unionization rates explain increasingly less of varying national economic performance and wage inequality. The exception to this generally pessimistic conclusion with respect to the unions' role in policy-making refers to data suggesting that the strong Scandinavian union systems are better able to protect against rising inequality than the other, more fragmented systems. By contrast, the defenders of the VoC perspective see the divergent arrangements as relatively robust and resilient (Hall and Gingerich 2009). As Thelen (2012) points out, the two sides of the argument are not focusing on the same trends, however: while VoC scholars emphasize continued employer coordination in many (although not all) CMEs, convergence theorists point to general trends and pressures on the side of labor, including declining labor strength, declining coverage of collective agreements and, more generally, declining social solidarity.

Policy Networks

The *policy-specific subsystem* spans the two arenas and includes the relevant political actors in the policy domain which may come from both, the parliamentary and the administrative arena. The policy-specific subsystem constitutes a *policy network* of actors specialized in the given policy domain (for the labor market example, see Knoke et al. 1996). It includes parliamentarians, members of government, public officials, lobbyists, experts, members of subnational governments, and journalists. The shape of a policy network is determined by the configuration of actors in the parliamentary and administrative arenas, as well as by the relationship between the two.

The relationship between the two arenas varies as a function of the problem pressure to which the subsystem is exposed, and as a function of the characteristics of the specific issues which are on the agenda of the subsystem. First, in ordinary times of 'normal problem pressure', the subsystem is mainly made up of the policy-specific specialists, i.e. the administrative arena is likely to dominate. In extraordinary times, however, when the daily routine of the policy-subsystem breaks down, it is extended to include the most important national political actors (see True et al. 2007). In other words, the focus shifts to the government and to the parliamentary arena – especially, but not exclusively, in majoritarian systems. Second, in labor-market policy in particular, there are specific issues which are reserved for treatment in the administrative domain. Thus, in most countries, industrial relations constitute the privileged domain for regulation by the social partners. In other words, depending on the problem pressure and the issue that dominates the labor-market policy agenda during a given period, the type of arena and of actors involved is likely to vary considerably from one country to the other.

The Labor Market Regimes

The domain-specific *policy legacy* is embodied in the institutions – formal and informal rules – that govern the policy domain in question and pre-structure the contemporary policy debate in decisive ways. For our purposes, we focus on the labor-market regimes of the six countries in our study. Labor market regimes can be characterize in two ways: by unemployment regimes; and by employment protection.

Combining two characteristics of unemployment regimes – their generosity and the extensiveness of active labor-market policies – with employment protection, we obtain a complex characterization of the labor-market regime of a given country. *Figure 3.2* presents the distribution of the OECD countries for which we have complete information on all three criteria for 2008, i.e. the year of the onset of the financial

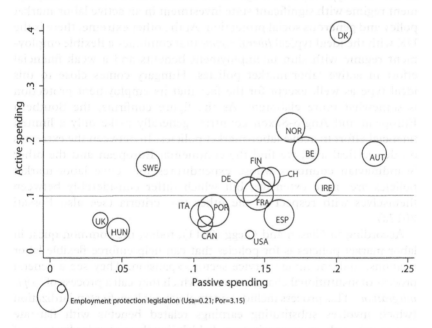

Employment protection legislation (Usa=0.21; Por=3.15)

Figure 3.2 Employment protection legislation and government expenditure for active labor-market policy (figures for 2008)

and economic crisis and the accompanying aggravation of the labor-market situation in our six countries. The horizontal axis in this figure corresponds to the generosity of the unemployment insurance. It is measured by the public expenditures for passive labor-market policies (as a share of GDP), divided by the unemployment rate. Not included are expenditures for early retirement. We divide the expenditures by the share of unemployed to control for the large differences in unemployment levels between the various countries. The vertical axis in the figure corresponds to the active labor-market policy effort. It is measured analogously by the public expenditures for active labor-market policies (as a share of GDP), divided by the unemployment rate. The level of employment protection is indicated by the size of the circle for each country: the larger the circle, the more elaborate the employment protection in the corresponding country.

Two of our six countries stand out clearly in *Figure 3.2*. At the one extreme, we find Denmark, which combines generous unemployment benefits with an extensive effort in active labor-market policy and rather limited employment protection. This is the country which comes closest to the ideal type of *'flexicurity,'* the combination of a flexible employment regime with significant state investment in an active labor-market policy and generous social protection. At the other extreme, there is the UK with the ideal typical *liberal regime* that combines a flexible employment regime with slim unemployment benefits and a weak financial effort in active labor-market policies. Hungary comes close to this ideal type as well, except for the fact that its employment protection is somewhat more elaborate. As the figure confirms, the Southern European and Anglo-Saxon countries generally make only a limited financial effort in active labor-market policies. In between the extremes on the vertical axis, we find the continental European and the other Scandinavian countries whose expenditures for active labor-market policies are more extensive, but which differ considerably between themselves with respect to the other two criteria (see also Fossati 2017a).

According to Clasen and Clegg (2011), today, the common quest in labor-market policies is for policies that can help enforce flexible labor relations, and encourage service sector expansion. They see a general process of institutional change at work, which they call a process of *'triple integration'*. This process includes unemployment benefit standardization (which involves substituting earnings related benefits with flat-rate payments), risk re-categorization (which involves standardization of benefit levels across working-age risk categories (unemployed, handicapped etc.), the abolition of certain benefit schemes and the intro-duction of conditionalities for receiving benefits), and the generalization of activation measures. As the contributions to their volume show, the UK, Denmark, and Germany moved most clearly in the direction of 'triple integration,' while France and Italy made only modest steps in this direction and Switzerland hardly moved at all (partly it even displays opposite trends).

More recently, policy-makers have paid particular attention to *activation policies*. Since 2000, the major objective of social security changed from passive compensation of social risks to setting indivi-dual behavioral incentives for both employers and benefit claimants to achieve labor-market integration (Hemerijck and Eichhorst 2010: 321). However, while all countries have introduced activation mea-sures, their characteristics vary considerably from one country to the other. Discussions of active labor-market policies in the literature tend to focus on the role played by sanctions in the re-integrative process – so called 'work-first' policies (Lødemel and Trickey 2001; Barbier and Ludwig-Mayerhofer 2004; Lødemel 2004), on the need to provide the unemployed with additional skills, and on the stimu-lation of labor-market re-entry (Daguerre 2007; Bonoli 2010, 2012; Fossati 2017b).

Building on this discussion, we propose a four-fold typology of labor-market policies that combines two aspects of labor-market regimes – generosity of unemployment insurance and employment protection – and, in a subsidiary way, also takes into account the active labor-market regime. *Table 3.3* presents this typology. We shall briefly sketch the country-specific labor-market policies. We begin with Denmark, the paradigmatic example of flexicurity, and Switzerland, a case of 'liberal flexicurity,' then turn to the dualization countries (Germany, France, and Italy), and end with the paradigmatic example of the liberal deregulation trajectory, the UK.

Table 3.3 *Typology of labor-market regimes*

Employment protection	Unemployment protection (generosity)	
	Low	High
Low	**UK** (liberal deregulation)	**Switzerland** (liberal flexicurity) **Denmark** (flexicurity)
High	**Italy** (severe dualization)	**Germany, France** (dualization)

Denmark: Flexicurity

In its heyday, the Danish model rested on the combination of three elements: flexible labor markets; generous unemployment benefits; and a strong emphasis on activation (Viebrock and Clasen 2009: 313–314): 'In a nutshell, the model promotes high occupational and geographical labor mobility via low employment protection, compensated by generous unemployment benefits and ambitious active labor-market policies aimed at skill improvement and activation of the unemployed.' Crucially, the concept of job security is replaced by employment security.

As Emmenegger (2010a: 290) explains, the Danish road to flexicurity has not been the result of 'policy making by wise policy designers taking into account the country's firm structure or proposing a trade-off between labor-market flexibility and job security'. The strategy's success does not explain its origin. Rather than having been deliberately designed, the flexicurity model is, at least in part, 'the result of the interplay between power resources, societal pressure and reform capabilities during a critical juncture'. Denmark did not have strict job security legislation and it had also done relatively little in the field of active labor-market policy (ALMP) until, under the pressure of unemployment peaking at 10 per cent, the Social Democratic government elected in 1993 adopted a series of reforms that transformed the Danish system of unemployment compensation (Bonoli 2012: 196). The 1993 reforms were a major step towards the introduction of 'flexicurity'. In exchange for their agreement to reorient unemployment policy in the direction of activation, the social partners obtained important concessions, such as a key role in the implementation of labor-market measures. The role of the social partners in this model has been pivotal. The liberal employment protection system with its relatively easy hiring and firing of workers became acceptable for trade unions thanks to a generous unemployment insurance, and vice versa for employers. Subsequent reforms (1998) further strengthened work incentives and employment assistance elements.

Eventually, in 2001, the Social Democrats lost power and for the next ten years – up to and beyond the period covered by our study, Denmark was governed by a centre-right coalition, supported by the radical populist right Danish People's Party (PF). Against the combined resistance of the left and the unions, and aided by the exogenous shock of the financial crisis of 2008, this cohesive government pushed through a series of far-reaching social reforms based on a program of combining tax freezes (highly effective in limiting the growth of social expenditures), welfare chauvinism (targeted cuts for social assistance, immigrants and young unemployed), and anti-unionism (exclusion of social partners from the implementation of labor-market policy, and break-up of the Ghent-system of administrating unemployment insurance) (Rathgeb 2013). Some observers suggest that these reforms have turned the 'flexicurity' model into something very different: according to these observers, the Danish active labor-market regime took on many elements of a 'work-first' regime in which sanctions are at least as important as incentives (Jørgensen and Schulze 2012), and which excludes the unions from both legislation and implementation. According to Schneider and Paunescu's analysis (2012: 740), by 2005, Denmark had moved so far as to become an LME. We are not entirely convinced, at least when compared to other activation regimes, as Denmark still seems to be have a comparatively generous and active regime.

Switzerland: Liberal Flexicurity

As observed in Chapter 1, Swiss unemployment has never reached the levels of the surrounding countries in Western Europe, even if it did increase in the 1990s and again in the Great Recession of 2008. Bonoli and Mach (2001) highlight the original combination of different policy elements, which seems to be particularly conducive to favorable labor-market performance: On the one hand, like Anglo-Saxon countries, Switzerland has a liberal and flexible labor market and a low tax wedge for low-skill employment (i.e. a low difference between what employees receive and what employers pays for their work), which favors employment creation in the low-skill service sectors. As explained by Emmenegger (2010b), this is a result of the weakness of the Swiss federal government that was unable to impose its will on employers' associations and either abandoned or diluted reforms of labor law. On the other hand, contrary to Anglo-Saxon countries, generous unemployment benefits with tight entitlement conditions, sector-specific industrial relations embedded in sectoral social partnership institutions, and an efficient vocational training systems, combine to provide highly skilled workers with sector-specific skills, which are much in demand in the Swiss labor market.

The unemployment insurance is a mandatory, generous insurance scheme for all employees that has been adapted several times after its belated introduction in 1984 – it was last updated just prior to our observation period in fall 2010. The 1995 reform, which was adopted after a series of urgent decrees had amended legislation in light of a dramatic increase in unemployment, was accompanied by measures incorporating concessions on the part of both social partners. On the one hand, in line with the demands of the business community, the reform reduced the duration for entitlements, which used to be unlimited, to a maximum of two years. On the other hand, the reform constituted a turning point from a rather passive labor-market policy to an active one. In line with the demands of the left, active labor-market policy measures were introduced for the first time. Moreover, the reform reinforced the financial basis of the insurance by increasing the contributions from 2 to 3 percent of salaries (1.5 percent each for employers and employees). An attempt to further reduce the benefits was defeated in a popular vote in 1997, indicating that one-sided measures of retrenchment have difficulties to pass the hurdle of the popular vote.

In Switzerland, the progressive extension of activation has not, however, been accompanied by greater benefit homogenization or policy coordination in line with the 'triple integration' model (Champion 2011). On the benefit side, reforms have above all aimed at tightening the access to unemployment and disability insurance benefits, but the benefit landscape has not been dramatically changed and the distinction between assistance and insurance-benefit levels has remained largely intact. Finally, it is important to mention that the Swiss unemployment insurance scheme also grants compensations for *short-time work*. This instrument is aimed at avoiding layoffs in companies facing hard economic times allowing them to decrease the number of working hours. During the period of reduced activity, employees receive short-time money, which corresponds to a partial unemployment benefit. Employers, for their part, save labor costs without losing the know-how of their employees. The current regulation is rather generous, as short-time money attains 80 per cent of the regular wages a maximum of 24 months.

Germany: Dualization as a Result of Hartz IV and Labor Market Reforms

With respect to the unemployment insurance, the Hartz IV legislation, introduced by the red–green governing coalition in 2005 as part of the Agenda 2010 reform package, marks a critical departure from the traditional German conservative welfare model towards more liberal models. This legislation restricted the idea of preserving the social status and the achieved living standard to the short-term unemployed (Seeleib-Kaiser and Fleckenstein 2006). The previously earnings-related unemployment benefits of unlimited duration were limited to 12 months (unemployment benefits I – Arbeitslosengeld I). After 12 months, the long-term unemployed receive only unemployment assistance (unemployment benefits II – Arbeitslosengeld II), which is no longer earnings-related and corresponds to the level of social assistance schemes (Second Book of the Code of Social Law – Sozialgesetzbuch Zweites Buch, SGB II). The former unemployment assistance was merged with the social assistance system, which constitutes a move towards 'benefit homogenization' in terms of the 'triple integration' model. The fact that unemployment benefits II (rather than the unemployment insurance) covers the vast majority of jobless benefit claimants in Germany today is yet another sign of benefit homogenization (Dingledey 2011). Structurally, even more thorough changes have been introduced: unemployment benefits II have two components: a support benefit (359 euros a month in 2010) for single adults plus supplements for other household members (paid for by the Federal Employment Agency (BfA)), and supplements for housing costs (paid for by the municipalities). The two parts are administered jointly by 356 newly created joint bodies of BfA and municipalities, which connect public employment services and municipal social assistance offices (Dingledey 2011).

As a consequence, the long-term unemployed 'experienced severe benefit cuts and lost any legal status protection' (Fleckenstein 2008: 180), and the German welfare state moved 'a significant distance towards an Anglo-American model of largely means-tested, flat rate jobless benefits' (Hassel and Williamson 2004: 13), 'a system organized more around poverty reduction (with activation) rather than income/ status maintenance for labor-market 'outsiders'' (Palier and Thelen 2010: 217).

Hartz IV not only integrated the unemployment insurance and social assistance, but was also aimed at the activation of the traditionally passive German welfare state. It introduced two sets of measures: 'positive activation,' i.e. social investment measures (such as occupational training programs) intended to improve the unemployed's chances of finding work, as well as 'negative activation,' which combines a reduction of benefits with more restrictive criteria for acceptable work and a sanction regime that punishes non-conforming behavior with benefit cuts, suspensions, or loss of benefits altogether. Hartz IV combines the 'enabling state' of positive activation with coercive measures of negative activation. However, spending on active measures has been scaled down significantly since the early 2000s (Dingledey 2010). Moreover, the implementation of the activation measures contributes to the dualization of the labor market: recipients of unemployment benefits II clearly receive less access to upskilling measures, and they are put under stronger pressure than recipients of unemployment benefits I to accept precarious jobs (Dingledey 2010: 22).

At the same time, labor-market reforms institutionalized a secondary labor market in Germany. In particular, Germany saw an increase in so-called 'mini-jobs' that have flourished in the less unionized service sector and at the service of the core sectors. Mini-jobs refer to low-level, part-time work that is not fully covered by social insurance contributions (Palier and Thelen 2010: 209). Currently almost 20 percent of low-skill service sector jobs are mini-jobs. Government policies facilitating the expansion of such jobs stand in rather stark contrast to other policies, especially the short-time work program that protects jobs, benefits and skills in manufacturing. This program is, however, largely constrained to benefit the core industrial workers, while 'Germany's efforts in the area of active labor-market policies for low-skill, hard-to-employ workers have been over the years far more uneven and lackluster' (Palier and Thelen 2010: 210).

France: Integrative Dualization

Just as in Denmark, it is impossible to point to one actor driving the labor market and welfare reforms in France (Palier 2010). These reforms were a reaction to past policy failures. They involved a large number of actors who, however, agreed to them for often very different reasons. Maybe most importantly, these changes were introduced at the margins (which facilitated their acceptance by major defenders of the core system) before being gradually extended, their expansion often leading to a change of their meaning within the system. Having been first introduced to comple-ment the system, they gradually became the base for a new pillar in the social protection system, arguably leading to a paradigmatic change of the whole system.

Just as in Germany, the French reforms resulted in an increasing dualization between insiders who benefit from unemployment insurance and outsiders who are assigned to social assistance, i.e. residual, means-tested benefits. Such reforms had already been introduced in the early 1980s (Palier and Thelen 2010: 213–216). Due in part to these reforms, the proportion of 'excluded people' increased, becoming one of the most pressing social issues of the late 1980s. New so called 'insertion policies' were introduced to deal with these problems, the most important of which was the RMI (revenu minimum d'insertion). By the time of our study, France had eight other social minimum income benefit programs with more than 10 percent of the French population receiving one of them at that time. The creation of these assistance schemes eased cuts in the unemployment insurance system by shifting people from insurance benefits to social assistance.

Changes in the financing of the system were also introduced in order to render it more employment friendly (Palier 2010). Like other social insurance schemes, unemployment insurance is financed through contributions levied on earnings. Employers pay more than employees, as the contribution rate is of 4 percent for the former and of 2.4 percent for the latter. During the 1990s, lowering the level of social contribution became the main employment policy in France. Some contributions were replaced by taxation. Thus, a new tax, originally aimed at replacing the social contribution financing by non-contributory benefits was created in the 1990s: contribution sociale généralisée (CSG), which is levied on all types of personal incomes, including wages, but also extends to capital revenues and welfare benefits). Today, CSG provides more than 20 per cent of all social protection resources and represents 35 per cent of health care resources.

In the 2000s, activation policies were added to this dual system. In 2001, the Jospin government created a tax credit, called prime pour l'emploi (PPE), which is a negative income tax for low-paid jobs (in-work benefits). In 2003, in the same vein, the Raffarin government aimed at increasing incentives to work by transforming the RMI into RMA (revenu minimum d'activité) for those having benefited from RMI for two years. Since 2009, a new scheme, called RSA (revenu de solidarité active), which combines a social minimum and a supplementary income given to those entering subsidized low-skill, low-paid jobs, has replaced RMI. As is observed by Palier and Thelen (2010: 216), these policy measures provided some check on the growth of poverty in France, but this did not prevent the increasing bifurcation in the logic of the two systems of social protection.

The unemployment insurance is currently organized around two bodies: the state-run pôle emploi and the bipartite UNEDIC (union nationale pour l'emploi dans l'industrie et le commerce). Pôle emploi was formed in 2009. Its aim is to provide jobseekers with a single point of contact for all employment-related services (registering, counseling, training, placing, and paying benefits). The main tasks of the UNEDIC, for its part, consist in administering the unemployment insurance scheme and in determining the benefits payment system. Despite the fact that it has long been a governmental agency, the UNEDIC has always been managed by the social partners. Both sides (unions and employers) have equal power in this scheme. More specifically, an agreement comes about if at least one organization of either side signs a new convention. Once an agreement has been reached, it has to be approved by the government. Usually, the government does not veto the provisions agreed upon by the social partners.

In theory, France offers one of the most accessible unemployment insurances among OECD countries. In reality, however, only one unemployed person in two draws benefits from the UNEDIC regime. This comparatively low coverage rate is due mainly to the fact that outsiders – jobseekers who formerly held short-term contracts, have never been employed, or are long-term unemployed – are not entitled to unemployment benefit.

Italy: Severe Dualization

The Italian unemployment benefit system is very complex, and highly segmented. Italy has seen two major reforms in 1997 and 2003, which modified the traditional employment policy mix and deeply transformed the rules that had been set up during the golden age of the post-war growth period (Jessoula et al. 2010: 562). Both reforms aimed at introducing some elements of the 'flexicurity' strategy into the Italian labor market.

Traditionally, the Italian protection against unemployment relied on a contributory unemployment insurance scheme and some special programs providing 'wage replacement benefits' in case of temporary working-time reduction without definitive dismissal. The unemployment benefits remained marginal until the 1991 reform of the unemployment insurance. Only in 2008 were benefit levels increased to reach 60 per cent of the previous wage (Ebbinghaus 2010; Anastasia et al. 2011). The special program of 'integration insurance' (*cassa integrazione guadagni*), adopted in 1947, targets employees in industrial firms with more than 15 employees. This is a unique Italian institution, which keeps the unemployed connected to their last employer. It provides large firms with the possibility to temporarily dismiss their workers in times of production difficulties – due for instance to bad weather or the general economic situation. This scheme is split into an ordinary (*cassa integrazione ordinaria* (CIG)) and an extraordinary (*cassa integrazione straordinaria* (CIGS)) scheme.[2] The extraordinary CIGS is for events of a 'non-transitory' character. Only about 40 per cent of the employees are covered by this special program. Moreover, the provision of these benefits is conditional upon a bargaining process between the government, the unions and employers. The unintended consequence of this institution is to severely restrict the workers' mobility, and it arguably constitutes a major obstacle to the introduction of flexicurity measures: jobless workers remain technically employed by their old firm and may not be inclined to look for a new job (Bonoli and Emmenegger 2010: 840).

---

[2] Furthermore, as a reaction to the economic crisis in 2008 the government set up an additional scheme called cassa integrazione in deroga.

In Italy, the high level of income protection for insiders is reinforced by their high job security, which is guaranteed by a rigid regulatory framework, one of the strictest among OECD countries. In particular, in 1966 individual dismissal was restricted by law to well-justified cases, and in 1970, Article 18 of the Workers' Statute prescribed that, in firms with more than 15 workers, employers were obliged to reintegrate fired workers if the Court declared dismissal 'illegitimate' (Jessoula et al. 2010: 566). The other side of the coin is the low level of protection of the great number of employees in small and medium firms, and, above all, of the outsiders. In the past, the employees in small and medium firms did not have access to the same job security as the insiders in the large firms, because they were not covered by Article 18 and they were not entitled to the generous benefits provided by CIGO and CIGS. Outsiders suffered from the lack of a universal social assistance scheme and from the low resources invested in active labor-market policies.

The first labor-market reform measures (introduction of a mobility allowance for insiders) adopted in 1991 followed the passive policy route. In the second half of the 1990s, the policy repertoire was enriched, but it remained characterized by a strong dualism: insiders continue to enjoy strong protection, while outsiders, mostly young workers, women and immigrants, are employed under precarious conditions. In other words, while flexibility was introduced, it was highly selective. Thus, the Treu reform (1997) provided for a gradual process of deregulation through the provision of so-called 'atypical' flexible contracts, and it introduced activation measures. The Biagi law (2003) proceeded further along the flexibility path. The policy innovations have not contributed to substantially reducing the traditional gap between insiders and outsiders, which is of particular importance, given the fact that the bulk of the large number of new jobs contributed to the positive trends in Italy's labor market since the late 1990s and up to the Great Recession were 'atypical' with 'non-standard' contracts. Moreover, the reform of the unemployment insurance went hand in hand with a weakening of the social assistance safety net (Jessoula and Alt 2010).

To sum up, in Italy, flexibilization has been introduced for the new entrants to the labor market, while employment protection for the insiders has not changed. Thus, 'Italy is increasingly characterized by a dualism between labor-market insiders protected by trade unions and labor market outsiders who carry the burden of adjustment' (Bonoli and Emmenegger 2010: 845).

UK: Laissez faire

The UK has moved farthest along the lines of the 'triple integration' model proposed by Clasen and Clegg (2010). Unemployment protection in the UK has de facto become a single-tier system while technically remaining a two-tier one consisting of a contributory and a means-tested component (Clasen 2010). In a major reform in 1996, the Jobseeker's Allowance (JSA) was introduced, which amalgamated contribution-based unemployment benefits (insurance) and means-tested social assistance for unemployed persons. Unusual in the international context, the levels of the two systems have never diverged much and the benefits provided are extremely low compared to other countries. Relative to average full-time earnings, the value of unemployment benefit dropped from 20 per cent in the late 1970s to about 14 per cent by 1990. In 2010, it was equivalent to 11 per cent of average earnings. Most coverage is means-tested protection (77 percent in 2009, compared to 21 percent contributory). The unemployed are always assessed for unemployment benefits first (unless a person has never worked previously) before proceeding to a means test that assesses whether they are entitled to claim assistance (Lødemel and Trickey 2001). Under some (special) conditions, the self-employed can also be entitled to benefits. By the establishment of JSA the government reinforced the coercive and also activating structure of the unemployment regime and simultaneously blurred the boundaries between contributory and non-contributory benefits (Lødemel and Trickey 2001).

In addition to the unemployment assistance and insurances schemes, there are several activation measures, so-called New Deals. These programs were originally initiated by the Labour government in 1998. By means of these activation measures, the government tried to reduce unemployment and welfare state dependency. These measures provide specific unemployed groups with enhanced training, voluntary work, and subsidized employment. The unemployed participating in such programs were supported by a personal adviser in one of the Jobcentres Plus, which considered the necessary steps to optimize their individual situation. Thanks to the cooperation between the public, private and voluntary sector the unemployed were put into alternative jobs (Trickey and Walker 2001).

Originally, the New Deals were developed for the young unemployed and targeted people between 18–24 years, who had been unemployed for at least 6 months (Martin 2004: 52ff.). However, the programs were then extended to also include unemployed older than 25, who have been unemployed for more than 18 months (New Deal 25+), workers older than 50 (New Deal 50+), for lone parents (New Deal lone parents), and for disabled (New Deal for disabled). Whereas the New Deal for young people and the New Deal for 25+ were mandatory, the other programs were voluntary and require motivation and active participation.

From the point of view of individual unemployed persons, benefit entitlement during the past two decades has become increasingly conditional on participating in work-related activities (Clasen 2010). The contributory principle has become increasingly irrelevant and work conditionality (in addition to need) increasingly important for determining the rights to benefits. Benefits have never been regarded as a 'social wage' and have at best been mildly earnings related. Homogenization has all but been achieved.

Conclusion

Summarizing the different aspects of the country-specific context structures, we find partially overlapping categorizations of the six countries according to the various aspects. However, the overlap varies depending on the categorization criterion, which makes for a patchy configuration of context structures and is likely to result in complex patterns of communication strategies.

With respect to the political communication system, the countries fall into two groups: France, Germany, and Switzerland, whose systems more closely follow the political logic; and Denmark, Italy, and the UK, whose systems follow the media logic. Second, as far as the political macro-context is concerned, the countries more or less fall into three groups. The first group consists of Denmark, Switzerland, and Germany – the consensus democracies, with highly coordinated, sector-specific policy networks, and coordinated market economies. Such structures are characteristic of small Western European open economies, such as Denmark or Switzerland. Other members of this group include the Benelux countries, Austria, or the other Scandinavian countries. Germany is the only large Western European country that more or less fits into this group. France and Italy constitute the second group: they are majoritarian democracies with state market economies and at best temporary concertation among the social partners. The main structural element distinguishing the two is the different strength of the state: while France constitutes the paradigmatic case of a strong state, Italy has a very large, but notoriously weak, state that is easily instrumentalized by social forces – such as the unions or political parties. This group represents the structural pattern of Southern Europe, which we also tend to find in the other countries in this region. The UK is the only member of the last group, which represents the Anglo-Saxon countries. It is characterized by a majoritarian democratic regime, pluralism in the administrative arena, and a liberal market economy. On each of the overall structural aspects, it is clearly set apart from the other two groups.

Third, with respect to policy-specific legacies, we can again distinguish four groups of countries. In spite of recent changes in the Danish labor-market regime, we still consider Denmark and Switzerland as the most likely representatives of the flexicurity regime. The overall welfare regimes of the two countries are not identical, and their labor-market policies are not quite the same either. Nevertheless, the labor-market regimes of the two countries seem to be closer to each other than they are to those of the other countries. This resemblance is a result of similar weaknesses of the left in the past (low job security), in combination with a strong liberal element, and a low domain-specific problem pressure in Switzerland, which allows the Swiss to maintain a rather generous unemployment insurance similar to the Danish one. In contrast to these two countries, Germany and the Southern European countries are characterized by an increasingly dualized labor market, which results from corresponding policies that distinguish between labor market insiders (who are well protected) and outsiders (who are only weakly protected). Italy is certainly the most extreme case of dualization in this group. The UK is again set apart, because its labor-market policies protect both insiders and outsiders only very superficially.

Table A3.1 *The news value criteria, ordered according to their overall importance in all six countries (by country: scale values[1]).*

Criterion	DK	CH	DE	FR	IT	UK	Total
Timing	1.50	1.24	1.52	1.11	1.59	1.14	1.35
Clarity	1.06	1.19	1.14	0.68	1.65	1.00	1.12
Timeliness	0.44	1.48	1.19	1.68	0.65	0.64	1.06
Credibility	0.63	1.05	1.29	0.95	0.94	0.50	0.93
Public interest	0.44	0.52	0.81	1.58	1.24	0.57	0.87
Information	0.56	0.71	0.62	1.37	0.82	0.50	0.78
Political basics	0.19	0.86	0.57	1.26	0.18	0.57	0.63
Newness	0.69	0.71	0.48	0.95	0.35	0.36	0.60
Professionalism	0.50	0.81	0.57	0.63	0.41	0.43	0.57
Critique	0.38	0.57	0.57	0.89	0.41	0.36	0.55
Closeness to public	0.06	0.14	0.43	0.47	0.82	0.71	0.43
Adaptation to format	0.81	0.14	0.38	0.32	0.41	0.43	0.40
Public opinion	0.38	0.29	0.19	0.16	0.47	0.36	0.30
Background info	0.25	0.29	0.33	0.53	0.00	0.21	0.28

Table A3.1 *(cont.)*

Criterion	DK	CH	DE	FR	IT	UK	Total
Conflict	**0.31**	0.19	**0.52**	0.26	0.18	0.00	0.26
Personality	**0.38**	0.19	0.14	0.11	0.18	**0.43**	0.22
Personalization	**0.44**	0.05	0.19	0.32	0.12	0.14	0.20
Polarization	0.19	0.19	0.29	0.26	0.12	0.00	0.19
Provocation	0.06	0.14	0.14	0.32	0.12	0.21	0.17
Visualization	0.19	0.05	0.19	**0.42**	0.06	0.00	0.16
Exciting story	**0.38**	0.05	0.10	0.16	0.12	0.21	0.16
Balanced	0.25	0.14	0.24	0.05	0.06	0.14	0.15
Commonsense	0.13	0.29	0.14	0.05	0.06	0.14	0.14
National values	0.25	0.10	0.05	0.16	0.24	0.07	0.14
Emotionality	**0.38**	0.10	0.10	0.05	0.12	0.14	0.14
Goodness	0.19	0.10	0.10	0.00	0.12	**0.36**	0.13
Expectations	0.19	0.10	0.19	0.00	0.06	0.21	0.12
Prominence + Prestige	0.13	0.10	0.00	0.16	0.00	0.14	0.08
Surprise	0.19	0.05	0.05	0.05	0.00	0.07	0.06
National symbols	0.06	0.00	0.00	0.11	0.00	0.00	0.03

[1] Scale ranges from 0 (unimportant) to 3 (most important). An average of 1 indicates that every respondent considers the criterion important, an average of 2 that every respondent considers it very important.

Table A3.2 *Factor analysis of 30 news value aspects (factor loadings, uniqueness, and Eigenvalues)*

Variable	Media logic	Information	Conflict	Uniqueness
Surprise	**0.66**	0.22	0.07	0.51
Personalization	**0.49**	0.00	0.06	0.76
Common sense	**0.47**	0.21	0.22	0.69
Good news	**0.46**	−0.14	−0.06	0.76
National values	**0.45**	−0.15	**0.42**	0.60
Prominence + prestige	**0.45**	0.17	0.24	0.71
Expectations of journalist	**0.43**	0.03	0.02	0.81
Adaptation to format	**0.41**	0.07	−0.01	0.83
Exciting story	**0.36**	0.20	−0.04	0.83
Clarity	**0.33**	−0.20	−0.16	0.82
Balance	**0.33**	0.18	−0.16	0.84
Credibility	**0.30**	0.14	−0.29	0.80
Background Information	0.22	**0.70**	−0.04	0.46
Information	−0.04	**0.58**	−0.09	0.66
Public interest	0.00	**0.53**	0.14	0.70
Visualization	0.23	**0.31**	−0.08	0.85
Timeliness	−0.06	**0.31**	−0.28	0.82

Table A3.2 *(cont.)*

Variable	Media logic	Information	Conflict	Uniqueness
Conflict	0.02	0.04	**0.55**	0.70
Individual person	0.11	0.03	**0.48**	0.75
National symbols	0.15	−0.14	**0.47**	0.74
Polarization	0.20	0.07	**0.35**	0.83
Closeness to citizens	0.18	0.09	**0.35**	0.83
Professionalism	**0.29**	**0.25**	**−0.34**	0.74
Critique	−0.11	**0.25**	**0.25**	0.86
Timing	0.26	−0.20	0.03	0.89
Newness	0.19	0.19	−0.21	0.88
Provocation	0.15	0.18	0.18	0.91
Emotionality	0.24	−0.14	0.21	0.88
Political basics	−0.03	0.17	0.05	0.97
Public opinion	0.23	0.04	0.09	0.94
Eigenvalue	**2.90**	1.90	1.90	

Table A3.3 *Factor analysis of seven statements about the relationship between policy-makers and journalists (factor loadings, uniqueness, and Eigenvalues)*

Indicator	Professional	Personal	Uniqueness
We make contact	**0.41**	0.33	0.72
Journalists make contact	**0.47**	−0.12	0.77
We invite journalists informally	**0.74**	0.41	0.29
Journalists invite us informally	**0.78**	0.26	0.32
We meet journalists outside of work	0.46	**0.59**	0.43
We know journalists personally	0.23	**0.69**	0.48
We are close friends with journalists	0.30	**0.66**	0.48
Eigenvalue	1.90	1.62	

4   The Variety of National Debates

Hanspeter Kriesi, Laurent Bernhard, Flavia Fossati,
Regula Hänggli and Christian Elmelund-Præstekær

Introduction

In this chapter, we discuss the specific issues that have given rise to public debates in each country during our period of observation. As we have argued, at any given point in time, the national policy-specific debates are likely to be characterized by 'Babylonian confusion': they focus on very different issues in different countries and their terminology varies from one country to the other, depending on the country-specific problem pressure, the country-specific policy legacy, and the stage of the issue-specific policy cycle in a given country. Political processes are generally characterized by stability and incrementalism – they incrementally develop the policy inventory that exists in a given policy domain. It is only occasionally that they enter critical periods of rapid and substantial change. The punctuated equilibrium model of policy-making takes this simple observation as its point of departure (True et al. 2007). In periods of incremental change, the specialized policy-makers who form the policy-specific subsystems are in charge. They are responsible for the routine modifications which are required every now and then in a given policy domain. During such periods, the public generally takes little notice of the policy process going on in the subsystem. In periods of crisis, however, a specific policy domain becomes a top priority of the key political leaders and policy-making shifts from the subsystem to top level politics. It is during such periods of punctuation that the public debate is most likely to become focused on the issue-specific policy process.

Against the background of the urgency of the labor-market problems in the aftermath of the 'Great Recession,' labor-market policies have generally entered a period in which punctuations have become more likely in all of our countries. Thus, our period of observation has been characterized by some form of punctuation in the labor-market policy domain in four of our six countries – Denmark, Germany, Italy, and the UK. In one other, Switzerland, a punctuation occurred just before the period we have selected for investigation. During the period we covered, both France and Switzerland witnessed only low-key debates on labor-market policy issues. This is a consequence of the constraints imposed by the political agenda: while incremental processing at the policy subsystems level can occur simultaneously in parallel, the processing at the top level can take place only serially. In other words, the political agenda at the top level becomes crowded very quickly and the processing at that level can thus address only very few issues at the same time (Jones 1994). Accordingly, at any given point in time, the probability that a certain issue is processed at the top level is quite low, even if the problem related to the issue is an urgent one that preoccupies the public a good deal. Thus, the financial and economic crisis had very serious consequences for many different policy subsystems, and, depending on the country-specific problem pressures and the strategies of the national leaders, these consequences were tackled in different orders of priority at different times, and, of course, in very different ways depending on the labor-market regime of the country in question.

The public debate does not, however, reflect only the agenda of the political system. It may also be a function of the media's own agenda, which may not necessarily coincide with the political agenda. Actors not part of the formal political process may attempt to put a given issue on the policy agenda, and the best opportunity they have to do so is by attracting the attention of the media for their cause. Thus, social movements typically stage protest events in the public sphere in order to catch the attention of the media which will increase their chances to obtain access to the policy agenda. In one of our countries, Italy, it was social movements who put the issues of the debate we selected for our study on the agenda. Professional experts and public intellectuals may use the media to raise an alarm and to contribute to the public issue-specific consciousness. Moreover, the media themselves may choose to put a specific issue on their agenda, by their investigating activities, or even by explicit mobilization attempts (Walgrave and Manssens 2000, Kriesi 2004). They have, indeed, done so in one of the countries in our study – Denmark.

We have selected our country-specific public debates as a combined result of our reading of the media during the period of our study and of our discussions with labor-market experts during our first interviews. For each country, we chose the most conspicuous issue in the unemployment policy domain during the period covered. *Table 4.1* presents the issues we selected and about which we interviewed our experts during the second interview. In three countries – Denmark, Italy, and the UK – we selected two issues, because we were not sure which one of

Table 4.1 *Issues for the selected public debates, by country*

	DK	CH	DE	FR	IT	UK
Debate 1	Activation	Mass dismissals	Hartz IV	Youth unemployment	Fiat	Comprehensive spending review
Debate 2	Youth unemployment				Education reform	Universal credit

Table 4.2 *Variables determining debate characteristics*

Variables	DK	CH	DE	FR	IT	UK
Problem pressure	Medium	Low	Medium	High	High	High
Problem structure	Skills	Skills	Precarity (long-term)	Precarity (youth/long-term)	Precarity (youth)	Youth
Policy cycle	Minor recent reform	Minor recent reform	Minor reform	No reform	No reform	Major reform, ongoing
Regime type	Active flexicurity	Liberal flexicurity	Dualization	Dualization	Dualization	Deregulation
Passive benefits	++	+	−	++	+	−
Activation	++	+	+	−	−	+
Job protection	−	−	+	+	++	−

the two would become more important during the period in question. As it turned out, one of the two issues clearly dominated in Denmark and Italy, while the second British issue was in fact a sub-issue of the first, more encompassing one.

Table 4.2, which provides an overview over the country-specific problem pressure, the stage of the policy cycle in the respective countries, and their labor-market regimes, allows linking these debates to the context conditions which we have presented in the previous chapter. *Table 4.3* provides two indicators for the intensity of the respective debates: the participation rate and the salience of the key issue-specific event in the period covered. The participation rate indicates the share of organizations represented by our respondents that took part in the debate. The debates are arranged according to this indicator which reaches from a high of 87 percent (for the British comprehensive

Table 4.3 *Indictors for the intensity of the issue-specific debates in fall 2010 (salience of key events and participation rates)*

Country	Debate	Event	Salience	Participation rate
UK	Spending review	Reform announcement	3.80	.87
DE	Hartz IV	Draft by government	3.50	.86
DK	Activation	Reform announcement	2.81	.81
IT	Fiat	Refusal by FIOM	3.39	.77
FR	Youth unemployment	Agreement on opening negotiations	2.80	.76
IT2	Education	Manifestations	2.89	.73
UK2	Welfare state	Universal credit	2.82	.56
DK2	Youth unemployment	Funds by EU's social foundation	2.47	.31
CH	Dismissals	Layoffs by Roche	2.61	.25

spending review) to a low of 25 percent (for the mass layoffs at a plant of Roche pharmaceutics in Switzerland). The second indicator for the intensity of the debate measures the salience of the key issue-specific event: respondents were asked to assess the importance of these events on a scale ranging from 0 (not important at all) to 4 (extremely important). As is shown in *Table 4.3*, the two indicators are closely, although not perfectly correlated (r=.74). Thus, the most important event was the announcement of the Comprehensive Spending Review (CSR) by the British government on October 20, 2010, with an impressive assessment level of 3.80.

In the UK, there was clearly a period of punctuation: against the background of a high problem pressure (see *Table 4.2*), the new government had launched an encompassing reform – the Comprehensive Spending Review – which included a major overhaul of the social insurance schemes: the universal credit proposal. As is fitting for our example of a deregulation regime, this new reform proposal followed the 'triple integration' model and involved cutting benefits and activation according to 'work first' principles. Unsurprisingly, this case of punctuation gave rise to the most intense public debate. Germany also experienced a rather intense debate, which was provoked by an incremental change of the major program in the policy domain, the modification of the Hartz IV reform that had first been implemented in 2005. As we have seen in the introduction, the problem pressure was less intense in Germany, but the effects of the crisis required a modification of Hartz IV, which first and foremost involved cutting benefits once again. The fact that the public debate in Germany focused on cutting benefits for people falling into social assistance is also quite typical for a dualization regime such as the German one.

The two Italian and one of the two Danish debates were also quite intense. All of them were put on the political agenda by challengers from below. In the Danish case, it was a media campaign that eventually succeeded in putting the issue of activation on the agenda of top-level politics, inducing the government to propose a minor reform of the activation policy – a key element of the Danish flexicurity regime. In the more important Italian case, an issue concerning the flexibilization of labor relations typical of the rigid dualization regime that characterizes Italy, it was the mobilization by the unions against Fiat industries that put the issue on the public and the political agenda. Similarly, the second Italian case also involved the mobilization by challengers, this time mainly researchers, teachers, and students who mobilized against the swingeing cuts made to the educational reform project ordered by the Berlusconi government. In this case, however, the mobilization from below only reinforced the salience of the issue that was already on the political agenda.

Finally, for different reasons, the Swiss and the French public debates on unemployment related issues during the period covered were not as intense as the debates in the other four countries. In Switzerland, just before our observation period, unemployment insurance had been the object of a direct-democratic vote – the typical Swiss version of punctuation. Although, compared to other countries, problem pressure has been low in Switzerland, as a result of the crisis the unemployment level had increased which required a restructuring of the financial situation of the unemployment insurance. As is typical for Swiss politics, once the direct-democratic vote had been decided, the issue disappeared from the public agenda and returned to the political subsystem. Since the overall problem pressure was low in Switzerland, there was no other issue ready to take its place in the unemployment policy domain. The unions tried to push the issue of mass layoffs, given that three highly publicized instances of massive layoffs occurred during the period we covered, but, as the indicators in *Table 4.3* show, it was not to be. In France, the public debate related to unemployment was dominated by the pension reform during the period we covered. This high-profile issue crowded out all the other issues in related policy domains. Meanwhile, the policy-makers in the subsystem agreed to tackle the problem of youth unemployment – an issue of particular importance in the dualized regimes of France and Italy.

We shall briefly present each one of the issues we selected in the remainder of this chapter. We follow the sequence of the regime types, beginning with the flexicurity regimes of Denmark and Switzerland, continuing with the dualization regimes and ending with the deregulation regime of the UK.

Denmark: Media Campaign on Activation

In the period under investigation, the unemployment issue enjoyed high salience in the Danish public. The public attention was, however, not primarily the result of the priority of the issue-specific policy process on the policy agenda of Danish politics, but it was above all due to a media storm on the Danish activation policy, and, to a minor extent, to a public debate on the steeply increasing rate of youth unemployment. We review the two debates separately.

The activation debate was important because, as we have seen, activation policy is one of the three pillars in the Danish flexicurity model (e.g. Bredgaard et al. 2006; Emmenegger 2010a). The quality and relevance of the actual content of the activation programs has been discussed regularly in the Danish public. This was, indeed, the case just prior to the period under investigation here. During summer 2010, a host of media stories revealed that unemployed people were enrolled in bizarre courses, such as courses on analyzing the handwriting of Hitler, enabling them to find their 'inner bird', or to build towers of spaghetti. The media also reported that at least one person was sent on job training at a brothel. This debate on such 'irrelevant' and 'meaningless' activation prompted the Minister of Employment, Inger Støjberg, to launch an internal task force to come up with adjustments to the activation scheme – an assignment that was due in January 2011. During September 2010, the media sporadically returned to these stories and provided new examples of the meaninglessness and the counterproductive consequences of an overly bureaucratic activation regime.

In October 2010 a regular 'media storm' (see Wien and Elmelund-Præstekær 2009) erupted as the broadsheet paper, *Berlingske Tidende*, launched a journalistic campaign on 'the great job circus' (*Det store jobcirkus*). The series was triggered by a case story on the activation practice of one of Copenhagen's major institutions situated in a street called Farvergade. The city of Copenhagen had no less than 800 uninsured unemployed assigned to the Farvergade project. Since the national law on activation prescribed a minimum of 25 hours of educational activity a week, one would have expected Farvergade to be humming with the activity of hundreds of jobseekers at any point in time. But the journalists never met more than 40 to 50 people during their frequent visits. *Berlingske Tidende* filed an application under the act of freedom of information and revealed that Farvergade provided only one-and-a-half hours of training a week. On this basis, the newspaper concluded that not only did the unemployed not gain access to the services they were entitled to, but also that the city council had enjoyed a major economic benefit as a result of this neglect.

The reason for accusing the city of fraudulent behavior is straightforward, but requires some additional information on Danish national activation law: Since the reform of unemployment policy by the center-right government, the activation policy has been administrated and implemented by the municipalities, while the national state is obliged to reimburse 35 percent (now 30 percent) of the benefits for uninsured unemployed people (i.e. for people who are not members of an unemployment fund). To provide the municipalities with an economic incentive to get people into jobs, the state has to reimburse not only 35, but 65 percent (now down to 50 percent) of the unemployment benefits once the municipality declares that an unemployed person is activated (assuming that activation is a first step towards a permanent job). Thus, the journalists argued that the municipality of Copenhagen collected the high reimbursement rate without really doing anything for the formally activated unemployed – the activation was, in fact, fake. This interpretation was shared by a high-ranking public official in the Copenhagen unemployment administration, who not only went public with his criticisms but also filed an official complaint to the Ombudsman.

In its journalistic campaign, *Berlingske Tidende* framed the Farvergade case as a symptom of a 'system failure' in the national law rather than merely an instance of municipal malpractice. In the following days, the newspaper wrote stories about similar experiences in other municipalities, and the national problem frame was reinforced by giving voice to university experts, representatives from the labor unions and the employers' organizations, the (left-wing) political opposition at the national level, and people knowing the system from within. Finally, the journalists referred the issue to the Labor Market Commission, consisting of nine independent experts, that had been earlier called upon by the government to provide advice as to how to enlarge the unsubsidized labor force: the Commission had published its final report in 2009 and had pointed to exactly the problems in the activation law revealed by the newspapers. It had proposed alternative regulations, but its proposal was not adopted by the government.

In mid-October, the Audit of the State Accounts published a report heavily criticizing another aspect of the activation policy. While the Farvergade project was supposed to activate the so-called job-ready unemployed, the Audit report concluded that the municipalities in general were performing poorly in their activation of the 'non-job-ready'. In fact, people outside the activation programs had higher chances of getting a job than those participating in such programs.

Finally, on October 19, the Minister of Employment promised to recalibrate the activation policy. As the government did not come up with concrete policy proposals, the media filled up the waiting time by pointing to even more troubles related to the activation policies. They suggested, for example, that municipalities did not activate the unemployed as quickly as prescribed by the law, or that the activation of people on sick leave paid too little attention to the conditions that had forced them out of their jobs in the first place. Moreover, the interest organization of the Danish municipalities, Local Government Denmark (KL), did not hesitate when it came to prescribing a cure-all answer. It was in the organization's declared interest to keep the activation policy at the municipal level and, accordingly, it came up with a list of elements that should be included in the activation reform from that point on – most of which were taken from the Labor Market Commission's final report.

By November 17, the government presented its own reform package, consisting of three bills (L67, L69, and L71). Besides some marginal adjustments, the key elements of these three bills included:
• reduced reimbursement rates from the state to the municipalities (L71). For the insured unemployed the rates were reduced from 50/ 75 percent to 30/50 percent and for the uninsured unemployed from 35/65 to 30/50 percent. The proposal was to reduce the public annual expenditures by approximately 70 million euros.
• similar reductions of the reimbursement rates for unemployed on sickness leave (L67). This was cost neutral for the municipalities collectively due to a simultaneous increase in the general subsidies from the state to the municipalities.
• delimitation of activation measures subject to the high reimbursement rate (L71). Specifically, activation via guidance and upgrading of skills especially designed for unemployed participations was no longer sufficient for the municipalities to obtain the high rate (i.e. no more courses in Hitler's handwriting or inner bird finding) – it would be possible to obtain the high rates only when activating the unemployed via formal and generally acknowledged education programs, via practical work training, or a subsidized job.

- introduction of a maximum cost (18,500 euros) of the six weeks of optional education for unemployed (L69). This initiative reduced the public annual expenditures by approximately 50 million euros. Later, when the new Social Democratic Prime Minister, Helle Thorning-Schmidt took office in fall 2011, this initiative was revoked.
- general reduction (from 2,500 to 1,800 euros) in the maximum annual cost of administration of one unemployed person's activation (L71). This was cost neutral for the municipalities collectively due to a simultaneous increase in the general subsidies from the state to the municipalities.
- some groups (not clearly defined) of sick unemployed were relieved for the demand of activation – without reduction in the reimbursement rate (L67).
- incitements for the municipalities to get unemployed on sickness leave into part time activation (L67)

All three bills were adopted by the parliament only one month after they were tabled, i.e. on December 17 – a time frame criticized by the unions for being too narrow to allow for sufficient public debate on the changes. The bills were adopted – without any substantial alterations – by the governmental coalition (i.e. the Liberals and the Conservatives), the Danish People's Party, and the Liberal Alliance. The left voted against the bills. The social liberals did, however, support L67. All changes were to be effected by January 1, 2011.

The government never really managed to frame the public debate. Instead a long list of actors seemed to agree that the government's reform did not respond properly to the problems encountered in the real world. Especially four arguments gained momentum during the debate in November and December: First, the parliamentary opposition and several specialized interest organizations (e.g. *Uddannelsesforbundet*) argued that the general reduction in reimbursement rates and the ceasing of activation of people off work due to sickness were nothing but a measure of retrenchment – it would not provide the municipalities with tools to get people into real jobs and it would only make it harder to help the weakest unemployed, i.e. people unfit for ordinary education and job training. Second, the parliamentary opposition, as well as specialized educational organizations and major labor unions (e.g. *3F*), argued that the new maximum costs of activation and education in conjunction with the incitement to activate people via temporary jobs would be counterproductive to the general ambition of the government to improve the skills of the unemployed. Third, the same actors argued that the new regulation would not put an end to economic speculation in the municipalities. In fact, the new regulation would have the same perverse effects as the old one, because public and private employers would be tempted to lay off regular employees and hire in people in temporary or subsidized positions instead – i.e. the municipalities would still be prompted to consider economic gains rather than the best interests of the unemployed when implementing the activation policy. Finally, university researchers and Local Government Denmark (*KL*) criticized the fact that the government kept formulating the active labor-market policy without any solid empirical evidence of possible effects and that the government did not alter the detailed control regime set up to monitor the municipalities as well as the individual unemployed. The municipalities were not granted more autonomy – or trust – to design their own individual solutions and ideas to get people in permanent jobs.

In December the Ministry of Employment demanded that the municipality of Copenhagen pay back a total of 390 million kroner (52 million euros or approximately 5 percent of the annual labor-market budget in Copenhagen) because of what the ministry saw as an illegal practice in Farvergade and multiple other places. This was a historically huge demand and the city council decided in early February to file a lawsuit against the state on the matter. Before the court case began in the summer of 2011 the state's claim was reduced to 65 million kroner (9 million euros), but at the time of writing the final verdict has yet to be delivered. Ironically, the very 25-hour rule that was the main driver of *Berlingske Tidende*'s journalistic campaign on the Farversgade case in particular, and the activation policy in general, was abolished by the government in early 2011 together with 45 other rules in order to 'get rid of the hassle,' as the Minister put it. These 46 instances of 'de-bureaucratization' were the result of the task force assignment mentioned above initiated by the Minister in summer 2010.

Turning to the issue of *youth unemployment,* some aspects relate to the issue of activation, but in general the unemployment issue was not as salient as the issue of activation. It is also more difficult to identify consistent streams of arguments in the coverage of youth unemployment – a lack of focus that perhaps stems from the following dilemma: on the one hand, the general issue of unemployment was, indeed, a salient issue in the period under investigation, and almost all actors agreed that the global economic downturn had the most negative consequences among the young in terms of an increasing unemployment rate. On the other hand, the media strove to put the Danish situation into a global – or at least European – perspective, and in comparison with many other countries (especially Spain, Italy, France, and Greece) the Danish youth enjoyed, as we have seen, a fairly high degree of employment.

However, even though the unemployment rate was low by international standards, it had quadrupled in just two years and the youngest generation was significantly more unemployed than any other generation. Thus, by national standards the issue of youth unemployment was important, arguably more important than the nation as such was willing to admit, as claimed by an editor at *Politiken*, a major center-left national newspaper. By the end of February 2011, the editor warned against the risk of creating yet another 'generation no-future' like the one in the 1970s. The issue did not make the front pages on a regular basis, but it was discussed to some extent during the period of investigation.

Thus, the general awareness of an increasing rate of unemployment among the young provided several labor unions with an opportunity to call for political action. However, no strong political demand was voiced to reform the active labor-market policy. The demands from various unions would merely calibrate the existing policies, and the opposition's so-called 'youth plan' presented in February 2011 did not aim at altering the fundamentals of the existing policy – it primarily promised to increase the capacity of the universities and other educational institutions. Moreover, this plan attracted only little attention and mostly negative comments.

Switzerland: The Calm After the Storm

In Switzerland, an intense debate on unemployment policy had been taking place in the weeks just before our observation period. The debate was part of the referendum campaign on a revised unemployment insurance law, on which the Swiss citizens had to vote on September 26, 2010. Such referendum campaigns are the typically Swiss version of punctuation of the routine policy process: they incite the whole country to debate the issues on the agenda of the public vote. On this particular voting day, 53 percent of Swiss citizens accepted the reform of the unemployment insurance supported by the federal government, right-wing parties, and business interest groups in a direct-democratic vote. The aim of the reform was to improve the financial situation regarding unemployment insurance. Over the previous seven years, the insurance had accumulated debts of 7.1 billion Swiss francs, since the country's average unemployment rate had proved to be higher (3.3 percent) than expected (2.5 percent). The reform was designed to tap additional revenues as well as to reduce the expenditures. Both chambers of Parliament agreed on an increase of wage contributions assumed by employers and employees from 2 to 2.2 percent. In addition, they decided to introduce a temporary 'solidarity percentage' for incomes between 126,000 and

315,000 Swiss francs. According to the Federal State Secretariat for Economic Affairs (Seco 2010), these two measures were expected to raise an additional 646 million Swiss francs per year, while cuts to benefits were expected to improve the financial situation of the insurance by another 626 million francs. Among others, these cuts included a closer linkage between the length of the contribution periods and the duration of entitlements (e.g. the unemployed qualify for daily allowances for a maximum of 18 months only if they have paid contributions for at least 18 months instead of the previous standard of 12 months), an extension of waiting periods for young people, as well as the abolishment of the possibility to extend the length of benefits in regions with high unemployment rates. In addition, time spent by unemployed people in public employment programs did not grant the right to benefit from additional benefits anymore. Labor unions and left-wing parties opposed these retrenchment measures, particularly those targeted at the young unemployed. In calling for a referendum, these actors had challenged the federal law adopted by Parliament in March 2010.

With the adoption of the law, unemployment policy largely disappeared from the public space, as the policy subsystem was now occupied with the details of the law's implementation, i.e. with the elaboration of the legal ordinance of the unemployment insurance (*Verordnung über die obligatorische Arbeitslosenversicherung und Insolvenzentschädigung*, AVIV), which had to be partially revised because of the reform adopted in the popular vote. There was little time for the elaboration of the ordinance, since the federal government announced that the revision would become effective by April 2011. In October 2010, the Federal Secretariat for Economic Affairs launched the corresponding consultation procedure (*Vernehmlassungsverfahren*). By January 2011, 83 political actors had taken the opportunity to comment on the blueprint issued by Seco. Fifteen organizations asked the federal authorities not to apply the new rules to persons who already had been unemployed. Calls for transitory measures were particularly fuelled by the circumstance that, as a result of the revised scheme, about 15,000 unemployed (roughly 10 percent of claimants) were expected to prematurely lose their entitlements by April 2011, thus leading to higher social assistance expenditures at the sub-national level. Nevertheless, the federal government stood firm. In March 2011, it decided to apply the new provisions pertaining to benefit duration to all recipients. In two respects, the government appeared more generous than the blueprint proposed by the Federal Secretariat for Economic Affairs, however. First, it refrained from raising the minimum monthly wage covered by the insurance from 500 to 800

Swiss francs. No less than 45 consulted organizations had criticized the planned increase. Second, the government agreed to double the period of employment required for the calculation of the contribution period for persons engaged in the cultural sector. In order to lobby for this change, some cultural professionals established a committee.

Public attention to the issue of unemployment was also constrained by the fact that, contrary to our other cases, Switzerland showed no obvious signs of economic weakness during our period of interest. As we have already seen in Chapter 1, its unemployment rate remained at a comparatively low level in spite of the Great Recession. The country had quickly found back to its path of prosperity.

The only employment-related topic focused on *the strength of the Swiss franc*. Its steady appreciation caused growing concern about Switzerland's international competitiveness. Somewhat ironically, the Swiss economy became a victim of its own success. The debt crises from which suffered many other countries had increased the attractiveness of the Swiss franc as a 'safe haven'. As a small, open economy, Switzerland proved to be very sensitive to currency fluctuations. The export share in relation to its gross domestic product (GDP) attains 40 percent. The European Union, and in particular Germany, are Switzerland's largest export markets. The Swiss currency had gained more than 12 percent against the euro in the previous 12 months, a development that alarmed Swiss exporters. The Swiss National Bank (SNB) had tried to curb the appreciation of the franc by buying massive amounts of euros in spring 2010, but was forced to abandon its interventions in June 2010, since it proved impossible to defend a targeted exchange rate of 1.40 SFr/euro. The SNB defended its interventions on the foreign currency market by arguing that it had at least been able to slow down the appreciation of the Swiss franc, which helped saving jobs and keeping the economy on track. In January 2011, the SNB reported an impressive loss of 26 billion francs on its foreign currency positions for 2010. Despite the fact that Swiss products and services had become much more expensive to sell abroad, most exporting companies did not cut jobs during our period of investigation.

There have been two major instances of mass dismissals, however, which were not directly related to the strength of the Swiss franc. On October 4, 2010, Alstom, a French engineering group, announced that it would cut 4,000 jobs from its power division, 750 of which were in its Swiss plant near Baden (Argovia). The company blamed the impact of the economic crisis on the coal and gas plant equipment markets. Roche, a Swiss pharmaceutical giant, planned to axe 4,800 jobs as part of a worldwide restructuring plan. The company released this announcement on November 17, 2010, stating that some 770 positions would be lost in Switzerland. Most importantly, Roche decided to close a diabetes diagnostic center in the canton of Bern. Both episodes triggered harsh reactions from labor unions. The scope of these events remained rather limited, however. They drew some media reports, most of which remained at the local level. Given that these events were sporadic and unique in nature, they did not give rise to any coherent debate about mass dismissals. This rather surprising result was attributable to the fact that Swiss companies accepted lower prices to maintain orders from abroad. This strategy let profit margins erode, but prevented companies from suffering a drop in demand. As a result, economic activity did not slow down.

Nevertheless, it was beyond dispute that a Swiss franc that stayed strong for a considerable period would cause great damage to the economy. However, the debate on the strong Swiss franc long remained at a very low level of intensity. This began to change only when the euro fell under 1.30 Swiss francs in December 2010. Several ideas emerged as ways of preventing a further appreciation of the domestic currency. These measures included pegging the franc to the euro, selling gold, accelerating inflation, introducing negative interest rates, limiting the inflow of capital, and paying salaries to cross-border workers in euros instead of Swiss francs. The Swiss Federation of Trade Unions also proposed the reintroduction of the so-called 'gentlemen's agreement' between the SNB and Swiss banks. In 1976, the latter had promised not to make use of speculative currency transactions to strengthen the Swiss currency. However, apart from labor unions, left-wing parties, and some isolated entrepreneurs and economists, no major political force called on the federal authorities to take action against the negative impacts of the strong franc.

Most importantly, the Swiss business community stuck to its notorious free market ethos. Economiesuisse, the most powerful business federation, called on companies to adapt to the challenge posed by the strong Swiss franc by diversifying their activities and increasing their productivity. Even Swissmem, the umbrella organization of export-oriented Swiss engineering and machinery industry, did not urge the government to take short-term measures. Although Swissmem had warned that the strong franc could result in up to 50,000 job losses, its demands focused on general economic conditions and were long term in nature, such as more money for innovation, new free-trade agreements with emerging markets, and maintaining both the flexible domestic labor market and the free movement of persons with the European Union. More pragmatically, many political actors rejected governmental measures to combat the strong Swiss francs because the Swiss economy had escaped a deep crisis by pointing its above-average performance in terms of growth and employment.

On January 14, 2011, the State Secretariat for Economic Affairs (Seco) invited representatives of the business community and labor unions to top-level talks regarding possible policy responses to the strong Swiss franc.[1] Swiss media referred to this talk as a 'crisis meeting'. Not surprisingly, the meeting came up with no specific measures to prevent the Swiss franc's appreciation. A statement issued by Seco (2011) pointed out that there was no consensus on what could be done in light of the strong franc. Participants only agreed on the independence of the Swiss National Bank to steer the country's monetary policy. After the meeting, the Federation of Swiss Trade Unions (SGB) criticized that no decision had been reached. Only on September 6, 2011, when the Swiss franc had almost reached parity with the euro, did the Swiss National Bank declare its new policy to fight against the overvaluation of the Swiss franc and to defend a minimum rate of 1.20 SFr/euro 'with the utmost determination'.

Germany: Adjusting Hartz IV

Between September and December 2010, the relevant public debate concerning unemployment was about the Hartz IV benefit reform. The reform of the Hartz IV benefit rates had become necessary following a ruling by Germany's highest court: On February 9, 2010, the *Federal Court* had declared the Hartz IV standard rates unconstitutional. It had instructed the federal government to render these rates more transparent and the calculation basis less arbitrary. The date set for these modifications was the end of 2010. In particular, the Constitutional Court claimed that the standard rate for children of benefit recipients should be based on their actual needs and not simply be calculated as a percentage of the standard rate for adults. Furthermore, additional earnings (Zuverdienst) should be regulated in a way that they increase incentives for recipients to accept further employment. In September and October 2010, the *government* worked out and agreed on a bill for the reform. Between October 2010 and February 2011, the debate about the reform of the Hartz IV legislation took place in the *parliamentary* arena. In this arena, the debate focused mainly on the standard benefit rate, on the so-called

[1] Amongst others, Economiesuisse, the Swiss Employers' Association (SAV), the Association of Small Business (SGV), the Federation of Swiss Trade Unions (SGB) as well as representatives of the engineering industry, the pharmaceutical industry, the watch industry, banking, tourism, and farming took part in this meeting.

education package (Bildungspaket), additional earnings for benefit claimants (Zuverdienst), and on financial support for municipalities.

The debate was prominently covered in the media because, since its introduction in 2005, Hartz IV legislation has been an important issue. However, it was not as prominently covered as it could have been because the unemployment rates were comparatively low, which decreased the perceived importance of the problem. In addition, there were other important debates taking place at the same time such as the debates about Stuttgart 21, the Castor transports (of nuclear waste), retirement age of 67 or the 2011 budget, which crowded out the unemployment issue from the public agenda.

After the Court's decision in February 2010, the government presented a draft bill for the reform of the Hartz IV benefit rates on 26 September, and agreed on a slightly modified version on October 20. The government basically proposed a five euro increase of the Hartz IV benefits (from 359 to 364 euro), and better conditions for children of benefit recipients and for municipalities. On December 3, the Bundestag (lower house) accepted the government's bill. The agreement was mainly based on the votes from the government coalition: the Christian Democratic Union–Christian Social Union alliance (CDU/CSU) and the Free Democratic Party (FDP). On December 17, the Bundesrat (the upper house in which the states are represented) came to a different decision and rejected the bill. In this chamber, the governing coalition parties were not able to command a majority. The governing coalition would have needed votes from the opposition. The opposition (SPD, Left, Greens) argued that the bill was still unconstitutional and non-transparent. Above all, it demanded a larger increase of the benefits than the five euro increase provided by the bill, and support for poor children in general (not only for children of benefit recipients). In addition, it called for a minimum wage.

Given the disagreement between the two chambers, a mediation committee (Vermittlungsausschuss) with members from both chambers was charged with finding a solution. After several meetings, a compromise was found on February 21, 2011. Four days later, both chambers officially accepted the suggested compromise: First, a limited benefits increase of five euros was maintained and introduced with retrospective effect as of January 1, 2010. An additional increase of three euros (plus inflation) was accepted for January 1, 2012. Second, poor children (not only children from benefit recipients) were to receive additional funds for education and participation in social and cultural activities. Included in this education package were school lunches, homework tutoring, and contributions to afternoon sports clubs and music lessons. The estimated costs for the educational package were ten euros per child per month. Third, minimum wages for temporary workers started to kick in on May 1, 2011. For approximately one million temporary workers, the minimum wage amounted to 7.6 euros an hour. Finally, municipalities received financial relief: starting on January 1, 2012, the federal government would increasingly subsidize costs of basic social assistance for retired people (Grundsicherung im Alter). After January 1, 2014, the federal state was to bear all the costs related to this kind of assistance. The compromise was accepted at last when the largest opposition party (SPD) also agreed to it. Thus, the governing coalition (CDU/CSU, FDP), together with the votes of the SPD, obtained a majority in the Bundesrat. The responsible minister, Ursula von der Leyen (CDU), called the agreement a joint project of the coalition and the opposition and considered it a reasonable solution. In particular, she pointed out that children and municipalities were to gain most from the agreement. She also recognized that the negotiations were hard. The Greens and the Left continued to disagree. Above all, they were concerned that the arbitrary basis for the calculation of benefits would give rise to renewed lawsuits before the Federal Constitutional Court. As a consequence, the member states (Bundesländer) where the Greens or the Left were part of the government coalition, such as Nordrhein-Westfalen, Bremen, Berlin, and Saarland, abstained from voting in the Bundesrat.

France: In the Shadow of Protest Politics

Strictly speaking, unemployment policies were not debated in any arena during our period of observation. The main reason relates to the fact that French politics focused the attention on the governmental pension reform. Accordingly, the public debate during our period of observation was dominated by the pension reform. The government proposed to raise the normal retirement age for public pensions from 65 to 67 and the anticipated retirement age from 60 to 62. As is usual in France, protests against the reform took place in the streets. United labor unions organized fourteen days of nationwide demonstrations from March 23 to November 23, 2010. The most attended events took place in September and in October 2010. According to labor unions, over two million people took to the streets in each of the seven demonstrations that occurred during these two months. In addition, there were some strike activities in the public transport sector, as well as blockades of motorways and of the access to oil refineries, leading to a serious fuel shortage. Despite this impressive mobilization, and the fact that polls taken in October revealed that a majority of the French population supported the strikes, both

chambers of Parliament approved the reform with some minor concessions. The Senate voted the law on October 26 and the National
Assembly on October 27. In a final effort to stymie the proposed reform,
defeated Socialist MPs appealed to the Constitutional Council. Since
their plaint was rejected, President Nicolas Sarkozy promulgated the
law on November 10, 2010.

One of the most striking features of the protest movement against the
governmental pension reform concerned the participation of numerous
students who joined the employees. They were worried that raising the
retirement age would worsen their job opportunities in the French labor
market. As noted in Chapter 1, the jobless rate for people under 25 years
reached 24 percent in France in fall 2010 – one of the highest levels
among OECD countries. Other problems include repetitive and poorly
paid internships, job instability, and low incomes. Moreover, young
people were being hit particularly hard by high rental costs. Some
media described the youth as a 'sacrificed generation'. Given that the
challenging situation in which young people found themselves had
attracted the public's attention, it was not surprising that the
problématique of youth unemployment remained in the public's focus
in the aftermath of the pension reform hype. The debate on youth
unemployment turned out to be low key, however. Policy measures
were decided in corporatist-like arrangements between the social
partners.

In fall 2010, the social partners agreed on opening negotiations
aimed at tackling the problem of youth unemployment. These negotiations can be traced back to a proposition expressed by François
Chérèque, the leader of the reformist labor union CFDT, during
a TV interview on October 25, 2010. Laurence Parisot, the president
of MEDEF, the most important employers' association, immediately
accepted taking part in these negotiations. Beyond the issue of youth
unemployment, the resumption of high-level talks between labor
unions and employers was of importance, as the protest movement
against the governmental pension reform had made such a *dialogue
social* impossible. By means of bilateral meetings with union leaders,
Ms. Parisot established a social agenda for 2011. Her proposition to
address four themes (employment, social protection, work conditions,
and industrial relations) was approved by labor unions on January 10,
2011. The only exception concerned the CGT, which as a consequence
of the passage of the pension reform had decided to only selectively
participate in these negotiations. With respect to the domain of employment, the social partners agreed on dealing with the problems of both
the young and the elderly as well as with the convention of the

unemployment insurance scheme on which an agreement had to be reached.[2] The negotiations on youth unemployment took place from February to July 2011, i.e. after the end of our period of observation. Altogether, the negotiations on youth (un)employment gave rise to four agreements, dealing with access to the labor market, access to accommodation facilities, apprenticeships, and internships, as well as the maintenance of young people in the labor market. The overall costs of the corresponding provisions were estimated at 155 million euros by the social partners.

The government, for its part, focused on the promotion of apprenticeships, since it was impressed by Germany's actions regarding this issue. In a TV speech held on November 16, 2010, President Sarkozy promised to double the number of apprenticeships, mentioning a study by Dares (2010) which showed that young people who completed an apprenticeship were much more likely to find a job. The objectives of Xavier Bertrand, the Minster of Labor, proved somewhat more realistic. He declared that he wanted to see the number of apprenticeships increase from 600,000 in 2010 to 800,000 in 2015. In order to encourage companies to hire young trainees, Bertrand proposed to introduce a bonus-malus system, which was eventually adopted by Parliament in July 2011. Firms with more than 250 employees which employed at least 4 percent of apprenticeships would receive a yearly payment of 400 euros for each contract, while those that failed to attain this level would be taxed between 0.05 and 0.2 percent on their overall salary bill, depending on the exact proportion of trainees. In addition, the government decided to spend 500 million euros on the modernization of training centers.

Italy: Fiat's Threat of Delocalization

In Italy during October 2010, at the time of our observation period, there were two debates related to unemployment. First, there was an ongoing dispute between Fiat's then CEO Sergio Marchionne and the unions, above all the left-wing CIGL, about the conditions under which workers should be forced to accept to avoid delocalizing the Pomigliano and Mirafiori factories to Serbia. Second, on November 25, 2011, the education minister Mariastella Gelmini finally managed to have the Italian parliament adopt a major education reform, which led not only to major

---

[2] As for the latter, negotiations began on January 24, 2011. With some minor exceptions, social partners agreed to continue most provisions of the 2009 convention on May 6. The labor union CGT was the only organization that refused to sign the text.

cuts in the educational budget but also to layoffs of public employees and a worsening of the working conditions, especially for young researchers and teachers at the academic level. These two debates, which at first sight might seem uncorrelated, generated a broad public discussion about the country's future and a wave of mobilizations of employees, unions, students, researchers, and 'precarious' workers (*precari*).

The first debate about the Italian automobile industry, the most important international firm of which is Fiat, refers to the issue of Italian labor-market flexibilization and to the issue of industrial relations bargaining practices established since the 1980s. Italy suffers from the characteristic 'vices' of the Southern European welfare state model: stagnant employment and rising unemployment levels. Typical for continental welfare states, an especially large share of the firms' costs derives from the inflexible labor market and the high taxes on labor (Levy 1999: 240–242). The inflexibility of the Italian labor market has already led to major political reform attempts in the past. As already pointed out in Chapter 3, a first step in this direction had been taken with the introduction of the Treu Reform in 1996–1997, which introduced the possibility of temporary contracts for both the private and public sector.

In 2003, the Biagi Law went a step further in this direction by paving the way for contracts that would allow firms to opt out of the national collective agreement and determine working conditions more liberally. Marchionne's move constituted a successful attempt to avoid the tenets of such a national agreement. He proposed agreements described by the unions as an exchange of 'rights' for 'work', and this precisely in the context of the economic crisis and after a two-year period of short-term work in Fiat's plants covered by the *Cassa integrazione* 'in deroga'.[3] In June 2010, after a long consultation and negotiation period, the workforce in the Pomigliano factory near Naples was requested to cast a ballot in favor of more restrictive employment conditions trying to reduce absenteeism, low productivity, labor cost, excessive coffee or lunch breaks, and strikes in order to save the factory and the jobs. The alternative proposed by Fiat was an immediate mass layoff and an industrial delocalization to Serbia. Faced with this stark option, the workers in Pomigliano eventually accepted the agreement with 63 percent of the votes, and prevented an outsourcing of the Fiat factory to Serbia. Essentially the same reforms were later also introduced in the Mirafiori

---

[3] The Cassa Integrazione in deroga is an additional short-term work program that was introduced specifically to fight against the rising unemployment as a consequence to the economic crisis 2008.

factory near Turin. There, the workforce was called to the ballot on January 13–14, 2011, and a majority of 54 percent accepted the agreement curtailing worker's rights[4] in exchange for the guarantee of further investments in the factory.

The Fiat proposal, which was supported by the government, also found support among two of the three most important labor unions – the metal workers' branches of CISL and UIL. However, the left-wing FIOM – the metal workers' branch of CIGL – opposed the proposal and argued that this agreement undermined the *Art. 1* of the Italian Constitution and especially the right to strike. This reference to the Constitution was used to raise a matter of principle against any regulation that might possibly constrain employees' rights. The split between the unions in this particular case revived old rivalries and put an end to a period of cooperation that had started with the advent of the left-wing Prodi government in 2006. At the same time, a series of protests and mobilizations organized mainly by the CIGL and supported by the Communist and radical left parties (Rifondazione Comunista, Sinistra Ecologia and Libertà, Italia dei Valori) took place against this 'disgraceful' trading of rights against work, which was seen as a precedent that could spread to other parts of the labor market.

This conflict about the Pomigliano contract was exacerbated and instrumentalized by the Berlusconi's government supporting Fiat's requests. Because of its disagreement with the new contract, the CGIL section FIOM was definitely excluded from industry-level representation inside Fiat factories. Fiat, on the other hand, was threatened by Confindustria, the main Italian employers' organization, that it would be expelled from the association by January 2012 if no adequate agreement were reached.

Another important labor-market policy reform, which is related to the debate on flexibilization reforms in Italy, refers to the introduction of the so-called *Collegato lavoro* (Law 183/2010) on November 24, 2010. This law applies particularly to workers in atypical contracts. Among other things, the *collegato* tried to rationalize dispute settlement procedures by reducing the period to appeal in court from 5 years to 270 days (Art. 30–31). Unions criticized this *collegato* especially because, as they saw it, the new procedures allowed employers to 'blackmail' their employees by confronting them with the choice between accepting the new clauses or quitting their job (Art. 31). Opponents from the left described

---

[4] New regulations include, for instance, the reduction of pauses from 40 to 30 minutes pauses; increases in production rhythm; the possibility of using lunch breaks to avoid overtime, mandatory overtime increased by 80 hours per year.

the arbitration procedure as an attempt to bypass Art. 18 of the workers' statute, according to which the recourse to a judge in case of layoff or labor disputes is mandatory. They regarded it as especially penalizing for atypical workers, who, because of the Biagi Law, already experienced a reduction of their contractual rights. These actors claimed that the new flexibility lacked a safety net whenever a precarious work situation would lead to unemployment.

Our observation period also coincided with the final part of the (since 2008) ongoing parliamentary debate on a far-reaching restructuring of the educational system. The first part of the Gelmini Law had been introduced for primary schools in September 2009, and for secondary schools in September 2010. During our observation period, a similar reform was finally approved for university education by the Chamber of Deputies on November 25, 2010, and by the Senate on December 23, 2010. President Napolitano signed the corresponding decree on December 31. Overall, the reform introduced massive budget cuts in this policy domain.

The debate on the last part of the Gelmini reform mobilized researchers, teachers, and students who were afraid of losing their jobs and who feared for the quality of education. Some of the catchphrases used during the protest on October 16 were 'Sapere bene comune,' 'Il sapere batte la crisi,' 'Non moriremo precari,' 'Noi la crisi non la paghiamo,' 'Per il futuro, per l'Italia,' or 'Siamo tutti Brontolo' in reference to the seventh Walt Disney dwarf, Grumpy, representing the 'angry worker' (De Santis 2010). Further massive protests against the Gelmini Reform, which sometimes degenerated into violent encounters, took place in different cities and universities during November 2010. On the weekend of November 29, the main slogan was 'Io non mi fido'. Another protest was registered briefly before the debates in the Chamber of Deputies on December 22, 2010.

Overall, these debates were rather intense. They launched a general discussion about Italy's future. The conflict opposed the left's opposition to the Berlusconi government. While the government parties, and the moderate unions (CISL and UIL) supported Fiat and Minister Gelmini, CIGL and the opposition parties from the radical left opposed the educational reform and the agreements with Marchionne.

UK: Imposing Austerity

In the United Kingdom, we witnessed the debate on a major reform during our observation period, a reform that was related to unemployment in different ways: the debate on the Comprehensive Spending

Review (CSR). The British general election – by which Members of Parliament (MPs) are voted into the House of Commons – took place on May 6, 2010. After 13 years of Labour government, the first coalition government of Conservatives and Liberal Democrats, under David Cameron, was formed and formally announced on May 12. Shortly after-wards, on June 22, 2010, the new Chancellor of the Exchequer, George Osborne, held his first budget speech and announced that the new gov-ernment intended to save £40 bn during the forthcoming legislative period (2010–2014). The consultation process and detail planning of the spending review then started. Osborne presented the definitive CSR proposal to the House of the Commons on October 20, 2010 (HM Treasury 2010d).

The CSR is relevant for the unemployment debate for two reasons: on the one hand, as announced by George Osborne, it entailed a massive layoff of public employees in different branches as a consequence of the overall budget reduction. On the other hand, the intended welfare spending cuts amounting to no less than £7 bn a year were to apply especially to housing facilities and childcare allowances. The Child Benefit entitlement conditions were to change from being almost uni-versal to relying on a strict means test. For the welfare state, the spend-ing review framed the cuts as 'fairness for the future' and stressed the need to reduce the welfare state dependency culture. In fact, it argued that the welfare state locked too many families into such a dependency cycle (HM Treasury 2010a: 26–27), while failing to provide chances/ services, which could stimulate individual initiative and social mobility. Furthermore, the Department of Work and Pensions (DWP) stressed the need to prevent fraud or payment errors, while supporting those who were genuinely in need. This 'fairness agenda' implied a massive restructuration in public service delivery that was to be addressed by means of the 'Universal Credit' reform, which, for our purposes, can be considered an especially relevant sub-debate of the more general debate on the spending review.

Iain Duncan Smith's speech 'Welfare for the 21st century' on May 27, 2010 and the corresponding white paper 'Universal Credit: welfare that works' further specified the government's intentions. The *'Universal Credit' reform* implied an extensive and far-reaching re-organization of the British welfare state system. By means of the so-called 'Work Programme' the British government intended to tighten the work-conditionality for benefit recipient and to re-introduce people into work more quickly and more efficiently. Substantial savings were expected to result from the decentralization and privatization of the benefit and service provision (HM Treasury 2010). This specific reform project was linked to the more general debate insofar as one part of the agreed upon debt reduction within the framework of the 'Spending Review' were to be borne by the DWP by means of the 'Universal Credit' reform. The plan was to reach an overall budget reduction of 26 percent by 2015 in the Department for Work and Pensions (DWP) (HM Treasury 2010). These economies were to be achieved mainly through the elimination of fraudulent benefit claims and unnecessary benefit payments, as well as by the overall restructuring of the welfare state benefit provision system (privatization and decentralization).

From September to October 2010, the DWP gave political stake-holders the opportunity to position themselves with respect to the planned reform. The plans of the Department for Work and Pensions were then made explicit on November 11, 2010, with a second speech by MP Duncan Smith (Duncan Smith; DWP 2010[5]). This announcement was followed by violent student protests in London. The motive of these protests and clashes were mainly the increasing tuition fees and the spending cuts (Hurst/Pitel 2010). In a second step, the welfare reform bill was introduced to parliament on February 16, 2011 (HC bill 197). Some goals of the welfare reform had already been set (Watson 2010). The centerpiece of the 'Universal Credit' Reform was the so-called 'Work Programme,' which was to be introduced in summer 2011 (DWP 2010). The Work Programme aimed to reform the welfare-to-work program of the British government (DWP 2010).

The introduction of 'Universal Credit' was a far-reaching reform that included all working-age benefits in the United Kingdom. The associated debate dealt with the problems inherent in the British welfare state, which was considered to be too complex, and too prone to abuse and dependency. The dearth and poor quality of education schemes were also to be addressed via this reform. During the period covered by our study, the government expressed its intentions, while the opposition and unions waited for measures to be specified before commenting on them. During the debate in our observation period, the emphasis was put on stimulating individual responsibility and promoting work with a work-first approach, which, as broadly assessed in the literature (Trickey and Walker 2001, Taylor-Gooby and Larsen 2005, Daguerre 2007, Taylor-Gooby and Stoker 2011), was the only reasonable measure to reduce welfare dependency. Another central point was the need to contain public spending, simplify public service delivery, and eliminate benefit overlaps, increasing efficiency and transparency. Finally, it was claimed that all of

---

[5] After this speech, the interested service providers were invited to tender for collaboration in the public sector. In January 2011 the tenders were published.

these measures would reduce the 'poverty trap' effect welfare benefits are held to imply.

The 'spending review' debate has been rather intense since the announced cuts were significant. With respect to welfare reform, the debate would become more intense once the details of the reorganization had been announced. At the time of our study, the reform intentions of the government were presented in a matter-of-fact manner and the opposition expressed its discontent in general terms. However, some collective actors from the left somewhat radicalized their action repertoire in light of the radical reform plans. In addition, we should mention protests by students, which occurred rather unexpectedly.

Conclusion

This detailed discussion of the national debates related to unemployment in our six countries during the period under investigation shows that only in one of our countries were these debates related to a major policy reform, a true punctuation of the routine policy process. This occurred in the UK, where the incoming government presented a major program to reform government activities, which crucially involved the reorganization of the welfare state in general, and of unemployment programs in particular. In Denmark and Germany, the labor-market policy debate was also related to policy reforms during our period, but these reforms were of a more limited scope. While not routine, they still constituted only minor modifications of the big programs that have been introduced in the past – activation policy in the Danish case, and Hartz IV in the German case. Given their more limited scope, the public debates on unemployment during the period of our investigation were less centrally focused on these two reform projects. Interestingly, while the German reform was an endogenous result of the policy process, the Danish reform was largely initiated by the mobilization of public opinion by the Danish media.

In two countries, there were no relevant unemployment-related policy debates during the period under study: in Switzerland, the referendum campaign on the reform of the unemployment insurance had taken place just before our investigation period, and the great debate on the strength of the Swiss franc and its consequences for the Swiss economy was still to come. In France, the pension reform had temporarily crowded out all other policies from the public sphere. Finally, in Italy, the major public debate on an unemployment related issue was not on public policy, but on the strategic decision of a key firm, which triggered an attempt of the unions to expand the conflict to

Table 4.4 *Aspects covered in the interviews with respect to the issue-specific debates in fall 2010, per country*

Aspects covered	DK	CH	D	F	I	UK
Events	Activation and youth	Dismissals	Hartz IV	Youth	Fiat and education	CSR and universal credit
Arguments	Activation and youth	Dismissals	Hartz IV	Youth	Fiat and education	CSR and universal credit
Discourse quality	Activation	Dismissals	Hartz IV	Youth	Fiat	Universal credit
Populism	Activation	Dismissals	Hartz IV	Youth	Fiat	Universal credit

the public sphere. The educational policy reform was only obliquely related to the issue of unemployment.

To conclude, *Table 4.4* shows the public debates about which we interviewed our policy-makers in the six countries involved in the study.

Part II

Political Actors and Their Assets

5   What Affects Power in the Labor Market Domain?

Laurent Bernhard

Introduction

Assuming that power lies at the core of politics, political science can be considered the study of power phenomena. According to Elster (1976: 249) 'power is the most important single idea in political science, comparable perhaps to utility in economics'. In a similar vein, realists in the domain of international relations conceive of power as the 'currency of politics' (see, for example, Mearsheimer 2001: 29). Indeed, the question of which actors own power is one of the oldest and most relevant in political science, as the famous community power debate reminds us (Dahl 1961). It is striking, however, that comparatively little attention is currently being paid to the explicit study of power.

To the extent that such examinations exist, they mostly focus on the influence of political actors in specific policy fields, specific decision-making processes, or political campaigns (e.g., Laumann and Pappi 1976, Knoke et al. 1996, Kriesi 1980, Fischer et al. 2009, Bernhard 2012). The present chapter proposes to perform a similar analysis by studying the power levels of political organizations involved in the labor-market domain.

This chapter centers on the role played by specific *actor types*. We will test two kinds of hypotheses in this regard. First, we will focus on direct effects. In this respect, national public administrations, and peak-level associations are expected to excel in terms of power. The latter category is subdivided into employers' associations and labor unions. These actors are hypothesized to be of crucial importance as they represent either capital or labor – the two most important production factors. National public administrations involved in the labor-market domain should enjoy above-average levels of power as well , since they are responsible for these issues. Governmental parties, for their part, may be particularly influential due to their ability to enact labor-market reforms. While the first hypothesis expects country-invariant differences, our second type of

99

hypotheses posits contextual specificities by looking at interactions between actor types and the institutional setting. More specifically, we expect interest groups to be less influential in liberal market economies and state-led economies than in coordinated or compound state-led contexts. The rationale behind this hypothesis relates to the fact that, in such contexts, these actors tend to be directly excluded from the political decision-making processes. Thus, peak employers' associations and peak labor unions should be less powerful in the United Kingdom and in France than in Germany, Denmark, Switzerland, and Italy. Furthermore, power levels of governmental parties are expected to be negatively related to their number in a given cabinet. Hence, when a given party rules alone (as was the case for the UMP in France during the period of investigation) it may prove to be more influential than if it is part of a coalition government. With respect to national public administrations, we expect them to enjoy considerably more power if they operate in a context of a strong state, which is exemplified by the French case.

Powerful Actor Types

This section addresses the theoretical question of who has power in the labor-market domain in Western Europe. We will first hypothesize that the inner circle is dominated by three national actor types: governmental parties, public administrations, and social partners, the latter consisting of the peak labor unions and employers' associations. The first two types of actors – governmental parties and national public administrations – are expected to be very influential as they tend to play a crucial role both in terms of labor-market regulation and social security schemes. The national public administrations are in charge of implementing and supervising these policies. They are thus in possession of technical expertise. Governments, for their part, are of primary importance in their ability to launch reform projects. Since the 1980s, the reform of the welfare state in general and of the labor market in particular has been on the top of the various governments' political reform agendas. These adjustments have been generally triggered by high levels of unemployment, economic globalization, and socio-economic change. In the realm of the labor market, national governments have mainly resorted to competition-driven institutional reforms. These efforts aimed at fostering employment by introducing more flexibility into the labor market, containing wages levels, reducing unemployment benefits as well as – usually to a lesser degree – promoting active labor-market policies (see Chapter 3).

Regini (2000) has observed that this general trend toward deregulation has been accompanied by widespread concertation. Indeed, governments all over Europe decided to involve social partners in the elaboration of numerous reform projects. This new form of tripartism is best exemplified by various 'social pacts' (Rhodes 2001) that have not only come about in countries with a strong tradition of social partnership in recent years (Baccaro and Simoni 2008). Since peak unions and peak employers' associations are part of these arrangements, these actors are still to be considered of primary importance in the labor-market domain. The scholarly literature has been primarily concerned with the role played by the major labor unions. This focus is justifiable because, in terms of economic governance, these actors can be considered as the only countervailing force to both the state and employers in the current neoliberal reform context (Boeri et al. 2002). In addition, labor unions have suffered from a considerable loss of members over the last few decades. This steadily decline prompts the question of whether labor unions are still able to exert a decisive influence on labor-market policies. This concern is all the more pertinent, as globalization tends to favor the (export-oriented) business community, providing employers with an exit option and making them less inclined to engage in concertation with labor unions.

Hassel (2006) argues that, under the conditions of monetarism and open markets, governments do not need unions anymore for solving the macroeconomic dilemma between fighting inflation and unemployment. However, given the governments' preferences for improving international competitiveness, wage moderation consented by unions is still of primary importance. The rationale behind this strategy relates to the assumption that wage restraint leads to higher profits, increased investments, economic growth, and eventually the creation of jobs. In other words, the shift from price stability to competitiveness as primary objective to achieve economic prosperity implies that the cooperation of labor unions still plays a crucial role. According to Pierson (1994), this also applies to welfare state reforms. He insists that even in liberal market economies where unions tend to be weaker than in coordinated market economies, these reforms are difficult to implement. Thus, in order to succeed in their reform endeavors, governments of any stripe face a huge incentive to seek union endorsement (Hamann and Kelly 2004). In this regard, it has to be highlighted that labor unions have shown that – despite their decline in terms of membership – they are still able to rather effectively resort to large-scale protest activities when combating unilaterally imposed retrenchment reforms. The substantial social mobilization potential of unions enables them to hold an 'ideological veto player position'

(Béland 2001) in labor-market politics. Even though unions cannot *a priori* be confident to succeed in blocking neoliberal reform plans, governments usually take a big risk if they do not take the unions' preferences into account.

More generally, the social partners' presumed extraordinarily high levels of power may arise from the fact that they have enjoyed a privileged position in most European countries since World War II. In many countries, employers' associations and labor unions co-manage social insurance schemes, thus providing organized economic interests with important resources, such as legitimacy and financial resources (Bonoli 2000), as well as technical expertise (Culpepper 2002). With respect to the latter, governments may, at least to a certain degree, depend on the necessary information acquired by social partners in order to design and implement labor-market reforms. From this perspective, these actors are thus best placed to assess the potentials and barriers of reforms. This aspect may constitute an additional reason for why governments decide to engage in concertation and why peak organizations are expected to excel in terms of power.

The degree of power of the three core actors in the labor-market domain (governmental parties, public administration, and social partners) is likely to vary from country to country, however. With respect to social partners, we expect the French and British peak organizations on either side of the class divide to display lower of levels of power than their German, Danish, Swiss, and Italian counterparts. Germany, Denmark, and Switzerland are commonly referred to as (neo-)corporatist systems of interest intermediation and policy-making (Lehmbruch 1979, Schmitter 1982). These institutional arrangements refer to the joint management of the national economy by state actors and the peak associations of the social partners (Siaroff 1999). In these three countries, there has been no general indication of a decline in corporatist institutions in recent years. The German system of interest mediation, which is characterized by centralized social partners, sectoral coordination, and bipartite wage bargaining due to the absence of state intervention (principle of *Tarifautonomie*) has not undergone any fundamental change in recent years. According to Thelen and van Wijnbergen (2003), this rather surprising result is attributable to the fact that centralized collective bargaining settings guarantee high predictability and labor peace. These outcomes are particularly appreciated by employers. However, it needs to be mentioned that Streeck (2009) observes a decline in the number of employees and workplaces covered by industry-wide bargains over the last fifteen years. In the case of policy-making, the government usually returns to corporatist concertation. One notable exception refers to the government of Gerhard Schröder that adopted an increased flexibiliza- tion of the labor market by co-opting labor unions in the framework of expert committees. Czada (2005) labels this new strategic form of con- certation as 'government by commission'. Denmark, for its part, stands for a social corporatist country (Katzenstein 1985). The country is char- acterized by centralized and encompassing social partners, national-level coordination, strong unions which, amongst other things, administer the unemployment insurance (Ghent system). In the domain of the labor market, Denmark is currently being praised by supranational organiza- tions for its 'flexicurity' approach to fight unemployment (see Chapter 3). This innovative system consistently came about as a result of national- level tripartite coordination promoted by the state (Woldendorp 2011). It should not be overlooked that corporatist policy formation ran into serious difficulties in the 1980s, as trade unions experienced major diffi- culties in adapting to changing macroeconomic conditions. Governments took a leading role in the process of corporatist exchange, in particular in times of economic adversity. Yet, it is striking that the employers in Denmark were instrumental in saving corporatist policy formation, which now takes place in a more decentralized way than before (Martin and Thelen 2007, Woldendorp 2011). This is in line with Swenson's (1991) finding according to which Danish employers have historically been the driving force behind centralization. In the case of Switzerland, its liberal variant of corporatism has remained remarkably stable both with respect to industrial relations and policy-making (Armingeon 1997, Oesch 2007). Cooperation between business and labor still occurs at a decentralized level, and the political process undoubtedly tends to be dominated by the right and the export-oriented business community. A peculiarity relates to the fact that direct-democratic institutions strengthen the bargaining position of comparatively weakly organized labor unions.

The three remaining countries studied here (Italy, France, and the United Kingdom) usually are classified as pluralist or at least non- corporatist. According to Treu (1994), concertation has been difficult to organize in Italy as a result of the fragility of collective bargaining and the low level of institutionalization. In addition, he states that political tensions have long hampered the difficult task of building a national consensus on economic and social issues. Things changed during the 1990s when several tripartite agreements were agreed on. The main motivation for this concertation proved pragmatic in nature, as they were primarily crisis-driven (Rhodes 2001). Technocratic governments aimed at qualifying Italy for the European Monetary Union (EMU) in a period that heralded the end of the traditional *partitocrazia*. They needed the involvement of employers' associations and trade unions. Peak organizations took the opportunity to enter this void by participating in negotiations, thus improving Italy's reform capacity. As a consequence of this rather successful concertation experience, Confindustria and the three union federations CGIL, CISL, and UIL may have gained new leverage, thereby increasing their levels of political power. However, these forms of concertation were not institutionalized and fell apart when Berlusconi came into power in 2001.

As considering Italy a corporatist country may be inappropriate, Schmidt (2008) has suggested the term of a compound state-led market economy in which the state intervenes in order to ensure enhanced coordination between labor and business in a kind of macro-level collaboration between employers, unions, and governments. In such a setting, we thus expect Italian peak associations to be more powerful than their French and British peers which operate in strictly non-corporatist contexts.

As far as France is concerned, the macro-institutional setting provides the state with tremendous power. Schmidt (2008) considers France the paradigmatic case of a 'state-influenced market economy'. Suffice it to mention that the conditions for corporatism are generally not met there. According to Hall (1990), the term 'neo-corporatism' is not applicable to France. The only exceptions concern the organizations of the *démocratie sociale* (Palier 2010), including the unemployment insurance which is managed by eight peak-level organizations (three employers' associations and five labor unions) having been recognized as 'representative' by the state after World War II. Apart from that, employers and unions tend to entertain antagonistic relationships. Moreover, the comparative literature classifies French labor unions as exceptionally weak. They suffer from pronounced ideological divisions, little internal cohesion, and a low membership density, especially in the private sector (Labbé 1996). As a result of a lack of institutional access and organizational flaws, the labor movement often adopts a radical action repertoire when disapproving governmental reforms. To the detriment of consensus, French governments often try to unilaterally impose retrenchment and deregulation in order to achieve their policy goals. Given the leadership of the state, organized economic interests are expected to be significantly less powerful than in the four countries discussed above.

The same pattern is to be expected in the British case. It would appear to be no coincidence that France and the United Kingdom are the only Western European countries where Hassel (2003) does not list any case of tripartite concertation from 1990 to 1999. Since the 1980s, the United Kingdom can be considered a liberal market economy

(Hall and Soskice 2001) in which the pure market logic prevails. Benefiting from the high concentration of power provided by the Westminster system, Margaret Thatcher deregulated industrial relations by imposing anti-union laws that enduringly weakened organized labor. Wage bargaining, for its part, has always primarily taken place in a decentralized manner in the United Kingdom, i.e., at the plant level (Howell 2006).

With respect to policy-making, the government is able to adopt policies without any coordinated cooperation, thus – at least to a certain degree – ignoring and sidelining their concerns. Anyway, in a pluralist system of arm's-length relationship between government and interest groups, policies are not primarily articulated by peak-level associations representing business and labor interest. As they do not hold an institutionalized privileged position, British economic interest groups are expected not to be very powerful.

As to governmental parties, we suggest their number to play a crucial importance. More specifically, we expect those ruling collective actors to be extraordinary powerful in the absence of coalition governments. At the time the empirical work was accomplished, only France had a single ruling party. Therefore, the Union for a Popular Movement (UMP) of Nicolas Sarkozy is expected to enjoy significantly more power than the remaining governmental parties. Quite exceptionally, the British government was composed of the coalition between Conservatives and Liberal Democrats. Two parties were also in power in Germany (Conservatives and Free Democrats), Italy (*Popolo della Libertà*, and Lega Nord after *Futuro e Libertà per l'Italia* of Gianfranco Fini had quit the government in November 2010), and Denmark (a minority government led by Liberals and Conservatives). In Switzerland, no less than five parties (Liberals, Christian Democrats, Social Democrats, Swiss People's Party, and the Conservative Democratic Party) composed the grand coalition government which contains seven members. Given their large number, Swiss governmental parties should thus display significantly lower levels of power.

Finally, with respect to the national public administration, we expect French actors to excel in terms of power. This hypothesis is derived from the fact that France is considered to constitute the paradigmatic case of a *strong state* (Badie and Birnbaum 1983). The country's centralized and concentrated structures, its relatively high degree of autonomy vis-à-vis the society, and its high degree of state interventionism allows the units of the public administration to exert a strong impact in any national policy area – including the domain of labor-market politics.

To sum up, we generally hypothesize governmental parties, public administrations, and social partners (i.e., peak labor unions and employers' associations) to excel in terms of power. With respect to social partners, we expect the French and British social partners to exhibit lower of levels of power than their peers of the remaining countries studied here. Regarding government parties, this is also expected to apply to Swiss parties, whereas the French UMP should be particularly powerful. Finally, the organizations of the French public labor-market administration are expected to outclass the authorities from the remaining countries.

Data and Operationalization

As is common practice in decision-making analyses (Kriesi 1980, Fischer et al. 2009), power is operationalized by a reputational indicator. The rationale for this approach rests on the assumption that political actors themselves are best suited for assessing the influence of their peers. Respondents received a list containing the most important organizations in their respective countries. In addition to the organizations which have been interviewed, this list includes those collective actors whose representatives refused to participate, some additional important state actors, as well as international and supranational organizations. With respect to the latter, we included the International Labour Organization (ILO), the Organisation for Economic Co-operation and Development (OECD), the European Council (EC), and the European Central Bank (ECB). The latter two supranational organizations did not appear on the Swiss list, since Switzerland is not member of the European Union. Respondents were first asked to name all organizations which, from their point of view, had been particularly influential. Second, they were asked to name the three most influential organizations. Third and finally, they had to select the most influential one among these collective actors. The most powerful actor obtained the value '3'. The following two organizations in terms of power were attributed a '2', and the remaining influential actors a value of '1'. Those organizations that were not considered particularly powerful were coded as '0'. In order to ensure comparability across countries, we decided to divide the power scores by the theoretical maximum (n x 3). The resulting *standardized indicator* has a theoretical range from 0 to 1, capturing the share of the possible power level an actor obtained in a given country.

With respect to actor types – the main independent variable – we distinguished between eleven categories. With respect to state actors, we drew the distinction between national public administrations and the remaining ones, which we label as 'other state actors'. With respect to economic interest groups, we included peak-level employers' association, peak-level labor union, other employers' associations, and other labor unions. In addition, we accounted for governmental as well as for non-governmental parties, i.e., parties which were not in power when our interviews took place. Finally, think tanks and research groups, citizen interest groups, and supranational organizations are considered, too. As far as the latter are concerned, we were able to analyze them only in the framework of the descriptive analysis, since representatives of supranational organizations were not interviewed. In order to account for contextual variances, we also included country dummies.

In addition to country and actor type dummies, two control variables were included into the multivariate analysis. First, we accounted for political actors' degree of centrality in the national networks by focusing on policy brokers. These actors were of strategic importance, as they connect other organizations which are not directly related to each other. In particular, when pronounced ideological differences exist within a network, *policy brokers* may be expected to be particularly influential (Diani 2003). The data used here refer to cooperative ties between the participating actors. From the list that is also used for the power measure, the respondents were asked to mention the organizations with which they had closely collaborated in the course of the last weeks. To operationalize the notion of policy brokers, we use Freeman's *betweenness centrality*. This widely used measure (Ingold and Varone 2011) calculates the number of times an actor is on the shortest path between two other actors. Second, we drew the distinction between specialists and generalist by making use of a dichotomous variable. It takes the value of '1' if an organization reports to allocates at least 80 percent of its personnel or its budget in the labor-market domain, and '0' otherwise.

Empirical Analysis

In the following, we shall proceed in two steps. First, we shall resort to descriptive analyses in which we will outline, for each of the six selected countries, the power levels of the various actor types as well as the ten most powerful organizations. Second, we shall turn to the multivariate analysis by focusing on the role played by specific actor types as well as the interaction between these actor types and country contexts.

Table 5.1 *The average power level of actor types, by country*

	Germany	Switzerland	Denmark	France	Italy	UK
National state actor	0.42	0.61	0.53	0.68	0.22	0.64
Peak union	0.35	0.39	0.31	0.16	0.30	0.37
Peak employers	0.33	0.45	0.36	0.24	0.39	0.27
Governmental party	0.33	0.13	0.27	0.41	0.22	0.46
Non-governmental party	0.19	0.01	0.23	0.05	0.07	0.13
Other state actor	0.17	0.07	0.06	-	0.10	0.24
Think- tank and research Institute	0.17	0.08	0.18	-	0.02	0.10
Other union	0.15	0.17	-	-	0.11	0.27
Citizen group	0.13	0.03	0.02	0.02	0.04	0.07
Supranational organizations	0.12	0.04	0.13	0.08	0.06	0.27
Other employers	-	0.17	-	-	0.06	-

Descriptive Analysis

Table 5.1 shows – for each of the six countries studied here – the level of power of various actor types. As expected, public administrations, peak-level employers and unions, as well as governmental parties appear to dominate the policy domain of the labor market. Indeed, these categories rank among the first four positions in each country. The remaining actor types generally display considerably lower levels of power. These first observations are in line with our first hypothesis. Nevertheless, *Table 5.1* suggests that the various categories are subject to some country-specific variations.

The national public administration turns out to be very strong in five out of six countries. The highest level of power is reached by the French public administration, thus supporting the view according to which a strong state strengthens the power of this actor type in labor-market policy. By contrast, the Italian public administration seems to be noticeably less influential. With respect to peak associations, French labor unions as well as French and British employers display comparatively low levels of power. At first glance, the results with respect to these three associations emerging from *Table 5.1* seem to be in line with the hypothesis that peak-level associations are less influential in state-influenced and pluralist market economies than in corporatist and semi-corporatist countries. The only exception with respect to this hypothesis concerns the British peak unions, which seem to enjoy a surprisingly high level of power. Regarding governmental parties, France and the United Kingdom stand out again. In these two countries, governing parties appear to be more powerful than in the Germany, Italy, Denmark and especially Switzerland where governing parties seem to be especially weak. This pattern confirms the rationale behind our hypothesis – an increasing of governing parties leads to a lower level of power.

As far as the remaining categories are concerned, it has to be mentioned that opposition parties as well as think tanks and research institutes enjoy a certain degree of influence in Germany and Denmark. The same applies to individual unions and other state actors in the case of the United Kingdom. While the former figure is probably due to the high level of decentralization of both the labor-market movement and industrial relations in the United Kingdom, the latter is attributable to the powerful Bank of England, which is the only British organization belonging to the category 'other state actor'. Citizens' interest groups are generally considered to be very weak. Only in the case of Germany do they attain a respectable level of power. We will address this issue later in the second part of this descriptive analysis. Supranational organizations also display rather low scores of power. These figures are in line with the notion according to which the labor-market policy domain in general and the issue of unemployment in particular are still characterized by a low degree of internationalization (Giugni 2010). However, it is noteworthy that British actors are the only ones to judge supranational actors to be somewhat influential.

Let us now take a closer look at the individual organizations' levels of power. *Table 5.2a* to *Table 5.2f* list the ten most powerful actors for each country. These rankings generally are in line with the patterns we found in *Table 5.1*. As is immediately obvious, the top rankings do not strongly vary

Table 5.2a *The ten most powerful actors in Germany*

	Organization	Actor type	Standardized power
1	Ministry of Labor (BMAS)	Public admin.	0.71
1	Federal Agency for Work (BA)	Public admin.	0.71
3	Conservatives (CDU-CSU)	Gov. party	0.40
4	Confederation of Trade Unions (DGB)	Peak union	0.35
5	Confederation of Employers' Associations	Peak employer	0.33
6	Institute for Employment Research (IAB)	Th.t. and res. in.	0.32
7	Parliamentary Labor Committee	Other state act.	0.29
8	Social Democrats	Non-gov. party	0.27
8	Free Democrats	Gov. party	0.27
10	The Left (Linke)	Non-gov. party	0.25
10	*Paritätischer Wohlfahrtsverband*	Citizen group	0.25

Table 5.2b *The ten most powerful actors in Switzerland*

	Organization	Actor type	Standardized power
1	Swiss Employers' Association (SAV)	Peak employer	0.64
2	State Secretariat for Economic Affairs (seco)	Public admin.	0.61
3	Confederation of Trade Unions (SGB)	Peak union	0.51
4	Unia	Other union	0.31
5	Small Business Association (SGV)	Peak employer	0.26
5	Travail.Suisse	Peak union	0.26
7	Social Democrats	Gov. party	0.21
8	Master Builders' Association (SBV)	Other employer	0.17
8	Swissmem (employers)	Other employer	0.17
10	Christian Democrats	Gov. party	0.15

Table 5.2c *The ten most powerful actors in Denmark*

	Organization	Actor type	Standardized power
1	National Labor Market Authority	Public admin.	0.67
2	Confederation of Trade Unions (LO)	Peak union	0.60
3	Confederation of Danish Employers (DA)	Peak employer	0.50
4	Ministry of Finance	Public admin.	0.40
5	Social Democrats	Non-gov. party	0.38
6	Liberals (Venstre)	Gov. party	0.33
7	Dansk Folkeparti (New Populist Right)	Non-gov. party	0.25
7	Danish Economic Council	Th.t. and res. in.	0.25
7	Economic Council of Labor Movement (AE)	Th.t. and res. in.	0.25
10	Socialist People's Party (SF)	Non-gov. party	0.23
10	Confederation of Danish Industry (DI)	Peak employer	0.23

Table 5.2d *The ten most powerful actors in France*

	Organization	Actor type	Standardized power
1	Ministry of Labor	Public admin.	0.71
2	*Présidence de la République* (Elysée)	Public admin.	0.65
3	MEDEF	Peak employer	0.63
4	Conservatives (UMP)	Gov. party	0.41
5	CGT	Peak union	0.33
6	CFDT	Peak union	0.28
7	FO	Peak union	0.20
7	Socialists	Non-gov. party	0.20
9	CGPME	Peak employer	0.16
10	CFTC	Peak union	0.15

Table 5.2e *The ten most powerful actors in the United Kingdom*

	Organization	Actor type	Standardized power
1	Department for Work and Pensions	Public admin.	0.64
2	Conservative Party	Gov. party	0.53
2	Trades Union Congress	Peak union	0.53
4	Liberal Democrats	Gov. party	0.38
5	Labour Party	Non-gov. party	0.36
6	Confederation of British Industry	Peak employer	0.33
7	Unite	Peak union	0.29
7	OECD	Supranational organization	0.29
9	Bank of England	State actor	0.24
9	Federation of Small Businesses	Peak employer	0.24
9	British Chambers of Commerce	Peak employer	0.24
9	UNISON	Peak union	0.24
9	ILO	Supranational organization	0.24

Table 5.2f *The ten most powerful actors in Italy*

	Organization	Actor type	Standardized power
1	Ministry of Labor	Public admin.	0.41
2	Confindustria	Peak employer	0.39
3	CGIL	Peak union	0.37
4	CISL	Peak union	0.30
4	Conservatives (Popolo della Libertà)	Gov. party	0.30
6	UIL	Peak union	0.24
7	Partito Democratico	Non-gov. party	0.22
8	Ministry of Finance	Public admin.	0.20
9	Council of Ministers	Public admin.	0.19
10	Lega Nord	Gov. party	0.15

among the six countries. The same categories appear at the top positions (i.e., public administrations, governmental parties, and peak-level employers and unions). With respect to *state actors*, the national public administrations in charge of the labor-market domain excel in terms of power. In five out of six countries, these actors rank first. The exception concerns Switzerland where the State Secretariat for Economic Affairs (Seco) occupies the second position. This result might be attributable to the comparatively weakness of the Swiss public administration. By contrast, the German case is particularly remarkable, as the Ministry of Labor (BMAS) and the Federal Agency for Work (BA) turn out to be *ex aequo* on top. Among the powerful state actors, there are two organizations which refer to the executive – the French Presidency and the Italian Council of Ministers. It is noteworthy that the former is considered by our French interview partners as the second most influential actor in the domain of labor-market policy, second only to the Ministry of Labor. These rankings confirm the extraordinary strength of the French state actors. In Denmark and Italy, the Ministries of Finance also belong to the most powerful organizations of the labor-market domain. We now turn to the remaining powerful state actors. It is interesting to observe that the German Parliamentary Labor Committee display a high level of power. This result can be explained by its important role in the context of the Hartz IV reform which occurred during our period of investigation. Finally, the Bank of England is the only central bank to appear among the ten most powerful actors in its country.

Let us now turn to the particularly powerful economic interest groups. As far as labor unions are concerned, their number among the ten most powerful organizations varies from country to country. In Germany and Denmark, there is only one labor union to fulfil this criterion – the German Confederation of Trade Unions (DGB) and LO of Denmark, respectively. The latter has proven to be very powerful, however. Indeed, LO ranks second in Denmark. There are three very powerful unions in Switzerland, Italy, and the United Kingdom. In Switzerland these actors include the two main peak-level organizations, Swiss Confederation of Trade Unions (SGB) and Travail Suisse, as well as Unia, the biggest union of the country and a member of the SGB. According to our analysis, the SGB turns out to be by far the most powerful Swiss labor union. In Italy, the three biggest union federations in terms of membership (CGIL, CISL, and UIL) find themselves among the most influential actors. As a result of the fractionalization of the Italian labor movement, no single organization displays very high levels of power, however. Taken together, these actors nevertheless constitute an important force in the labor-market domain. In the United Kingdom, the Trades Union Congress (TUC) is considered by our interview partners as the third most important British actor. The two remaining powerful unions (Unite and UNISON) seem to enjoy a much lower level of power than the umbrella organizations to which both are affiliated. Finally, there are four peak-level unions which rank among the ten most powerful actors in France: the big three organizations (CGT, CFDT, FO) and, rather surprisingly the Christian-Democratic CFTC. As is the case in Italy, the mainly ideologically driven cleavage between unions prevents the emergence of a very powerful single union actor.

On the side of *employers' associations*, the big peak-level associations appear to be very important in terms of power. This especially applies to Switzerland, where the Swiss Employers' Association (SAV) proves to be the single most influential organization of labor-market policy. In addition, three other employers' associations (Small Business Association, Swissmem, and the Master Builders' Association) belong to the country's ten most powerful actors. In Denmark, Italy, and France, the most important peak-level employers' associations (DA, Confindustria and MEDEF) can be considered crucial players, as they all rank among the top 3 in their country. In Denmark and France, there is one additional umbrella employers' association which is of importance (DI and CGPME). In Germany, only the Confederation of Employers' Association (BDA) belongs to the ten most powerful actors. Rather surprisingly, it does not attain a very high level of power. The same holds true for the British employers. However, it has to be pointed out that there are no less than three peak-level organizations in the British top ten ranking (Confederation of British Industry, Federation of Small Businesses, and the British Chambers of Commerce).

We now highlight the most powerful *parties*. Many governmental parties appear in the rankings presented in *Table 5.2a* to *Table 5.2f*. This applies to the French UMP – the only party among the six countries studied here not dependent on any coalition partner – as well as to the leading parties (at the time of writing) of the coalition governments of Germany (CDU-CSU), Denmark (Venstre), the United Kingdom (Conservative Party), and Italy (Popolo della Libertà). The respective 'junior coalition partners' all display lower levels of power. They are included among the top ten in Germany (Free Democrats), the United Kingdom (Liberal Democrats), and Italy (Lega Nord), but not in Denmark, where Conservatives do not feature. In Switzerland, no single Swiss party turns out to be very influential; only the Social Democrats and the Christian Democrats belong to the ten most powerful actors. This is not the case for the three remaining governmental parties (Swiss People's Party, the Free Democrats, and the small Conservative Democratic Party). According to our indicator, powerful opposition parties are available in Germany (Social Democrats and Greens), France (Socialists), and in Denmark (Social Democrats, Danish People's Party and Socialist People's Party). It is particularly noteworthy that the Social Democrats are considered to be the most powerful party of Denmark, despite the fact that they were not in power at the time of our interviews. Finally, we should mention that there was no powerful party operating outside the parliamentary arena in the six selected countries.

Beyond state actors, economic interest groups, and parties, three organizations of the category 'research institutes and think tanks' find their way into the list of most powerful organizations. It is striking, however, that these actors are closely associated with powerful actors. The German Institute for Employment Research (IAB) belongs to the Federal Agency for Work (BA), the Danish Economic Council of the Labor Movement is financed by LO, and the Danish Economic Council is financed by the government, although it enjoys a wide margin of independence when it comes to issue policy recommendations. As far as citizens' interest groups are concerned, the *Paritätische Wohlfahrtsverband* of Germany is the only organization of this kind to enter a top ten ranking. A major reason for this exception may be attributable to the organization's moderate approach, which relies on scientifically substantiated information. Among supranational organizations, only British actors consider them to be of some importance, as both the OECD and the ILO appear among the ten most powerful actors in the case of the United Kingdom. The institutions of the European Union invariably exhibit low levels of power, thus confirming that social and economic policies still predominantly pertain to the national level.

Multivariate Analysis

Table 5.3 presents the results of four OLS regression models explaining the political organizations' standardized levels of power. In order to check for the robustness of our results, we decided to resort to a blockwise procedure. Model I estimates the effects of the indicators outlined above (i.e., actor types, country dummies, betweenness scores, and labor-market specialists), with citizens' groups and Germany serving as reference categories for actor types and countries, respectively. The hypothesized interactions between countries and peak-level associations are added to model II, while model III accounts for the interactions between countries and state actors as well as between countries and governing parties. Finally, model IV includes all interaction terms. Generally, the explanatory power of the regressions models is rather high. The share of explained variance, expressed by means of adjusted R^2, ranges from 0.57 (model I) to 0.64 (model IV).

With respect to the first hypothesis, the results prove very robust across the four models. National state actors, governing parties, peak-level employers' associations, and peak-level labor unions are found to be significantly more powerful than citizens' interest groups. These results consistently support our theoretical expectations. The magnitudes of these estimated effects turn out to be quite impressive. This especially

Table 5.3 *OLS regression models explaining actors' power levels*

	Model I	Model II	Model III	Model IV
Switzerland	−0.074	−0.077	−0.039	−0.042
	(0.038)	(0.037)	(0.038)	(0.038)
Denmark	0.025	0.018	0.015	0.012
	(0.041)	(0.040)	(0.038)	(0.038)
France	−0.093[*]	−0.069	−0.122[**]	−0.123[**]
	(0.039)	(0.045)	(0.038)	(0.045)
Italy	−0.089[*]	−0.097[*]	−0.104[**]	−0.111[**]
	(0.040)	(0.039)	(0.037)	(0.037)
United Kingdom	−0.011	0.010	−0.023	−0.003
	(0.042)	(0.044)	(0.039)	(0.041)
National state actor	0.424[***]	0.425[***]	0.363[***]	0.352[***]
	(0.059)	(0.059)	(0.060)	(0.060)
Other state actor	0.001	0.009	−0.031	−0.031
	(0.067)	(0.067)	(0.064)	(0.063)
Peak employer	0.218[***]	0.233[***]	0.216[***]	0.206[***]
	(0.050)	(0.061)	(0.047)	(0.057)
Other employer	0.155	0.164	0.113	0.118
	(0.092)	(0.091)	(0.087)	(0.086)
Peak union	0.180[***]	0.219[***]	0.185[***]	0.201[***]
	(0.042)	(0.051)	(0.039)	(0.048)
Other union	0.098[*]	0.098[*]	0.078	0.073
	(0.050)	(0.049)	(0.047)	(0.046)
Governmental party	0.197[***]	0.200[***]	0.233[***]	0.229[***]
	(0.044)	(0.044)	(0.049)	(0.048)
Non-governmental party	0.062	0.059	0.066	0.064
	(0.039)	(0.039)	(0.037)	(0.036)
Think tank and res. institute	0.044	0.050	0.041	0.040
	(0.048)	(0.048)	(0.045)	(0.045)
Betweenness	0.709[***]	0.782[***]	0.731[***]	0.839[***]
	(0.165)	(0.171)	(0.155)	(0.162)
Specialist	0.039	0.032	0.033	0.034
	(0.037)	(0.037)	(0.035)	(0.035)
Peak employer * France		0.000		0.070
		(0.087)		(0.084)
Peak union * France		−0.100		−0.042
		(0.069)		(0.067)
Peak employer * UK		−0.276[*]		−0.261[*]
		(0.132)		(0.123)
Peak union * UK		−0.048		−0.036
		(0.099)		(0.092)

Table 5.3 *(cont.)*

	Model I	Model II	Model III	Model IV
Public admin. * France			0.333**	0.346**
			(0.124)	(0.126)
Gov. party * France			0.197	0.202
			(0.120)	(0.121)
Gov. party * Switzerland			−0.176*	−0.170*
			(0.071)	(0.070)
Constant	0.083*	0.077*	0.091**	0.088*
	(0 .036)	(0.036)	(0.34)	(0.034)
Observations	117	117	117	117
Adj. R^2	0.57	0.58	0.63	0.64

* $p < 0.05$, ** $p < 0.01$, *** $p < 0.001$.
Standard errors in brackets.
Reference categories: Germany (country) and citizen groups (actor type).

holds true for public administrations. According to the estimation results disclosed here, these actors display average standardized power scores that surpass those obtained by citizens' interest groups by 0.4 points. The corresponding effects for the three remaining powerful categories are approximately half as much. In addition, *Table 5.3* reports significant positive coefficients for the remaining labor unions ('other unions'). However, this is only the case regarding the first two models. Nevertheless, these results suggest that these actors also tend to play an important role as far as labor-market policies are concerned.

We now turn to the interaction hypotheses. Peak-level labor unions are not statistically weaker in the United Kingdom and in France than in the remaining four countries in which corporatist settings are available, thus contradicting the impression gained from the descriptive analysis. Hence, this hypothesis has to be rejected. This also holds true for the case of the French employers' associations, as the interaction between France and peak-level employers' turns out to be insignificant. According to models II and IV, the British peak-level employers' associations display significantly lower levels of power. These findings are in line with my theoretical expectations. However, this result has to be qualified. Indeed, the multivariate analysis only contains one peak-level employers' association – the Federation of Small Businesses (FSB) – as both the Confederation of British Industry and the British Chambers of Commerce are missing. Since these two organizations were considered the most powerful ones in this actor category by our interview partners, it is highly questionable whether this result would still hold true if they had been included in the multivariate analysis. As is shown in models III and IV, the contextual hypothesis about the French governmental parties has to be rejected. The differences across countries that have been detected in the descriptive analysis are obviously not large enough to attain statistical significance. However, the results for Swiss governmental parties indicate that they display significantly lower levels of power. This result corroborates our theoretical expectations. Finally, *Table 5.3* reveals that public administration proves to be more powerful in France than in the other five countries. Thus, this finding confirms the hypothesis according to which a strong state provides the public administration with an extraordinary degree of power.

As far as the control variables are concerned, the analysis shows that the degree of betweenness centrality exerts a positive impact on power. Policy brokers in a given national labor-market network can thus be considered highly influential actors. However, organizations specialized in the labor-market policies are not found to enjoy more power than generalists. Finally, some country-level effects emerge from this multivariate analysis. Italian and French organizations tend to display lower levels of power. These results might be due to the fact that political organizations involved in the labor-market domain are characterized by a generally high level of fragmentation in these two countries.

Conclusion

This chapter set out to map and explain the power of political organizations involved in West European labor-market politics. As the main determinant of power, we focused on the role played by specific actor types. With respect to direct effects, national public administrations, peak-level associations (employers as well as labor unions), and governing parties have been shown to be extraordinarily influential. This result turned out to be in line with the arguments we developed in the theoretical part of this contribution.

Our second type of hypotheses pertained to interactions between these powerful actor types and the institutional setting provided by the six countries under scrutiny. Contrary to our theoretical expectations, peak-level organizations did not prove to be less powerful in liberal and state-influenced market economies (respectively represented by the United Kingdom and France) than in the remaining four countries. In other words, this analysis suggests that peak-level employers and unions are similarly influential across the six country contexts studied here. In addition, the hypothesis that the average power of these actors is higher in contexts in which one single party is ruling (France) also had to be rejected in the framework of the multivariate analysis. It is fair to mention, however, that this association as rather close to attain statistical significance. In the framework of our analysis of interaction effects, two hypotheses were confirmed. First, Swiss governing parties have been shown to be comparatively weaker than the governing parties in the remaining countries. The second significant association relates to the reinforcing effect caused by a strong state on its public administration. Thus, governmental actors of the remaining five countries lack the centralized authority and the administrative capacity of the French state.

Despite these notable context-specific differences, this analysis suggests that similarities across countries are much stronger than dissimilarities when it comes to the distribution of power in the West European labour market domain. Indeed, the same types of actors have been shown to be influential in all six country contexts. In light of the great variation in terms of institutional arrangements, this conclusion is far from being trivial.

6   The Labor-Market Policy Space

Flavia Fossati

Introduction

Over the last decade, labor-market policy reforms have been the subject
of scholarly research because they are the primary instruments used to
achieve an encompassing restructuration of the European welfare and
production regimes. Scholars such as Bonoli and Natali (2012) argue
that these reforms transformed welfare states from being (passive) secur-
ing arrangements towards schemes which (actively) promote labor-market participation (Torfing 1999; Gilbert 2002). In fact, these activating
measures seem to meet new social needs (Bonoli 2006) that have arisen
because of the changing economic context and which are characterized
by phenomena such as labor-market tertiarization (Iversen and Wren
1998), changes in social structures (ageing and feminization of the labor
markets) (Esping-Andersen 2009) or the growing shares of unemployed, precarious and atypical workers (Berton, Richiardi and Sacchi
2009). The problem pressure of the post-industrial production environment, and especially the context of permanent austerity (Pierson 1996),
limit government's ability to rely exclusively on decommodifying passive
benefits or employment protection legislation (EPL) to reduce unemployment. Hence, alternative solutions had to be found. Most European
welfare states reformed their unemployment schemes by introducing
active labor-market policies (ALMPs). These "novel"[1] strategies aiming
at improving the efficiently and the long-lastingness of workers'
re-commodification diffused all over Europe because supra- and
international organizations, such as the Organization for Economic
Cooperation and Development (OECD) or the European Union with
the European Employment Strategy (EES), and networks of political
elites proposed these strategies as viable alternatives to a mere "race to

---

[1] The novelty of activation policies is of course debatable since in Sweden such strategies
have been applied since the 1950s. However, the massive diffusion of these policies
legitimates their characterization as "new" instruments.

the bottom" (Casey 2004; Daguerre and Taylor-Gooby 2004; Daguerre 2007).

In the light of this *activation turn* (Bonoli 2010 and 2013), the question arises as to whether the political conflict in labor-market policy is still merely unidimensional and only revolves around the labor/capital conflict over the level of passive benefits. In fact, following authors such as Bonoli and Natali (2012) or Häusermann (2010), who reached the conclusion that in several social policy areas preferences are becoming increasingly *multidimensional* and at times lead to "modernizing" reforms and novel political coalitions, the present contribution analyses whether the conflict in labor-market policy has pluralized as well (see also Fossati 2017a).

This chapter analyses, first, how many dimensions characterize the labor-market conflict and whether, as argued in the literature, an additional conflict related to the *re-commodifying* and *activating* strategies can be identified. Second, we address the question of whether different labor-market regimes or countries are characterized by *similar* or *different* national policy conflict structures. While authors such as Handler (2003 and 2004) or Jessop (1993) argue that the workfare model introduced in the US diffused and influenced European policy-making (Deacon 2000) leading to an overall convergence of policy schemes, the representatives of the power resources approach (PRA) and of the Varieties of Capitalism (VoC) literature stress the persistence of national divergences (Esping-Andersen 1990; Taylor-Gooby 2005; Bonoli 2006; Thelen 2012). In an institutionalist perspective, the introduction of similar activation schemes may lead to different outcomes in different countries. In fact, these authors claim that, due to their interaction with pre-existing institutional settings, i.e., the welfare state *legacies*, the stakeholders in different contexts prefer and priorities (i.e., allocate higher salience to) specific reform measures or policy mixes to address the challenges of high unemployment (Fossati, 2017a).

Here, I propose a theoretical framework that tries to reconcile these different strands of the literature by arguing that the political elites feature the same political conflict structure on the traditional *state/market*[2] conflict dimension in all six countries featured in our study. This is because during periods of crisis, politicians – regardless of their ideological position – are less likely to propose measures increasing welfare expenditures. Accordingly, the political conflict on the state/market axis can be expected to be homogeneous even across different countries/ regimes. Conversely, we expect that the elites' views differ on the second (and more recent) political conflict, namely about *activation*. In fact, the

---

[2] Here we use *economic* and *state/market* conflict synonymously.

implementation of ALMPs is recognized as a mostly low-cost and employer-friendly alternative to increasing passive effort (Häusermann and Palier 2008). Finally, since the regime-specific conflict dimensionality is determined by the actor configuration in the political space, we analyses the *potential* for policy coalitions separately for the different labor-market regimes.

The focus of this chapter is on assessing the configuration of *objective* coalitions (Ossipow 1994). Objective coalitions are composed of political actors who share similar policy preferences and similar belief systems, but do not necessarily cooperate with one another (Sabatier and Weible 2007). Chapter 7 will complement the present analysis and focus on the actual cooperation patterns, i.e., the *subjective* coalitions. Subjective coalitions may deviate from the preference-based coalitions because of strategic considerations or debate-specific alliances.

To answer these three research questions (two-dimensional structure, similarity/difference of conflicts, and coalition patterns) the theoretical argument will be developed in five steps: first, we will explain why it can be expected that the general structure of the labor market-specific political space is composed of more than one basic political conflict. Then, the explanatory model will be presented. Following Thelen's (2012) re-theorization of the VoC approach and considering the differences in problem pressures and welfare state legacies, we develop expectations about the factors influencing the regime-specific political preference structure. Third, by means of a factor analysis we test the hypothesis whether the labor-market policy space has become two-dimensional. Indeed, we can show that *two* political conflicts emerge. We identify a first conflict that deals with traditional labor-market policies (state/market) and a second that deals policies targeting the new social risks (activation). Fourth, we develop expectations about the coalition structure that characterizes the labor-market conflict and analyse the regime-specific actor constellations. Finally, by means of a cluster analysis we assess whether stakeholders belonging to the same party family or actor group, favor the same political measure-mix in the different countries. The final section summarizes the findings.

Theoretical Considerations

The Conflict in Labor Market Policy: The Economic and the Activation Dimension

Traditionally, the main political conflict in social policy in European countries is represented by conflicts concerning the generosity and universality of *passive benefits*, as well as the role and degree of state intervention (Esping-Anderson 1990; Kitschelt 1994). It goes back to the general conflict between labor and capital, which structured the modern party system (see Lipset and Rokkan 1985 [1967]; Bartolini 2000). One of the first authors to link this political conflict and the relative distribution of power (resources) explicitly, to explain differing *social policy* developments in different countries, was Korpi (1980, 1983). He argued that, depending on the mobilization of unions and their structure (split/unified) and labor/left party incumbency in government, social policy differed from one country to the other. By consequence, the basic political conflict in social and labor-market policy can be synthesized by an axis opposing on the one side *state*-interventionist and on the other *market*-oriented policy solutions. In more detail, policy positions from the left, which are proposed for instance by social-democratic parties and unions, promote generous unemployment and pension benefits, universalistic insurance models, public job creation or minimum wage regimentation, with the aim being to insure (blue-collar) workers against the traditional industrial labor-market risks. Furthermore, left political actors insist on the necessity of introducing or expanding universalistic welfare state efforts to lower social stratification by mitigating market distortions (Esping-Anderson 1990). Conversely, market solutions promote a reduction in state intervention and passive unemployment spending, abolishing minimum wages or liberalizing and flexibilizing labor relations. Political actors on the right hence support measures that do not alter the original social stratification, which do not interfere with the labor-market mechanisms, and which oppose an overly universalistic and redistributive welfare state.

We maintain that, today, this straightforward political conflict about the degree of state intervention and generosity is no longer able to accurately capture the preferences and hence the political contention in labor-market policy, because the occupational structure (Kriesi 1998; Oesch 2006), the needs (Bonoli 2005) and, thus, the political preferences (Rueda 2006) of the labor force have dramatically changed. In fact, generous insurance benefits (unemployment or pension) serve first and foremost the workers in standard employment relations who reach the necessary contribution payments, while they represent suboptimal protection for the increasing share of non-standard employed workers (Bonoli 2006). Labor market outsiders, such as employees with a non-continuous work biography, or women with caring duties who work part time, encounter difficulties in reaching the necessary contribution years to be entitled to full pension or unemployment benefits. These new risk structures, which have arisen in a context of reduced steering capacity of governments, preclude the possibility of meeting these needs simply by increasing the decommodification efforts. These challenges have led to a partial change in the welfare state paradigm (Bonoli and Natali 2012: 1–4) and highlight the necessity of analyzing the consequences of these structural shifts in more detail (Rueda 2005; Taylor-Gooby 2005; Bonoli 2006). In fact, because of rising structural unemployment (Ebbinghaus 2006), the most pressing goal of modern welfare states is to *re-commodify* workers (Bonoli and Natali 2012; Bonoli 2013). Social investment measures (Gingrich and Ansell 2011; Morel, Palier and Palmer 2012), and, in the labor-market domain, *activation* policies, are the strategies that have prevailed in the most recent welfare state reforms all over Europe, starting with the third-way programs (New Deals) under Labor in the UK (1997) (King and Wickham-Jones 1999), the recently introduced Universal Credit (DWP 2010; Smith 2010) or the Hartz IV legislation in Germany (Fleckenstein 2008).

Overall, ALMPs constitute a remedy for the advancing liberalization of labor markets, because they are judged not only to be effective in reducing unemployment but also less expensive (Giddens 1998; Jensen 2012; Morel, Palier and Palmer 2012). However, these novel social policy strategies are likely to change the elites' underlying political preferences, influence the conflict dimensions in labor-market policy and thus influence the public debate.

Labor Market Conflicts: Similarity or Difference Across Regimes?

We suggest that all six countries included in our sample can be characterized by a two-dimensional conflict structure that includes a state/market and pro/contra activation expansion axis. There are several different reasons why activation policies may be contested. First, these may be subject to debates in countries with high problem pressures or which have suffered most from the recent crisis (dualizing countries and the UK) and who want to implement such strategies; however, activation schemes may be contested as well in countries which already use such policies. In the flexicurity countries, activation schemes have already been implemented but the political conflict might revolve around issues such as expanding or reforming the current institutions. By consequence, the question which arises is rather whether these challenges and reform pressures give rise to similar or different conflicts in the various regimes. In fact, in the scholarly literature different activation types are identified (Barbier and Ludwig-Mayerhofer 2004; Daguerre 2007; Bonoli 2010). Accordingly, it is plausible that the conflict structure is country specific and depends on the labor-market regime legacies, the problem pressures and the elites' ideas about what kind of activation strategy is best suited to solving the national challenges (see Fossati 2017a).

This specific research question can be embedded in a broader scholarly debate, which focuses on whether welfare state policies are converging on a neoliberal trajectory or diverging in country-specific pathways. The relevant discussion can be traced back to Scharpf (1981), to the PRA (Esping-Andersen 1990) or to the VoC literature in the 2000s. However, so far, no consensus has developed about whether these reforms lead to an overall *convergence* in policy solutions or whether *path-dependent* solutions prevail. Authors such as Handler (2003 and 2004), Gilbert (2002) and Jessop (1993) identify a clear-cut *convergence* of the European countries towards the US workfare model because of a generalized diffusion of coercive activating policies. Similarly, authors such as Ferrera and Gualmini (2004), Graziano (2007) and Bertozzi and Bonoli (2002) argue that we assist to a (partial) *integration* of supranational guidelines, especially those developed by the European Employment Strategy (EES), into the national unemployment policies. These authors suggest a kind of "European convergence route". By contrast, authors such as Esping-Andersen (1990 and 1996) and Clasen and Clegg (2011) insist on the *diversity* of national responses to the upheavals in the economic and productive structure. This strand of the literature stresses the importance of considering policy legacies and path-dependencies when discussing recent labor-market or unemployment reforms.[3]

In labor-market policy, the country-specific differences in the ALMP[4] arrangements become evident when analyzing their composition instead of merely measuring the *resources* invested in activation policies, as proposed instead by Gallie and Paugam (2000). In fact, while these authors propose to characterize welfare state regimes in terms of the percentage of Gross Domestic Product (GDP) invested in the ALMPs, which of course is a very crude measure for any kind of welfare performance as argued by Green-Petersen (2004), following Barbier and Ludwig-Mayerhofer

---

[3] Koistinen and Serrano (2009) distinguish a fourth strand in the literature, which argues that convergence depends on the dimensions of the analysis, as for instance policy field (see Hinrichs and Kangas 2003 for pension reforms). This last distinction was deemed less relevant in the context of this contribution, which clearly focuses only on one policy field.

[4] The analytical distinction which captures the characteristics of the political conflict characterizing the different labor market regimes across Europe was developed for unemployment policy by Gallie and Paugam (2000). The authors classify countries and policy measures according to three policy variables: 1) the amount of coverage; 2) the level and duration of the coverage; and 3) the overall share of ALMPs. In these terms, however, their classification results in an amplification of the model proposed by Esping-Anderson (1990) and Ferrera (1996) because "activation" is used just as an additional criterion to characterize the generosity of the four welfare regimes.

(2004) ALMPs should be characterized depending on the strategy these pursue to re-commodificate unemployed workers. The authors distinguish between typically Nordic ALMPs focusing on enhancing the human-capital resources of the individual unemployed person and the liberal variant, which instead is characterized by so-called workfare or work-first measures, which stress the need to swiftly re-introduce workers to the labor market principally by means of (negative) incentives and sanctions. An even more sophisticated theoretical approach to differentiating activation policies is proposed by Bonoli (2010), who distinguishes these measures depending on: i) the degree of human-capital investment; and ii) their degree of "pro-market employment orientation" (see also Bonoli 2013). Overall, he discerns four different activation strategies: the occupational, the incentive, the assistance and the up-skilling models[5]. Similarly to Barbier and Ludwig-Mayerhofer (2004), Bonoli (2010) argues that in the Anglo-Saxon countries incentive reinforcement policies were preferred. These measures, which are also known as "workfare" policies, aim at increasing the conditionality to prevent welfare state dependency, but contemporaneously keep the efforts of human-capital investment rather low. In the Nordic countries, the policies are instead in line with the social investment framework, i. e., "up-skilling" and employment assistance schemes are implemented (cf. Jensen 2012). Finally, Bonoli argues that in the continental welfare states "occupation"-oriented ALMPs were introduced in the 1980s and 1990s, which focused on keeping the unemployed busy while failing to invest in their skill profiles. Daguerre (2007) makes a similar argument when summarizing Barbier and Ludwig-Mayerhofer's (2004) discussion of a possible continental ALMP scheme. In her understanding, these continental ALMPs focus on maintaining the social networks of the unemployed.

Critically assessing this last typology, it must be noted however that the characterization of the continental ALMP strategy is rather vague and

---

[5] The first ideal type is the *occupational* model, which comprehends policies such as the creation of job schemes in the public sector and which is characterized by a low "pro-market employment orientation" and weak human capital investment. The other three categories share a high pro-market employment orientation but diverge in terms of human capital investment. Measures to reinforce the *incentives* to re-enter the labor market swiftly without investing in the skills of the unemployed encompass, for instance, time limits on recipiency, benefit reductions and increased conditionality on passive benefits. Furthermore, there are measures with a medium level of human capital investment, which are meant to *assist* the unemployed while looking for a job, by means of counseling services, job search programs or job subsidies. Finally, there are *up-skilling* policies, which combine a high pro-market employment orientation and a high degree of human capital investment. Such measures principally involve job-related vocational training measures.

tentative. Overall, the most important insight given by this regime-specific distinction of ALMP schemes is that activation (as welfare state performance in general) should not be differentiated simply based on the monetary effort, as suggested by Gallie and Paugam (2000), but that, depending on the priorities, rather different activation schemes may emerge (cf. Barbier and Fargion 2004).

Considering this scholarly discussion about (partially) diverging or converging national pathways, we would like to test whether the political *conflict* is the same in each country or whether (one or both) conflicts differ in line with the divergence literature. In fact, based on the varieties of activation literature, it is plausible that the second conflict axis differs between countries depending on the ideological "orientation", and hence on the concrete arrangement of activation measures.

In the following sections, we first give a brief description of the operationalization and the methodology we use to analyze whether the political conflict in labor-market policy is characterized by more than one dimension. Then, we present the result of the regime specific factor analyses and present the models, which support our expectations that the political conflict is indeed two-dimensional. According to the expectations we are able to show that the different regimes are characterized by different activation axes and thus corroborate the point made by the literature on labor-market divergence. In a final step, we turn to the third research question and theorize on the actor coalitions and on whether these are similar or differ between regimes by means of cluster analysis.

Operationalization and Methods

The present analyses rely on semi-structured telephone interviews with the major policy-makers[6] who are active in the domain of labor-market policy, i.e., parties, unions, state bodies, administrations and social movement organizations (SMOs).[7]

To operationalize the conflict structure, we rely on questions about political actors' preferences with respect to policy measures and their assessment of the relative importance of these measures.[8] We selected

---

[6] For the response rate by country, see Chapter 1.

[7] Interview partners were chosen as representatives of the major decision-making organizations who are experts of unemployment policy within the specific organizations. The relevance of those included in the analyses was cross-checked with two experts per country and validated by means of media analyses; see Chapter 1.

[8] The emprirical section draws some data and analyses from Fossati (2017a), however, the present chapter adds an additional case, namely the UK, and uses a different approach to identify coalitions (cluster analyses).

Table 6.1 *Operationalization of the conflict dimensions characterizing labor-market policy*

	State	Market
1. Conflict dimension	1) The use of state programs to create jobs (state job) 2) Raising the minimum wage (minimal wage)	3) Reduction of unemployment benefits (reduction benefit) 4) Flexibility of working hours (work hours) 5) Loosening of hire and fire legislation (hire-fire)
	Generous activation	Non-generous activation
2. Conflict dimension	6) More retraining possibilities for the unemployed (training) 7) The promotion of short-time work (short-time)	8) Promotion of labor-market reintegration (reintegration) 9) Tougher sanctions for those who refuse to accept an appropriate job (sanction)

those items that are theoretically best suited to capture the economic dimension (state/market) and the different activation models (Nordic, liberal and occupational). We also paid attention to choosing variables which best allow discrimination between the different actors' positions, i.e., which have the largest possible variance. We excluded items which were too generally formulated to capture specific labor-market preferences (such as "social inequality should be reduced") or uncontested items (such as "solidarity with the unemployed should be increased") and which accordingly do not represent a political *conflict*.[9]

Overall, we selected nine measures related to labor-market and unemployment benefits to define the preference structure (see *Table 6.1*).

To operationalize the economic conflict, we selected two indicators which capture the *generosity of passive benefits* and the degree to which the state engages in regulating social policy. The first item refers to the creation of jobs by the state. Especially in continental welfare states but also in social-democratic countries, the expansion of public employment is a way of preventing unemployment and is associated with a leftist position and with generous assistance to the unemployed. Second, we rely on the item "raising the minimum wage," which corresponds to a

---

[9] For more details on the exact question wording, the descriptive statistics and correlation tables, see *Table A6.1* to *Table A6.9* in the appendix.

state-led intervention to guarantee decent living standards to workers (prevent in-work poverty).

To operationalize the *market orientation* of the first dimension, we have one item which captures preferences for retrenching passive benefits ("reduce unemployment benefits"). Furthermore, there are two items which capture preferences for lower and more flexible EPL ("loosening of the hire and fire legislation" and "increasing working-hours flexibilisation").

With the available data, we can operationalize two activation strategies. The human-capital activation type is measured by two items referring to the promotion of skills: the promotion of (re)training programs and the promotion of short-time work, a measure for preserving/retaining human capital within a firm (Estevez-Abe et al. 2001, Thelen 2001, Sacchi et al. 2011). The second activation type mostly relies on the swift reinsertion of the unemployed along the lines of the "occupational" model (Bonoli 2010), and is captured by one item referring to labor-market "reintegration", i.e., increasing placement effort, and one referring to negative incentives ("increasing sanctions when an unemployed person refuses a job which is deemed appropriate"). Thereby, sanctions in case of non-compliance with the activation requirement is most often enacted by monetary disincentives, for instance by freezing or reducing the cash transfers (Kemmerling and Bruttel 2006; Trickey and Walker 2001; Clasen and Clegg 2011). The dimensionality of the political space is analyzed by means of an exploratory factor analysis including the nine items shown in *Table 6.1* above. For each item, we constructed an indicator which considers both the actor's *position* on a given measure and the *salience* of the measure for the actor. The combined indicator was developed by multiplying standardized salience and position for each actor. This strategy, which involves weighing position by salience, gives less weight to positions on measures, which the actor considers irrelevant and allows capturing only the most significant conflicts in labor-market policy. Weighting position by salience is a necessary strategy because political actors are likely to have a stance on all issues, however, they may judge them differently in terms of relevance. Whilst an actor's position on a given policy measure is gauged on a scale ranging from 1 to 5 (strongly disagree–strongly agree), we operationalized a measure's salience by asking our respondents to indicate the most important measure on the list we submitted to them, the three most important measures, and the three least important measures. The resulting salience indicator allocates three points to the most important measure, two points to the other two important measures, zero points to the three least important measures and one point to the remaining ones. Finally, an exploratory factor analysis[10] was run and the solutions were rotated orthogonally (varimax rotation). The non-governmental organization Attac Germany was excluded from the analyses because it proved to be an outlier in the pooled model, which includes the actors of all six countries. Since this organization is only of minor importance in this policy domain, its exclusion seems to be legitimate.

To assess the stability of the actor constellation, two different types of checks were run. First, instead of including all types of actors, the analyses were re-run with the parties and the social partners, i.e., unions, employers' associations and state bodies. These actors are deemed to be the most influential players and hence can be expected to decisively shape labor-market policy conflict structure. Moreover, the analyses were performed without issue salience weightings. In these additional analyses, the actor constellations were found to be stable both with the reduced actor sample and with and without weighting by salience.

Analyzing the Structure of Labor-Market Policy Space in Western Europe

The *pooled* analysis shows that when including all 124 political actors (except for Attac Germany) in a single model, the nine items load on two distinct factors, as highlighted in bold in *Table 6.2*.

Factor one is the economic factor (state-market), while factor two is the activation factor. On the economic dimension, the state-orientation is clearly captured by the items "increasing the minimum wage" and "increasing efforts in public job creation", which load negatively (both with −0.64). Interestingly, the *market orientation* (positive scores) of the economic dimension is instead defined in terms of increasing the "sanctions" (0.62) if an unemployed person refuses an appropriate job and in terms of the reduction of passive unemployment benefits (0.61). Also, the items which capture the degree of job protection, i.e., "flexibilizing of working hours" (0.57) and "loosening of hire and fire legislation" (0.45), load rather weakly on factor 1 and thus seem to be overall less relevant than other items in determining the political conflict in labor-market policy. As expected, the activation factor involves the items "increasing (re)training efforts" (0.41), "short-time work regulations" (0.36) and "(re)integration of unemployed in the labor market process" (0.36). However, in the pooled analysis this second factor has an eigenvalue conspicuously smaller than 1 and by consequence should not be

---

[10] Missing cases were recorded as neutral both in position and salience; they represent only between 2 and 5 percent.

Table 6.2 *Pooled factor analysis (all actors, all countries)*

Items	Factor 1	Factor 2
Sanction	0.62	0.06
Reduction benefit	0.61	0.04
Work hours	0.57	−0.21
Hire-fire	0.45	0.00
Minimal wage	−0.64	0.16
State job	−0.64	0.20
Training	−0.29	0.41
Short-time	−0.02	0.36
Reintegration	−0.08	0.36
Eigenvalue	2.18	0.54
Explained variance	90.57	22.50
N	124	124

Note Attac Germany was excluded from the sample.

considered an independent underlying factor. As described in the next section, this finding can be explained regarding the big differences in activation schemes that become visible when estimating regime specific models. In other words, on the activation dimension we find *functionally equivalent* policy conflicts, which depict different *combinations* of variables depending on the institutional setting. Accordingly, as expected by the convergence literature, we find *similar* preferences on the economic axis across countries but *differences* in terms of ALMP preferences. At this point it is useful to have a detailed look at the regime-specific labor-market policy conflict structure.

In *Table 6.3* and *Table 6.4*, the results of the regime-specific factor analyses are presented. We distinguish between the three regimes that were introduced in Chapter 3 – flexicurity (Denmark and Switzerland), dualization (Germany, France and Italy) and deregulation (UK). In *Table 6.3* we show the loadings of the items on the economic factor (state-market) and in *Table 6.4* we present the results for the second factor, which deals with activation policies. Overall, the results, which are supported by the country-specific analyses,[11] show that in all regimes/countries an economic and an *activation* axis exist. Thus, it can be concluded that the political conflict in these six western European countries circles

---

[11] See the Appendix for country-specific solutions. The country-specific analyses reveal that the conflict structure is rather similar for the countries belonging to the same regime, even though smaller deviations can be seen, in particular for Germany.

Table 6.3 *First factor by country: State versus market*

	Flexicurity	Dualized	Deregulated
Items	Denmark and Switzerland	Germany[1], France and Italy	UK
Sanction	0.52	0.58	0.89
Reduction benefit	0.71	0.51	0.85
Work hours	0.46	0.71	−0.41
Hire-fire	0.46	0.55	0.38
Minimal wage	−0.53	−0.76	−0.39
State job	−0.31	−0.72	−0.68
Training	−0.11	−0.30	−0.27
Short-time	0.00	0.20	−0.05
Reintegration	−0.09	−0.02	−0.13
Eigenvalue	2.12	2.71	2.52
Explained variance	60.45	81.09	50.88
N	40	67	16

[1] Attac Germany was excluded from the sample.

around two types of strategies to organize labor markets and to fight unemployment. However, even though in all regimes this two-dimensional structure clearly appears, it also becomes evident that, on the second dimension the *precise* conflict configuration must be assessed separately for the flexicurity, the deregulation or the dualization type.

Turning to the details of the findings summarized in *Table 6.3*, in all three regimes the items "increasing sanctions," "reduction of benefits," "flexibilizing working-hours," "hire-and-fire regimentation," "increasing the minimum wage" and "investing in public job creation" determine the state/market factor, except for the fact that in the UK "minimum wage" pertains to the activation axis. Furthermore, the results indicate that the state/market dimension is above all defined by the variables "investment in public job creation" (state job), "increasing the minimum wage," "reductions of benefits" and "increasing sanctions for unemployed," as indicated by their high loadings.

The variation on this first conflict dimension among the three regimes is minimal, and concerns merely the magnitude of the loadings. In more detail, while in the flexicurity countries "reduction of benefit" (0.71) is the most important item for the market orientation, in the dualized countries it is the flexibilizing of working hours (0.71). In the UK, it is the sanctioning of unemployed people who refuse to accept an appropriate job (0.89). In both the flexicurity and the dualized regimes, "increasing the "minimum wage" (−0.53/−0.76) is the best indicator for state interventionism, whereas in the UK it is the "introduction of state jobs" (−0.68).

Table 6.3 also reveals another interesting finding: the conflict structure in the UK seems to be comparable the one present in the dualizing countries. This can be explained to some extent by reference to the similarity of the problem pressure. In fact, the increasing dualization of labor-market insiders and labor-market outsiders is a weighty problem in both regimes and by consequence, even though the regimes are different, the most salient policy measures seem to coincide.

In sum, even though the composition of the economic factor shows some minimal regime-specific peculiarities, it can be nonetheless stated that a convergent political conflict structure exists. In detail, this conflict opposes a generous and state-interventionist position, captured by either an increased effort in public job-creation schemes or generous minimum wage regulation, and a market-oriented labor-market regimentation defined by lowering the generosity or increasing the conditionality of passive benefits.

While the results for the economic factors show similarities among the different regimes, the story for the activation dimension (*Table 6.4*) is one of regime-specific difference.

Table 6.4 *Second factor by country: Activation*

Items	Flexicurity	Dualised	Deregulated
	Denmark and Switzerland	Germany[1], France and Italy	UK
Sanction	−0.23	−0.09	0.19
Reduction benefit	−0.07	−0.26	−0.12
Work hours	−0.33	−0.13	−0.35
Hire-fire	0.03	−0.16	−0.31
Minimal wage	0.22	−0.05	−0.57
State job	0.61	−0.02	0.26
Training	0.48	0.40	−0.18
Short-time	0.59	0.35	0.24
Reintegration	0.22	0.66	0.77
Eigenvalue	1.42	1.95	1.35
Explained variance	0.46	25.84	27.25
N	40	67	16

[1] Attac Germany was excluded from the sample

In the flexicurity countries the empirical analyses show that the key measures determining the activation factor are "increasing public job creation" (0.61), "short-time work expansion" (0.59) and "training" (0.48). This combination of measures rather clearly mirrors the strong human-capital orientation of the flexicurity regimes, which prioritizes high state effort in terms of educational investment and the preservation of skills, for instance by means of short-time work. By contrast, in this labor-market regime "reintegration" and hence an occupational-oriented activation results to be quite irrelevant, with a negligible loading of 0.22.

The lower salience of reintegration policies in these countries can be explained by the overall rather low problem pressure (see Chapter 1). Moreover, during our debate period in Switzerland, just a few mass-dismissals occurred and were acknowledged as marginal events in the national press. Thus, the Swiss case does not achieve more than anecdotal relevance, especially when compared to other European countries, where the economic crisis hit the labor market severely and redundancies were an almost daily occurrence. Furthermore, the dualization problem is of marginal importance in the flexicurity countries, not least because of the low unemployment rates and of the good performance of the activation schemes. Accordingly, the political conflict on the activation axis, rather than revolving around the question of how to reintegrate unemployed persons into the labor market, focused on the question of whether it is necessary or not to introduce (additional) short-time schemes to prevent firms from losing their highly skilled collaborators and hence their know-how (Sacchi, Pancaldi and Arisi 2011).

Finally, also public job creation is a salient issue in flexicurity countries. The controversy about this issue is not so surprising because the state already effectively and efficiently regulates the labor markets. Especially in Switzerland, public job creation, and state effort more generally, encounter resistance from a strong market–liberal coalition and therefore become salient political issues. Thus, in Switzerland and Denmark the activation conflict refers on the one hand to the question of whether it is necessary to increase the state effort to introduce additional activation policies. On the other hand, a specific emphasis seems to be put on the retention of skills and retraining, not least because short-term schemes are often combined with additional training requirements.

A different picture emerges in the dualizing countries – Germany, France and Italy – where the most important determinant of the activation axis is "reintegration into the labor market" (0.66), followed by "training" (0.40) and, in only last place, short-term work (0.35). Unlike the flexicurity countries, where the debate focuses on the pros and cons of increasing state effort to retain the skilled workforce in the labor market by means of short-time measures and public job creation, in the dualization countries the insider–outsider debate is highly salient. Thus, a heated conflict about the necessity to strengthen the efforts to reintegrate the labor-market outsiders and the strategies to do so defines the conflict on the activation axis. In the dualizing countries, the short-term issue is markedly less controversial. In fact, in times of crisis in these countries it has become a common strategy to face labor-market challenges, and rising unemployment figures in particular, by means of short-term work schemes (Sacchi, Pancaldi and Arisi 2011), to avoid the loss of what is often the only source of family income, as is typical for male breadwinner welfare systems. In the crisis that developed after 2008, the trend to expand short-term work schemes made a quantum leap. Accordingly, rather than being a conflictive issue like in Denmark and Switzerland, where it structures the political preference patterns, short-term work was a widely agreed upon measure and accordingly is not particularly important in determining conflict structure.

Finally, the activation axis in the deregulated UK is clearly different from the dualized countries even though it shows a parallelism with respect to the most important item, "reintegration," which in this context clearly stands for workfarist re-commodification measures (Barbier and Ludwig-Mayerhofer 2004). Rather surprisingly, the activation axis in the UK shows also a negative reaction to the concept of "increase the minimum wage" (−0.57). Accordingly, the political actors are either in favor of reintroducing the unemployed into the labor market by means of workfarist reintegration policies or support an increase in the minimum wage. Thus, the activation conflict in the UK is completely different from the one in the flexicurity and in the dualization countries. Admittedly, this conclusion is based on scant information[12] and is rather difficult to interpret because it seems to link issues such as "reintegration policies" and "minimum wage schemes," which, at first sight, appear to belong to rather different dimensions. We will nonetheless try to make sense of the findings in *Table 6.4.*

The most plausible argument in our view is that the political conflict in this Liberal Market Economy (LME) is marked by the overall very flexible and liberal economic environment, which represents a challenge not only for the people who are already unemployed but also for those who receive low wages. In fact, as argued by Taylor-Gooby and Larsen (2005), in liberal countries the most important new social risk

---

[12] This country is the only representative of the deregulating system, and we could collect only 16 interviews.

constellation is related to low or obsolete skills, as well as to (long-term) unemployment. Accordingly, the focus of the activation axis might in this case not be exclusively related to the needs of the unemployed or labor-market outsiders, i.e., to preferences for or against increasing activation efforts, but more generally to the improvement of the situation for the precarious employees (cf. Oesch 2006), who are disproportionately at risk of being laid off or earning a poverty wage. Consequently, in the UK political actors appear to be either favorable to increasing labor-market reintegration efforts, which in this context are foremost workfarist activation policies as for instance the New Deals introduced by Labour in 1997, or they plead for an increased minimum wage[13], as in the Spending Review announced by the conservative government coalition in autumn 2010 (HM Treasury 2011), which foresaw cuts in welfare benefits (childcare etc.). The earning losses for those workers could of course be compensated with increased salaries. Accordingly, it is plausible that above all, political actors from the left promote measures that allow compensating these losses by means of sustainable wages.

In sum, whereas the structure of the economic conflict dimension is rather consistent between the different countries and is defined by the conflict over "sanction" and "work-hours" (decreasing generosity and increasing flexibility) versus "state job" and "minimum wage" (increasing generosity), the activation factor is clearly regime specific. Its composition, however, rather clearly reproduces the classification of the countries in the three labor-market regimes and in the three different activation ideologies, i.e., liberal (deregulation), human capital (flexicurity) and occupational (dualization), and thus nicely corroborates the findings of the varieties of activation literature (Barbier and Ludwig-Mayerhofer, Torfing 1999; Bonoli 2010).

Actor Constellations in the Labor-Market Policy Space

Hypotheses

In the following, the objective actor constellations and the differences between the coalitions in the three labor-market regimes will be analyzed focusing especially on the major players active in this field, i.e., parties, unions, employers' associations and the state bodies. To assess the

[13] Interestingly, the UK is – with France – one of the few countries with a minimum wage regulation (Bonoli 2007: 29), which, according to Bonoli functions as another way of insuring labor market participants instead of welfare state policies. However, in the UK the minimal wage is set at 37.4 percent of the full-time average earnings, making it extremely low compared with France's 55.3 percent.

Table 6.5 *Expected coalition composition in flexicurity, dualized and deregulated labor markets*

Activation dimension	Economic dimension	
	State	Market
Pro activation	**MODERN LEFT** - Greens - Communists - Unions (white collar) - Social movement organizations	**THIRD WAY** - State bodies, administration, research institutes - Progressive liberals or right-wing parties
Against activation	**TRADITIONAL LEFT** - Social-democratic parties - Unions (blue collar)	**TRADITIONAL RIGHT** - Employers' associations - Conservative government parties

coalition structures and the placement of the actors in the policy space we rely on the results of the factor analyses. Before illustrating the actual configurations, we however derive several hypotheses about the coalition patterns.

In detail, we hypothesize that four different coalitions may be identified in the field of labor-market policy, depending on their preferences with respect to the economic and the activation axes. *Table 6.5* presents our expectations with respect to the composition of these four coalitions.

In the first quadrant, we expect the modern left coalition, i.e., a coalition which endorses a flexicurity strategy characterized by strong passive and active labor-market policy measures. The political actors favoring such solutions represent people with preferences for redistribution and strong activation effort. We expect that people with left-libertarian values and labor-market outsiders to be represented by actors belonging to the "modern left" (Kitschelt 1994). Libertarian people, and well-educated citizens, can be expected to endorse this policy strategy because of their professional choices. In fact, working in occupations characterized by interpersonal work-logic (Oesch 2006; Kriesi 1998) might sensitize them to the needs of the unemployed and thus reinforce their preferences for generous state intervention. At the same time, these (well-) educated people recognize the need to improve the skills of the jobless and to re-train them in order to help them back into employment. We expect these left-libertarian people to be represented foremost by Green parties and white-collar unions. Moreover, we expect this modern coalition of the left to also include opposition parties (as, for instance, the Communists) which have no governmental – and hence budgetary – responsibility and consequently do not fear electoral punishment for suggesting the retention of high levels of welfare state support and even increasing them in the domain of activation.

In the bottom left quadrant, we expect the *traditional left* coalition, i.e., a coalition focusing above all on passive benefits and job-security regulations. We expect actors representing labor-market insiders in particular to be placed in this coalition. In line with Rueda (2006), it can be expected that social-democratic parties endorse pro-insider policies, particularly in the dualizing countries where the insider–outsider divide is most pronounced. We expect these insider actors to favor rather strong state intervention in terms of the traditional measures for guaranteeing employment or earning security, and to be skeptical with respect to activation measures which focus primarily on labor-market outsiders and by consequence do not accommodate their primary clientele. Together with the blue-collar unions, we expect them to be placed in the lower left quadrant.

The *third-way* coalition located in the top right quadrant is expected to favor increasing activation measures combined with a strong market orientation. Here, we expect to find political actors who are most likely to be influenced by the supranational consensus, which combines the neoliberal insistence on balancing the budget with the understanding that it is essential to provide labor-market access and enable outsiders to re-enter the labor market as quickly as possible, even at the cost of reducing traditional passive benefits to finance ALMPs. Overall, these third-way actors can be expected to include government authorities and public administrations, as well as progressive liberal or right-wing parties (Daguerre and Taylor-Gooby 2004; Stiller and van Gerven 2012). However, it is also plausible to assume that highly skilled workers (represented by white-collar unions), who are less likely to become unemployed, prefer a less costly welfare state and hence from a rational-choice perspective endorse reductions in welfare state effort and increasing re-commodification effort.

Finally, in the *traditional right* coalition at the bottom right quadrant we expect to find primarily employers' organizations and conservative/right-wing liberal mainstream parties, for whom the current welfare state effort is big enough and who give priority to budgetary rigor over the expansion of any kind of welfare state benefit (Esping-Anderson 1990). As argued by Huber and Stephens (2001), right-wing/conservative parties are characterized by preferences for subsidiarity and self-reliance, and by consequence can be expected to be against not only an expansion of passive, but also of active, state effort (cf. Miles and Quadagno 2002).

This fourfold coalition structure, however, is not the only conceivable option in terms of actor constellations. The recent critique of the dualization literature discloses another possibility: a broad coalition on the left including both traditional and modernizing left forces. This hypothesis is based on the evidence proposed by authors such as Emmenegger (2009), who shows that both insiders and outsiders have the same (or very similar) labor-market policy preferences, or Schwander (2012) who shows that social-democratic parties do not target exclusively labor-market insiders in their electoral campaigns but address also the outsiders. In the light of the inconclusiveness of these theoretical expectations, we introduce a dotted line in *Table 6.5* which illustrates the alternative hypothesis assuming that insiders and outsiders may be represented by a single left coalition. The common denominator of this coalition would be preferences for generous state intervention, while the degree of activation policies could instead be expected to be a subject of debate.

Analyzing Actor Constellations in the Labor-Market Policy Space

The empirical findings of actors' positioning in the issue-specific policy space, which is defined by the economic and the activation axes, are presented in *Figures 6.1 to 6.3*. The coalitions, which are defined by means of a cluster analysis[14] based on the similarity of their preferences (factor scores on the state/market and on the pro/contra activation dimension), are encircled with a dotted line. The first insight that appears from these figures is that the coalitions are located slightly differently than expected by the first set of hypotheses, where we find a broad left coalition between "modern" and "traditional" forces, which include different actors such as unions, Greens and social-democratic parties.

However, when looking more closely at the composition especially of the left coalitions, we find that neither of the hypothesized clusters can be fully corroborated. In fact, we do *not* find that social-democratic parties, as expected by Rueda (2006), are located in a traditional left coalition, nor do we find that these always belong to the leftist coalition in the first place. What the result does show is that the positioning of social-democratic parties depends on the country at stake. In more detail, we find that in the flexibilizing countries, the Danish Socialist Party (SPD)

[14] The cluster analysis was performed by means of the *kmeans* command in STATA, based on both the state/market and the pro/contra activation factor scores. Four groups were requested.

and the Swiss Socialist Party (SP) are both located in the third-way coalition, whereas the broad left coalition is composed by unions and SMOs. The findings for the dualizing countries are supportive of the Rueda-based argument because social-democratic parties are clearly located in the traditional-left quadrant; however, these parties belong to different coalitions (left or centrist). Finally, in the UK, we actually find just three major coalitions: a united left, a centrist coalition and a right coalition. Interestingly, also in the UK, the socialist party (Labour) is located in the centrist coalition.

Flexicurity Countries

Figure 6.1 shows the four coalitions in the flexicurity countries. The left coalition is composed of two Swiss union federations (Travail Suisse

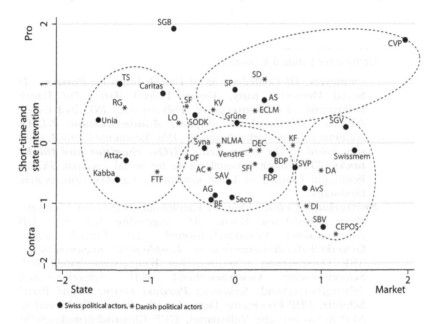

● Swiss political actors, ✳ Danish political actors

Figure 6.1 Actor configuration in the flexicurity countries (Denmark and Switzerland)

Legend
Clusters: result of a cluster analysis.
Denmark: Unions: *AC* Akademikernes Centralorganisation, *FTF* Confederation of Professionals, *LO* Confederation of trade unions; ***Employers' organizations***: *DA* Confederation of Danish

and Unia), the coordinating organ of the Swiss cantons (SODK), the Danish union federations (LO and FTF), the Swiss NGOs Caritas, Attac and Kabba, as well as the Danish red–green alliance (RG), the Socialist Folkeparti (SF) and the Danish Folkeparti (DF). Surprisingly, the Swiss confederation of trade unions (SGB), the unions of the Swiss white-collar employees (AS) and the Swiss Greens belong to the third-way coalition, which favors a more liberal and market-oriented passive benefit strategy. In the third-way coalition we further identify the Swiss Social Democratic Party (SP), the Danish Social-democratic Party (SD), the Swiss Christian-Democratic Party (CVP) and the Danish Economic Council (ECLM), which is an advisory board to the labor movement.

The actor constellation in Denmark and Switzerland thus suggests that in countries where welfare state benefits are generous and contemporaneously problem pressure in terms of unemployment

---

Caption for Figure 6.1 (cont.)

Employers, *DI* Confederation of Danish Industry; **Parties:** *SD* Social Democrat party, *Venstre* Liberal Party, *DF* Dansk Folkepartis, *KF* Konservative Folketsparti, *RG* Red–Green Alliance, *SF* Socialist Folkeparti; **Administration:** *NLMA* National Labour Market Authority, *DEC* Economic Council, advisory board to the government; **NGOs, charities and think-tanks**: *SFI* Danish national centre for social research, *ECLM* Economic Council of labor movement, *CEPOS* Conservative think-tank.

Switzerland: *Unions*: *Unia, KV* Kaufmännischer Verband Schweiz, *Syna* Arbeitslosen Kasse, *AS* Angestellte Schweiz, *SGB* Scherizerischer Gewerkschaftsbund, *TS* Travail. Suisse Gewerkschafts-dachorganisation; **Employers' organizations:** *SBV* Dachverband Schweizerischer Baumeisterverband, *SGV* Schweizerischer Gewerbeverband, *SAV* Schweizerischer, Arbeitgeberverband, *Swissmem*; **Parties:** *Gruene* Grüne Partei Schweiz, *FDP* Freisinning Demorkatische Partei, die Liberalen, *SVP* Schweizerische Volkspartei, *CVP* Christlichdemokratische Volkspartei, *BDP* Bürgerlich Demokratische Partei, *SP* Sozialdemokratische Partei; **Administration:** *BE* Canton Bern, *AG* Canton Argau, *SODK* Conference of the cantonal social ministers, *SECO* State Secretary for Economic Affairs; **NGOs, charities and think-tank**: *Caritas* Switzerland, *Attac* Switzerland, NGO, *Kabba* NGO on behalf of the unemployed, *AvS* Avenir Suisse.

level is comparatively low[15], actors facing government responsibility are less likely to endorse an expansion of passive benefits. In fact, in the left cluster, merely the Danish red–green alliance (RG), some unions and social movement organizations can be identified. Interestingly, the actors belonging to the left coalition diverge widely with respect to activation preferences. Whereas the Danish white-collar union FTF is rather against expanding training, short-term and public job creation, i.e., pro-outsider policies, the other left unions are in favor of such activation measures.

The heterogeneity within the left coalition supports the expectations that these actors face particular challenges deciding whether to endorse activation policies and whether to address rather insider or outsider (Rueda 2007; Schwander 2012). In terms of coalition no clear distinction between left-pro-insider and left-pro-outsider actors can be found, rather they form a heterogeneous coalition basing on their common left stance on the state/market dimension.

Moreover, the figure shows that, contrarily to the expectations, the social democratic parties are located in the third-way cluster and thus do not share the preferences of the left coalition endorsing the expansion of welfare benefits. Rather, these parties seem to engage for outsiders by endorsing activation (training, short-term and public job creation) but, against the interest of their former core constituencies, are willing to keep the status quo or eventually even reduce passive benefits. This finding challenges the argument made by Rueda (2007) that social democratic parties represent the labor-market insiders and rather lends support to the argument made by Schwander (2012) that social democratic parties target, along with insiders, also outsiders and thus also strongly engage for labor-market activation possibly even more than for passive benefits.

Unexpectedly, we find a centrist cluster of actors, which are character-ized by a neutral position on the state/market dimension and by a ten-dency to moderately oppose expansive activation measures. The actors belonging to this coalition include state bodies from Switzerland

---

[15] In 2010 youth unemployment (as percentage of the youth labor force) for Denmark reached 13.8 percent and in Switzerland 7.2 percent. As compared to the UK (19.1 percent), Italy (27.9 percent) and France (22.5 percent), these figures are very moderate. The only exception to this pattern is Germany, with just 9.7 percent youth unemploy-ment. The low level of problem pressure can also be documented by figures for long-term unemployment (as percentage of the unemployed). In 2010 Denmark had 19.1 percent and Switzerland 34.3 percent of long-term unemployed. Compared to France (40.1 percent), Germany (47.4 percent) and Italy (48.5 percent), these again indicate a good performance of the Swiss and Danish labor markets. Only the UK has similarly low levels of long-term unemployment (32.6 percent) (Source: OECD key tables).

(the cantons Aargau and Berne and the State Secretary for Economic Affairs (SECO)) and Denmark (NLMA and DEC) as well as the Danish liberal party Venstre and the Swiss liberal party FDP, both the Swiss conservative BDP and the Danish conservative (KP) parties, as well as the Swiss employers' organization (SAV).

These findings clearly contradict the hypothesis that state bodies and administrations in Denmark and Switzerland should endorse a third-way strategy because of their contact to international and supranational bodies of experts. On the contrary, we find that state bodies and administrations are rather skeptical of activation measures and overall are oriented towards preserving the status-quo.

Last, the traditional right coalition is composed as expected of the employers' organizations (SGV, Swissmem, SBV in Switzerland and the DI, DA in Denmark), the Swiss Peoples' Party (SVP) and the think tanks CEPOS and Avenir Suisse. Similarly to the left coalition, also the right coalition is very homogenous on the state/market axis but rather heterogeneous on the activation axis. This result nicely endorses the findings of previous studies, arguing that a multidimensional policy space may give rise to flexible, issue-specific coalitions (Häusermann 2006 and 2010). Given the similarity of their position on the activation axis, it is plausible that the employers' organization Swissmem cooperates with the social movement organization Attac, even though such cooperation would be unconceivable for instance with respect to passive unemployment benefits.

Dualization Countries

As in the flexicurity countries, in the dualizing regimes (*Figure 6.2*) an actor constellation characterized by four coalitions (left, centrist, third way and right) emerges. However, the allocation of the different types of actors in the four groups is less clearly structured than in Denmark and Switzerland. First, it appears that the unions are spread across the left, centrist (center-left) and third-way coalitions and the Italian UIL is even placed in the traditional right coalition. In the Italian case, the differences between the unions can be explained to some extent by their ideological fragmentation (Kriesi 2007). In fact, the findings that the liberal UIL is closer to the political right and the Roman Catholic CISL is located in the third-way coalition, as is the Swiss Christian-democratic party CVP in Switzerland, is comprehensible. Rather surprising is instead that the formerly communist union CIGL is located not with the COBAS in the left coalition but in the moderate centrist group along with the German unions IGM and DGB, the Italian party Lega or the Social Democrat party in Germany.

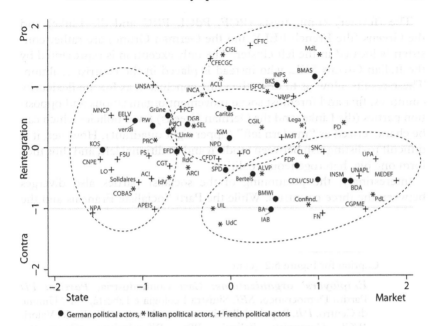

Figure 6.2 Actor configuration in the dualising countries (Germany, France and Italy)

Legend
Clusters: result of a cluster analysis.
France: Unions: *Solidaires, UNSA* Union nationale des syndicats autonomes, *CFECGC* Confédération française de l'encadrement, *CFDT* Confédération française démocratique du travail, *CFTC* Confédération Française des Travailleurs, *CGT* Confédération générale du travail, *FSU* Fédération syndicale unitaire; *Employers' organizations: CGPME* Confédération Générale des Petites et Moyennes Entreprises, *MEDEF* Mouvement des entreprises de France, *UNAPL* La confédération interprofessionnelle des professions libérales, *UPA* Union Professionelle Artisanale; ***Parties:*** *UMP* Union pour le Mouvement Populaire (UMP), *PS* Parti Socialiste, *FN* Front National, *PCF* Parti Communiste Français, *LO* Lutte Ouvrière, *NPA* Nouveau Parti Anticapitaliste, *FO* Force Ouvrière, *EELV* Europe Ecologie Les Verts; ***Administration:*** *MDT* Ministère du Travail; **NGOs, charities and think-tanks:** *AC!* Agir contre le Chômage!, *APEIS* Association Pour l'Emploi, l'Information et la Solidarité, *CNPE* Comité national des privés d'emploi CGT, *MNCP* Mouvement National des Chômeurs et Précaires, *SNC* Solidarités nouvelles face au chômage.
Italy: Unions: *COBAS* Confederazione dei Comitati di Base, *UIL* Unione Italiana del Lavoro, *CISL* Confederazione Italiana Sindacati dei Lavoratori, *CIGL* Confederazione Generale Italiana del Lavoro;

The (former) communists (PCF, PdCI, PRC and die Linke) and the Greens (the French EELV and the German Grüne) are rather consistently located in the left cluster. The only exception is represented by the Italian Greens SEL, who instead is placed in the centrist coalition. These results allow us to draw the same conclusion as for the flexicurity countries: first and foremost social movement organizations and opposition parties (die Linke, and the German Greens) favor policies which can be characterized as "modern left" (upper right quadrant). However, it is difficult to distinguish between modern and traditional left, and thus they form one big, heterogeneous coalition.

Interestingly, the positioning of the socialist parties also diverges between the three countries. While the Parti Socialiste Français and the

---

Caption for Figure 6.2 (cont.)

Employers' organizations: Conf Confindustria; *Parties: PD* Partito Democratico, *SEL* Sinistra Ecologia e Libertà, *UdC* Unione di Centro, *PdL* Popolo della Libertà, *Lega* Nord, *IdV* Italia dei Valori, *PdCI* Comunisti italiani, *PRC* Rifondazione Comunista; *Administration: MdL* Ministero del Lavoro, *INPS* Istituto Nazionale Previdenza Sociale; *NGOs, charities and think-tanks: ISFOL* Istituto per lo Sviluppo della Formazione Professionale dei Lavoratori, *ACLI* Associazioni Cristiane Lavoratori Italiani (ACLI, patronato CISL), *ALVP* Movimento Associazione Lavoratori Vittime del Precariato, *INCA* Istituto Nazionale Confederale di Assistenza (patronato CIGL), *ARCI* Associazione di Promozione culturale, *RdC* Rete della Conoscenza.

Germany: *Unions: KGA* Koordinierungsstelle gewerkschaftlicher Arbeitslosengruppen, *IGM* Industriegewerkschaft Metall, *Verdi* Vereinte Dienstleistungsgewerkschaft, *DGB* Deutscher Gewerkschafts Bund; *Employers' organizations: BDA* Bundesvereinigung der Deutschen Arbeitgeberverbände; *Parties: Linke* Die Linke, *CDU/CSU* Christlich Demokratische Union/ Christlich Soziale Union, *NPD* Nationaldemokratische Partei Deutschlands, *FDP* Freie Demokratische Partei/ Die Liberalen, *SPD* Sozialdemokratische Partei Deutschlands, *Gruene* Grüne Partei Deutschland; *Administration: BKS* Bundesvereinigung kommunale Spitzenverbände, *BMAS* Bundesministerium für Arbeit und Soziales, *BWM* Bundeswirtschaftsministerium, *BA* Bundesagentur für Arbeit; *NGOs, charities and think-tanks: Caritas* Deutschland, *EFD* Erwerbslosenforum, *Attac* Deutschland, *INSM* Initiative Neue Soziale Marktwirtschaft, *PW* Paritätischer Wohlfahrtsverband, *Bertels* Bertelsmannstiftung, *IAB* Institut für Arbeitsmarkt und Berufsforschung.

Italia dei Valori are in the left coalition, the German SPD belongs to the centrist group, which in the light of the fact that it was the social-democratic party that proposed the liberal-leaning Hartz IV reforms, might not surprise after all. Finally, and as an absolute outlier, the Partito Democratic in Italy seems to belong to the right coalition.

The state bodies and administrationsl which were expected to be in the third-way coalitionsl are consistently located moderately on the right and diverge widely on the activation axis (right coalition). Interestingly, a similar pattern has been detected also for the state bodies in Denmark and Switzerland. Conversely, the Italian Ministry of Employment and the German Ministry for Social Affairs behave as expected and are located in the third-way coalition favoring an active reintegration policy. The corresponding French office is neutral and thus belongs to the centrist coalition, while the German Bundesagentur für Arbeit (BAA) is clearly located in the right coalition.

The hypothesis that the conservative government parties pertain to the right coalition can be corroborated at least to some extent for the dualizing countries. In fact, both the German CSU/CDU and the Italian PdL meet these expectations; only the French UMP is part of the third-way coalition and endorses activation strategies, in particular reintegration and training measures, which are the items with high factor loadings and which determine the regime-specific activation factor.

Interestingly, in the dualizing countries the right coalition is extremely divided on the state/market dimension but has a very homogeneous stance in refusing increasing activation effort (especially training and reintegration measures). These actors thus seem to disagree foremost on whether employment conditions should be liberalized further, an issue which has been pushed particularly by employers' organizations and government parties in the dualizing countries to countervail the rigidities of the continental welfare states. Conversely, issues linked to activation seem less debated and/or relevant.

Deregulated Country

In the UK (see *Figure 6.3*), we find just three coalitions, a coalition each on the left, in the center and on the right; the fourth cluster is represented by the New Policy Institute, a non-governmental organization that seems to have rather extremist preferences and results to be isolated from the other political actors. In the UK, the unions (Unison, Trade Union Congress and Unite), the Scottish National Party and the Greens are located in the left coalition. These actors prefer a pro-labor-market reintegration policy orientation rather than increasing the minimum wage,

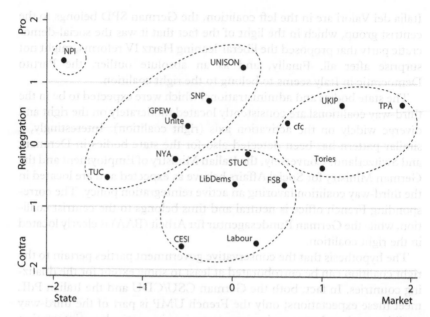

Figure 6.3 Actor configuration in the liberal country (United Kingdom)

Legend

Clusters: result of a cluster analysis.

United Kingdom: *Unions*: *TUC* Trade Union Congress, *STUC* Scottish Trade Union Congress, *UNISON* Public service trade union, *Unite* The Union; *Employers' organizations*: *FSB* Federation of Small Business; *Parties*: *GPEW* Green Party, *Tories* Conservative Party, *Libdems* Liberal democrats, *Labour* Party, *SCNP* Scottish National Party, *UKIP* United Kingdom Independence Party; *NGOs, charities and think-tanks*, *NPI* New Policy Institute (independent think-tank), *Cfc* Centre for Cities, *CESI* Centre for Economic and Social Inclusion, *NYA* National Youth Agency, *TPA* Taxpayers' Alliance.

accordingly they seem to care foremost for the interests of the labor-market outsiders, i.e., the unemployed, rather than engaging to prevent in-work poverty. Thus, as for the other regimes, also in the UK the left coalition is composed by unions, opposition parties and social movement organizations and is very heterogeneous both on the state/market and on the activation dimension.

Somewhat unexpectedly for a social-democratic party, Labour is located moderately to the political right and belongs to the centrist coalition. In terms of activation preferences, Labour does not prioritize the reintegration of the unemployed in the labor market but is decidedly in favor of increasing the minimum wage. This finding is thus rather compatible with Rueda's (2006) expectation that social-democratic parties represent the interests of labor-market insiders because increases in minimal wage benefit first and foremost labor-market insiders. The other actors, who are part of the centrist coalition with the Labour Party, include the Liberal Democrats, the Scottish Trade Union Congress (STUC), the FSB – the only employers' organization we succeeded in interviewing in the UK – and the think tank CESI.

To interpret the results with respect to the right coalition, we should keep in mind that in the UK the composition of the activation axis in differs slightly from the one in the other regimes. At first sight, in fact, the right coalition coincides with the third-way coalitions in the other countries and is located in the upper right quadrant. However, in the deregulating country the right coalition favors a strong-market orientation and focuses on increasing the efforts to reintegrate the unemployed as opposed to *guaranteeing a minimal wage* to prevent in-work poverty. In other words, these actors favor work-first measures (reintegration) rather than increasing protection for labor-market insiders and thus cannot be considered a third-way coalition. The right coalition in the UK is composed by the nationalist UK Independence Party, the conservative Tories and two SMOs (Centre for Cities and the Taxpayers' Alliance).

In sum, across all three regimes, the most consistent finding is clearly the one concerning the employers' associations, which, in all countries, are located in the rightist coalition, often joined by conservative governing parties. In contrast, the composition of the left, centrist and third-way coalitions vary by regime.

In detail, we could show that social movement organizations, unions and opposition parties cluster in the left coalition and accordingly endorse generous passive benefits, but that these cannot be distinguished in terms of whether they support pro-insider or pro-outsider policies. Thus, at coalition level the results concerning the representation of insider and outsider are inconclusive.

Moreover, we found that social-democratic parties in the flexicurity countries pertain to the third-way coalition and, by consequence, are at best for a preservation of the status-quo with respect to passive benefits while supporting an expansion of activation policies. Conversely, the findings for the dualizing countries are more in line with the expectations of Rueda (2007); in fact, both the French Socialist Party and the Italian Italia dei Valori support traditional left policy measures (lower left quadrant) and pertain to the left coalition, while – not surprisingly – German SPD is located in the centrist coalition.

This result rather nicely supports our expectations that socialist parties should not be expected to implement *exactly the same* policies independently of the institutional context in which they are embedded in. In fact, in the flexicurity countries where insider protection is unchallenged and the insider/outsider divide is less pronounced, traditional left actors might focus more on novel clienteles rather than engage to preserve traditional workers' privileges. In the dualizing countries, the socialist parties instead might still be concerned with defending the insiders' interest against novel claims especially because with the high levels of problem pressure social policy increasingly develops into a zero-sum game where ameliorations for one group necessarily implies cuts in other domains.

In sum, the present analyses show that the political contest is two-dimensional and revolves around a state/market axis that results to be very similar in all regimes, and an activation axis that instead is regime-specific. Furthermore, we corroborated the theoretical expectation that the political contest and hence the actor constellations depend on the institutional legacies and eventually on the problem pressure. Thus, as suggested by Thelen (2012), future research should concentrate on assessing the institutional starting points and how these influence reform trajectories and actor constellations.

Conclusion

The aim of this chapter was to unveil the structure of the *labor-market space* in six western European countries and to evaluate whether the conflict structure is two-dimensional and whether it is similar or different across countries. Moreover, since the conflict structure is determined by the actor configuration, we also described the preference-based coalition patterns in the different regimes (see also Fossati 2017a).

Overall, in analyzing labor-market space dimensionality it could be shown that the economic dimension is rather regime invariant, i.e., in the three regimes the same items capture the state/market political conflict. It was another story for the activation conflict, which instead depends on whether the country has a flexicurity, a dualizing or a deregulating labor-market legacy.

In this respect, we argued that, because of the changing socio-economic context, political actors are confronted with new social needs, especially those of the long-term unemployed (Bonoli 2005), and that these are above all accommodated by means of activation and re-commodification policies. In the light of the convergence/divergence debate, the question was raised whether in all countries exactly the same political conflict space can be expected. We argued that the labor-market policy preferences differ because of institutional legacies, in particular the activation models implemented in each country. In the flexicurity countries (Denmark and Switzerland), a strong orientation towards a generous and human-capital activation practice was expected and we could show that the political contention in these countries is mainly about whether it is necessary to increase state efforts in the activation domain by means of expanding short-time work or creating employment in the public sector. In the dualization regime, which is characteristic of France, Italy and Germany, the labor force is split into insiders profiting from rather generous benefits and an increasing share of workers with precarious or atypical contracts. Here, the political conflict on the second (activation) dimension was shown to be defined by activation preferences relating to reintegration. The UK, as the only representative of the deregulation model, is characterized by both very low passive benefits and rather low activation efforts, which, moreover, are conditional and incentive based. Furthermore, in the UK there is a large share of the population working in underpaid service jobs, which needs additional protection. This might be a reason why, in this country, the activation axis does not only concern preferences for workfarist reintegration measures but has a second polarity that captures the preferences for an increase in the minimum wage.

The regime-specific composition of the activation axis supports the expectations that the state/market conflict is similar across countries and regimes, whereas the difference in the activation dimension rather supports the literature on national divergence. Thus, given the rather high between-country variation in conflict structure, the comparative political economy literature – which argues that different institutional legacies lead countries to endorse different reform trajectories (Esping-Anderson 1996; Taylor-Gooby 2005; Thelen 2012) and hence confront them with slightly different political conflicts – can be supported. In fact, as the analyses show, the nine items used to operationalize the political conflict structure in labor-market policy are perceived to represent *functionally equivalent* conflict dimensions, but the specific composition of the conflicts clearly depends on the regime characteristics.

Finally, we reported several interesting findings with respect to the actor constellations. The flexicurity and the dualizing regimes are characterized by four different coalitions – left, centrist, third-way and right, respectively – and in the UK by three major coalitions, which are discernible in terms of left–right placement. Overall, the most consistent finding concerns the employers' organizations which clearly and consistently are part of the right coalition. We could then show that contrary to the expectations, state bodies and administrations pertain to the centrist coalitions which endorse a moderate retrenchment on both policy dimensions. Moreover, the argument by Rueda (2007) that social democratic parties favor traditional left policies could partially be corroborated. In fact, the French Parti socialiste and the Italian Italia dei Valori could be shown to belong to the left coalition and be located in the lower left quadrant. Conversely, the German social democrats and Labour belong to the center-left coalition, the Swiss and the Danish to the third-way coalition and the Partito Democratico very surprisingly to the right coalition.

This heterogeneity of social democratic positions and coalition patterns suggests that organizations belonging to the same party families may have different preferences depending on institutional context, and supports our expectations that institutional starting points are pivotal in understanding the elites' policy proposal (Fossati 2017a).

We also challenge current practices in welfare state research which capture actors' positions basing merely on preferences for policy types or amount of spending, without considering that these preferences are influenced and hence can be understood only *within* a particular institutional context and against the background of specific challenges as for instance high unemployment figures.

Table A6.1 *Interview statement wording*

1	State job	The use of state programs to create jobs.
2	Minimal wage	Raising the minimum wage.
3	Sanction	Tougher sanctions for those who refuse to accept work that is deemed appropriate for them.
4	Reduction benefit	Reduction of unemployment benefits.
5	Workhours	Flexibility of working hours.
6	Hire-fire	Loosening of hire and fire legislation.
7	Training	More retraining possibilities for the unemployed.
8	Short-time	The promotion of short time work – the ability of employers to reduce workers' hours when orders are low.
9	Reintegration	Reintegration in the labor market should be actively promoted.

Table A6.2 *Correlation table*

	Sanction	Reduction benefits	Work hours	Hire-fire	State job	Minimal wage	Training	Short-time
Sanction	1.00							
Reduction benefit	0.53	1.00						
Workhours	0.29	0.26	1.00					
Hire-fire	0.28	0.24	0.35	1.00				
State job	−0.36	−0.41	−0.39	−0.27	1.00			
Minimal wage	−0.31	−0.29	−0.52	−0.28	0.50	1.00		
Training	−0.19	−0.12	−0.18	−0.07	0.29	0.23	1.00	
Short-time	−0.02	−0.05	−0.09	0.09	0.10	0.01	0.18	1.00

Note: N = 124 (Attac Germany has been excluded from the analyses).

Table A6.3 *Descriptive statistics all countries*

	Variable	Mean	St.dev.	Min.	Max.
1	State job	0.23	0.43	−1.00	1.00
2	Minimal wage	0.22	0.38	−0.66	1.00
3	Sanction	−0.03	0.31	−1.00	1.00
4	Reduction benefit	−0.15	0.31	−1.00	1.00
5	Workhours	0.07	0.26	−0.33	1.00
6	Hire-fire	−0.06	0.26	−0.66	1.00
7	Training	0.36	0.35	−0.66	1.00
8	Short-time	0.15	0.29	−0.33	1.00
9	Reintegration	0.42	0.34	−0.5	1.00

Note: N = 124 (Attac Germany has been excluded from the analyses).

Table A6.4 *Descriptive statistics Switzerland*

	Mean	St.dev.	Min.	Max.
State job	0.11	0.36	−0.33	1.00
Minimal wage	0.13	0.37	−0.33	1.00
Sanction	0.05	0.30	−0.33	0.66
Reduction benefit	−0.06	0.33	−0.66	1.00
Work hours	0.15	0.35	−0.33	1.00
Hire-fire	−0.11	0.24	−0.66	0.33
Training	0.28	0.39	−0.33	1.00
Short-time	0.10	0.30	−0.33	0.66
Reintegration	0.41	0.40	−0.50	1.00

Note: N = 24.

Table A6.5 *Descriptive statistics Germany*

	Mean	St.dev.	Min.	Max.
State job	0.19	0.36	−0.33	1.00
Minimal wage	0.30	0.47	−0.66	1.00
Sanction	−0.12	0.30	−1.00	0.33
Reduction benefit	−0.19	0.28	−1.00	0.33
Work hours	0.04	0.23	−0.33	0.66
Hire-fire	−0.08	0.16	−0.33	0.17
Training	0.26	0.38	−0.66	1.00
Short-time	0.20	0.26	−0.17	1.00
Reintegration	0.39	0.33	−0.33	1.00

Note: N = 21 (Attac Germany has been excluded from the analyses).

Table A6.6 *Descriptive statistics Denmark*

	Mean	St.dev.	Min.	Max.
State job	0.03	0.43	−1.00	1.00
Minimal wage	0.01	0.19	−0.33	0.66
Sanction	−0.07	0.31	−0.66	0.66
Reduction benefit	0.02	0.28	−0.33	0.66
Work hours	0.11	0.22	−0.33	0.66
Hire-fire	−0.11	0.17	−0.33	0.17
Training	0.33	0.37	−0.17	1.00
Short-time	−0.06	0.19	−0.33	0.33
Reintegration	0.53	0.35	0	1.00

Note: N = 16.

Table A6.7 *Descriptive statistics France*

	Mean	St.dev.	Min.	Max.
State job	0.42	0.45	−0.33	1.00
Minimal wage	0.38	0.40	−0.33	1.00
Sanction	−0.02	0.21	−0.33	0.33
Reduction benefit	−0.22	0.30	−1.00	0.17
Work hours	0	0.33	−0.33	0.66
Hire-fire	−0.03	0.42	−0.33	1.00
Training	0.48	0.30	0	1.00
Short-time	0.13	0.24	−0.33	0.66
Reintegration	0.40	0.34	0	1.00

Note: N = 25.

Table A6.8 *Descriptive statistics Great Britain*

	Mean	St.dev.	Min.	Max.
State job	0.30	0.41	−0.66	1.00
Minimal wage	0.10	0.23	−0.33	0.66
Sanction	−0.13	0.33	−1.00	0.33
Reduction benefit	−0.27	0.43	−1.00	0.33
Work hours	0.14	0.13	0	0.33
Hire-fire	0	0.23	−0.66	0.33
Training	0.34	0.25	0	1.00
Short-time	0.11	0.13	0	0.33
Reintegration	0.37	0.31	0	1.00

Note: N = 16.

Table A6.9 *Descriptive statistics Italy*

	Mean	St.dev.	Min.	Max.
State job	0.29	0.46	−0.33	1.00
Minimal wage	0.32	0.37	−0.33	1.00
Sanction	0.09	0.36	−0.66	1.00
Reduction benefit	−0.16	0.16	−0.33	0
Work hours	0.04	0.19	−0.33	0.33
Hire-fire	−0.03	0.23	−0.33	0.66
Training	0.43	0.33	0	1.00
Short-time	0.38	0.37	0	1.00
Reintegration	0.46	0.32	0	1.00

Note: N = 22.

7   Beliefs or Interests
What Is the Driving Force Behind Coalition Formation?

Laurent Bernhard

Introduction

The aim of this chapter is to analyze the coalition structure of the labor-market domain in six Western European countries (Germany, France, Italy, United Kingdom, Denmark, and Switzerland). The fact that our examination pertains to a time-specific period (from October 2010 to January 2011) prompts the question of whether the coalition structure is driven by long-term characteristics or rather short-term considerations made by political actors. According to the very influential advocacy coalition framework (ACF) developed by Sabatier (see Sabatier and Weible 2007), coalitions in a given policy system are based on shared beliefs. However, we will argue that the ACF offers a valuable but insufficient explanation of the process of coalition formation in the short run. This is due to the fact that this theoretical approach largely disregards both the self-interests of political actors and the incentives provided by the institutional setting. When accounting for these two aspects, divergences in terms of beliefs cannot automatically considered an insurmountable obstacle to coalition formation. In the following, we shall examine under which conditions the coalition structure is characterized by a classical left–right divide as opposed to cross-camp cooperation patterns in the labor-market domain during our period of investigation. As will be developed in the next section, the latter is expected to occur to the extent that incongruent veto players are available in a given arena in the presence of a policy reform project.

Camp and Cross-camp Cooperation

Among the theoretical approaches for understanding the role of coalitions in the domain of policy analysis, the *Advocacy Coalition Framework (ACF)* is, without any doubt, the most important one. The ACF has been developed by Paul Sabatier and Hank Jenkins-Smith

154

(Sabatier 1987, Sabatier 1988, Sabatier and Jenkins-Smith 1988, Jenkins-Smith 1990).

In these contributions, the authors have argued that policy change occurs in policy-domain specific *subsystems*. These subsystems can be conceived of as networks of a variety of actors who are concerned with influencing public policy in a particular domain. The ACF thus tends to take an all-embracing view of the policymaking community. Policy subsystems are composed of a limited number of advocacy coalitions. The 'glue' that holds the members of these coalitions together is their common *belief systems*. Sabatier and Jenkins-Smith (1993) conceptualize a three-tiered hierarchical structure of beliefs. At the broadest level are deep core beliefs. As they involve fundamental values, they are not policy-specific in nature. At the next level are policy core beliefs which are applications of deep core beliefs that span the entire policy subsystem. The final level consists of secondary beliefs. They are relatively narrow in scope and address specific aspects of the policy in question. The ACF considers possible that coalition members will disagree on secondary beliefs, but postulates that such disagreement will be limited. Since the approach argues that coalitions are homogenous in terms of belief systems, advocacy coalitions are expected to be very stable both in terms of longevity and membership composition.

Advocacy coalitions seek to translate their shared beliefs into public policies. Thus, these coalitions play a crucial role when it comes to policy-making. The policy subsystem usually is expected to be characterized by one *dominant coalition*. Since this coalition controls the executive, it is able to exert a strong influence on public policies. The remaining coalitions are less powerful and nevertheless try to modify the policy direction. Given that the ACF postulates a high degree of stability within a given policy subsystem, it is consistent that significant policy change is believed to primarily occur as a result of external shocks, including changes in the government composition, policy changes in other subsystems, or public opinion reversals (Sabatier and Jenkins-Smith 1999). More minor policy changes can stem from policy learning which takes place in subsystems, especially as far as technical domains are concerned.

The ACF has been criticized on various grounds (Szarka 2010, Nowlin 2011). With respect to the examination at hand, there are two theoretical objections particularly worth considering. First, the approach does not consider political actors' short-term interests (Schlager 1995). The neglect of the latter aspect is largely due to the fact that the ACF takes a long-term perspective. Given that Sabatier (1988) is interested in time frames of at least a decade, it is all too understandable that he regards the political actors' interests as being part of the belief structure. Thus, he does not need to draw the distinction between these two analytical elements. In the short run, however, interests and beliefs cannot be expected to converge. More specifically, political actors may engage in 'ad hoc coalitions' (Mahoney 2007) that are not necessarily based on shared beliefs. Such atypical coalitions characterized by heterogeneous beliefs of their participants are formed in the short run in order to achieve policy change. Such attempts may often prove not to be successful or only to lead to policy adjustments. However, the ACF overlooks the possibility that such alliances can sometimes bring about major policy change. Temporary strategic coalitions motivated by short-term interests have been shown to have lasting impacts on policy trajectories. Indeed, *cross-class coalitions* between segments of organized business and labor played a crucial role in shaping the European welfare state (Swenson 1991, Iversen 1999, Häusermann 2010). In the scholarly literature, this phenomenon constitutes probably the most intriguing example of coalitions that are not based on common core beliefs.

According to a second recurrent criticism, the ACF assumes that actors build coalitions independently of the political institutions in which they are embedded (Kübler 2001, Jegen 2003). In the Western European context for instance, Kriesi et al. (2006) show that the national network structures – despite a common European framework – considerably differ within a given policy domain. Thus, the incentives provided by the domestic institutional setting may exert a decisive influence on the actors' coalition behavior and consequently on policy outcomes. Given that the realm of the labor market can still largely be considered a national affair characterized by a great deal of variety, the integration of institutions may play a major role for the present analysis. The ACF has been implicitly developed against the background of a pluralist system. In order to apply the framework to corporatist (as well as authoritarian) regimes, Sabatier and Weible (2007) have introduced the notion of the 'coalition opportunity structure' in a recent revision of the approach. Besides the degree of openness of political systems (which basically corresponds the number of venues to enter decision-making bodies), the authors mention the degree of consensus needed for policy change. This aspect is expected to structure the actors' coalition formation behavior. More specifically, the availability of corporatist arrangements implies a rather high level of cooperation between labor unions and employers' organizations. In a similar vein, consensus democracies (as opposed to majoritarian democracies) should witness, at least to some degree, some cooperation between the left and the right. According to this view, the most powerful parties should belong to the same coalition in consensus democracies. Hence, cross-class and cross-partisan coalitions may be more likely to come about in these contexts. Among the six countries analyzed in our study, these two characteristics (consensus democracy and extensive corporatism) apply to Germany, Denmark, and Switzerland. By contrast, France, Italy, and the United Kingdom are commonly referred to as both majoritarian and non-corporatist contexts. From this perspective, a sharp coalitional divide between camps (i.e. left-wing parties and unions on the one hand and right-wing parties and employers' associations on the other hand) should be observable.

However, the contribution of Thelen (2012) highlights the fact that political actors have recently formed atypical coalitions for the purpose of bringing about policy reforms in all kinds of regimes. In other words, cooperation patterns are not always attributable to the general institutional context. In the following, we shall argue that two circumstantial factors are crucial for explaining the coalition structure. First, the coalition structure is expected to depend on *the presence of a reform project* in the labor-market domain. If this condition is not met, political actors rely on a default strategy, which consists in working with those organizations with which they share the same core beliefs. In such a situation, the coalition structure is based on the fundamental antagonism that is prevalent in a given policy area (Kriesi and Jegen 2001). In the domain of labor-market politics, the traditional interest-based conflict pertains to the opposition between labor and capital in all Western democracies, a cleavage that, indeed, lies at the heart of the division between left and right. In the absence of reform proposals there is no need for cross-camp cooperation. Thus, the labor-market elites are hypothesized to be structured along the left–right divide in such circumstances.

Second, in those cases in which reform projects are available, cross-camp cooperation is expected when actors on a given side are not able to bring about policy change on their own. Recent studies suggest that narrow coalitions based on shared beliefs may not be broad-based enough to encourage substantial policy change (see Ansell et al. 2009). Reform support coalitions may thus be obliged to enlarge their base by joining forces with actors who do not share the same beliefs. Among the potential coalition partners, veto players are of particular importance. Borrowing from the definition of Tsebelis (2002), a veto player is an actor whose agreement is required for a policy change. In cases of two or more veto players who do not belong to the same camp (either left or right), cooperation between these crucial actors should be observable. The rationale behind this hypothesis is that policy reform takes place only if these incongruent veto players are able to find a compromise. By contrast, if veto players are on the same ideological side, no cooperation between left and the right is to be expected. Thus, deviations from the standard cooperation pattern (sharp coalitional divide between left and right) should be observable in the presence of *incongruent veto players*.

To identify those actors who possess veto player status, the prevailing rules of the game as well as the power distribution among the relevant actors need to be considered at the level of the *arenas* in which a given reform takes place. Theoretically, there are at least five loci in which such policy-related changes can occur: the administrative arena; the parliamentary arena; the corporatist arena; the direct-democratic arena; and the judicial arena. The range of participating actors varies from arena to arena. Most obviously, parties are the relevant actors in the parliamentary arena. Social partners (employers' associations and unions) are the key actors in the 'corporatist arena'. The direct-democratic arena tends to be open to all types of actors. The judicial arena typically is reserved to specialized actors such as lawyers. Finally, the administrative arena is always composed of state actors and – depending on the case at hand – of a few or many others actor types. Applied to our analysis, the five main reform projects that were present in the selected countries during our period of investigation basically were located in only two different decision-making arenas. The reform of the German Hartz IV legislation, the British spending review, and the activation reform in Denmark took place in the parliamentary arena. Both the Italian case of the FIAT factory of Pomigliano and the French negotiations on youth unemployment were waged in the 'corporatist arenax'. Therefore, possible incongruent veto players are parties as far as Germany, the United Kingdom, and Denmark are concerned and social partners (employers or labor unions) in the cases of France and Italy. In order to identify these crucial actors, we will present the institutional rules and – with respect to parties – at the distribution of power in Parliament. In Switzerland, there has been no policy reform having taken place during our period of interest. Thus, the coalition structure is expected to be based on the political organizations 'default mode', which refers to a classical left–right divide.

In Germany, the two chambers of Parliament displayed diverging majorities during our period of interest. While the governmental coalition composed of Conservatives (CDU-CSU) and Liberals (FDP) held 331 of 622 seats in the lower house (*Bundestag*), it had lost its majority in the upper house (*Bundesrat*) in May 2010. Since the reform of the Hartz IV legislation required the approval of both chambers of Parliament (the amendment fell into the so-called *Zustimmungsgesetze*), this change in majority provided the Social Democrats and the Greens with a veto player status. To achieve a reform, the right thus depended on the approval of the left. These circumstances required the right (Conservatives, and Liberals) and the left (Social Democrats, and the Greens) to find a compromise solution. Parliamentary bargaining usually takes place in joint committees (*Vermittlungsausschüsse*) in Germany (Lehmbruch 1976). As a consequence, we expect cross-camp cooperation patterns between parties. The four big parties should be regrouped in the same main coalition. By contrast, the employers' associations and labor unions are expected to be part of separate component coalitions.

In the United Kingdom, the government coalition formed in 2010 by the Conservatives and Liberal Democrats enjoyed a comfortable majority in Parliament in order to enforce the spending review plan. Therefore, these parties were not reliant on other actors (notably the Labour Party). Given this distribution of power, there is no incongruent veto player in the case of the United Kingdom. Thus, the British coalition structure is expected to be characterized by camp cooperation. The two governmental parties are expected to closely work together and should be found in the same component coalition in opposition to organizations from the left. In addition, employers' association should join forces with the parties on the left, while labor unions are expected to coalesce with the left.

A similar coalition pattern should be detectable among the political elites of Denmark. With respect to the parliamentary arena, the ruling Liberals and Conservatives formed a minority government. Thus, in order to get through adjustment of the activation policy, these moderate right parties depended on the new populist right (DF), which constitutes a congruent veto player. The three parties on the right are thus expected to be located in the same coalition along with employers. Parties on the left should form the other main coalition along with the labor unions.

In France and Italy, the two countries where reform proposals in the 'corporatist arena' were available, we expect cross-class coalitions between the relevant unions and employers' associations. This hypothesis is derived from the fact that a reform requires an agreement between the representatives of labor and capital, as both sides usually have equal power in the corporatist negotiation arena. Thus, social partners can be conceived of as incongruent veto players. Regarding the FIAT factory of Pomigliano, the transition to more flexible working conditions that were envisaged by the employers had to be agreed on by the three relevant unions. In the case of France, the requirements tend to be less restrictive than in most other countries. A reform usually comes about if – among the eight 'representative' social partners (five unions and three employers' associations) – at least one organization on either side signs a given agreement. This rule also applied to the negotiations on youth unemployment that took place during our period of investigation. Strictly speaking,

Table 7.1 *Expected cooperation patterns, by country and arena*

	Switzerland	Germany	Denmark	France	Italy	UK
Parliamentary arena	CC	C-CC	CC	CC	CC	CC
Corporatist arena	CC	CC	CC	C-CC	C-CC	CC

CC: Camp cooperation
C-CC: Cross-camp cooperation

it is not the single organizations which have veto player power in French corporatism, but the representatives of capital and labor as a whole. Nevertheless, we also expect coalitions between social partners there. With respect to the parties, we expect sharp coalitional divisions between the left and the right in France and Italy.

Table 7.1 summarizes our hypotheses. We expect cross-camp coalition patterns in three instances. This is due to the presence of incongruent veto players in the arena in which a given reform project took place. Germany should witness cross-partisan coalitions between the major organizations of the right (Christian Democrats and Liberals) and the left (Social Democrats and the Greens). In France and Italy, we should detect cross-class coalitions as far as social partners are concerned. At the same time, we expect labor unions and employers' association not to be regrouped in the same coalition in Germany and a sharp divide between left and right parties in France and Italy. In the remaining three countries, we hypothesize camp cooperation both with respect to parties and economic interest groups. These expectations are based on the fact that either reform projects were missing or congruent veto player settings available in the arenas in which these attempts occurred.

Data and Operationalization

To identify the coalition structure in labor-market elites, we rely on the cooperative ties between the organizations involved. In the framework of the second wave of interviews, respondents were presented with a complete list of organizations we had included in the first interview. These persons were asked to mention the organizations on the list with whom they had closely collaborated in the course of the then last few months. After they had gone through the list, we asked them to indicate the three organizations with whom they had collaborated particularly closely, and finally, we asked for the one organization among the three with whom they had most closely collaborated. We recorded this information in a square N x N matrix in which rows and columns consist of the same political organizations. A collaborative relationship is indicated by a '1,' a particularly close relationship by a '2,' and the closest collaborative tie by a '3' (see Bernhard 2012 for a similar approach).

In Italy and the United Kingdom, some important organizations in the labor market refused to participate in our study. As the absence of these actors is very likely to provide us with a biased picture of the coalitional structure, we added the five most powerful missing organizations for each of these two countries. To that end, we used the power indicator outlined in Chapter 5. The supplementary organizations for Italy were the Ministery of Labor (MdL), the *Istituto Nazionale per la Previdenza Sociale* (INPS), the carmaker FIAT, the Communist Party (PRC), and the social movement ALVP; for the United Kingdom were the Department for Work and Pensions (DWP), the Confederation of British Industry (CBI), the British Chambers of Commerce (BCC), the Adam Smith Institute (ASI), and the Institute of Economic Affairs (IEA). We decided to mirror the values of the available ties. For example, if a representative of actor A told us that their organization had a particularly close relationship with missing actor B, we also coded the tie directed from B to A with a '2'. This procedure leaves us with 22 organizations for Italy and 19 for the United Kingdom. It also needs to be mentioned that we removed the two far-right parties – NPD (Germany) and *Front national* (France) – from the analysis. These organizations turn out to be isolated, i.e. they are not connected to other actors at all.

To study the coalition structures based on this type of data, we draw on block-model analysis, which allows for distinguishing between structurally equivalent groups of actors on the basis of an analysis of the cooperative relationships. Structural equivalence is met when two or more actors jointly have similar ties with third actors independently of the ties they have with each other. A block model consists of two elements (Wasserman and Faust 1994: 395): (1) a partition of actors in the network into discrete subsets called positions; and (2) for each pair of positions a statement of the presence or absence of a tie within or between the positions. We will make use of the CONCOR algorithm which applies successive splits to the network. In the first step, the procedure breaks down the campaign-specific set of actors into two structurally equivalent groups. Subsequently, each group is broken down into another two structurally equivalent sub-groups, and so forth. Due to the small number of observations, we will stop the procedure after the third step. For each country, we will present the results pertaining to two, four and eight blocks. Most attention will be given to the two-blocks solutions as they display the main schisms among the labor-market elites. Given the rather rigid logic of CONCOR, this is open to criticism. To validate our results, we will make use of an alternative, more flexible block-modelling method. The classical hierarchical clustering using corrected Euclidean (HC) algorithm does not apply splits to all available blocks, but successively to one single block.

Empirical Analysis

Table 7.2a to *Table 7.2f* present the composition of the various component coalitions for the six countries under scrutiny. The first split produced by CONCOR separates the two basic coalitions – blocks A and B. Subsequently, each of the two blocks is divided into two components. These blocks obtain numerical labels (blocks 1 to 4). At the level of the eight blocks solutions, we add a lower-case letter (a or b) to the block marks. Wherever possible, we will also comment the result of the HC procedure.[1] The overviews presented in the *Table A7.1* to *Table A7.6* characterize the eight blocks in terms of density, power, and number of coalition members.

In the following, we will present the results of the network analysis for each of the six selected countries. We will begin with showing the cases which witnessed a policy reform proposal in the parliamentary arena (Germany, the United Kingdom, and Denmark). Subsequently, we will present the coalition structure for France and Italy where the 'corporatist arena' was affected. Finally, we will deal Switzerland where no major policy reform took place during our period of investigation.

Germany

As far as Germany is concerned, CONCOR tends to separate the powerful organizations from the marginal left and the labor unions (see *Table 7.2a*). Note that all veto players the (Christian Democrats, Free Democrats, Social Democrats, and Greens) belong to the same block. This result is consistent with our hypothesis about the cross-partisan coalition structure. The Social Democrats even find themselves in the inner core (block 1) along with the Christian Democrats and the two main public administrations in the labor-market domain (BA and BMAS). The inner circle is composed of the last three

---

[1] The HC procedure cannot be applied to the Italian and British cases. These networks contain missing data with respect to the ties between two added organizations. Unfortunately, the Pajek program is not able to perform this algorithm with missing data.

Table 7.2a *Blocks produced by CONCOR for Germany*

Block A		Block B	
Block 1	Block 2	Block 3	Block 4
CDU/CSU (1a)	Greens (2a)	Linke (3a)	IGM (4a)
BMAS (1a)	BKS (2a)	KOS (3a)	DGB (4a)
BA (1a)	FDP (2a)		
	BDA (2a)	EFD (3b)	Verdi (4b)
SPD (1b)	BMWi (2a)	Attac (3b)	
	IAB (2a)		
	PW (2b)		
	Caritas (2b)		

mentioned organizations. Those organizations which belong to block 2 are less powerful. Block 2b contains two citizen-interest groups (PW and Caritas), while block 2c includes several actor types: two parties (Free Democrats and Greens); two state actors (BMWi and BKS); one research institute (IAB); and the employers' association BDA. In line with our theoretical expectations, the unions are cut off from the employers' association BDA. They are located in block 4, whereas the far left organizations (Linke, KOS, EFD, and Attac) form a separate component (block 3). The alternative splitting method basically confirms the results of CONCOR, as it arrives exactly at the same composition with respect to the first two main blocks (not shown here).

United Kingdom

With respect to the United Kingdom, the two hypotheses which postulate traditional partisan and class cleavages are also confirmed. Indeed, the CONCOR solution presented in *Table 7.2b* suggests that the British labor-market policy was structured along a left–right divide during our period of interest. Block A contains amongst others the Tories, the Liberal Democrats, the peak employers' associations CBI, BCC, and FSB as well as the Department for Work and Pensions (DWP). Apart from the FSB, all these actors are regrouped in block 1a. This component of very powerful organizations clearly constitutes the inner core of the British labor-market elites. Among the political organizations assigned to block B, we find all four labor unions included in our

Table 7.2b *Blocks produced by CONCOR for United Kingdom*

Block A		Block B	
Block 1	Block 2	Block 3	Block 4
Tories (1a)	UKIP (2a)	Labour (3a)	NPI (4a)
LibDems (1a)	IEA (2a)		Green (4a)
CBI (1a)		STUC (3b)	
DWP (1a)	NYA (2b)	TUC (3b)	Unite (4b)
BCC (1a)			UNISON (4b)
FSB (1b)			
ASI (1b)			
CESI (1b)			
cfc (1b)			

analysis as well as the parties on the left. The Labour Party occupies a structurally distinctive position, as it forms a component on its own (block 3a).

Denmark

Let us now turn to the Danish context. As is the case for the United Kingdom, CONCOR separates the left from the right in *Table 7.2c*. In line with our hypotheses, the coalition structure seems to have corresponded to this classical antagonism based on shared beliefs. Block A is composed of right-wing parties, the employers' association, and the Ministry of Employment. The right parties find themselves in the Block 1, whereas the two governmental parties (Venstre and KF) form a sub-coalition on their own (block 1a). The new populist right party (DF), which tolerated the governmental coalition of the latter two parties, finds its way into block 1b. It is striking to note that the ties between these two blocks are only strong in one direction. The two parties of the government block report to have closely collaborated with the new populist right. In network analyses, such an asymmetrical relationship is a sign of a power-relation (Kriesi 1980). In this case, the DF has the power, and the government depends on it. This unilateral pattern may reflect their attempts to obtain the approval of DF regarding the reform of the activation policy in the parliamentary arena.

It also needs to be mentioned that block 2a includes two powerful actors: the employers' association DA and the Ministry of Employment. Block 2b, for its part, is composed of four research institutes. The second

Table 7.2c *Blocks produced by CONCOR for Denmark*

Block A		Block B	
Block 1	Block 2	Block 3	Block 4
KF(1a)	DA (2a)	SF (3a)	AER (4a)
Venstre (1a)	MoE (2a)	SD (3a)	LO (4a)
DF (1b)	DI (2b)	RGA (3b)	FTF (4b)
	SFI (2b)		AC (4b)
	Cepos (2b)		
	EC (2b)		

main component (block B) is formed by parties from the left and labor unions. The former are regrouped in block 3 and the latter in block 4. The main left parties SD and SF are part of block 3a, while the extraordinary powerful labor union LO finds itself in block 4a along with its own think tank AER.

France

CONCOR first divides the French organizations in terms of power. Those actors who enjoy direct access to the decision-making arenas are regrouped in block A. It includes the relevant labor unions, all employers' associations, the Ministry of Employment, and the governmental party UMP. Thus, the eight representative social partners all are included in the same main component, thereby confirming the cross-class coalition hypothesis. As is shown in *Table 7.2d*, the three big labor unions (CGT, CFDT, and FO) form a separate sub-coalition along with UNSA, a moderate and steadily growing organization (block 2). The other component of powerful actors (block 1) distinguishes between those actors who can be considered to form the inner core (UMP, Ministry of Employment, and employers' organizations) and two rather centrist labor unions (CFE-CGC which represents the interests of management staff and the Christian Democrat CFTC).

Block B is almost exclusively composed of weak actors. The only exception concerns the Socialists. They find themselves in the first component (block 3) along with three other left parties (EELV, LO, and PCF). The Socialists subsequently form a component with the Greens (EELV), since they have closer ties with them than with the two far left parties. This lineup confirms the absence of cross-pattern coalition

Table 7.2d *Blocks produced by CONCOR for France*

Block A		Block B	
Block 1	Block 2	Block 3	Block 4
UMP (1a)	FO (2a)	PS (3a)	FSU (4a)
MdT (1a)	CFDT (2a)	EELV (3a)	Solidaires (4a)
CGPME (1a)			NPA (4a)
Medef (1a)	CGT (2b)	LO (3b)	
UNAPL (1a)	UNSA (2b)	PCF (3b)	AC! (4b)
UPA (1a)			APEIS (4b)
			CNPE (4b)
CFE-CGC (1b)			MNCP (4b)
CFTC (1b)			

patterns in France. The second block of weak actors consists of peripheral actors of the left on one hand (the unions Solidaires and FSU, as well as the far-left party NPA) and the four social movement organizations which act in defense of unemployed people on the other. AC!, APEIS, CNPE, and MNCP are commonly referred to as 'the gang of four'. These findings are confirmed by the HC algorithm (not shown here). The composition of the two main blocks proves to be identical to the solution produced by CONCOR. The first block of powerful actors regroups the six most important labor unions, while the second one corresponds to the inner circle mentioned above.

Italy

In the case of Italy, the first split accomplished by CONCOR produces two blocks of comparable size. As expected, the social partners find themselves in the same main coalition, thus confirming our cross-class coalition hypothesis. With respect to parties, the line-up shown in *Table 7.2e* corresponds to the hypothesized opposition between the left and the right, whereas the former are located in the second main coalition (block B) which is mainly composed of weak actors. It turns out that this block is entirely composed of actors from the left (parties, minor unions, and citizen groups). The main opposition party PD constitutes a block of its own (block 3a). By contrast, the big three peak unions (CGIL, CISL, and UIL) find themselves in the first main block along with the employers of Confindustria and FIAT, state actors (Ministry of Labor, and INPS), and the parties on the right (PdL, Lega) as well as the centrist UdC. There are two powerful sub-coalitions in the Italian labor-market domain. The

Table 7.2e *Blocks produced by CONCOR for Italy*

Block A		Block B	
Block 2	Block 3	Block 2	Block 3
PdL (1a)	FIAT (2a)	PD (3a)	IdV (4a)
Confindustria (1a)	UdC (2a)		PRC (4a)
Lega (1a)		ARCI (3b)	COBAS (4a)
ISFOL (1a)	UIL (2b)	RDC (3b)	PdCI (4a)
ACLI (1a)	CGIL (2b)		SEL (4a)
	CISL (2b)		INCA (4a)
MdL (1b)			
INPS (1b)			ALVP (4b)

Table 7.2f1 *Blocks produced by CONCOR for Switzerland*

Block A		Block B	
Block 2	Block 3	Block 2	Block 3
SVP (1a)	SGB (2a)	SP (3a)	AS (4a)
Swissmem (1a)	BDP (2a)	GPS (3a)	
FDP (1a)	Caritas (2a)		Attac (4b)
CVP (1a)	Syna (2a)	KV (3b)	KABBA (4b)
SBMV (1a)	TS (2a)	Unia (3b)	
SGV (1a)			
	SODK (2b)		
SAV (1b)	AG (2b)		
Seco (1b)	BE (2b)		
	Avenir Suisse (2b)		

first regroups amongst other the governmental parties and Confindustria in block 1a, the second the three big unions in block 2b. The cooperation occurring between these two blocks refer to social partnership, i.e. cooperation between Confindustria and the labor unions.

Switzerland

In the case of Switzerland, CONCOR produces a first split that, to a large degree, corresponds to the expected split between left and right (see *Table 7.2f1*). Block A is composed of all right-wing parties, employers' associations, and cantons. The first sub-coalition of this block includes the major

168   *Laurent Bernhard*

Table 7.2f2 *Blocks produced by hierarchical clustering (corrected Euclidean) for Switzerland*

Block 1	Block 2	Block 3
Swissmem (1a)	Attac (2a)	Seco
AvSuisse (1a)	KABBA (2a)	
FDP (1a)	AS (2a)	
BDP (1a)	GPS (2a)	
SBMV (1a)	SP (2a)	
SVP (1a)		
CVP (1a)	KV (2b)	
	Unia (2b)	
AG (1b)	TS (2b)	
BE (1b)	SGB (2b)	
SODK (1b)		
Syna (1b)		
Caritas (1b)		
SAV (1c)		
SGV (1c)		

parties from the right, all employers' associations studied here, as well as the State Secretariat for Economic Affairs (Seco). Block 1 can thus be considered the dominant coalition of Swiss labor-market politics. The inner core of this block consists of block 1b, as it is formed by the two most powerful actors: Seco and the Swiss Employers' Association (SAV). Rather surprisingly, three unions (SGB, Syna, and TravailSuisse) and a charity (Caritas) also belong to Block A, however. This result is not in line with my hypothesis. A closer look reveals that these actors form a separate sub-coalition (block 2a) along with the BDP, a newly formed moderate-right party that separated itself from the Swiss People's Party (SVP). The other sub-component (block 2b) includes three cantonal actors (SODK, AG, and BE) as well as Avenir Suisse, a neoliberal think tank. The second main coalition (block B) only consists of seven organizations, all of which belong to the left. Block 3 is composed of the core left (Social Democrats, Greens for block 3a, as well as Unia, and KV for block 3b, both of which defend the interests of employees). More peripheral actors are located in block4: the radical citizen organizations Attac and KABBA are regrouped in block 4b, while the moderate association of Swiss clerks (AS) finds itself in block 4a.

The more flexible hierarchical clustering algorithm provides some crucial additional information (see *Table 7.2f2*). The first split separates

Seco from the remaining 23 organizations. This prominent position is probably due to the fact that most organizations report having closely collaborated with this state actor, which was in charge of organizing the ordinance of the unemployment insurance, the final step in order to implement the reform of the unemployment insurance that had been accepted in the popular vote in September 2010. As expected, the two divides give rise to a left and a block from the right (Block1 and Block 2). This result clearly lends support to my hypothesis, which postulates a sharp contrast between these two camps. On the side of the right, three components emerge: the core right (1c), the satellite right (1a), and the cantons (1b). The left coalition comprises the labor unions (2b) as well as the remaining actors from the left (2a).

Conclusion

This chapter has examined the coalition structure of the labor-market elites during our period of investigation. Against the background of the advocacy coalition framework (ACF), we have argued that both institutional and circumstantial factors need to be accounted for in order to understand the logic guiding the political organizations' coalition behavior in the short run. Coalitions are not necessarily based on shared core beliefs. They sometimes arise as a result of strategic choices made by political actors. In the theoretical section, we have outlined two conditions under which collective actors engage in cross-camp cooperation, which are characterized by extensive cooperation between left and right parties or employers' associations and labor unions. We have hypothesized that the presence of both a reform project and incongruent veto players in a given arena lead to these atypical configurations. The empirical analysis lends support to our theoretical refinement of the ACF. In line with our hypotheses, Germany displayed cross-partisan cooperation patterns and France as well as Italy cross-class coalitions. By contrast, we have found classical camp cooperation patterns in all other instances. To be sure, these contextual differences point to the importance of specific situational configurations.

Our empirical analysis invites the conclusion that the political actors' interests as well as the institutional contexts at the level of a given arena play a crucial role. While core beliefs certainly are decisive when taking a long-term perspective, we have established that political actors do occasionally cooperate across the class divide in the short run. This finding confirms the usefulness of the distinction between objective and subjective coalitions (Ossipow 1994). Political organizations that do not share the same policy preferences from an objective point of view (see Chapter 6) nevertheless occasionally decide to join forces. In other words, political organizations have been shown to exhibit a certain degree of strategic flexibility. This stimulating insight can be illustrated by our finding that cooperation between social partners can be more intensive in France and Italy than in countries that are generally recognized as being fully corporatist (Germany, Denmark, and Switzerland). In a similar vein, the labor-market elites of Switzerland – a paradigmatic case of a bargaining democracy – was basically structured along the left–right divide during our period of investigation. These intriguing examples show that coalition behavior of political actors is time-dependent. From a researcher's perspective, this fact reminds us of a major limitation of the present analysis. Its cross-sectional nature provides us with only a snapshot of the lineup of the labor-market elites at a given point in time. Longitudinal data would allow studying evolving and changing coalition structure. Amongst other things, scholars could compare phases of policy equilibrium with instances sudden of major policy change in a given policy area (Baumgartner and Jones 1998).

Table A7.1 *Block characteristics for Germany*

Block	1	2	3	4	5	6	7	8	Power	N
1a Inner core	*1.50*	0.00	0.39	0.33	0.00	0.00	0.33	0.00	1.83	3
1b Social Democrats	0.00	-	0.33	0.00	0.00	0.00	0.00	0.00	0.27	1
2a Satellite of inner core	**2.00**	**0.67**	*0.43*	0.17	0.08	0.00	0.17	0.00	1.41	6
2b Charities	**1.17**	**1.50**	0.50	**3.00**	0.25	0.00	0.00	0.00	0.40	2
3a Far-left groups	0.00	0.00	0.00	**1.00**	*0.50*	**1.00**	**2.25**	**1.50**	0.33	2
3b SMOs	0.00	0.00	0.00	0.00	**2.25**	*1.50*	0.50	**1.50**	0.16	2
4a Main labor unions	**2.00**	**1.50**	0.25	0.00	**1.00**	0.25	*1.50*	**1.00**	0.49	2
4b *Verdi*	**0.67**	**1.00**	0.17	**1.00**	**1.50**	0.50	**2.00**	-	0.16	1

Densities within a given block are italicized; densities between blocks higher than 0.5 are written in bold.

Table A7.2 *Block characteristics for the United Kingdom*

Block	1	2	3	4	5	6	7	8	Power	N
1a Government	*1.93*	**0.71**	0.00	0.00	**0.60**	0.50	0.00	0.20	2.13	5
1b Employers	**1.24**	*0.00*	0.29	0.33	0.50	0.00	0.00	0.00	0.53	4
2a UKIP and IEA	0.00	**0.71**	*2.00*	0.00	0.00	0.00	0.00	0.00	0.10	2
2b *National Youth Agency*	0.00	0.33	0.00	-	0.00	0.00	0.00	0.00	0.07	1

Table A7.2 *(cont.)*

Block	1	2	3	4	5	6	7	8	Power	N
3a *Labour Party*	**0.60**	0.00	0.00	0.00	-	0.00	0.00	0.00	0.36	1
3b Peak labor unions	0.50	0.25	0.00	0.00	0.00	*1.00*	0.00	**2.00**	0.73	2
4a NPI and Greens	0.00	0.13	0.00	0.00	0.00	**1.50**	*0.00*	**1.75**	0.02	2
4b Single labor unions	0.20	0.13	0.00	0.00	**2.00**	**2.50**	0.00	*1.00*	0.53	2

Densities within a given block are italicized; densities between blocks higher than 0.5 are written in bold.

Table A7.3 *Block characteristics for Denmark*

Block	1	2	3	4	5	6	7	8	Power	N
1a Government Block	*2.50*	**2.00**	**1.00**	0.25	0.00	0.00	0.00	0.00	0.58	2
1b New populist right	0.00	-	0.75	0.00	0.00	0.00	0.00	0.00	0.21	1
2a Inner core	0.50	0.50	*2.00*	**1.13**	0.50	0.00	**1.50**	**1.00**	1.17	2
2b Research institutes	0.25	0.25	**2.13**	*0.25*	0.25	0.25	0.50	0.50	0.69	4
3a Main left parties	0.00	0.00	0.50	0.00	*2.50*	0.00	**2.00**	**1.00**	0.60	2
3b *Red–green alliance*	0.00	0.00	0.00	0.00	**1.00**	-	0.50	0.00	0.15	1
4a *LO+*	0.00	0.00	**1.50**	0.00	**1.00**	0.00	*2.00*	0.25	0.85	2
4b Other labor unions	0.50	**1.00**	**1.00**	0.00	**1.25**	0.00	**1.25**	*2.00*	0.33	2

Densities within a given block are italicized; densities between blocks higher than 0.5 are written in bold.

Table A7.4 *Block characteristics for France*

Block	1	2	3	4	5	6	7	8	Power	N
1a Gov. and employers	*1.60*	**1.00**	**1.00**	**0.58**	0.42	0.08	0.11	0.00	2.09	6
1b Moderate labor unions	**0.83**	*2.00*	**2.25**	**1.00**	0.50	0.00	0.00	0.00	0.28	2
2a Main labor unions 1	**1.17**	**1.00**	*2.00*	**1.50**	0.50	0.25	0.00	0.25	0.48	2
2b Main labor unions 2	**1.33**	**1.25**	**1.75**	*1.00*	0.75	0.25	**0.67**	0.25	0.40	2
3a Moderate left parties	0.00	0.25	**2.00**	**1.50**	*2.00*	0.50	**0.67**	**1.00**	0.23	2
3b Far-left parties	0.08	0.25	0.75	**1.75**	0.50	*1.00*	**1.50**	**1.25**	0.04	2
4a Far-left groups	0.00	0.00	0.17	**0.67**	0.00	0.33	*0.83*	**1.75**	0.14	3
4b SMOs	0.04	0.00	0.25	0.38	0.50	0.50	**0.75**	*2.17*	0.07	4

Densities within a given block are italicized; densities between blocks higher than 0.5 are written in bold.

Table A7.5 *Block characteristics for Italy*

Block	1	2	3	4	5	6	7	8	Power	N
1a Government parties+	*0.40*	**1.70**	0.10	0.93	0.20	0.00	0.00	0.00	0.87	5
1b Public administration	**1.70**	-	0.25	0.17	0.00	0.00	0.00	-	0.50	2
2a FIAT and UDC	0.40	0.25	*0.00*	0.67	1.00	0.00	0.08	0.00	0.09	2
2b Big labor unions	0.40	0.33	0.00	*0.67*	1.00	0.00	0.08	0.00	0.91	3
3a *Partito Democratico*	**0.60**	0.00	0.00	**3.00**	-	0.00	0.17	0.00	0.22	1
3b SMOs	0.20	0.00	0.00	**1.00**	0.00	*1.00*	0.00	0.00	0.11	2
4a Far-left organizations	0.03	0.00	0.00	0.39	1.33	0.00	*1.00*	0.20	0.48	6
4b *ALVIP*	0.00	-	0.00	0.00	0.00	0.00	0.20	-	0.06	1

Densities within a given block are italicized; densities between blocks higher than 0.5 are written in bold.

Table A7.6 *Block characteristics for Switzerland*

Block	1	2	3	4	5	6	7	8	Power	N
1a Right	*0.47*	**2.08**	0.17	0.00	0.08	0.08	0.00	0.00	1.25	6
1b Inner core	**0.83**	*1.50*	0.10	0.00	**1.25**	0.00	0.00	0.00	1.00	2
2a Labor unions 1	0.23	**2.00**	*0.60*	0.15	0.50	0.30	0.20	0.30	1.00	5
2b Cantons	0.08	**1.75**	0.35	*0.67*	0.00	0.25	0.00	0.00	0.26	4
3a Left parties	0.00	0.00	0.50	0.00	*0.00*	0.50	0.00	0.00	0.22	2
3b Labor unions 2	0.00	**1.25**	**0.80**	0.00	0.00	*0.00*	0.00	0.00	0.43	2
4a *Angestellte Schweiz*	0.00	**1.00**	**1.20**	0.50	0.00	**1.50**	-	0.00	0.11	1
4b SMOs	0.00	0.00	0.50	0.00	0.00	**2.25**	0.50	*1.00*	0.01	2

Densities within a given block are italicized; densities between blocks higher than 0.5 are written in bold.

8   Action Repertoires for Shaping the Debates

Laurent Bernhard

Introduction

Tilly (1978) introduced and popularized the concept of action repertoires to identify the forms of protest used by Social Movement Organizations (SMOs) in modern capitalist societies. Tilly made three specific claims. First, he maintained that political actors do not pick from an elaborated catalogue of theoretically available activities, but rather from a more limited number of options. In Tilly's (2008:14) words: 'claim making usually resembles jazz and *commedia dell'arte* rather than ritual reading of scripture. Like a jazz trio or an improvising theater group, people who participate in contentious politics normally have several pieces they can play but not an infinity . . . ' Second, by comparing the protest repertoires across time and space, Tilly observed that such performances markedly differ from context to context. In his view, collective actors draw on repertoires they have developed in order to suit a historically specific setting. Third, when looking at how repertoires evolve and transform, Tilly noticed that radical innovations are rare. Changes tend to be incremental in nature and take place within the limits set by the established repertoire. To put it simply, history may constrain the choices of actors (Tarrow 2008).

Against the background of Tilly's claims, this chapter proposes to study the action repertoires of all kind of collective actors in the context of present-day politics. We will focus on the question whether there are country-specific differences in this regard. To that end, we will examine three kinds of activities the relevant organizations involved in the labour-market domain employed for shaping the various debates on unemployment. The first type of actions refers to the very general distinction between two basic modes of action: insider tactics and outsider tactics. As Jasper (2006: 10) points out, political organizations face the choice of whether to play to inside or outside audiences. In the remaining part of this chapter, we will consider the conditions under which political actors resort to two specific outside-oriented actions. We will study the use of protest politics as well as the opportunities provided by the Internet. Whereas the former refers to classical and familiar forms of actions, the latter constitute a major innovation with respect to the political organizations' toolkits. More specifically, we will analyze to what degree the various actors adopt Web 2.0 applications.

Outside and Inside Activities

Drawing on the literature on interest- group involvement, this chapter distinguishes between inside-oriented and outside-oriented activities (Kollman 1998, Kriesi et al. 2007). The former are designed to directly influence decision-making in the parliamentary and administrative arenas. The latter refer to strategies intended to influence such decisions indirectly by appealing to the public – either by means of media-related activities or as a result of direct mobilization efforts.

Regarding the activities used by collective actors during our period of investigation, we would like to draw a very simple distinction between countries that witnessed public debates of high or rather high intensity and the one in which public debates was of low intensity. Based on the characterization of the various debates (see Chapter 4), we thus hypothesize that political actors relied much more on outside-oriented strategies in Germany, France, Italy, the United Kingdom, and Denmark than in Switzerland. Since the debates which took place in these five countries were linked to political decisions, political actors might also have decided to more heavily make use of inside strategies. Thus, we expect Swiss actors to have been less active regarding both kinds of activities than their counterparts of the remaining countries.

Beyond contextual factors, the strategic orientation might depend on actor-related characteristics. First, the action repertoire is expected to be a function of issue ownership (Budge and Farlie 1983: 271). Political organizations 'own' an issue in the sense that voters consider them as most competent at handling a given problem. The theory of issue ownership states that the advantage arises from reputations the actors have developed for effective policy making on certain issues. Political actors have what Petrocik (1996) describes as a history of attention, initiative, and innovation toward these problems, which leads voters to believe that some specific actors are more sincere and committed to doing something about them. As far as the issue of unemployment is concerned, it is the left which enjoys this kind of reputational advantage. Thus, left-wing actors are hypothesized to go public in this domain. Right-wing actors, by contrast, may prefer resorting to inside-oriented strategies.

Second, the strategic orientation might depend on the actors' level of power. The default strategy of powerful actors is likely to pertain to the political inside sphere. As Schattschneider (1975 (1960)) pointed out, the expansion of the scope of conflict is the 'weapon of the weak'. These actors need to appeal to the public as a consequence of their lack of access or support in the administrative and parliamentary arenas. Therefore, political actors should employ more inside (outside) activities the more (less) powerful they are.

Finally, the characteristics of a given actor should be taken into account. In this analysis, we distinguish between five types of actors: political parties; government; economic interest groups; citizens' interest groups, think tanks and research institutes. Among these actors, political parties are expected to play a very active role with respect to public-oriented strategies. Parties constitute the main organizational channels linking the individual citizens to their representatives in the policy-making process. They are continuously seeking public attention for electoral reasons. Public-oriented strategies are thus crucial for them. The same may hold true for citizens' interest groups, which typically lack direct access to the decision-making arenas. By contrast, economic interest groups and governmental actors may excel in terms of inside-oriented strategies, given that they usually have a privileged access to the decision-making arena.

This analysis draws on the interviews our research team conducted with representatives of the most important political organizations involved in the labour-market domain. As far as the action repertoire is concerned, our respondents were presented a list of the following 41 activities: Outside-oriented activities

1. Media conference
2. Media statement
3. Mobilization of prominent political figures
4. Mobilization of prominent figures in sport, culture, science
5. Interviews
6. TV appearances
7. Letters to the editor
8. Advertisement
9. Billboards
10. TV ads
11. Homepage
12. Blogs
13. Newsletters
14. Social networks
15. Twitter

16. Telephone marketing
17. Own publication
18. Direct mailing
19. Public gatherings
20. Flyers
21. Stands
22. Door-to-door canvassing
23. Protest and demonstrations
24. Support committees
25. Sponsorships

Inside-oriented activities
 1. Provide decision-makers with information
 2. Contacting MPs directly
 3. Contacting cabinet members directly
 4. Contacting the administration directly
 5. Contacting (other) political parties directly
 6. Contacting (other) associations directly
 7. Carry out internal consultations
 8. Participation in consultations (initiated by government)
 9. Participation in commissions (initiated by government)
10. Participation in parliamentary commissions
11. Negotiations with MPs
12. Negotiations with members of the cabinet
13. Negotiations with the administration
14. Negotiations with (other) parties
15. Negotiations with (other) associations
16. Taking legal action

In the framework of the second wave of interviews, respondents were asked to mention those activities their organization had been using over the then past few months. This question was designed to capture the debate-specific action repertoire. Based on these answers, we construct two summary indicators: one for the 25 outside activities and the other for the 16 inside activities. These measures represent the extent to which the political organizations used the full range of outside and inside activities.

This analysis includes four types of independent variables. To assess the role played by the contexts, we introduce country dummies. Switzerland will serve as reference category. In addition, the actors' ideological orientations are measured on a self-reported left–right scale which reaches from 0 (completely right) to 10 (completely left). We create a dummy variable, which takes the value of '1' for those organizations which display values

Table 8.1 *Descriptive analysis of the action repertoire indicators, by country*

	Outside	Inside
France	11.1 (1)	9.4 (1)
United Kingdom	10.3 (2)	6.4 (4)
Germany	9.1 (3)	8.6 (2)
Italy	9.0 (4)	7.2 (3)
Denmark	7.5 (5)	5.9 (5)
Switzerland	4.7 (6)	4.5 (6)
All	8.5	7.1
Number of activities	25	16

higher than '6'. Power, for its part, is operationalized by a reputational indicator introduced in Chapter 5. Finally, we distinguish between five actor types: political parties; economic interest groups; citizens' interest groups; state actors; think tanks and research institutes. Again, we use dummy variables, whereas the economic interest groups constitute the reference category. To put the results in perspective, we also include the general action repertoire in the multivariate analysis. In the first wave of interviews, respondents were asked to mention, among the same 41 activities, those their organization generally employs when it comes to the issue of unemployment. The construction of this indicator corresponds to our measure for the debate-specific action repertoire.

Table 8.1 shows, for each country analyzed here, the number of activities the political organizations involved in the labour-market domain utilized during our period of scrutiny. The rank orders are represented in brackets. These figures tend to lend support to the hypothesis according to which Swiss actors were less active than those of the remaining countries. Indeed, Switzerland displays lower values than Denmark, Italy, France, United Kingdom, and Germany with respect to each of the two debate-specific indicators. Swiss actors only used 4.7 outside tactics and 4.5 inside tactics on average. The corresponding figures are highest for France, where the corresponding figures are of 11.1 and 9.4, respectively. These suggest that outside and inside activities are not mutually exclusive. A closer look at the strategic orientation (not shown here) that all actors indeed do combine inside with outside tools.

Let us now turn to the multivariate analysis. In addition to the two debate-specific modes of action (i.e., outside and inside strategies), *Table 8.2* presents the corresponding general repertoires. The first model presented shows that German, French, British, and Italian organizations relied significantly more on outside activities than their Swiss peers (which serve as reference category here) during our period of investigation. These results are in line with our hypothesis. Yet, the coefficient for Denmark turns out to be insignificant, which is contrary to our theoretical expectations. It is fair to say, however, that it is close attaining the 5 per cent error level. It is interesting to note that the second model of *Table 8.2* suggests that there are no contextual differences when it comes to the general outside activities. In other

Table 8.2 *Ordered probit regressions models explaining outside and inside action repertoires*

	Outside debate	Outside general	Inside debate	Inside general
Germany	0.984**	0.023	1.252***	0.083
	(0.336)	(0.325)	(0.358)	(0.336)
Denmark	0.697	−0.120	0.927*	−0.745
	(0.395)	(0.397)	(0.418)	(0.395)
France	1.440***	−0.223	1.499***	−0.673*
	(0.327)	(0.308)	(0.339)	(0.315)
United Kingdom	1.241**	−0.247	0.897*	−0.359
	(0.387)	(0.375)	(0.402)	(0.378)
Italy	1.151***	0.601	1.211***	0.369
	(0.347)	(0.337)	(0.364)	(0.341)
Left	0.716***	1.033***	−0.416	−0.265
	(0.216)	(0.224)	(0.217)	(0.213)
Power	−0.256	0.619	1.678*	1.633*
	(0.737)	(0.739)	(0.773)	(0.765)
Parties	0.240	0.824**	−0.468	−0.093
	(0.258)	(0.264)	(0.270)	(0.266)
Citizens' groups	−0.322	0.142	−0.439	−0.268
	(0.337)	(0.337)	(0.351)	(0.347)
State actors	0.116	−1.410**	0.724	−0.754
	(0.418)	(0.436)	(0.435)	(0.432)
Think tanks and research institutes	−0.484	−0.496	−1.252*	−1.472**
	(0.460)	(0.445)	(0.508)	(0.462)
Observations	105	107	105	107
Pseudo R^2/ Adj. R^2	0.068	0.112	0.079	0.068

Reference groups: Switzerland (country), economic interest groups (actor type).
* $p < 0.05$, **$p < 0.01$, ***$p < 0.001$; standard errors in parentheses.

words, Swiss actors have been less active with respect to outside activities only as far as our period of interest is concerned. Regarding inside-oriented strategies, the observed pattern perfectly fits our contextual hypothesis. According to the third model, Swiss organizations are consistently found to have relied less on inside strategies than the remaining actors. Again, this deviation is found to be contingent on the selected time frame. The fourth model even reports that collective actors in France tend to generally resort less to inside-oriented strategies than in the other five countries. This result certifies that the French decision-making arenas are particularly difficult to access.

There are also some revealing findings on the actors' level. With respect to the debate-specific outside strategies, *Table 8.2* displays only one significant association. Organizations on the left are found to more heavily rely on outside activities. This is in line with the first hypothesis we have formulated at the actors' level. By contrast, less powerful organizations as well as parties and citizens' groups did not resort more to outside tactics, thus contradicting our second and third actor-related hypotheses. The results for the general outside repertoire (second model of *Table 8.2*) suggest that political parties tend to be more active toward the outside world during 'ordinary' politics, while the opposite seems to hold true for state actors. As far as the inside strategies are concerned, *Table 8.2* reports a significantly positive effect of the organizations' degree of power. This finding lends support to the view that powerful actors have made use of their privileged access to the decision-making arenas. In addition, think tanks and research institutes are less prone to resort to inside strategies than the other actor types. As is shown in the fourth model, these patterns are not limited to the debates but general in nature.

Protest Politics

Both scholars of social movements and interest groups draw the distinction between information politics and protest politics (Keck and Sikkink 1998, Beyers 2004, Jasper 2006, Opedal et al. 2012). The former refers to the collection of credible information and their introduction into the public sphere. The latter deals with the organization of collective action in general, and with the staging of protest events in particular. In the following, we shall focus on the political actors' use of protest activities. On the contextual level, the extent to which political actors resort to protest activities is expected to depend on the dominant strategies that have been traditionally adopted by the authorities in dealing with challengers (Scharpf 1984). In line with the idea developed by Kriesi et al.

(1995), challengers are expected to radicalize their action repertoire in contexts in which their demands have usually been met with exclusive reaction patterns. The concept of dominant elite strategies seems to be particularly well suited for the analysis at hand, as the conflict between government and challengers has been historically waged in the labour-market domain. In his encompassing examination of the political mobilization of left in Western Europe, Bartolini (2000) shows that the state authorities of some countries reacted to the emerging labour movement by strongly restricting the fundamental freedoms during the late nineteenth and the early twentieth century. Among the countries studied here, such repressive strategies have been employed in Germany, France, and Italy. By contrast, the Swiss, Danish, and British legacies are characterized by a far higher degree of inclusion. With respect to the general action repertoire, it follows that political actors are expected to more heavily rely on protest activities in Germany, France, and Italy than in Switzerland, Denmark, and the United Kingdom. Regarding the time frame considered in this study, it might have been the case that the radical spending cut plans of the British government triggered some protest activities, however. Thus, we expect the United Kingdom to display higher levels of contention than in Denmark and Switzerland during our period of scrutiny.

On the actor-related level, we hypothesize protest activities to be primarily used by the left. Protest politics domain has historically been employed by the left in the labour market. By contrast, taking to the streets tends to be frowned upon by the right. Only in instances of astonishing weakness is it inclined to resort to protest politics (Kriesi et al. 1995). Given that the right was in power in all selected countries during the time frame considered here, the right is expected to prefer the conventional action repertoire. Hence, a marked difference between the left and the right should be detected with respect to protest politics. In addition, the use of protest activities might be negatively related to the level of power. Finally, citizens' interest groups should be more likely to resort to this strategy. The rationale behind these hypotheses relates to the fact that weak actors and citizens' interest groups typically lack direct access to the decision-making arenas. Consequently, they may feel obliged to call attention to the public by radicalizing their action repertoire.

Roughly one in three organizations reports having made use of the activity 'protest and demonstrations' during our period of interests. As expected, there is considerable variation on the country level. In France, no less than 68 per cent of the interviewed actors engaged in protest politics. Of course, much of this widespread contention was linked to the opposition against the governmental pension reform we have outlined in Chapter 4. However, representatives of labour unions also mentioned that protest activities were organized at a local level in order to avert mass dismissals that had been announced by private firms at that time (such as the low-cost airline Ryanair, and Molex, an American electronic-parts maker). In addition, the social movement organizations which act in defence of unemployed people (AC!, APEIS, CNPE, and MNCP) held their annual demonstration in Paris. Partly due to a low participation level, this event did not attract the news media's attention, however. These examples confirm that protest politics in general and demonstrations in particular generally plays an important role in France (Fillieule and Tartakowsky 2008).

Italy displays the second highest score. 44 per cent of the included actors did resort to forms of protest. These instances were performed by the left and mainly referred to the two major debates that revolved around the question of unemployment in autumn and winter 2010/11, i.e., the reform on education and the case of *Pomigliano* (see Chapter 4). In Germany, there are 33 organizations that relied on protest activities. To some extent, these actions were directed against the Hartz IV legislation – the debate we selected for the analysis at hand. Two demonstrations organized by marginal groups representing unemployed people took place in Oldenburg (October 2010) and in Berlin (January 2011). In the United Kingdom, some protests occurred against the Spending Review plans. Even though opponents were long hesitant to resort to this kind of actions, 29 per cent of the organizations included in our sample reported to have done so. Labour unions in particular turn out to have been active in the realm of protest politics. By contrast, we find almost no contentious action in Denmark and Switzerland. Indeed, only one organization in each country utilized this type of action in our period of interest. We also need to mention that the use of protest and demonstration also strongly varies between actor types. Not surprisingly, governments – as well as think tanks and research institutes – never engage in such activities.

The probit regression estimations presented in *Table 8.3* reveal that Germany, France, the United Kingdom, and Italy excel in terms of debate-specific protest politics. The first model exhibits significant positive effects for these countries compared with Switzerland (which serves as reference category). This finding lends support to our contextual hypothesis. Regarding to the general action repertoire, we find that protest politics is usually more likely to occur in the three countries characterized by a repressive tradition against political outsiders (i.e., France, Germany, and Italy). Turning to the actors' level, the results first of all unambiguously show that protest politics are a matter of the left. This holds true for the organizations' debate-specific as well as for their general

Table 8.3 *Probit regression models explaining protest activities*

	Protest debate	Protest general
Germany	2.128**	6.637***
	(0.714)	(0.801)
Denmark	0.933	−1.026
	(0.890)	(0.916)
France	2.678***	5.868***
	(0.697)	(0.770)
United Kingdom	1.490*	0.084
	(0.738)	(0.914)
Italy	2.118**	6.302***
	(0.688)	(0.797)
Left	1.832***	7.845***
	(0.424)	(0.808)
Power	−3.560*	−1.702
	(1.665)	(1.709)
Parties	0.623	0.744
	(0.680)	(0.577)
Citizens' groups	0.093	0.087
	(0.754)	(0.72)
Economic interest Groups	1.266	1.244
	(0.741)	(0.767)
Constant	−3.366**	−5.913***
	(0.907)	(0.804)
Observations	105	105
Adjusted R^2	0.492	0.642

Reference groups: Switzerland (country), state actors and think tanks and research institutes (actor type).
* $p < 0.05$, ** $p < 0.01$, *** $p < 0.001$; standard errors in parentheses.

behaviour. These findings are thus in line with our first actor hypothesis. In addition, protest activities tend to have been used by weak actors during our period of investigation. However, this proves not to be the case in general, thus yielding only partial support for the power hypothesis. Finally, it is noteworthy that we do not find any differences with respect to actor types when controlling for their ideological positioning, their levels of power as well as for their country belongings. This result runs counter our third actor-related hypothesis.

New Social Media

McAdam et al. (2001) state that tactical repertoires are not only shaped by characteristics of the political authority, but also as by technological developments. For instance, the occurrence of the print media played an important role in shifting the repertoire from the local to the national level during the eighteenth and nineteenth century (Tilly 1995). Today, the Internet and social media pervades our daily lives. The emergence of new information and communication technologies (ICTs) has led political actors to resort to several internet-based applications over the last decade (Gibson and Römmele 2008). As a consequence of the growing importance of the Internet in today's world, these tools have been adopted very rapidly. It is thus not surprising that nowadays online campaigning tools belong to the standard repertoire employed by political actors (Kluver et al. 2007). Until recently, internet based campaign involvement of the latter has been characterized by a lack of interactivity with citizens. The flow of information proved predominantly one-sided, as political elites controlled their messages by providing target groups with static content they often duplicated from other media sources and then simply published on their websites (Vergeer et al. 2011). In other words, political actors have long resorted to so-called Web 1.0 campaigns. By contrast, Web 2.0[1] features allow users to play a much more active role. Thanks to blogs, forums, and social networking sites, the citizen public can easily exchange political ideas and opinions.

In the following, we shall analyze the degree to which political organizations have adopted these new social media. The proliferation of new ICTs should not be conceptualized as a linear process. Taken together, the existing literature suggests that the extent to which political organizations rely on internet tools still considerably varies across countries. However, there has been very little research on cross-national comparisons to date, as most studies have been grounded in a single-context approach (Anstead and Chadwick 2009).

When it comes to the contextual level, the spread of the technology in a given country may moderate the political actors' decision to engage in Web 2.0 mode of campaigning (Norris 2001, Gibson et al. 2008). In the absence of elaborated theoretical models, we will first hypothesize that the use of new social media depends on the technological development in

---

[1] The term Web 2.0 was coined by O'Reilly (2005) in 2003.

a given country at a certain point in time. The idea guiding this hypothesis is that political actors face greater incentives to resort to online tools if the internet has achieved a high level of usage. Even though a convergence pattern is observable, the size of the internet audience still varies across countries. Figures about the internet penetration rate show that Italy lags far behind the remaining five countries studied here. According to the ICT Internet Database provided by the International Telecommunication Union (ITU) the share of internet users was of 53.7% for Italy in 2010, whereas the remaining countries exhibit much higher percentages that are characterized by a rather small range from 80.1 (France) to 88.7 (Denmark).

Political communication basically consists of three main actors: the political actors, the media actors, and the citizen public (Gibson and Römmele 2008). The communication and mobilization strategies of the political elites have long been mediated by the mass media, which determine the attitudes and behaviours of both the elites themselves and the citizen public. From the perspective of the political actors, Web 2.0 applications can be conceived of as opportunities to bypass traditional media in order to get their messages across.

The choice to revert Web2.0 may depend on the macro-structural context. More specifically, the media opportunity structure is expected to play a major role in shaping the way political elites communicate with citizens. The main idea guiding our second contextual hypothesis is that the availability of independent media encourages greater use of Web 2.0. The incentives to circumvent traditional mass media may thus be more pronounced in contexts characterized by a greater differentiation between the political system and the media system. According to the very influential typology of Hallin and Mancini (2004), the independence of media systems can be conceptualized in terms of professionalization and commercialization. Professionalization refers to the autonomy, distinct professional norms, and public service orientation of journalists, while commercialization refers to prevailing market orientation of the media. Therefore, we expect political organizations to more heavily rely on the functionalities of Web2.0 in highly professionalized and commercialized country contexts. Following Hallin and Mancini (2004), these combined peculiarities apply to liberal media systems, which are present in Anglo-Saxon countries. Among the countries studied here, we thus expect British actors to more heavily make use of this kind of innovations than their continental European counterparts.

Our first actor-related hypothesis states that parties are more likely to resort to Web 2.0 platforms than the remaining collective actors. Even though it is probably exaggerated to claim that 'every day is election day' in modern democracies (Morris 1999), political parties are in anticipation to the next elections under constant pressure to communicate with citizens nowadays. Parties can signal the causes they defend to the public by reverting to various communication channels. The innovative Web 2.0 platforms can be considered handy ways to get in touch with their broad constituencies, especially with their supporters and activists. Furthermore, the ideology of collective actors may explain variations in terms of the use of new ICTs (Ward and Gibson 2009). Given their more participatory and grass-roots culture, organizations on the left may be particularly taken by the possibilities provided by the new social media. As the aspect of inter-activity lies at the heart of these new tools, the left is expected to more heavily rely on Web 2.0 than the right, which might prefer the top-down model of the Web 1.0 era.

With respect to the dependent variable, we again constructed a summary indicator. It is obtained by simply adding the three Web 2.0 activities available in the list of activities: blogs, social networks (such as Facebook), and Twitter. Our indicator ranges from 0 to 3 and measures the extent to which the political organizations used the full range Web 2.0 applications. Let us now turn to the descriptive analysis. It appears that blogs, social network services, and Twitter have been much more widely employed in the United Kingdom than in the five remaining countries. The scope measure indicates that British actors use slightly more than two Web 2.0 applications on average. Italian, German, French, and Danish political organizations use about one such tool. By contrast, Swiss actors can be considered digital laggards, as their mean score only attains 0.3.

The multivariate analysis confirms the impression gained from the descriptive analysis. *Table 8.4* shows that British actors excel in terms of Web 2.0 usage, since the coefficients for the five other countries prove insignificant vis-à-vis the United Kingdom, which serves as reference category. This result thus lends support to our second contextual hypothesis according to which the innovations of blogs, social networks, and Twitter are more heavily used in liberal media systems. It needs to be highlighted that Lilleker et al. (2011) also found that Web 2.0 modes of communication are much more developed in the United Kingdom than in Continental Europe. Given that Italy does not fall apart, this analysis suggests that the use of Web 2.0 is not related to the internet penetration rate. Thus, our first contextual hypothesis regarding technological devel-opment has to be rejected. As far as the level of the political organizations is concerned, *Table 8.4* reports no significant association with respect to the debate-specific Web 2.0 repertoire. However, political parties are shown to generally more rely on these innovations than the remaining actor types.

Table 8.4 *Ordered probit regression models explaining Web 2.0 activities*

	Web 2.0 debate	Web 2.0 general
Switzerland	-2.088***	-1.337**
	(0.461)	(0.437)
Germany	-1.064*	-0.736
	(0.442)	(0.440)
Denmark	-1.368**	-1.457**
	(0.481)	(0.480)
France	-1.193**	-0.918*
	(0.431)	(0.428)
Italy	-0.969*	0.195
	(0.449)	(0.470)
Left	0.376	0.333
	(0.241)	(0.239)
Power	-0.435	1.033
	(0.867)	(0.860)
Parties	0.527	1.066***
	(0.296)	(0.298)
Citizens' groups	0.015	0.168
	(0.387)	(0.377)
State actors	-0.097	-1.107
	(0.543)	(0.571)
Think tanks and research institutes	-0.356	-0.358
	(0.537)	(0.506)
Observations	105	107
Pseudo R^2	0.135	0.191

Reference groups: United Kingdom (country), state actors and think tanks and research institutes (actor type).
$* p < 0.05$, $** p < 0.01$, $*** p < 0.001$; standard errors in parentheses.

Conclusion

According to Tilly, the repertoires of political actors are limited, context-specific, and slow to evolve. Tarrow (2008) observed that the claims made by Tilly have been usually taken for granted by scholars and thus only rarely been subject to empirical investigation. This chapter is based on a mapping of the activities employed by labour-market organizations in the debate-specific setting. We have focused on three kinds of categories: inside-oriented and outside-oriented activities, protest politics, and new social media.

Our analysis has established that political organizations make use of a considerable range of both outside-oriented and inside-oriented activities. As most organizations engage in strategic multitasking, their action repertoires prove to be polyvalent. This finding challenges Tilly's observation that collective actors tend to use a small range of performances. By contrast, our results suggest that context still matters a lot. This finding is in line with Tilly's second claim. Indeed, our analysis reveals some significant country-specific differences in all three kinds of actions studied here.

Probably the most striking findings emerged from the domain of protest politics. While Swiss and Danish actors were reluctant to make use of contentious actions, the latter turned out to be very present in France, Italy, Germany, and the United Kingdom. There is no doubt that protest politics belongs to the standard repertoire of the left in these three Continental European countries for historical reasons. However, the fact that we find a lot of protest in the United Kingdom is due to a debate-specific characteristic, i.e., the radical spending cuts announced by the government of David Cameron in autumn 2010. This example shows that political actors are not always the 'slaves of their history', but also able to use strategic options they are less familiar with.

Finally, our snapshot about the adoption of new social media suggests that, while the uptake of innovative Internet functionalities takes place at varying speed, political organizations are quick in adding new Internet functionalities to their action repertoires. In accordance with Tilly, these applications do not replace the other forms of collective action. The latter are thus very likely to persist, as political actors tend to rely on existing forms.

Part III

Communicating in Public

9 Framing Strategies
Important Messages in Public Debates

Regula Hänggli

Introduction

In this chapter, we aim to gain a better understanding of how news content is built by investigating the messages (i.e., arguments) of the debates in our six countries. We want to know which messages are important to the public, and why they become important. Exploring the determinants of message importance is relevant for at least two reasons. First, knowing more about determinants of strong messages in public opinion is relevant in the light of political representation. Studies on representation have long assumed that 'the mass public, standing to the side, forms its opinions on its own and then transmits them to elites through the various modes of democratic action available to them' (Klar et al. 2012, see also Kuklinski and Segura 1995, Disch 2012). However, the formation of mass public opinion is unlikely to work so independently. Political actors' framing strategies may greatly influence the preferences of the masses. Second, exploring the determinants of message importance is relevant for yet another reason: An important part of the framing process is under-investigated, namely '[T]he relative roles of parties and movements in taking leadership roles in framing issues in the media is an important and understudied aspect' (Ferree at al. 2002: 296). Thus, this chapter also sheds some light on the frame-building process (also called elite framing, e.g. by Klar et al. 2012) by investigating which messages are important in the public and why. In this view, a message is (part of) a frame and provides a certain interpretation of an issue (Entman 1993: 52).

The results show that the salience of a message for one's own organization (salience hypothesis), message resonance (resonance hypothesis), and the promoter's power (power hypothesis) can be crucial. The influence of these factors is dependent on the debate type. Based on our sample, we investigate three different types of debates: parliamentary debates; corporatist debates; and debates without a policy-reform goal.

Determinants of Message Importance

Our general approach for conceptualizing the relationship between political actors and the mass media is an actor-oriented political process model, as introduced by Wolfsfeld (1997). In Wolfsfeld's model, the political process is likely to be the driving force in this relationship. The reasons he provides for this hypothesis are numerous, but most importantly, he suggests that the mass media are much more likely to react to political events than to initiate them. This is in line with Sigal's idea (1973) that by releasing news, political actors take the first step toward making news. Following this line of research, we analyze the determinants of message importance by exploring the behaviour of the political actors in this paper.

In greater detail, literature on agenda and frame building suggests taking the *salience of a message for the political organizations* into consideration to explain the salience of a message in the news media. Furthermore, research on social movements has shown that message *resonance* (the extent to which others – opponents, allies, etc. – ascribe salience to a message) is important. In addition, literature investigating news bias shows that *power* is crucial, too. Finally, we explore message characteristics such as extremity, polarization (degree of disagreement regarding a message), politicization (= salience of the message for one's own organization multiplied by its polarization), origin of the message (pro- or contra-argument), and congruence with dominant schema. In the analysis, none of these message characteristics have been shown to be relevant for message importance and are mostly omitted. Congruence with dominant schema was not measured and was not used in the statistical analysis.

Promoted Messages: Salience of Message for the Organizations

We start by looking at the political actors and use the distinction between importance of a message in the public debate (=the debate in the media, dependent variable) and the salience of a message for the actors' organizations (independent variable). Importance means the same as salience. In order to avoid confusion, however, we use the term 'importance' when we speak about the public debate and the term 'salience' when we talk about political actors.

The influence of salience at the issue level has been investigated: Studies of agenda building have confirmed that the salience of issues for the organization is positively related to the importance of issues in news media (Kiousis et al. 2006). At the message level, it has been shown for direct-democratic campaigns that the message's salience for an actor's own organization is very decisive (Hänggli 2012a, 2012b). The theoretical idea behind this factor is that journalists follow the political actors based on the professional norms in journalism. In Western democracies, the neutral-informational professional journalism is dominant (Hallin and Mancini 2004). Based on this neutral-informational journalistic norm, the media should give an accurate account of important events, actors and messages within the institutionalized arenas of the political system and make the political process transparent for the citizen public. The journalists are expected to disseminate information as neutral chroniclers and impartial observers. This norm is in line with the mirror approach, which conceives of the media as a mirror of political reality (e.g. McQuail 1992, Schulz 1976). Thus, we expect that the messages which the political actors consider to be salient are important in news media coverage too. We call this the *salience hypothesis*.

Resonance

We assume that not only does the salience of a message for one's *own* organization matter, but that it is relevant whether *other* organizations perceive it as salient too. In particular, we expect that messages which are also salient for the opponent, i.e., the other side, have a particularly high chance of becoming important messages in the media. Salience for the other side is analyzed by message resonance. Accordingly, this hypothesis is called the *resonance hypothesis*. It is in line with Koopmans' (2004) idea of resonance. For him, resonance is the extent to which other actors such as opponents or allies react to a given message. A message that finds resonance has a higher chance of being further diffused (see also Hänggli and Kriesi 2010). We do not rely on the extent of reactions because we did not ask for message-specific reactions for all messages. Instead, message resonance occurs if political actors of *both* sides conceive a message as salient. If it is salient only for one side, the message is one-sided. Combining resonance with the message's salience, we arrive at three types of messages: first, messages that are highly salient for both sides are defined as resonant messages; second, messages that are highly salient only for one side are known as one-sided; third, messages that remain below the threshold for high salience are considered to be secondary or irrelevant messages.

The Power of Speakers

Numerous studies have shown that media attention is biased toward the more powerful actors (e.g. Galtung and Ruge 1965, Gans 1979, Schulz

1997, Hänggli 2012a, 2012b). In other words, the actors who dominate the decision-making process seem to get preferential access to the media (Danielian and Page 1994). The journalists rely on powerful actors because they provide a particularly convenient and regular flow of information and they also have a high news value. Relying on powerful actors makes writers more efficient at their job because it eliminates the need to double-check facts (Hackett 1985). As a consequence of this overrepresentation of powerful actors in the media, the content also represents primarily the views of these elites. Along this line of argument, the so-called 'indexing hypothesis' predicts that '[m]ass media news professionals (...) tend to "index" the range of voices and viewpoints (...) according to the range of views expressed in mainstream government debate about a given topic' (Bennett 1990b: 106). Based on this idea of indexing, we expect the salient messages of the *powerful* actors to become particularly important in the public debate (*power hypothesis*).

Debate Type

When looking at how news content is built, it is common to distinguish between 'institutional-driven' and 'event-driven' public debates (Livingston and Bennett 2003, Lawrence 2000). Institutional-driven public debates are *institutionally staged*, which means that they take place in the parliamentarian, corporatist, direct-democratic, or judicial arena and are initiated by political actors. Since the institutions set the agendas of news organization, these debates can be anticipated, planned, and administratively managed. Boorstin (1977) called them pseudo-events because of their lack of spontaneity. By contrast, other debates seem driven by the impact of spontaneous *external events*. In these cases, political actors and institutions often respond to the news agenda rather than set it and are less likely to shape the stories than in institutionally driven debates. The Fukushima nuclear disaster is an example of an external event that triggered many responses. Lawrence notes that event-driven public debates are 'more volatile and difficult for officials to control or to benefit from and are more open to challengers' (20). The Swiss debate was driven by an external event whereas the other five debates were institutionally staged.

There are important differences between the institutionally staged debates. As introduced in Chapter 4, they took place in two different arenas with a different range of participating actors and a different degree of publicly available information. Both factors influence the mechanisms that make a message important. We call debates staged in the

Table 9.1 *Debate type, debate content, and intensity*

Country	Debate type	Debate	Intensity
UK	Parliamentary Debate	Spending review	3.3
D		Hartz IV	3.0
DK		Activation	2.3
IT	Corporatist Debate	Fiat	2.6
FR		Youth unemployment	2.1
CH	No Policy Reform	Dismissals	0.7

parliamentary arena 'parliamentary debates', whereas debates in the corporatist arena are labelled 'corporatist Debates'. In these corporatist debates, the government (plus social partners) holds a monopoly on information. The British spending review, the reform of the German Hartz IV legislation, and the activation reform in Denmark took place in the parliamentary arena and constitute our parliamentary debates (see *Table 9.1*). By contrast, both the French negotiations on youth unemployment and the Italian case of the Fiat factory of Pomigliano were waged in the corporatist arena. We define them as 'corporatist debates'.

In Switzerland, no policy reform took place during our period of interest and we did have a low-key issue. The debate was initiated by an external event: the dismissal of workers by corporations. We classify this debate as 'debate without a policy reform'. This debate type is less controlled by institutional actors and the arguments of a secondary debate (strength of the Swiss Franc) dominated the discourse. *Table 9.1* also shows that the most intense debate (see Chapter 4) was the debate on austerity in the UK. The Swiss events of mass dismissals were least important.

The salience and resonance effects are expected to be dependent on the debate type. Both of these effects seem to be unimportant in *debates without a policy reform* because political actors do not prepare these debates. By contrast, messages which are salient and resonant have a particularly high chance of becoming important messages in the media *in parliamentary and corporatist debates* because the political actors have a leading role in both types. Regarding salience, we expect that its influence is strongest in parliamentary debates. Corporatist debates are more confidential. Only under specific circumstances the details become public. For instance, if a political actor strategically goes public to find more support, if investigative journalists find out newsworthy facts, or if an information leak occurs. For resonance, the policy-specific coalitions in the domain of labour-market policy identified in Chapter 7 become relevant. For the present purposes, we use the two basic blocks A (=pro) and B (=contra) and blocks 1 and 2 within the basic block A. We assume that these coalition structures remain more or less the same for different labour-market policy debates. This is in line with the idea of the advocacy coalition framework approach, which characterizes coalitions by their high level of stability (Sabatier and Weible 2007). We expect resonance *between* basic blocks A and B to be crucial in parliamentary debates, whereas in corporatist debates resonance *within* block A, i.e., between block 1 and 2, is crucial because the opposing actors, the social partners and the government, belong to block A (pro-coalition). Power is explicitly expected to be important regardless of the debate type (power hypothesis). Powerful actors often have resources at their disposal which allow them to react to external events in a timely manner (Wolfsfeld and Sheafer 2006: 338).

Alternative Explanations

There are other potentially relevant factors: Extremity, polarization, politicization, and origin of the argument (pro- or contra-argument). First, it might be the case that an *extreme* position helps a message to become important because it contains news value (Schulz 1997). The opposite can be true as well: extreme positions do not influence message importance. They might be explicitly suppressed by the media. As a third alternative, the extremity of position might not influence message importance but could be more influential for the salience of a message for a political actor: an extreme position on an argument makes it salient for the actor who takes such a position. Second, the degree of disagreement regarding a message (i.e., polarization) could be decisive for its importance in a public debate. Based on news value theory (Schulz 1997), one could expect that disagreement increases the news value of a message and makes it interesting for journalists to report on. Thus, it might directly increase the importance of the message. At the same time, however, the opposite might be the case as well. Valence messages (messages with a high level of agreement by political actors) potentially become very strong in communication and in thought because – similar to valence issues (Schneider 1972) – actors and voters take only one side on them. Valence messages, however, bear the risk of being less debated because they are uncontroversial.

Taking strategic negotiation into consideration, one can also expect that polarization matters *indirectly* in cases where the government has no dominant position. Scharpf (1997: 11, 126) observed that policy change either is 'problem-oriented' or 'interaction-oriented'. In the problem-oriented case, the political actors can focus on the best solution whereas in the interaction-oriented case distributive bargaining and side payments come to the fore because the agreement of an incongruent veto player is needed. In these interaction-oriented cases polarization matters because the different coalitions have to find a solution on disagreed arguments, or disagreed preferences. We conceive it as an indirect effect because polarization increases salience which then effects message importance. Applied to our cases, it means that in Germany, France, and Italy, polarization influence message salience because the negotiation mode is characterized by interaction. In these cases, incongruent veto players were available, the coalition pattern went across-camp (see Chapter 7) and the government had no dominant position. Instead, the government had to care for interaction and the incongruent veto player were powerful enough to block the policy reform.

Third, politicization corresponds to the salience of the message for one's own organization multiplied by its polarization. Politicization is expected to matter as a function of salience and polarization. Fourth, it is possible that the origin of the arguments matter. Pro-arguments might have an advantage because they are sponsored by the governments' side and are more credible. Alternatively, contra-arguments might be more newsworthy because they bring in a conflict to the governments' side. In the statistical analysis, none of these alternative explanations proved to be influential for debate importance. Nevertheless, in certain individual cases these factors add to the explanation and are then reported (see below). Finally, we also use congruence with dominant schema as an explanatory factor in the German case. Entman (2004) claims that frames incongruent with dominant schemas are blocked from spreading by common culture. Since we did not measure the arguments' congruence with dominant schema, it has not been included in the statistical analysis.

Operationalization

We operationalized the theoretical concept of the messages by the arguments provided by the actors to justify their positions. We used eight to fourteen debate-specific arguments from the six debates that took place in the six investigated countries (see Chapter 4). The data set was structured accordingly. The unit of analysis was the argument, with seventy arguments in total. In the second interview, the political actors were asked which one of the debate-specific arguments had been most important for the public debate. This question constituted our dependent variable. The resulting variable corresponded to the share of actors who considered a given argument as the most important one in the corresponding debate. This indicator for the overall importance of an argument for the debate was to be distinguished from the salience of an argument for the actors' organizations. For message salience, we asked the political actors for each message whether it was the most important for their own organization, or belonged to the three most important messages for their own organization. Their answers were coded as 1: the most salient argument for their own organization, 0.5: the three most salient arguments, 0: non-salient arguments. To characterize the salience of an *argument* (=unit of analysis), we took the *average* of salience of all organizations. *Power* is operationalized by a reputational indicator as introduced in Chapter 5. It is measured at the organizational level and standardized. For our unit of analysis (message), we calculated the mean power of those political actors who evaluated a message as most important for their organization.[1] For *resonance*, we first needed to define two sides. In order to identify the two competing sides, we used the coalition patterns as introduced in Chapter 7. The combined blocks 1 (inner core of block A) and 2 (non-inner core) constitute the block A (=pro) and the combined blocks 3 (inner core actors of block B) and 4 (more peripheral actors of block B) constitute block B (=contra). *Resonant messages in parliamentary debates and in debates without a policy reform are* defined as being salient for both block A and block B. Resonant messages in Corporatist Debates are defined as being salient overall as well as salient for block 1 and block 2. The threshold for overall salience is set arbitrarily: We use the mean (salience = 0.2) of those messages that were at least moderately salient and/or important (salience/importance in debate > 0.0) to distinguish highly salient messages from less salient ones. We do not rely on the mean or median of *all* messages because many messages did not play any role. For resonance, we rely on the same benchmark as for overall salience. Thus, if a message is salient overall (salience > 0.2) and both coalitions conceive it as salient (salience for block A or block 1 > 0.2 and salience for block B or block 2 > 0.2), the message is resonant. Defined in this way, there were 13 percent resonating (n = 9), 14 percent one-sided (n = 10) and 73 percent secondary or irrelevant (n = 51) messages. Finally, extremity was the deviation of the middle position on the arguments and polarization is the standard deviation of an argument position across the actors.

---

[1] Alternatively, one could use a stacked file with an argument for each political actor as the unit of analysis (each argument is listed separately for each political actor). The first option is chosen because most of the influencing factors are at the argument level. In any case, the results do not vary.

Table 9.2 *Correlation matrix of message debate, salience, resonance and power*

	All debates	Parliamentary debates	Corporatist debates	No policy reform
	Debate	Debate	Debate	Debate
Salience	0.53	0.72	0.45	0.15
Resonance	0.43	0.46	0.68	−0.11
Power	0.61	0.68	0.45	0.75
N	70	35	23	12

Results

Overall: Influence of Salience, Resonance, and Power on Debate Importance

As a first step, we looked at correlations between the key factors. The first column of *Table 9.2* looks at all debates together, followed by correlations for each debate type. Across all debates, the salience of an argument for the organizations (salience), resonance, and sponsorship by a powerful actor (power) correlate at above 0.4 with importance for the debate (debate). This result supports our general expectations. Regarding variations in different debate types, we see that all of these effects become stronger in parliamentary debates. Salience is most highly correlated with importance in this debate type, as expected. Resonance is most highly correlated with debate importance in corporatist debates, whereas in debates without a policy reform, power is most crucial. These results do not contradict our hypotheses. However, we did not have a specific expectation that resonance is most important in corporatist debates and power is most crucial in debates without a policy reform. Obviously, you have to be powerful to be able to suppress a debate.

To check whether the bivariate relationships hold when we control other factors, we ran a regression analysis. In *Table 9.3* and *Table 9.4*, the dependent variable is the importance of the argument in the public debate. *Table 9.3* includes all three independent variables and controls for country effects with country dummies. Model 1a looks at all debates, whereas model 1b excludes the debate without a policy reform. This debate type is investigated in model 1c.[2] In the first

---

[2] We did not run a model with interaction terms for debate types for two reasons. First, the mechanisms are not expected to be the same in all three debate types. Second, the model would not pass the linearity test.

Table 9.3 *Factors influencing importance of arguments in public debate*

	Model 1a: All debates	Model 1b: Parliam. and corpor. debates	Model 1c: Debate without policy reform
Salience	0.076	0.220[+]	−0.679[+]
	(0.47)	(1.35)	(−1.53)
Resonance	0.094°	0.141**	0.113
	(1.92)	(2.74)	(0.93)
Power	0.537***	0.306°	1.408**
	(3.66)	(2.00)	(3.74)
UK	−0.024	−0.029	
	(−0.56)	(−0.71)	
Denmark	0.021	0.024	
	(0.46)	(0.55)	
Italy	0.028	0.022	
	(0.58)	(0.51)	
France	−0.024	−0.033	
	(−0.56)	(−0.83)	
Switzerland	−0.017		
	(−0.40)		
Constant	0.014	0.014	0.023
	(0.41)	(0.43)	(0.44)
Observations	70	58	12
Adjusted R^2	0.37	0.44	0.55

t statistics in parentheses.
[+] $p < 0.2$, ° $p < 0.10$, * $p < 0.05$, ** $p < 0.01$, *** $p < 0.001$.
Note: Model 1c: Does not pass the linearity test ($F(3, 5) = 37.09$***).

Table 9.4 *Factors influencing importance of arguments in public debate*

	Model 2a: Parliam. debates	Model 2b: Corpor. debates	Model 2c: Debate without policy reform
Salience	0.450*	0.444[+]	−0.359
	(2.14)	(1.63)	(−1.28)
Power	0.254	0.413[+]	1.217**
	(1.14)	(1.52)	(3.88)
UK	−0.006		
	(−0.18)		

Table 9.4 *(cont.)*

	Model 2a: Parliam. debates	Model 2b: Corpor. debates	Model 2c: Debate without policy reform
Denmark	0.012 (0.32)		
Italy		0.049 (0.88)	
France			
Switzerland			
Constant	−0.002 (−0.07)	−0.039 (−0.76)	0.010 (0.20)
Observations	35	23	12
Adjusted R^2	0.48	0.21	0.55

t statistics in parentheses.
$^{+} p < 0.2$, $^{\circ} p < 0.10$, $^{*} p < 0.05$, $^{**} p < 0.01$, $^{***} p < 0.001$.
Model 2a: Power is significant at the $p = 0.27$ level.

model (1a), we see that only power has a highly significant effect. The results of model 1b show that resonance significantly influences the argument's importance in parliamentary and corporatist debates (in line with the resonance hypothesis). Both, salience of an argument for the organizations, as well as promotion by a powerful actor, only tentatively increase the importance of the argument in the debate (in line with the salience and the power hypothesis but not as significant as expected). Model 1c indicates that neither salience nor resonance increase the importance of an argument in debates without a policy reform (as expected by the salience and resonance hypotheses for this debate type). By contrast, salience even reduces the importance of an argument! In this debate type, power is particularly important.

In *Table 9.4*, we look at all debate types separately to get at the effects of salience and power more in detail. We leave resonance aside because we only have nine resonating arguments. Models 2a show that the salience hypothesis can be supported for parliamentary debates. For corporate debates, salience also increases message importance but this influence is significant only at the 0.2 level because this debate is less directed towards the public and the number of cases (n=23) is quite small. Salience is unimportant in debates without a policy reform, as expected. Power is most important in debates without a policy-reform goal, but is not significant at conventional levels in the other two debates. We think that a larger number of cases and/or content analysis data would make the effect more significant. In addition, salience and power are very highly correlated in parliamentary debates (corr. = 0.84). Parliamentary debate helps powerful actors to make their arguments salient also for other actors. Thus, power does not really add to explain argument importance in these cases.

The small number of cases, the low level of significance, and the non-linearity in model 1c need to be acknowledged and addressed as limitations regarding the present models. We nevertheless show these models because they overall support the bivariate relationships and are further supported by the more detailed individual results below. In addition, we rely here on one observation for each organization and are convinced that these mechanisms become more significant when we use different type of data. Overall, the results all go in the same direction and we conceive them as indicative results for future research.

Individual Cases: Influence of Salience and Resonance on Debate Importance

Next, we explore the effect of salience and resonance on importance for the relevant arguments in more detail. Relevant arguments are those *that are either salient or important* (Salience > 0.2 or Debate > 0.2). The left-hand side in *Figures 9.1a–f* respectively refers to the arguments which were more salient for the pro-coalition than for the contra-coalition and vice versa for the right-hand side. For each argument, two columns are presented. The first column shows salience of the argument (=salience) and the second column shows its importance in the public debate (=debate). The 'R' indicates resonating messages. As mentioned above, a message is resonating if both coalitions conceive the message as salient. Below, we will discuss the arguments in the order of their importance in debates.

Parliamentary Debates

In the parliamentary debates, we see that salience and resonance indeed matter for debate importance: salient messages for political actors were also important for the public debate, with the exception of the 'job seekers', the 'long-term unemployed', and the 'skills-needed' arguments. In the Spending Review debate and in the Hartz IV reform, at least one message was emphasized by both camps. By contrast, in the Danish activation debate, no message resonance occurred. To understand what is going on, let us look more closely at these three debates.

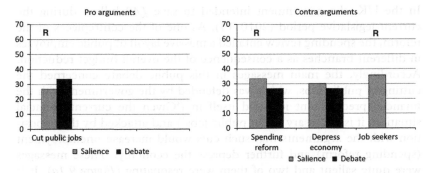

Figure 9.1a Comprehensive Spending Review (UK)

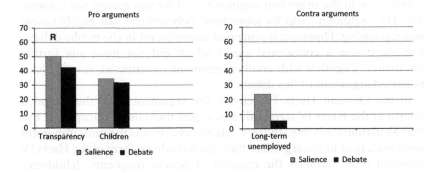

Figure 9.1b Hartz IV adjustment (Germany)

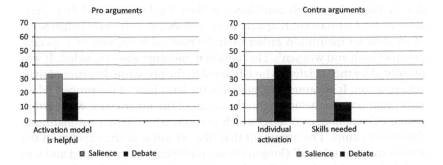

Figure 9.1c Activation policy (Denmark)

In the UK, the government intended to save £40 billion during the current legislative period (2010–14). As one of the centrepieces of the reform, the spending review entailed a massive layoff of public employees in different branches as a consequence of the overall budget reduction. Accordingly, the main messages in this public debate concerned the cutting of public jobs, which was defended by the government with the financial predicament it found itself in ('Given the current financial situation, it is necessary to cut public jobs') and attacked by the opposition with the arguments that such cuts would increase unemployment (spending reform) and further depress the economy. These messages were quite salient and two of them were resonating (*Figure 9.1a*). It is not exceptional that not all three messages are resonating. Each side normally has one or two resonating messages (see campaigns in direct-democracy, Hänggli 2012b). 'Depress economy' was less general in comparison to the other two arguments and for this reason not resonating. The argument 'help for jobseekers' (job seekers) was highly salient and resonating. However, it remained unimportant in the public debate, because it was a consensual aspect which did not need any further discussion. Together with another argument (incentives), it is the least polarized argument of this debate.

In the German Hartz IV reform, the argument that 'the intended reform of the Hartz IV standard rates makes them more transparent and the calculation basis less arbitrary' (transparency) was the most important argument, next to the argument that 'the intended reform of the Hartz IV standard rates supports the children of benefit recipients' (children). *Figure 9.1b* shows that the 'transparency' message was also highly salient, and that it did resonate. The fact that this argument became the most important one has to do with the fact that the Federal Court had declared the Hartz IV standard rates unconstitutional. The reform then had to modify the standard rates for this reason. Ferree et al (2002: 289) stated that Germans have high confidence in their legal system and that 'decisions of the German court appear as *ex cathedra*, the ultimate judgements of an abstract institution rather than the particular opinion of a specific group of men and women'. The 'children' message was one-sided. It was promoted by the socialists who belonged to the pro-camp because of their veto position. It became most salient in the last phase of the process when only organizations belonging to the camp of the inner circle was participating (*Vermittlungsausschuss*) which explains why it is not resonating in the contra camp. The argument that 'the reform is at the expense of the long-term unemployed' (long-term unemployed) was one-sided and was mainly ignored in the public sphere. This relates to the fact that it was incongruent with dominant schema in German society. In a dualized labour-market regime, the long-term unemployed are part of the system and have to be tolerated. This argument is also highly polarized. Using Entman's (2004) term, it was an ambiguously contested matter, which bears the risk of being blocked.

In the Danish activation debate, the argument that 'activation should be much more individual, and not everybody needs to follow the same plan' (individual activation) became most important in the public debate. This specific argument is most important because of the criticisms and problems related to the individual activation programs, and particularly because the media revealed that unemployed people were enrolled in bizarre adult education courses, such as courses on analyzing the handwriting of Hitler, enabling them to find their inner bird, or to build towers of spaghetti (Chapter 4). In *Figure 9.1c*, we see that this message was one sided. The pro-side emphasized most that the 'current Danish activation model is helping the unemployed get back into employment' (activation model is helpful). This message is one-sided too. The argument that 'activation provides the unemployed with skills which the labor market will need after the crisis' (skills needed) was most salient for the contra-organizations. It was again one-sided but less important in the public debate, because it was crowded out by stories on irrelevant and meaningless individual activation (individual activation) and the great job circus (unfortunately, no argument was covered on this aspect). Obviously, the two sides did talk past each other (these messages also did not resonate *within* coalition A, as is the case in Corporatist Debates, not shown). No resonance occurs because, first of all, the government did not really need to care about the criticism. It commanded a parliamentary majority and had no problem in getting through its proposals: The government presented a reform package for the activation regime on November 17, which was already adopted by the parliament one month later. Second, the government seemingly did not fear that the critical voices had any chance of winning strong popular support for their position or might bring about trailing poll standings – in such a situation the government might have taken the critique more seriously. Much of the critique was raised by the unions and the left-wing parties and highlights that the dispute had an ideological core. Third, the government slightly altered the original bills during the legislative process. The minister said that she had listened to (some of) the critique voiced by the municipalities' organization and that through the alteration the municipalities saved some money. Even though the alteration did not change the proposed new general rules, and might be seen as merely technical, it was enough to stop the media storm.

Corporatist Debate

The key finding for corporatist debates is that the important messages were resonating *within* block A. There was only little dialogue across all actors (between block A and B, not shown). This finding is associated with the fact that the negotiations on industrial relations and on youth (un)employment were a corporatist-like arrangement between the social partners and the government, who both belong to block A. Actors who were not involved in the corporatist-like arrangements (actors from block B identified in Chapter 7) did debate less about the topic, but instead were more concerned about other debates.

Let us look at messages that are highly salient or important in the corporatist debate. In the Italian industrial relations debate, the public debated about 'delocalization of industry' (to avoid major delocalization of Italian industry, it is important to ask for major flexibilization of labour conditions). This argument was so important because Fiat asked its workforce in the Pomigliano factory near Naples to cast a ballot in favour of more flexible employment conditions in order to save the factory and the jobs. The alternative proposed by Fiat was instead an immediate mass layoff and a consequent industrial delocalization to Serbia. The Fiat proposal was broadly accepted: It was supported by the government and by two of the three most important labour unions. The most important labour union (CGIL, block 2) rejected the Pomigliano agreement. Ultimately, workers in Pomigliano ended up accepting the agreement with 63 percent of the votes, and prevented an outsourcing of the Fiat factory to Serbia.[3] In other words, the threat of delocalization was helpful in finding support for more flexible employment conditions. It also made the argument so important because of its consequences. For the pro-coalition, the economic aspects (competitiveness and costs) also received priority. For the contra-coalition, flexibilization as a measure to reduce unemployment (flexibilization of collective labour agreement) was most salient. They disagreed with this argument. It did not become more important because the alternative of an industrial delocalization was very newsworthy. It dominated the debate and crowded out other views.

In *Figure 9.1e*, we see that the argument of 'number of people in vocational training' (vocational training) was salient, resonating and important in the French public debate. It was highly present because the government focused on the promotion of apprenticeships and in

---

[3] Since we were unable to interview main employers' organizations, the salience of this argument is probably underestimated.

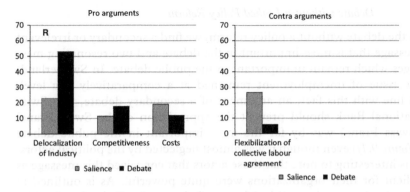

Figure 9.1d Industrial Relation (Italy)

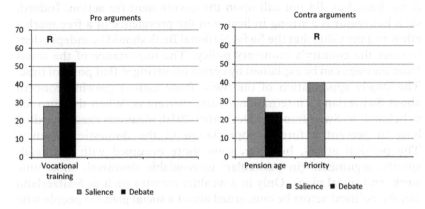

Figure 9.1e Youth unemployment (France)

a TV speech held on November 16, 2010, President Sarkozy promised to double the number of apprenticeships. 'Increasing the pension age disadvantages youth employment'(pension age) was one-sided and still rather important in the public debate. The 'priority' argument (tackling youth unemployment should be declared as a national priority) was resonating but did not appear in the media because political actors broadly agreed with one another (like the job seekers argument in the UK). It was the second least polarized argument. For both debates, we can state that the messages are resonating only *within* coalition A. They do not resonate *between* coalition A and B (not shown). Thus, we have dialogue among social partners and the government.

Debate without a Linked Policy Reform

In the debate without a policy reform, we find a secondary or irrelevant message that is most important in the debate and two resonating messages which remain unimportant in the public debate. In Switzerland, the issue of unemployment remained at a comparatively low level. In line with this fact, an argument of a secondary debate, 'the Swiss National Bank should prevent the appreciation of the Swiss Franc' (Swiss Franc) was by far the most important in the public debate (*Figure 9.1f*) even though it was almost neglected by the political actors. It is interesting to note that those actors that conceived this message as salient for their organizations were quite powerful. As is outlined in Chapter 4, no major political force called upon the Federal authorities to take action against the negative impacts of the strong franc. In other words, powerful actors clearly realized the challenge posed by the strong Swiss franc but did not call upon the government for action. Indeed, such behaviour is a strong indicator of the prevalence of a free market ethos and the value that the Swiss National Bank should be independent to steer the country's monetary policy. The importance of the Swiss franc message can be explained by events occurring at that point of time. The steady appreciation of the Swiss franc caused growing concern about Switzerland's international competitiveness. When the euro fell to below 1.30 Swiss francs in December 2010, ideas emerged regarding how to prevent a further appreciation of the domestic currency. The political actors, however, were more occupied with dismissal-specific arguments (in particular: unavoidable dismissal, short-time work, and social plan). Only in a wealthy country such as Switzerland can the political actors be concerned about a social plan for people who

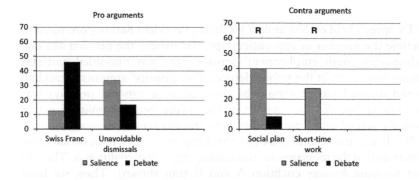

Figure 9.1f Mass dismissals (Switzerland)

lose their jobs and talk about the prevention of mass dismissal. These arguments also did not find high media resonance because the problem was not large.

Alternative Explanations

We end this chapter by looking at alternative explanations for the importance of arguments in public debates. It is not shown but worthy of mention that extremity does not prove to significantly increase the importance of an argument in the models. By contrast, extremity of positions seems to be related to the salience of an argument for one's own organization than to debate: Those arguments on which actors have a clear position tend to be more salient to them. If the dependent variable is salience, extremity is a significant influencing factor. Furthermore, polarization, politicization, and the origin (pro- or contra-argument) are insignificant. Thus, polarization has no *direct* influence on importance in debate.

In a final step, we investigate Scharpf's idea about whether strategic interaction plays a role. As mentioned in the theoretical part, in the interaction-oriented cases, polarization might increase salience and in such a way *indirectly* influence debate importance. In Germany, France, and Italy, incongruent veto players were available. Thus, in these countries, the negotiation mode is interaction-oriented (see third column of *Table 9.5*). One could expect the most polarized message to become salient here because the actors have to negotiate these aspects. Otherwise, the incongruent veto player can block the reform. In other words, we expect to find a positive correlation between polarization and salience in these cases. The first column in *Table 9.5* shows that polarization correlates positively with salience in the German, and Italian (and the Swiss) case, but not in France.

Table 9.5 *Correlation of salience and polarization*

a) *Parliamentary debates*

Corr.	Debate	Negotiation mode
−0.37	Spending review (UK)	Problem-solving
0.35	Hartz IV (Germany)	Interaction
−0.44	Activation (Denmark)	Problem-solving

Table 9.5 *(cont.)*

b) *Corporatist debates*

Corr.	Debate	Negotiation mode
0.25	Fiat (Italy)	Interaction
−0.07	Youth unemployment (France)	Interaction

c) *Debate without policy reform*

Corr.	Debate	Negotiation mode
0.63	Dismissals (Switzerland)	Problem-solving

Thus, in one case (France), we find no support for our expectation whereas in the two other cases (Germany and Italy, plus in the Swiss debate, see below), we find weak support at first glance. However, if we look at the cases more in detail, the idea of indirect influence has to be rejected. In Germany, the correlation is indeed positive, but weak. Two of the most polarized arguments – long-term unemployed and overcoming Hartz I – did not find salience and were rather ignored, which supports Entman's idea that contested (i.e., polarized) arguments bear the risk of being blocked. If we exclude these two arguments, the correlation is still weak. It even slightly decreases. It means that our expectation cannot be uphold. In Italy, correlation is again positive but weak. To explain the weak relationship, we look at the two most polarized arguments (costs and flexibilization of collective labour agreement). They belong to the salient arguments of the debate but did not become most salient. This can have two reasons. First, another argument – the possibility of industrial delocalization – was dominating the public debate. The importance in the public debate and the consequences of delocalization made this other argument salient for the political actors. Second, some of the actors resist flexibilization as long as social security is broadly lacking for mid- and outsiders. There might be too little security in Italy for flexibilization or reducing costs. As long as flexibilization is no option, they do not empha-size it. In the French corporatist debate, the interaction-oriented negotia-tion mode is not represented in the correlation at all. It is unclear why this occurs. It might have to do with the fact that the president used a TV speech to promote apprenticeships and in such a way set this aspect on the agenda. Finally, we see the highest correlation (0.63) in the Swiss case (*Table 9.5*). Since there is no incongruent veto player in this case, we did not expect a strong correlation in this case. We can only speculate about explanations. One reason might be that no discussion took place yet. A discussion in the parliament or between the government and social partners can produce a common understanding of the problem at stake and in such a way distract the political actors from their original salience and re-prioritize the salience of their arguments. Another reason might be that the political culture is consensual and actors want to discuss arguments on which they disagree.

Conclusion

Summarizing the results, we first note that, the salience hypothesis works as expected: it is the political actors who introduce the most important messages into the public discourse in parliamentary debates. The same also tends to be true in corporatist debates. Further research should elaborate more on the details of why a message becomes public in this debate type: In the French case, the main message of the contra-coalition (vocational training) was in the public because the president used it in a TV interview. In this debate type, information leaks and strategic manoeuvering are more important than in parliamentary debates because the messages are not necessarily in the public debate. The political or the media actors need a reason to go public. Regarding the debates without policy reform, an irrelevant message was on the top of the public debate. As expected, in this type of debate, message salience does not increase its importance.

Second, and in line with the resonance hypothesis, resonating messages generally find more importance in parliamentary and corporatist debates, whereas resonance does not increase the importance in debates without a policy reform. In the Danish parliamentary debate, however, we found no resonating messages because the government did not enter into the discussion. Furthermore, for corporatist debates, we can state that messages are resonating *within* coalitions but not *across* coalitions. In this debate type, non-participating actors keep out of it. Future research should show whether non-participating actors also avoid commenting in highly important debates like a Euro crisis summit. In other words, we want to know whether resonance across coalitions is also irrelevant in such cases. Third, with respect to the power hypothesis, the policy-specific power of a political actor is crucial for the importance of an argument in all debates. This influence is particularly strong and significant for debates without a policy reform.

10   The Positioning of Actors in Public Debates

Hanspeter Kriesi and Regula Hänggli

Introduction

At first glance, the public debate in one country is seemingly unrelated to the debate in another country. In the activation debate in Denmark, for instance, prominent discussion points referred to whether activation should be more individual, whether it is helping the unemployed to get back into employment, or provides the unemployed with the skills needed after the crisis. In the UK, by contrast, it was argued that it was necessary to cut public jobs given the prevailing financial situation. Since different issues are discussed in the various countries, the arguments vary greatly from one country to the other. Thus, one can question whether it makes sense to make a comparison of arguments *across* countries. However, as we have shown in previous chapters, to some extent at least, the domain of labor-market policy is structured similarly in all six countries discussed in our study, and the policy-specific actors align in similar configurations of coalitions, too. This leads us to expect that the country-specific debates (i.e., position of the actors on the debate-specific arguments) are also driven by similar forces. More specifically, we expect that they are structured by similar ideological positions of the actors involved.

In the present chapter, we take our cues from Sabatier's ACF-paradigm. Following Sabatier and Jenkins-Smith (1993) we can conceptualize the actors' belief systems as a three-tiered hierarchical structure (see Chapter 7 for a more detailed discussion). At the most abstract level, we find deep core beliefs. These involve fundamental values and ideas, which are not policy-specific. Policy-core beliefs constitute the next level; here, as you might expect, we have the deep core beliefs of a policy domain. The final level consists of secondary beliefs, which address specific aspects of the policy domain in question. The arguments exchanged in the debates can be considered as secondary beliefs. In this chapter, we would like to investigate the link between these debate-specific arguments, on the one hand, and policy-core and deep core beliefs, on the other. The policy-core and deep core beliefs were investigated in Chapter 6. We treat them here as influencing factors (independent variables) of positions on arguments. To the extent that the debate-specific arguments are closely linked to the actors' more fundamental beliefs, and to the extent that these links are similar across countries, the bewildering kaleidoscope of debate-specific arguments may be more apparent than real. The policy legacies may be different from one country to the other, as well as the configuration of actors. In the final analysis, however, the underlying pattern of the debate may be the same across countries – at least to a considerable extent, and this is what we hope to show below.

After presenting the theoretical considerations that guide our analyses, we begin the empirical part by describing the beliefs at the more abstract levels – the core beliefs and policy-core beliefs. Next, we present the secondary beliefs – arguments exchanged in labour-market policy debates – in two steps. First, we introduce general, all-purpose arguments that are applied by labour-market policy specialists independently of the specificities of a given debate. Then, we turn to the arguments of the specific debates that we are studying in the various countries. Finally, we shall test the relationship between the more abstract beliefs and the general arguments, on the one hand, and the debate-specific arguments, on the other.

Theoretical Argument

We are not interested in all possible core beliefs, but only in those which are relevant for the labour-market policy domain, i.e., these core beliefs that refer to the actors' fundamental economic orientations. Given that labour-market policy is a key component of the classic economic left–right divide, we expect that, for the specialists in this particular policy domain, policy-core beliefs are closely associated with their overall economic core beliefs. In other words, we expect them, in terms of core beliefs, to divide straight-forwardly along class lines into a pro-state left and a pro-market right. The key hypothesis guiding the analysis in this chapter is that these core-beliefs have a strong influence on the actors positioning in the more specific debates, independently of the country-specific characteristics of these debates. Thus, we reduce debates to their most basic structures to understand the underlying and generalizable patterns. We expect that, indeed, the positions of the actors on the debate-specific arguments can, to a large extent, be explained by their core beliefs as well as by the positions they use to adopt with respect to the general arguments in labor-market policy.

There is one aspect of labour-market policy that is likely to be not as closely related to the core beliefs as the other measures that are usually debated in this domain – activation. With respect to activation policies, the analysis in Chapter 6 has already shown that different institutional legacies lead to different configurations of preferences and, by implication, to different reform trajectories. If activation-related ideas and preferences are not integrated into the common deep core belief structure, we can expect that activation-related ideas will be less powerful at the debate level. This expectation draws on insights from framing analysis. Thus, Entman (2004: 14) maintains that the most inherently powerful frames are those that are 'fully congruent with schemas habitually used by most members of society'. Gamson (1992: 135) and Wolfsfeld (1997: 32) make similar points in discussing the concept of 'cultural resonance'. Frames that employ more culturally resonant terms have a greater potential for influence. The classic economic left–right conflict is such a culturally resonant theme.

Core Beliefs and Policy-core Beliefs

Let us first address the level of the core beliefs, which we assume to be at the roots of the debate-specific arguments. We have three types of measures to operationalize core beliefs and policy-core beliefs (*Appendix 10.1* provides the exact wording of the questions used for the operationalization):

1. the actors' self-placement on the left–right scale, which is the most general and the most frequently used way to get at their core beliefs;
2. their answer to a question about the fundamental distinction between state intervention and a self-regulating market economy: 'do you desire a [country] with more state intervention in the economy, or would you prefer a purer free market economy?';
3. their answers to the policy measures as operationalized in Chapter 6, where we distinguish between two dimensions of the labour-market policy space: a state-market dimension and an activation dimension.

Our general expectation of a close association between core beliefs and policy-core beliefs refers in particular to the state-market dimension uncovered in Chapter 6. The activation dimension, as argued above, may not be part of these core beliefs.

We have submitted the four indicators of core beliefs – positioning on the left–right scale, the state intervention/free-market-economy scale, and the two dimensions of the labour-market policy space – to an exploratory factor analysis. *Table 10.1* provides the results of two separate analyses – one with the activation dimension, and one without it. As is immediately apparent, the activation dimension is hardly at all associated with the

Table 10.1 *Factor analysis of indicators of core beliefs*

Variable	Factor1 = ideology	Uniqueness	Factor1 = ideology	Uniqueness
Left–right self-placement	0.79	0.38	0.78	0.39
State-free-market-economy	0.88	0.23	0.88	0.23
State-market dimension	0.82	0.33	0.82	0.32
Activation dimension	−0.14	0.98	.	.
Eigenvalue	2.08		2.06	
N	120		120	

Table 10.2 *Positioning on the activation dimension as a function of core beliefs, by country type: OLS regression coefficients and t-values*

	All	Flexicurity CH-DK	Dualization D-F-I	Deregulation UK
	b/t	b/t	b/t	b/t
Ideology	−0.11	−0.45**	0.06	−0.06
	(−1.39)	(−3.12)	(0.64)	(−0.23)
Constant	0.00	0.08	0.01	−0.01
	(0.06)	(0.62)	(0.13)	(−0.05)
Adjusted R^2	0.01	0.18	−0.01	−0.07
N	120	40	64	16

other three indicators. These three indicators, however, form a strong factor, which we shall take as our index for the actors' core ideology, i.e., for their position on the (policy-) core beliefs. Negative values on this index indicate a position on the left, while positive values correspond to a position on the right. The activation dimension will serve as an additional indicator of the policy-core beliefs. Positive values on this dimension indicate support for activation measures, negative values opposition to such measures.

To get a better understanding of the relationship of the way the activation dimension is related to the core beliefs, we have run four straightforward OLS-regressions to predict the actors' positions on the activation dimension based on their positions on the core beliefs (see *Table 10.2*). The first regression covers all six countries, whereas the other three refer to the three groups of countries we distinguished based on their labor-market legacy. The only group of countries, where the activation dimension is somewhat related to the actors' core beliefs is the flexicurity group – Denmark and Switzerland. More detailed analyses show that this effect is observable in each one of the two countries. The effect is highly significant, but still not very strong. In both countries, the left is more in favour of activation than the right. In the other four countries, no such differences can be observed. This confirms once again (see Chapter 6) that activation is generally not closely associated with the traditional conflict structure in the domain of labour-market policy. An implication of this result is that activation-related beliefs open opportunities for new alliances across the traditional left–right divide.

General Arguments in Labor Market Policy

In order to get at the more specific policy beliefs, we asked the actors a series of questions about the arguments that are generally used in the debates on unemployment as well as the key arguments that have been used in the specific national debates we have studied in more detail. These arguments are messages used to justify the actors' position during the debates. We shall also use the term 'frame' for these arguments. According to Entman's (1993: 52) highly influential definition, *framing* is defined as follows: 'To frame is to select some aspects of a perceived reality and make them more salient in a communicating text, in such a way as to promote a particular problem definition, causal interpretation, moral evaluation, and/or treatment recommendation.' The arguments we have submitted to the specialists in the labour-market policy domain actually are selective in the way suggested by this definition. Actors endorsing a general argument such as 'the unemployed should be more adaptable to the needs of the labor market' at the same time select a problem definition and causal interpretation of unemployment (for them, unemployment has a lot to do with the lack of flexibility on the part of the unemployed), promote a particular solution (the unemployed should be more adaptable), and provide a moral evaluation (it is the unemployed themselves who are to blame for their predicament). Even if the various aspects remain largely implicit in the argument, the actors' interlocutors and the general public who receive a message that is framed by such arguments can be expected to understand the connotations of the arguments in terms of the various aspects involved in a frame.

For the operationalization of the general arguments, we have asked our respondents about their position on fifteen standard arguments which are regularly advanced in debates on unemployment (for the exact wording of the questions, refer to *Appendix 1*). *Table 10.3* presents the country means for the fifteen arguments, which are ordered according to their means

Table 10.3 *Average positions on 15 statements on employment policy, by country, and standard deviations*[1]

Country	Denmark	Switzerland	Germany	France	Italy	Great Britain	Total	St.dev.
Social equality	0.50	0.71	0.96	0.85	1.22	1.12	0.90	1.10
Reintegration	*1.06*	*0.83*	*0.86*	*0.81*	*0.92*	*0.77*	*0.87*	*0.83*
Solidarity	0.29	0.44	0.43	**0.86**	**0.51**	0.31	0.50	1.15
Responsibility employers	0.27	0.39	0.45	0.44	0.53	0.41	0.42	1.20
Well off	**-0.21**	0.44	0.35	0.24	0.42	0.48	0.30	1.51
Negotiation	0.02	0.21	0.38	0.45	0.42	0.33	0.31	1.40
Standard of living	0.23	0.25	0.17	**0.54**	**0.42**	0.10	0.30	1.23
Adaptation	0.27	0.33	0.17	0.04	0.33	0.27	0.23	1.49
Lack of competitivity	***0.52***	*-0.21*	*-0.28*	*0.25*	***0.66***	*0.31*	*0.19*	*1.57*
Accept loss	**0.39**	**0.25**	0.13	-0.11	-0.06	**0.33**	0.13	1.48
Responsibility unemployed	0.06	**0.29**	0.12	-0.08	0.05	**0.23**	0.11	1.42
Responsibility state	**-0.25**	-0.10	-0.07	**0.41**	**0.32**	-0.12	0.06	1.48
Conditional benefits	-0.08	0.06	-0.21	-0.13	-0.20	-0.04	-0.10	1.24
Natives	*-0.10*	*-0.12*	*-0.18*	*0.00*	*-0.07*	*-0.27*	*-0.11*	*1.23*
Young	*-0.27*	*-0.25*	*-0.31*	*-0.46*	*0.00*	*-0.10*	*-0.24*	*1.10*

[1] the statements in italics have not been used for the creation of the index.

from top (arguments receiving the greatest support) to bottom (arguments receiving the least support).

Two statements have clearly received the largest endorsement from our labour-market specialists: the general argument calling for a reduction of social inequality, and the one calling for the active promotion of the 'reintegration of the unemployed into the labor market'. This is to indicate that labour-market specialists in all our countries are generally sensitive to the rising inequality in our societies, and that they generally are quite favourably disposed with respect to activation measures. We have used the reintegration statement for our operationalization of the activation scale (see Chapter 6). Overall, these specialists are also in favour of 'strengthening the solidarity with the unemployed', they believe that 'the employers should take on more responsibility,' that 'the well-off should contribute more to the financing of unemployment benefits', that 'the negotiation position of the employees should be strengthened,' and that 'the unemployed should be able to maintain their standard of living'. However, they also expect the unemployed to be 'more adaptable to the needs of the labor market,' even if they hardly expect them 'to accept certain losses (such as longer commutes or changes of residence)' and give only lukewarm support to the idea that 'the unemployed should take more responsibility for themselves'. Overall, they do not expect 'the state to be responsible for ensuring that there is a job for every individual willing to work.' Three arguments tend to be rejected by most of our respondents. These are the arguments claiming that 'the employment opportunities for the young should be improved at the cost of the older generations,' 'the native workforce should be given preferential treatment,' and that 'those who have contributed little should also receive limited benefits when they are unemployed.' This indicates that, although youth unemployment has been identified as a key structural problem of contemporary European labour markets, our respondents tend to disagree with policies that intend to solve this problem on the back of older generations. Neither do they generally want to pursue solutions which penalize foreign workers, nor do they favour making unemployment benefits conditional on contributions.

The last column in *Table 10.3* provides the standard deviations per argument, which is a measure of the agreement among the specialists on a given argument. As this measure shows, there is, obviously, more agreement for the arguments that find large support as well as for those that tend to be generally rejected. Disagreement is more pronounced for the arguments with a mean closer to zero. The greatest disagreement (std. dev.=1.57) is to be found for the general argument claiming that 'the capacity of our country to compete in economic terms at the international level is insufficient.' This general item aims at a structural explanation for the difficulties on the labour market of a given country. As a comparison of the country-means in *Table 10.3* shows, the answers to this statement vary strongly across countries, which reflects realistic assessments of their countries competitiveness on the part of our respondents: thus, Italy and Denmark are much less competitive by their country's labour-market specialists than Germany and Switzerland by theirs, with France and the UK taking intermediary positions.

We do not wish to comment on all the country-specific differences with respect to these arguments, but we would like to add three points. First, the Italian and French specialists clearly distinguish themselves from the rest by their more decisive support for solidarity with the unemployed and for the notion that the unemployed should be able to maintain their standard of living. Much more than their colleagues from the other countries, they also insist on the state's responsibility to create jobs for everyone who is willing to work. Second, the Danish, Swiss, and British specialists are more ready than the rest to expect the unemployed to accept certain losses and to take on more responsibility on their own. Finally, the Danish experts are more critical than the rest of the idea to have the well-off contribute more to the financing of unemployment benefits and they are particularly critical of expecting the state to create jobs for everyone.

To summarize the information contained in the answers to these fifteen arguments, we have factor-analyzed the fifteen statements. We have performed two types of analysis – one with weighted arguments and one unweighted. The weights for the first analysis correspond to the salience of a given argument for the organization in question. To determine this salience, we asked the respondents to indicate the three most important arguments as well as *the* most important argument for their organization (see *Appendix 10.1* for the wording of the corresponding questions). Both types of factor analyses indicate that four of the fifteen arguments (those about reintegration, lack of competitiveness, natives and the young) do not contribute anything at all to a common scale, neither in the one-factor nor in the two-factor solutions. This means that they do not have anything in common with the remaining arguments and refer to aspects which are quite specific. For the remaining eleven arguments, surprisingly, the unweighted solution, which does not consider the organization-specific salience of the various items, provides stronger scales than the weighted one. Both types of unrotated analyses show that there is just one dominant factor. The corresponding results are presented in *Table 10.4*. The summary scales take on positive values for positions asking the unemployed to

Table 10.4 *Factor analysis of 11 statements on
employment policy, weighted and unweighted statements*

Variable	Weighted factor1	Unweighted factor1
Accept loss	0.75	0.81
Adaptation	0.73	0.79
Responsibility unemployed	0.67	0.74
Conditional benefits	0.37	0.60
Standard of living	−0.57	−0.66
Well off	−0.64	−0.73
Responsibility state	−0.55	−0.74
Responsibility employers	−0.53	−0.74
Social equality	−0.66	−0.80
Negotiation	−0.70	−0.81
Solidarity	−0.69	−0.83
Eigenvalue	4.40	6.20

make additional sacrifices and to take on more responsibility of their
own, whereas they have negative values for positions that demonstrate
solidarity with the unemployed and ask for a stronger negotiation position of the employees.

There is a very close relationship between our index for the core beliefs
and these scales for general arguments. The correlation between the two
is of the order of r=.86. Across all the countries, a pro-market ideology
goes hand in hand with a framing of employment policy which asks the
unemployed to make more sacrifices, while a pro-state position is associated with a framing that demonstrates solidarity with the unemployed.
However, even if the association between the actors' overall ideology and
their general framing of unemployment is very close, it is not perfect,
which means that the general framing of unemployment policy by the
actors is, to some extent at least, influenced by factors other than their
overall ideological position, too. As is shown by the analysis of the determinants of the general arguments in *Table 10.5*, such additional factors
refer to the country differences with respect to the overall tone of framing:
the present analysis confirms what we have already seen when inspecting
the country differences on the individual items: independently of their
overall ideology, in Italy and France, labour-market specialists use frames
which generally show more solidarity with the unemployed than their
colleagues in the remaining four countries. Moreover, a pro-activation
position (which tends to be characteristic of the left at least in some

Table 10.5 *Relationship between general arguments and core ideology (OLS-regression coefficients and t-values for unweighted and weighted policy-core scale)*

	Unweighted	Weighted
	b/t	b/t
Ideology	0.91***	0.88***
	(21.53)	(20.14)
Activation	−0.16**	−0.11*
	(−3.27)	(−2.18)
Switzerland	−0.25	−0.24
	(−1.84)	(−1.75)
Germany	−0.25	−0.31*
	(−1.76)	(−2.14)
Denmark	−0.09	−0.06
	(−0.65)	(−0.37)
France	−0.50***	−0.50***
	(−3.71)	(−3.57)
Italy	−0.59***	−0.56***
	(−4.34)	(−3.96)
Constant	0.31**	0.31**
	(2.97)	(2.88)
Adjusted R^2	0.82	0.80
N	120	120

countries as we have seen above) is also significantly, although much less tightly, associated with solidarity with the unemployed.

Debate-specific Arguments

For each debate, we have tried to identify the key arguments of the competing camps. Depending on the country, we identified between ten and fourteen arguments, which we submitted to our respondents, asking them to position themselves with respect to each individual argument. As the reader may recall, in each country, the governments, all of which were centre-right, constituted the pro-camp. This camp always included the employers and business interest associations and other actors allied to centre-right, as well. By contrast, the contra-camp included the centre-left opposition and the unions as well as actors allied to them (see Chapter 7). For each country, *Appendix 10.2* includes the list of all debate-specific arguments. The arguments are ordered according to the average support they receive in a given country. For each argument,

Table 10.6 *Overview of debate-specific arguments, per country*

	Number of arguments	Average	Supported by left	Supported by right	Supported by both	Rejected by both	SD	Consensual (SD<1)	Polarizing (SD>=1)
Denmark	10	−0.4	3	1	3	3	1.3	1	2
Switzerland	12	−0.1	3	5	2	2	1.3	1	4
Germany	12	−0.2	5	3	1	3	1.4	1	6
France	14	−0.4	3	3	8	0	1.2	2	5
Italy	11	0.8	1	4	3	3	1.2	4	3
UK	13	0.8	1	6	4	2	1.2	3	4

the tables in the appendix also provide the standard deviation (an indicator for the extent to which an argument is polarizing, and which varies between 0 and a maximum of roughly 2), as well as the average positions of the actors from the right and the left, as well as the difference between these two averages. *Table 10.6* provides some summary descriptive information for these more detailed tables.

Table 10.6 shows that, overall, the number of arguments from the two camps is quite well balanced, even if arguments of the right dominate to some extent in Italy and the UK, while arguments of the left are somewhat privileged in Denmark. The French debate is exceptional to the extent that a majority of the arguments is supported by both camps, although not to the same extent. For example, in France both sides agree to some extent that the young are a sacrificed generation and that the access to jobs for the young should be facilitated, but agreement on the left with respect to these two arguments is much more pronounced. This means that, in spite of an overall positive attitude to the arguments used for justification in France, there is still a considerable difference in the framing between left and right, because the right often only pays lip-service to arguments that the left strongly endorses. There is also one argument that polarizes almost to the extreme in France – the left unanimously and strongly adheres to the argument that 'raising the pension age works against the young', while the right unanimously and strongly opposes it. Overall, the degree of polarization on the arguments (as indicated by the average country-specific standard deviations) is rather similar across all six countries, which suggests that the debates were similarly conflictive and can, indeed, serve as 'functional equivalents', as intended by our original selection.

We have also subjected these arguments to a factor analysis in order to find the common latent dimension(s) underlying these justifications of the actors' positions in the debates. Since these arguments are

Table 10.7 *Factor analysis of debate-specific arguments, per country*

arguments (see appendix 2)[1]	DK	CH	DE	FR	IT	UK
a5-a11-a2-a2-a4-a12	−0.37	−0.59	0.89	0.55	0.90	0.88
a10-a1-a6-a9-a8-a11	0.72	1.00	0.89	−0.91	0.89	−0.97
a4-a1-a5-a13-a5-a9	−0.35	0.84	−0.94	−0.66	0.91	−0.91
a2-a4-a11-a1-a1-a8	−0.86	−0.06	0.66	−0.76	0.92	0.55
a1-a2-a4-a12-a2-a7	0.49	1.00	0.81	−0.29	0.63	0.85
Eigenvalue	1.76	3.07	3.56	2.24	3.66	3.56
N	16	24	19	25	17	15

[1] The numbers of items refer to their numbers in the table in Appendix 2. The numbers are listed in the sequence of the country columns: DK-CH-DE-FR-IT-UK.

debate-specific and vary from one country to the other, we are obliged to do such an analysis separately for each country. This implies that, given the limited number of respondents per country, we have to restrict the number of arguments for the analysis. We have chosen the 'strength' of an argument as the criterion for the selection of the arguments for this analysis. For each country, we have selected the five arguments that turned out to be of greatest strength in the country-specific debates (for the identification of the 'strong' arguments, see the next chapter). The strongest arguments are printed in bold in the tables of *Appendix 10.2. Table 10.7* provides the results of the factor analyses: in all the countries, the unrotated analysis results in just one single factor.

The arguments in a given row of the table vary from one country to the other, of course, but for our present purposes, this is of secondary importance. Not all the arguments load on the country-specific factor either. For example, the fourth argument (a4) in the case of Switzerland ('multinationals dismiss more easily in Switzerland than in other countries') does not load at all on the common factor, although it has been a strong argument in the debate. This is, however, also of secondary importance for our analysis here. What is crucial from our point of view is that overall, with one possible exception, the five strongest items in each country-specific debate constitute a strong scale (as indicated by the factor loadings and the Eigenvalues). The exception concerns Denmark, where the common dimension underlying the strongest arguments is weaker than in the other countries. This is no accident, because the Danish debate was about activation, which, as we already know from Chapter 6, is much less closely associated with the core ideology of labour-market specialists. As we have already observed as well, this means that activation debates are likely to be more open to cross-camp coalitions and justifications.

Multivariate Analysis

In a final step, we now attempt to predict the actors' positions on the debate-specific arguments based on their core ideology and their positions on the general arguments. Given that we have only few cases for each country, and given that the factors for core beliefs and general arguments are highly correlated, we created a summary index for the left–right conflict consisting of core beliefs and general arguments for this analysis, which simply corresponds to the average of the two factors. *Table 10.8* provides the results of the corresponding regression analyses. In the first part of this table, we look at each country separately. In all the countries except Denmark, the index for core beliefs explains roughly three-quarters or more of the actors' positions in the country-specific debates. In other words, these positions are determined by the same ideological factors in all the countries, except Denmark. And these core beliefs, as we have seen, refer to the classic left–right divide. The activation dimension has a much weaker effect on the debate-specific arguments. In two countries – Switzerland and the UK – this effect is significantly negative, which suggests, as we would have expected on the basis of a simple left–right divide, that the experts who are more in favour of activation are also more in favor of solidarity with the unemployed in the specific debate than those who demand more sacrifices from the unemployed.

The Danish results in *Table 10.8a* are particularly interesting because they indicate to what extent the positioning in the Danish debate on activation during the period covered by our study is different from what we would have expected based on a simple left–right divide. In Denmark, the left generally supports activation policies more than the right – as is indicated by a sizeable negative correlation between our index for core beliefs and the activation dimension (r=−.61), a correlation that is much higher than in our six countries overall (r=−.20). Given that the Danish debate was a debate on activation, the positive effect of the core beliefs on the debate-specific arguments confirms this general preference of the left for activation. However, once we control for this general preference of the left, it turns out that the activation dimension in Denmark has a positive, although not quite significant, effect on the debate-specific arguments. This means that the experts from the right tended to argue in favour of the specific activation measures taken by the right-wing government, while,

Table 10.8 *Relationship between core ideology, general arguments and debate-specific arguments (OLS-regression coefficients and t-values)*

a) *by country*

	DK	CH	DE	FR	IT	UK
	b/t	b/t	b/t	b/t	b/t	b/t
Ideology	−0.57	0.36	0.17	0.78**	0.39	0.84**
	(−1.23)	(1.84)	(0.51)	(3.41)	(1.08)	(3.33)
Activation	1.05*	−0.23	−0.07	0.02	0.27	−0.18
	(2.84)	(−2.08)	(−0.49)	(0.23)	(1.00)	(−1.55)
General argument	1.58**	0.36	0.72*	0.07	0.73	0.19
	(3.09)	(1.82)	(2.70)	(0.27)	(1.44)	(0.80)
Constant	−0.59*	−0.14	−0.02	0.16	0.14	0.08
	(−2.89)	(−1.98)	(−0.14)	(1.84)	(0.69)	(0.68)
Adjusted R^2	0.59	0.87	0.71	0.86	0.75	0.87
N	16	24	18	23	17	15

b) *all countries*

	All
	b/t
Ideology	0.52***
	(4.90)
General argument	0.40***
	(3.80)
Switzerland	−0.16
	(−1.12)
Germany	0.00
	(0.01)
France	0.20
	(1.30)
Italy	0.14
	(0.81)
Denmark	0.58**
	(3.28)
General argument DK	−1.93***
	(−11.20)
Activation	−0.08
	(−1.52)
Activation Denmark	−0.95***
	(−3.87)
Constant	−0.00
	(−0.02)
Adjusted R^2	0.78
N	113

given the measures taken by this government, the specialists from the left tended to reject the arguments that the Danish activation policy was an unmitigated success and that it helped unemployed back into work.

Ultimately, however, the limited effect of the core beliefs (in terms of its significance) on the debate-specific positions of Danish labor-market specialists can be attributed to the fact that the experts' positions on the debate-specific arguments were much less polarized than the experts in the specific debates in all the other countries. Once we divide the experts into two camps – the left (with below average index values on core beliefs) and the right (with above average index values on core beliefs) – and compare the average positions of the two camps on the key arguments in the debate, the exceptionally low extent of polarization among Danish specialists comes out very clearly:

Country	Polarization
Denmark	4.1
France	6.2
UK	7.9
Switzerland	8.7
Germany	11.3
Italy	11.5

This finding shows that first, strategic action is at play. If political actors disagree with the activation reform, they do it for strategic not for substantive or ideological reasons. Substantively, Danish actors widely support flexicurity as the low polarization shows. However, they act strategically here. The centre-right government has tried to abandon the model for ten years but failed. As a consequence, the left has voted down all suggestions going into this direction. Second, this finding is in line with the fact that the Danish debate was triggered by a media campaign that eventually succeeded in putting the issue of activation on the agenda of top level politics, inducing the government to propose a minor reform of the activation policy. Thus, the Danish actors did not act because of a conflict within society but reacted as a consequence of disclosed examples of meaningless and irrelevant activation.

The specificity of the Danish situation is confirmed if we put these differences into perspective by analyzing them in the context of the debate-specific positions of the labour-market specialists from all six countries (see *Table 10.8b*). Overall, the core beliefs have a very strong positive effect on the arguments exchanged in the specific debates we studied. However, the equally strong negative interaction effect for the core beliefs in the Danish debate shows that this is much less the case in Denmark. Overall, the activation dimension has no effect, but in Denmark it tends to have a negative (although not significant) effect, indicating that those who are generally in favour of activation (the left) tend to be somewhat less positive about activation in the specific debate (=debate-specific arguments) than the right in this particular debate. Apart from the Danish exception, the debate-specific positions of the actors can be very well explained (to 76 percent) by their core beliefs, as operationalized by a combination of their ideological position and their position on the general arguments on unemployment-related issues. There are no other country-specific factors involved. All the other country-dummies do not have any effect, nor do we find any effect for other country-specific interactions with core ideology and general arguments (not shown here in detail). This means that, apart from the Danish debate, the arguments exchanged in the country-specific debates have been some versions of the arguments which are generally exchanged in the debates on unemployment, and which are, in turn, dependent on the classic ideological positions taken by the actors in economic policy debates.

Conclusion

In this chapter, we have introduced the (policy-) core beliefs of the actors as well as their positions on the general and debate-specific arguments (frames). The purpose of this chapter has been both descriptive and theoretical. It was our intention to demonstrate that behind the smoke-screen of highly idiosyncratic, country-specific debates on unemployment we find the same ideological positions and general arguments on unemployment across Europe. We indeed could show this general pattern. In addition, as we saw in the Danish case, the influence of core beliefs or of general arguments in a policy field on a debate is reduced if strategic action or reactive behaviour is at play.

The demonstration of the general pattern provides some good news and some bad news. The good news is that, despite the apparent differences, the policy debates on unemployment are actually very similar across Europe. This means that, in this particular policy field at least, conflict is structured in very similar ways across Europe and Europeans have much more in common than at first meets the eye.

There is another piece of good news here: the fact that activation is not fully assimilated into the classic conflict between left and right implies that activation-related beliefs open up opportunities for new alliances across the traditional left–right divide. There is some bad news here too, however: the fact that, with the exception of Denmark, all these country-specific debates are intimately linked to the classic left–right divide suggests that these debates lack new ideas and are led in ways that are less than promising for novel solutions to the pressing problem of unemployment.

Appendix 10.1   Operationalization – original questions

Core beliefs and policy-core beliefs

- We often talk about left–right polarity in politics. On a scale from 0 to 10, 0 being far left, 10 being far right, where would you position your organization?
- Do you desire a [country] with more state intervention in the economy or would you prefer a purer free market economy? (1=state intervention, 5=free market economy)
- The State–market and the activation dimensions are taken from Chapter 6, based on the three separate factor analyses the results of which are presented in Tables 6.3 and 6.4. For the present purposes, the results of the three separate analyses have been merged into a single variable for each one of the two dimensions.

General Arguments

Questions for the actors' *position* on the arguments: Please look at list... On this list, you will find fifteen statements on employment policy. The first statement is... How much does your organization agree with this statement? Please indicate a number from 1 (we completely disagree) to 5 (we completely agree).

- The well-off should contribute more to the financing of unemployment benefits.
- Social inequalities should be reduced
- Solidarity with the unemployed should be strengthened
- The unemployed should be able to maintain their standards of living

- The unemployed should be more adaptable to the needs of the labour market
- The unemployed should be willing to accept certain losses (e.g. longer commutes, changes of residence...)
- The state is responsible for ensuring that there is a job for every individual willing to work
- Employers should take on more responsibility
- The negotiating position of employees should be strengthened
- Those have contributed little should also receive limited benefits when they are unemployed
- The capacity of our country to compete in economic terms on an international level is insufficient
- The unemployed should take more responsibility for themselves
- Employment opportunities for the young should be improved at the cost of the older generations
- The reintegration of the unemployed into the labour market should be actively promoted
- The native workforce should be given preferential treatment

For the analysis, these five-point scales were transformed to the range of −2/+2, such that positive values indicate agreement, and negative values disagreement with the statement.

Questions for the *salience* of general arguments:
- Let's look at this list (of the fifteen arguments) again. Please could you indicate which three issues are the most important for your organization?
- Which one issue was the most important?

Debate-specific Arguments

Question for the actors' *position*: Please look at list... You will find a variety of arguments that have come up in the debate over [country-specific issue]. Please indicate on a scale of 1 to 5 to what degree your organization agrees with these statements. (1=completely disagree, 5= completely agree).

For the analysis, these five-point scales were transformed to the range of −2/+2, such that positive values indicate agreement, and negative values disagreement with the statement.

Questions for the *salience* of the argument
- Please could you indicate three arguments that were the most important for your organization in the [country-specific] debate.
- Which of these arguments was the most important for your organization?

Appendix 10.2   Debate-specific arguments, summary of question wording and descriptive statistics, per country

DK Item	Activation Label	Mean	Std. Dev.	Left	Right	Right–left
a8	for voluntary enrolment	−0.7	1.5	−0.8	−0.6	0.2
a9	extension to new groups	−0.6	1.2	−1.4	−0.3	1.1
a1	**unmitigated success**	−0.5	1.0	−1.2	−0.2	1.0
a2	**prone to abuse by employers**	−0.2	1.4	1.2	−0.8	−2.0
a7	prone to wage dumping	−0.2	1.5	0.8	−0.6	−1.4
a3	equal grants in public and private jobs	0.2	1.4	1.0	−0.2	−1.2
a4	**provides needed skills**	0.3	1.4	0.6	0.1	−0.5
a10	**helps unemployed back into work**	0.4	1.1	−0.2	0.7	0.9
a6	regular jobs instead of internships	0.6	1.2	1.8	0.1	−1.7
a5	**more individualized activation**	1.5	0.8	1.8	1.4	−0.4
	Average position	0.1	1.3	0.4	0.0	−0.4

CH Item	Mass dismissals Label	Mean	Std. Dev.	Left	Right	Right–left
a12	make frontier workers bear the costs	−1.2	0.9	−1.3	−1.1	0.1
a7	sanctioning managers who dismiss employees	−0.9	1.3	0.0	−1.5	−1.5
a8	dismissed workers easily find new job	−0.4	1.0	−1.3	0.2	1.5
a4	**multinationals dismiss more easily in CH**	−0.2	1.0	−0.2	−0.3	0.0
a5	increase protection for older employees	0.0	1.5	1.0	−0.8	−1.8
a10	loss of know how	0.0	1.3	0.7	−0.6	−1.3
a11	**appreciation of SFR has to be avoided**	0.2	1.2	0.6	−0.1	−0.8
a2	**need for social plan**	0.4	1.6	1.2	−0.2	−1.4
a3	information of local authorities	0.5	1.6	0.9	0.1	−0.8
a1	**dismissals are unavoidable**	0.5	1.7	−1.0	1.6	2.6
a9	short-term work is better than dismissal	0.6	1.2	0.9	0.4	−0.5
a6	**against dismissal protection**	0.7	1.3	−0.6	1.6	2.2
	Average position	0.0	1.3	0.1	−0.1	−0.1

DE Item	Hartz IV Label	Mean	Std. Dev.	Left	Right	Right–left
a11	**refuses minimum wage**	−1.3	1.3	−2.0	−0.6	1.4
a4	**sets standards for modern social policy**	−1.1	1.1	−1.8	−0.4	1.3
a9	lowers level for jobs subject to social insurance	−0.9	1.0	−0.8	−1.0	−0.2
a7	improvement for handicapped	−0.7	1.3	−1.7	0.3	2.0
a3	accomplice of employers	−0.5	1.5	0.2	−1.3	−1.6
a1	abandon Hartz IV	−0.4	1.8	0.8	−1.4	−2.2
a2	**provides transparency**	−0.4	1.6	−1.6	0.9	2.4
a8	fishy compromise	−0.3	1.6	1.0	−1.7	−2.7
a6	**supports disadvantaged children**	0.1	1.3	−0.7	0.9	1.6
a5	**unemployed bear the costs**	0.2	1.7	1.6	−1.2	−2.8
a10	costly new regulation for additional income	0.3	1.5	0.9	−0.1	−1.0
a12	provides financial relief for cities	1.3	0.8	1.7	1.1	−0.6
	Average position	−0.3	1.4	−0.2	−0.4	−0.2

FR Item	Youth unemployment Label	Mean	Std. Dev.	Left	Right	Right–left
a5	sanction firms without apprentices	−0.2	1.5	0.4	−1.0	−1.4
a3	jobs for young - for social partners	0.1	1.2	0.0	0.2	0.2
a10	obligation to stay in apprenticeship firm	0.1	1.0	−0.4	0.9	1.2
a8	state task to help the young to get job	0.2	1.5	1.1	−1.0	−2.1
a4	improve job orientation in schools	0.2	1.5	−0.8	1.8	2.6
a9	**raising pension age works against the young**	0.3	1.9	1.7	−1.8	−3.5
a14	neglect of youth unemployment	0.5	1.2	0.7	0.4	−0.3
a6	employment incentives for firms	0.8	1.6	0.5	1.4	0.9
a1	**young are sacrificed generation**	0.9	1.3	1.6	0.1	−1.5
a11	provide help for job search	1.0	1.0	1.4	0.9	−0.5
a2	**improve vocational training**	1.1	1.1	0.8	1.7	0.9
a7	priority for the young in urban areas	1.1	1.1	1.3	1.0	−0.3
a12	**jobs for the young - national priority**	1.6	0.8	1.7	1.4	−0.3
a13	**facilitate access to jobs (e.g. transportation)**	1.6	0.6	2.0	1.1	−0.9
	Average position	0.7	1.2	0.9	0.5	−0.4

IT Item	Industrial relations Label	Mean	Std. Dev	Left	Right	Right–left
a3	atypical contracts contribute to growth	−1.2	0.9	−1.6	−0.6	1.0
a2	**for individualization of labour contracts**	−1.1	1.3	−1.9	0.0	1.9
a4	**flexibilization necessary to avoid delocalization**	−0.8	1.3	−1.6	0.4	2.0
a10	cassa integrazione only postpones dismissals	−0.6	1.2	−0.6	−0.6	0.0
a1	**for flexibilization of collective labour agreements**	−0.5	1.7	−1.6	1.1	2.7
a8	**flexibilization necessary for competitiveness**	−0.3	1.4	−1.1	0.9	2.0
a5	**labour costs need to be reduced**	−0.1	1.7	−1.3	1.6	2.9
a7	for permanent positions	0.7	1.5	1.6	−0.6	−2.2
a11	for universalistic benefits	1.4	0.8	1.6	1.3	−0.3
a9	for innovation and research	1.6	0.6	1.8	1.4	−0.4
a6	for investment in education	1.8	0.4	2.0	1.4	−0.6
	Average position	0.1	1.2	−0.2	0.6	0.8

UK Item	Spending review Label	Mean	Std. D	Left	Right	Right–left
a5	limited accessibility of social housing	−1.2	0.9	−1.5	−0.7	0.9
a6	fit to work	−0.6	1.4	−1.4	0.8	2.2
a7	**pro targeted safety net**	−0.6	1.3	−1.2	0.6	1.8
a3	creates dependency culture	−0.4	1.3	−1.0	0.8	1.8
a8	**maximize earnings from work**	−0.3	1.5	−0.3	−0.2	0.1
a10	too much fraud	−0.2	1.5	−0.7	0.8	1.5
a13	increase sanctions	−0.2	1.5	−0.9	1.2	2.1
a12	**necessary to cut public jobs**	0.0	1.5	−0.7	1.4	2.1
a4	consider household income	0.5	1.4	0.1	1.3	1.2
a11	**cutting jobs depresses economy**	0.9	1.4	1.5	−0.4	−1.9
a2	more incentives for re-entering work	1.2	0.6	1.3	1.0	−0.3
a9	**spending reform increases unemployment**	1.3	1.0	1.6	0.6	−1.0
a1	help active job-seekers	1.4	0.7	1.6	1.0	−0.6
	Average position	0.1	1.2	−0.1	0.6	0.8

11 Inside the Interaction Context

Laurent Bernhard

Introduction

This chapter considers the strategic interaction between the actors involved in the various debates under scrutiny. According to Jenkins (1981: 35), strategies refer to the overall *plan for action*, the blueprint of activities with regard to the mobilization of resources and the series of collective actions. In recent decades, there has been an increased interest in studying the strategic decisions adopted by political actors involved in campaigns and other contexts. In elaborating their action plans, political actors consider the rules of the game, the actors' configuration as well as the behaviour of their adversaries. However, to date the literature has almost exclusively focused on the analysis of single actors (Green-Pedersen and Mortensen 2010). In other words, political scientists have been limited in their ability to move beyond this rather isolated perspective by examining what Kriesi (2004: 77) calls the interaction context, where the interplay between the various actors come into view.

This contribution attempts to provide answers to the question of what matters inside the interaction context. To that end, we will make use of a content analysis of those press releases the labour-market elites produced during our period of interest. These documents were taken from the organizations' web pages. This examination includes four out of the six selected countries: the United Kingdom, France, Germany, and Switzerland. We decided to remove Denmark and Italy from the analysis for different reasons. In Denmark, we were not able to collect a representative sample, since many political organizations do no publish their press releases online. With respect to Italy, the documents did not prove to be uniform in nature. Communications produced by some organizations tended to resemble more press reviews than press releases. Especially documents produced by political parties often contained statements made by prominent figures in the mass media (TV shows, press, and news agencies). Thus, a part of the elite documents did not refer to unfiltered input material destined to the media.

Analyzing the actions and reactions among the political actors is a challenging task. With the data at hand, the probably most obvious approach would be to study the various documents longitudinally by looking at the ways in which elite actors react to press releases aired by their fellows. However, this direct data analysis strategy is not a feasible option in the present case, as it turned out that no single document explicitly referred to another one. For this reason, we propose to study the interaction context rather indirectly by focusing on three basic strategic choices. First, we will examine the political actors' event management. As will be exposed in this chapter, most press releases were indeed published in relation to institutional events set by decision-makers. These events can be conceived of as 'actions', whereas publishing a press release constitutes a possible 'reaction'. Hence, studying whether and how the labour-market elites reacted to major debate-specific events will, admittedly to a limited extent, tell us something about the inner workings of the interaction context. Second, we will analyze the content of the messages selected by the various political organizations, an aspect which indeed lies at the heart of any public engagement. In this respect, we will focus on the question of message convergence. To what extent do opposed actors address the same considerations in a given debate? Third, we will shed light on the phenomenon of negative campaigning. We will examine some basic patterns by focusing on both the senders and the targets of actor-related attacks.

Identifying Major Events

We identify the major debate-specific events by using those press releases the various labour-market organizations produced in the framework of the selected debates. This approach might be subject to criticism, as we do not take a source that is independent of the documents we study here. We concede that we are not able to account for events that have not been publically addressed at all by means of press releases. However, we believe these events to be rather insignificant, given that political actors usually react to the most important events. Thus, we feel confident to have included the most relevant instances. In the following, we shall outline the major debate-specific events for each of the selected country cases.

In the case of the British debate on austerity, the selected press releases were published in relation to two events – the announcement of the

Comprehensive Spending Review (CSR) by then Chancellor George Osborne on October 20, 2010, as well as the publication of the so-called Welfare Reform White Paper, which substantiated the introduction of the Universal Credit on 11 November 2010 (see Chapter 4). Altogether, the selected British labour-market elites produced 97 press releases about these two major events. The CSR can be qualified as having been much more important, however. Indeed, an overwhelming majority of the documents considered (79 out of 97 press releases) addressed the Comprehensive Spending Review launched by the coalition government.

Regarding the adjustment of the Hartz IV reform in Germany, the corresponding press releases cover the period from September 20, 2010 to January 31, 2011. The relevant organizations published 79 press releases altogether. Hence, the debate pertaining to the adjustment of Hartz IV turns out to have been of rather high intensity from a political actors' perspective. We have identified no less than 15 major events, in response to which the various organizations aired press releases. These events were all institutional in nature, as they were clearly structured along the legislative decision-making process. The first event referred to the draft bill made public by the Federal Ministry of Labor on September 27, 2010, while the last one pertained to the launching of the Joint committee (*Vermittlungsausschuss*) whose objective was to find a compromise solution after that the two Chambers had not been able to find common ground. The large number of institutionalized events illustrates that the decision-making process was characterized by a considerable amount of bargaining and therefore turned out to be much more complicated in the German than in the British case, which also occurred in the parliamentary arena. Due to the fact that no single event attracted a large number of press releases, we decided to treat the whole parliamentary debate as one major event.

In Switzerland, the labour-market elites promulgated 39 press releases about the aspect of dismissals from October 1, 2010 to January 31, 2011. Twenty-nine of these documents reacted to two events – the announcements made by Alstom on October 4, 2010 and by Roche on November 17, 2010. The first case of redundancies was waged much more intensively, since it triggered 23 reactions (as opposed to the 6 press releases about the dismissals by Roche). The ten remaining press releases dealt with rather minor dismissals (such as Mayr-Melnhof, Clariant, and Karl Mayer) as well as with the issue of abusive dismissals of labour representatives (two documents).

As far as France is concerned, there were 32 press releases revolving around the topic of youth unemployment. Strikingly, these documents referred to 20 different events, many of which were not coherently related to each other, as they touched upon various aspects. In addition, these events often only triggered the reaction of one single organization. In other words, there were many isolated cases. The only event of some magnitude pertains to the social partners' negotiations on youth unemployment (see Chapter 4). On January 10, 2011, social partners agreed on a so-called social agenda, i.e., the major employers' associations and labour unions established the topics and a schedule for the most important negotiations to be organized in 2011. There are ten press releases which should be appreciated in the context of these corporatist negotiations. Thus, particular attention will be devoted to this event in the empirical analysis.

Event Management – Engagement and Positioning

Public debates refer to all public-oriented communication related to a particular issue in a given time frame (Kriesi et al. 2012). They consist of a varying number of participating political actors who attempt to control their fellow politicians, the media, and the public in order to impose their favoured positions, sub-issues, and messages. To gain the media's attention and obtain support among citizens, these actors usually stage institutionalized or so-called 'pseudo-events'. This section is devoted to the analysis of event management, which consists of two interrelated aspects – engagement and positioning. At its most basic level, any strategic action consists of two choices: altering the salience of certain issues and the positions toward them (Kriesi et al. 2008). When faced with an issue-specific event, political actors have first to decide whether to address it in public. Those who abstain from reacting purse what Meguid's (2005) calls a *dismissive strategy*. It is very likely that only a low-key debate will take place if a majority of the political elites chose this strategic option. On the contrary, actors who react will politicize the issue at stake and thus contribute to the emergence of an intensive public debate. What is more, those actors who have made the choice to react to a given event will have to adopt a position. Basically, they can either support or reject the announced issue-specific decision. In Meguid's (2005) terminology, the former option is identified as *accommodative strategy* and the latter one as *adversarial strategy*.

With respect to the first choice, we expect that the *decision-making arena* has a decisive influence on the actor types willing to politicize the issue of unemployment. The basic idea is that each arena has its dominant actors, which are more likely to take part in the public debates. As has been outlined in Chapter 4, the policy-specific decisions occurred in two different venues in the various countries during our period of investigation. Given that the most important events took place in the 'corporatist arena' in France (negotiation on youth unemployment) and Switzerland (instances of mass dismissals), we expect the labour unions and the employers' associations to have been more likely to have reacted to these events than the remaining actor types (state actors, political parties, and social movements, think tanks and research institutes). By contrast, the policy-specific contest was carried out in the parliamentary arena as far as the German and the British debates are concerned. Thus, we expect the issue-specific events to have massively attracted political parties in these two countries. However, the remaining actors should have been much more active in the case of the United Kingdom. This hypothesis is derived from the fact that the austerity measures were much more radical in nature and far-reaching in scope than the minor adjustment of the German Hartz IV legislation. Hence, we expect the state actors, the employers' associations, the labour unions, and the social movement organizations to have heavily gone public when it comes to events related to the British debate on austerity. In other words, we expect a more pluralistic picture of elite participation in the United Kingdom.

Regarding the second choice, we assume the positioning towards events to be based on the actors' fundamental beliefs. Since the cleavage between labour and capital lies at the heart of labour-market politics, the degree of support towards the issue-specific decisions which are made public is expected to reflect the basic *antagonism between the left and the right*. Thus, the parties from the left as well as labour unions are hypothesized to take adversarial stances from those expressed by the right-wing parties, the employers' associations, and state actors. The latter are assumed to support the camp of the right (i.e., to pursue an accommodative strategy) as all countries under investigation were governed by a right-wing majority during our period of interest. However, we propose to specify this beliefs-based hypothesis in two respects. First, we need to account for the *radical right*, which nowadays, along with the left and the moderate right, constitutes the tripolar structure of the political space in Western Europe (Kriesi et al. 2008). We expect these actors to reject the issue-specific solutions proposed by the traditional right. Given that these actors are not in government, they should not be supportive. To the extent that parties from the radical right decide to react to events, they are thus expected to rely on adversarial strategies. Second, the opposition between left and right should appear less pronounced in the case of *France*. This theoretical expectation is rooted in the fact that social partners engaged negotiations designed to establish a so-called 'social agenda' during our time frame of interest which included the rather uncontroversial problem of youth unemployment (see Chapter 4). Public reactions towards these decisions might have been less conflictive than in the remaining cases (mass dismissals in Switzerland, Hartz IV adjustment Germany, and the spending review in the United Kingdom).

As to the basic strategic choices – reaction and positioning – we coded the salience and the direction of each document at the level of the included collective actors. Our measure for reaction simply corresponds to the number of press releases a given organization published on the respective domains of interest during our period of investigation. Concerning the indicator about position, we coded the direction of each press release by using three different values: '1' for a supportive stance towards the decision or reform proposal at stake, '0.5' for a neutral or ambivalent statement, and '0' for a rejection. For each political actor, we calculated the average score. Hence, values higher (lower) than 0.5 imply an accommodative (accommodative) strategy.

We now turn to the examination of the event management hypotheses. We will proceed in two steps. The first part is devoted to the actors' decision of whether to participate in the debates of interest. We will begin with taking a comparative perspective, before we will go more into detail by reporting on each country case separately. In the second part, we will focus on participating actors in order to look at their positioning towards the selected events.

Engagement

As is visible from *Table 11.1*, the British elites proved to be most active during our period of investigation. On average, the 18 organizations studied here issued 5.4 press releases in relation to the debate on austerity. Next in line are the German actors, with 3.5 documents pertaining to the adjustment of the Hartz IV legislation. The Swiss organizations, for their part, published 1.6 press releases about the topic of dismissals, while we found only 0.4 documents per collective actors as far as the French case about the negotiations on youth unemployment are concerned.

However, the various actor types markedly differed in their likelihood to go public across the four countries under scrutiny. As expected, political parties turned out to be most active in Germany. The four included opposition parties published almost 9 press releases on average. The corresponding figure is of 5.5 for the two government parties (CDU and FDP). The remaining actor types proved to be less assiduous. Whereas citizen groups issued almost 4 press releases, the involvement by

Table 11.1 *Average number of press releases and positioning (in actors) by actor types*

	United Kingdom	Germany	Switzerland	France
State actors	10.0 (1.00)	1.3 (0.67)	0.8 (0.50)	0.0 (–)
Government parties	3.0 (1.00)	5.5 (0.84)	0.0 (–)	0.0 (–)
Opposition parties	8.8 (0.01)	8.8 (0.00)	0.0 (–)	0.0 (–)
Employers' associations	3.3 (0.72)	1.0 (1.00)	0.0 (–)	1.3 (0.75)
Labour unions	8.3 (0.00)	1.3 (0.00)	6.0 (0.00)	0.6 (0.40)
Citizen groups	1.5 (0.50)	3.8 (0.00)	0.0 (–)	0.0 (–)
Think tanks & research inst.	0 (–)	0.3 (0.50)	0.0 (–)	0.0 (–)
Mean (N)	*5.4*	*3.5*	*1.6*	*0.4*
N	*97*	*76*	*39*	*10*

labour unions (1.3), state actors (1.3), and employers' associations (1.0) as well as think tanks and research institutes (0.3) turned out to be far below the country average. In the British case, we find similar levels of public engagement regarding the political parties. Again, parties in opposition (8.8 press releases per organization) are found to have been somewhat more active in the public realm than government parties (3). In contrast to the German case, three actor types turn out to have been much more dedicated to the debate under scrutiny. The probably most striking feature concerns the involvement of the economic interest groups. Both employers and labour unions exhibit a much higher level of participation in the United Kingdom. With an average of more than 8 press releases, the four labour unions included in the study seem to have been particularly involved in the debate on austerity, while the mean score for the three British employers' association is of 3.3. According to *Table 11.1*, there also seems to be a marked difference with respect to state actors. The impressive number of 10 press releases needs to be nuanced, as the Department for Work and Pensions is the only representative of this category. Overall, we observe a less pronounced domination by political parties in the British case than in Germany. In line with our hypothesis, elite participation in the public debate followed a more pluralistic pattern. This statement still holds true when accounting for the finding that citizen groups and organizations belonging to the category 'think tanks and research institutes' issued slightly more press releases in the framework of the German debate.

The most striking characteristic of the Swiss and French cases pertain to the fact that the entirety of the selected press releases originated from only two actor types. In Switzerland, the six labour unions accounted for an impressive average of 6 press releases. Besides that, some state actors went public. The labour-market authorities of two cantons (i.e., the Swiss member states) wrote the remaining press releases in response to dismissal cases. While we expected a huge engagement by labour unions, the absence of public statements by employers' associations does not lend support to our theoretical expectation as far as the Swiss case is concerned.

Consistent with our engagement hypothesis, *Table 11.1* shows that only employer associations and labour unions published press releases regarding the corporatist negotiations on youth unemployment that occurred in France during our period of interest. The fact that the remaining actors refrained from using this communication tool lends support to the view that this domain was dominated by social partners. With an average of 1.25 press releases, the 4 proved to be slightly more active than the 8 labour unions (0.63).

Table 11.2 provides a detailed overview of the press releases the selected British labour-market organizations issued on the CSR and on the welfare reform during the months of September, October, and November 2010.[1] With respect to the Comprehensive Spending Review, our hypothesis according to which a large diversity of actor types addressed its announcement is confirmed. As is visible from *Table 11.2*, most organizations completed at least one press release. The exceptions concern the Department for Work and Pensions (which focused on the welfare state reform), the Liberal Democrats (who did not hold portfolio in the domains of the economy and social affairs) as well as the two research institutes NPI and CESI. Despite the fact that the political decision-making process took place in the parliamentary arena, the debate on the CSR was by no means restricted to political parties and state actors. It is striking to observe that the actors from the left were much more active than those from the right. Left-wing parties (Labour, SNP, and Greens) published 28 press releases, and the labour unions 33. With respect to the latter, two organizations (TUC and UNISON) proved to be particularly assiduous. By contrast, the Conservatives and the three main employers' associations released only 13 communications altogether. Beyond that, the United Kingdom Independence Party (UKIP) issued 2 press releases. A striking feature of the CSR debate relates to the fact that many actors anticipated the event, as 33 documents were published before the announcement.[2]

---

[1] Press releases by the Taxpayers' Alliance are not included here, since we were not able to collect these documents in the aftermath of the debate on austerity.

[2] This was due to the fact that the Chancellor of the Exchequer had communicated this date in the framework of the so-called Osborne speech on June 22, 2010. The high number of press releases in the run-up to the CSR announcement can be interpreted as attempts by the various actors to influence the government budget decisions.

Table 11.2 *Engagement and positioning (in brackets) of the British labor-market elites*

Organization	CSR	Welfare reform	Total
State actors			
Department for Work and Pensions	0 (–)	10 (1)	10 (1)
Parties			
- Governmental parties			
Conservatives	3 (1)	3 (1)	6 (1)
Liberal Democrats	0 (–)	0 (–)	0 (–)
- Non-governmental parties			
Labour Party	12 (0)	3 (0)	15 (0)
Scottish National Party (SNP)	9 (0)	2 (0.25)	11 (0.05)
Greens	7 (0)	0 (–)	7 (0)
United Kingdom Independence Party (UKIP)	2 (0)	0 (–)	2 (0)
Economic interest groups			
- Employers' associations			
Confederation of Business Industry (CBI)	4 (1)	0 (–)	4 (1)
British Chambers of Commerce (BCC)	3 (0.67)	0 (–)	3 (0.67)
Federation of Small Businesses (FSB)	3 (0.50)	0 (–)	3 (0.50)
- Labour unions			
Trades Union Congress (TUC)	14 (0)	0 (–)	14 (0)
Unite	1 (0)	0 (–)	1 (0)
UNISON	13 (0)	0 (–)	13 (0)
Scottish Trades Union Congress (STUC)	5 (0)	0 (–)	5 (0)
Citizen groups			
Centre for Cities	2 (0.5)	0 (–)	2 (0.5)
National Youth Agency	1 (0.5)	0 (–)	1 (0.5)
Think tanks and research institutes			
New Policy Institute (NPI)	0 (–)	0 (–)	0 (–)
Centre for Economic and Social Inclusion (CESI)	0 (–)	0 (–)	0 (–)
	79	**18**	**97**

The distribution of press releases shown in *Table 11.2* reinforces the impression that the CSR proved to be much more salient than the disclosure of welfare state reform.[3] In fact, 13 out of the 18 press releases pertaining to the latter event originated from the two main promoters of the Universal Credit (UC), i.e., the Department for Work

[3] Given the reform's radical orientations, the widespread lack of public statements in general, and adversarial stances in particular, is worth mentioning. A possible explanation for this finding relates to the fact that the Comprehensive Spending Review forced most political actors to neglect the welfare issue. In addition, the reform plans probably were difficult to communicate to a broader audience, as they turned out to be very complex and technical in nature.

Table 11.3 *Engagement and positioning (in brackets) of the German labour-market elites*

Organization	Hartz IV
State actors	
Federal Employment Agency (BA)	3 (1)
Ministry of Labour and Social Affairs (BMAS)	1 (1)
Ministry of Economics and Technology (BMWi)	0 (–)
Union of Communes (*Kommunale Spitzenverbände*)	1 (0)
Parties	
- Governmental parties	
Conservatives (CDU-CSU)	7 (1)
Liberals (FDP)	4 (0.67)
- Non-governmental parties	
Social Democrats (SPD)	7 (0)
Greens	7 (0)
The Left (*Die Linke*)	21 (0)
National Democratic Party (NPD)	0 (–)
Economic interest groups	
- Employers' associations	
Confederation of Employers' Associations (BDA)	1 (1)
- Labour unions	
Confederation of German Trade Unions (DGB)	4 (0)
IG Metall	0 (–)
Verdi	0 (–)
Citizen groups	
Paritätischer Wohlfahrtsverband	8 (0)
Attac	0 (–)
KOS	3 (0)
ELF	7 (0)
Caritas	1 (0)
Think tanks and research institutes	
IAB	1 (0.5)
Bertelsmann Foundation	0 (–)
INSM	0 (–f)
	76

and Pensions (10 press releases) and the Conservative Party (3 press releases). In addition, the reform of the welfare benefit scheme triggered only some reactions by the Labour Party and the SNP. Thus, the pluralistic pattern of elite participation only observed in the overall debate on austerity only applies to the announcement of the Comprehensive Spending Review.

The overview provided in *Table 11.3* displays the distribution of the press releases on the German Hartz IV reform across the various political organizations. As we have shown previously, the dominance by political party reflects the fact that this minor reform took place in the parliamentary arena. Looking more closely, it turns out that *Die Linke* was particularly active, as the far-left party published 21 press releases. To a lesser extent, citizen groups exhibited a high degree of engagement. Four out of five organizations of this actor category (Caritas, ELF, KOS, and *Paritätischer Wohlfahrtsverband*) published a total of 15 public statements. In line with our reading of the debate that the adjustment of Hartz IV did not pertain to the social partners' domain, the powerful German economic interest groups (i.e., employers and labour unions) published only five press releases on Hartz IV altogether. Nevertheless, we need to mention that many organizations participated in this debate. Among the labour-market organizations under scrutiny, only five abstained from making use of this communication tool – the Ministry of Economics and Technology, National Democratic Party, the Bertelsmann Foundation as well as the two labour unions IG Metall and Verdi.

As emerges from *Table 11.4*, the redundancies by Alstom (23 press releases) and Roche (six press releases) attracted most attention. The big difference between these two cases is attributable to the fact that three national labour unions Unia, Syna, and Angestellte Schweiz (AS) enjoyed contractual partner status in the former, while the latter relied on in-house labour representatives who were not affiliated to any union. Thus, these organizations turned out to be much more active with respect to Alstom. As far as state actors are concerned, the Canton of Argovia tried to limit the damage in terms of job loss in the Alstom quarrel. The same applied to the Canton of Berne in the case of the dismissals by Roche. These state actors communicated with restraint, however, as they negotiated behind closed doors with the concerned firm in order to reduce the magnitude of the job losses.

With respect to the three Swiss events, a closer look at the individual organizations reveals that Unia, the country's biggest labour union, was the only organization to react to all these cases. The white-collar union Angestellte Schweiz did so concerning the dismissal announcements by Alstom and Roche, while the blue-collar union Syna went public regarding the Mayr-Melnhof case. These reaction patterns thus followed a 'sectoral logic'. It needs to be highlighted that the peak labour unions had to contain themselves as labour disputes are meant to take place at the plant-level in Switzerland, i.e., between the firms in question and single labour unions. It is thus consistent that employers' associations and parties

Table 11.4 *Engagement and positioning (in brackets) of the Swiss labour-market elites*

Organization	Alstom	Roche	Others	Total
State actors				
State Secretariat for Economic Affairs (SECO)	0 (–)	0 (–)	0 (–)	0 (–)
Cantonal Ministers of Social Affairs (SODK)	0 (–)	0 (–)	0 (–)	0 (–)
Canton of Argovia (AG)	1 (0.5)	0 (–)	0 (–)	1 (0.5)
Canton of Berne (BE)	0 (–)	2 (0.5)	0 (–)	2 (0.5)
Parties				
- Governmental parties				
Swiss People's Party (SVP)	0 (–)	0 (–)	0 (–)	0 (–)
Social Democrats (SP)	0 (–)	0 (–)	0 (–)	0 (–)
Liberals (FDP)	0 (–)	0 (–)	0 (–)	0 (–)
Christian Democrats (CVP)	0 (–)	0 (–)	0 (–)	0 (–)
Conservative Democratic Party (BDP)	0 (–)	0 (–)	0 (–)	0 (–)
- Non-governmental parties				
Greens	0 (–)	0 (–)	0 (–)	0 (–)
Economic interest groups				
- Employers' associations				
Swiss Employers' Association (SAV)	0 (–)	0 (–)	0 (–)	0 (–)
Small Business Association (SGV)	0 (–)	0 (–)	0 (–)	0 (–)
Swiss Master Builders' Association (SBV)	0 (–)	0 (–)	0 (–)	0 (–)
Swissmem	0 (–)	0 (–)	0 (–)	0 (–)
- Labour unions				
Swiss Federation of Trade Unions (SGB)	0 (–)	0 (–)	1 (0)	1 (0)
Travail Suisse	0 (–)	0 (–)	0 (–)	0 (–)
Unia	7 (0)	4 (0)	7 (0)	18 (0)
Syna	8 (0)	0 (–)	1 (0)	9 (0)
Swiss Employees (AS)	7 (0)	0 (–)	1 (0)	8 (0)
Association of Commercial Employees (KV)	0 (–)	0 (–)	0 (–)	0 (–)
Citizen groups				
KABBA	0 (–)	0 (–)	0 (–)	0 (–)
Attac	0 (–)	0 (–)	0 (–)	0 (–)
Caritas	0 (–)	0 (–)	0 (–)	0 (–)
Think tanks and research institutes				
Avenir Suisse	0 (–)	0 (–)	0 (–)	0 (–)
	23	**6**	**10**	**39**

on the right often take the decentralized setting of industrial relations as a pretext for not reacting to these events.[4]

---

[4] Based on information collected in the framework of our interviews, it turns out that Swiss peak employers' associations usually do not go public in cases of mass dismissals. Indeed, their representatives observed that they refrain from commenting on decisions taken by single firms. They do not consider themselves as a moral authority. In addition, organized business often lacks precise background information, which may lead a given firm to fire people.

Table 11.5 *Engagement and positioning (in brackets)*
of the French labour-market elites

Organization	Negotiations
State actors	
Ministry of Labour	0 (–)
Presidency (Elysée)	0 (–)
Parties	
- Governmental parties	
Conservatives (UMP)	0 (–)
- Non-governmental parties	
Socialists (PS)	0 (–)
Communists (PCF)	0 (–)
Greens (EELV)	0 (–)
MODEM	0 (–)
Front national (FN)	0 (–)
Lutte ouvrière (LO)	0 (–)
Nouveau parti anticapitaliste (NPA)	0 (–)
Economic interest groups	
- Employers' associations	
MEDEF	2 (0.50)
CGPME	1 (1)
UPA	1 (0.50)
UNAPL	1 (1)
- Labour unions	
CGT	1 (0)
CFDT	0 (–)
Force ouvrière (FO)	0 (–)
CFE-CGC	1 (0.50)
CFTC	2 (0.50)
UNSA	1 (0.50)
FSU	0 (–)
Solidaires	0 (–)
Citizen groups	
AC!	0 (–)
MNCP	0 (–)
APEIS	0 (–)
CGT Chômeur	0 (–)
SNC	0 (–)
	10

As we have already shown, the ten French press releases about corporatist negotiations were all published by social partners. *Table 11.5*
reveals that employers' associations and labour unions respectively went
public on five occasions. However, the use of press releases was not

limited to organizations that took part in this decision-making process. The labour union UNSA as well as UNAPL, the umbrella organization of liberal professions, each issued one press release on the topic, although they did participate in these negotiations. This is due to the fact that these organizations have historically not been accepted as negotiation partners by the French state. Inversely, two organizations belonging to the inner power circle of French corporatism did not make use of press releases in relation to the bipartite negotiations at hand. This concerns the two labour unions CFDT and FO. Finally, we should mention that these documents were aired after informal meetings between the actors involved, at the beginning of the negotiations youth unemployment as well as in the framework of annual press conferences some organizations scheduled in January 2011.

Positioning

As is evident from *Table 11.1*, we find a clear opposition between the left and the right regarding the positioning of those organizations that went public by utilizing press releases. Whereas state actors, government parties, and employers' associations tended predominantly to endorse the reform plans, opposition parties, and labour unions took an adversarial stand. As expected, this cleavage proved to be less pronounced in the French negotiations on youth unemployment than in the remaining country cases. The results are thus in line with our hypotheses about the actors' positioning.

In the United Kingdom, actors from the left unequivocally rejected the discussed austerity measures. The figures placed in brackets in *Table 11.1*, which equal 0 for all organizations (with the exception of the SNP), are rather unambiguous in this respect. The left called the government to reconsider its reform plans. By contrast, right-wing parties and British business tended to back the reform. However, some intra-camp nuances in terms of support emerge from *Table 11.2*. Whereas the Conservatives and the Confederation of Business Industry (CBI) fully endorsed the reform plans in public, the British Chambers of Commerce (BCC) and especially the Federation of Small Business (FSB) expressed some concerns. The latter basically welcomed the government's objective to cut the public deficit, but nevertheless urged the coalition to maintain vital spending on infrastructure. In light of these public statements by organized business, our expectation about an unconditional backing of the CSR by the right needs to be nuanced. As far as the radical right is concerned, UKIP took a hostile position. The party specifically rejected the 'Strategic Defence and Security

Review' which was part of the CSR and aimed at an 8 per cent reduction of the defence budget, on the grounds of national security. This adversarial stance confirms our hypothesis about the positioning of the radical right. Yet, it is interesting to note that the UKIP went public when a security issue was at stake. This example illustrates that actors from the radical right are not very likely to address classical redistributive topics. With respect to the Universal Credit reform, a similar picture emerges. The two participating parties from the left (Labour and SNP) basically opposed the reform. By contrast, the documents published by the Tories and the DWP all contained supportive statements towards Universal Credit, thus confirming the expectations about the actors' positioning.

Regarding the positions taken by the various collective actors' publically engaged in the Hartz IV adjustment, numbers presented in *Table 11.3* suggest that this policy debate also corresponded to the classical cleavage between the left and the right. Whereas the former basically pursued an accommodative strategy by supporting the reform, the latter pronounced themselves against it. We need to mention, however, that both state actors and government parties did not completely endorse the discussed proposals. This is attributable to respectively one actor of these actor categories. The association of German municipalities raised some concerns, as it feared to have to bear the financial burden of the adjustment. In addition, the Liberals publically warned their coalition partners from the CDU-CSU not to succumb to the demands of the left. Finally, it is interesting to observe that citizen groups took an adversarial stake in the German case, while these actors adopted a neutral orientation as far as the British debate on austerity is concerned.

As is shown in *Table 11.4*, the two types of active organization markedly differed in the dismissal cases regarding their publically expressed positioning in Switzerland. The various labour unions took an adversarial position by expressing deep concern and being outraged about the firms' sudden announcements. By contrast, the cantonal authorities took a more moderate stance by calling for negotiations to reduce the number of dismissals and to find socially acceptable solutions for those who would have to leave the companies.

In the French case, as is visible from *Table 11.5*, social partners took a neutral or even a supportive stance toward the corporatist negotiations. The only exception concerns CGT, the country's biggest labour union, which refused the propositions made by employers. The widespread lack of adversarial strategies is consistent with our hypothesis about the French case, which comes close to a peaceful setting between negotiating actors. Finally, we would like to highlight that for the remaining press

releases on youth unemployment (not shown here), we observe
a pattern that resembles much more the classical antagonism between
left and right. This is especially the case as far as political parties
are concerned. The right-wing government party UMP pursues an
accommodative strategy, while the Socialists and the Front national
follow an adversarial logic.

Message Convergence

We turn now to the second step of our analysis, which is concerned
with the aspect of message convergence. Political actors generally devote
great attention to the framing of issues (Slothuus 2010). They carefully
choose which messages to emphasize and how to discuss them in the hope
of influencing the opinions of the targeted public (Bernhard 2012).
According to the saliency theory introduced by Budge and Farlie
(1983), political actors try to *selectively emphasize* certain considerations
by placing most attention to the type of messages that favour themselves
and give correspondingly less attention to those which favour their opponents. As opposed to changing citizens' preferences, rhetorical efforts are
directed toward influencing the criteria on which citizens base their
decisions by increasing the salience of certain messages. The theory of
issue ownership states that the advantage arises from reputations the
actors have developed for effective policy making on certain issues.
The political actors have what Petrocik (1996) describes as a history of
attention, initiative and innovation toward these problems, which leads
voters to believe that one of them is more sincere and committed to doing
something about them. Thus, 'issue ownership' appears to provide political organizations with the kind of advantage that Riker (1996) would
describe as 'dominance'. The crucial aspect behind this advantage is
credibility, which is created by the accumulated historical evidence of
the activities related to the issue in question.

Accepting that each issue has different aspects and that the actors
involved in a policy debate enjoy different reputations, we can assume
that the opposing camps rely on different types of messages. For instance,
the left can make a claim to have a credible commitment to solving the
problem of unemployment by improving the workers' labour-market
conditions. The right can similarly make a claim to have a credible
commitment to this issue by promoting flexible labour-market institutions. Following the issue ownership logic, the two opposing sides are very
likely to 'talk past each other' (Budge and Farlie 1983), i.e., to place
emphasis on different kind of aspects. We thus generally expect a *low
degree of message convergence* during the public debates selected here.

Again, we expect the French actors to slightly deviate from their peers in the three other countries under investigation. Given the rather uncontroversial nature of the negotiations between social partners about youth unemployment, the message convergence is expected to display higher levels in France than in Germany, the United Kingdom, and Switzerland.

Our indicator for message convergence is based on a measure proposed by Kaplan et al. (2006):

$$\text{Convergence} = 1 - \left| (S_{Li} - S_{Ri})/(S_{Li} + S_{Ri}) \right|$$

where S_{Li} and S_{Ri} are the salience that the organizations from the left (L) and from the right (R) devoted to the various arguments of the debates. To that end, we assigned the messages available on the press releases to a message categorization we established inductively. We proceeded for each country case separately. In the framework of the present content analysis, messages refer to all kind of statements political actors use in order to convince the readers of press releases from their respective policy positions. The level of the coding occurs at a low level of aggregation. The range of the used convergence measure ranges from 0 (no convergence) to 1 (full convergence).

As expected, the actors from the left and the right tend to past talk each other. There is a clear tendency to emphasize different kinds of messages. The coding of the various press releases reveals that the degree of message convergence varies across countries, however. In line with our hypothesis, our indicator exhibits a higher level in France (0.43) than in the remaining countries (0.21 in the United Kingdom, and 0.23 in Germany). We need to mention that we were not able to calculate this indicator for the Swiss case, given that all actors from the right decided to sit out the topic of mass dismissals (see above).

When looking at the level of single messages, we observe that, despite some marked differences, the actors on either side decided to put emphasis on three identical aspects: the necessity to launch negotiations, the youth's difficult situation in the French labour market, and the objective to reduce the level of unemployment in this age category. In the United Kingdom and Germany, opposing actors relied on very different kinds of considerations. Actors from the left relied on three main messages. First, labour unions and left-wing parties maintained that cuts on this scale would harm the economy by hindering the recovery. They called the CSR a gamble with growth and jobs. In addition, the left opposed the spending reviews on the grounds that the cuts would hit the poor, the sick, and the vulnerable. Third, the opponents described the budget strategy as ideologically driven and considered austerity a political choice, not an economic necessity. By contrast, actors from the right emphasized the necessity of their reform plans, their objective to improve work incentive, as well as the requirement to maintain vital infrastructure. However, both sides agreed on the basic goal to foster growth and create jobs. In Germany, the left primarily urged the necessity to increase benefits of Hartz IV in order to combat poverty. Moreover, many press released called into question the constitutional conformity of the bill proposed by the government. The right focused on the government's competence in social matters. Regarding the time target, government parties and state actors repeatedly maintained that they were 'on track'. Actors from the left and the right nevertheless displayed some convergence in one respect. Both sides deplored that the German communes would be the loser of the planned adjustment.

Negative Campaigning

Finally, we consider the phenomenon of negative campaigning by asking who attacks whom and why. Drawing on theories of decision making under risk, Riker (1996) argues that negative campaigning is pervasive in policy debates. Indeed, political elites are always able to 'go negative'. However, the magnitude of these attacks is expected to depend on the actors' position in a public debate. The reform camp offers an alternative to the status quo that is not completely understood and is vulnerable to deliberate distortion by the defenders of the status quo. Although the reformers always have the possibility of attacking their adversaries, they have an incentive to point out that the reform proposal constitutes an opportunity to do something about these deficiencies and that the proposed reforms will be effective. By contrast, defenders of the status quo have typically nothing to defend positively. The status quo is visible to all and not subject to transformation by rhetorical reinterpretation. The asymmetrical incentives posed by the setting of issue-specific debates lead us to the *structural positioning hypothesis* according to which defenders of the status are more likely to attack those actors who call for a reform (Bernhard 2015).

Applied to the cases selected for this analysis, we expect organizations not represented in government (i.e., collective actors from the left and from the radical right) to attack moderate right actors during the debates in Germany, the United Kingdom, and Switzerland. Taking into account both the arena and the magnitude of the reform, we expect the main senders of these attacks to be opposition parties in Germany (parliamentary arena and minor reform), labour unions in Switzerland (corporatist arena), and all kind of opposition actors in the United Kingdom (parliamentary arena and major reform). As far as the main targets are concerned, government parties and state actors are expected to receive most attacks in Germany and the United Kingdom as the debates took place in the parliamentary arena. With respect to Switzerland, the employers are hypothesized to constitute the main target in the framework of the controversy on mass dismissals. Finally, the level of attacks should display a comparative low level in France. Besides the rather uncontroversial nature of the youth unemployment issue, the fact that the negotiation between social partners tends to blur the barriers between status quo and reform camps renders these actors an unattractive target.

As far as the coding of negative campaigning is concerned, we focus on instances of explicit attacks directed at other actors (Ansolabehere et al. 1994). Following Nai (2013), we do not consider issue-related attacks (i.e., criticism of the issue position taken by other actors) as manifestations of negative campaigning. We accounted for up to three actor-specific attacks per document. The patterns of negativity will be presented in the form of matrices which will contain both the originators and the targets of the coded attacks.

The occurrence of negative campaigning turns out to be highly context-dependent. The highest proportion of attacks is found in Switzerland (0.69 attacks per press release), and Germany (0.68), followed by the United Kingdom (0.42), and France (0.19). The low ratio found in France lends support to our expectation that attacks are rare when a policy domain is dominated by negotiations on a rather uncontroversial issue. As is visible from *Tables 11.5 to 11.8*, most attacks were launched by actors from the opposition (i.e., actors from the left or from the radical right) in the four countries studied here. In the United Kingdom, this was the case in no less than 40 out of 41 attacks. The instances of negative campaigning stemmed from left-wing parties, the United Kingdom Party, and the various labour unions. The grey area in *Table 11.5* shows that all these attacks were directed at the government in its broadest sense (government in general, Conservative Party, and members of the government). The only attack that took the opposite direction originated from the Tories and targeted the Labour Party.

In the German case, the political parties proved to be particularly prone to rely on negativism, as they were responsible for 35 attacks. However, we need to mention that one party decided massively to go negative. *Die Linke* launched 23 attacks, which corresponds to more than one attack per press release on average. Nevertheless, the overall pattern of the 51 attacks proves to be slightly less one-sided than in the United Kingdom. According to the figures presented in *Table 11.6*, 41 attacks follow the hypothesized pattern. These attacks originated from left-wing parties (SPD, Greens, *die Linke*),

Table 11.6 *Attacks during the austerity debate in the United Kingdom*

	Gov.	Tories	Cameron	Osborne	Duncan Smith	Clegg	Labour	Attacks	Attacks/ pr. rel.
Tories							1	1	0.17
Labour		1	1		2	1		5	0.33
SNP	4		1	1				6	0.55
Greens	3			1				4	0.57
UKIP	2							2	1.00
TUC	5							5	0.36
UNITE	1							1	1.00
Unison	6	1	2	3				12	0.92
STUC	2			3				5	1.00
	23	2	4	8	2	1	1	41	

the Confederation of German Trade Unions, and citizen groups (ELF, KOS, PW). Targeted actors included the government in general, state actors (BA and BMAS), members of the government (Merkel, von der Leyen, Westerwelle), and government parties (CDU-CSU, FDP). With respect to the latter, the Conservatives and the Liberals received 17 attacks altogether, which is much more than in the United Kingdom (where we observed only attacks directed at the Tories). Four attacks run in the opposite direction, i.e., from the right to the left. As is visible from *Table 11.6*, these cases all emanated from the CDU and targeted left-wing parties. Interestingly, we also report two intra-camp attacks. The far-left party criticized the Social Democrats (one press release targeted the party, the other one Franz-Walter Steinmeier, a prominent figure of the SPD). Finally, the final category of negative campaigning refers to overall attacks. *Die Linke* decided attacked so-called 'Hartz IV parties' (which include the CDU, the FDP, the SPD, and the Greens) on four instances. This attack strategy is no coincidence, as it reveals the important role played by the moderate left in the context of the parliamentary bargaining on the adjustment of the Hartz IV scheme. Given that Social Democrats and the Greens, due to their majority in the German upper house, were able to block any proposal made by the government from the right, it is consistent that the far-left party put some pressure on these two parties when it became clear that the policy solution had to be found in the framework of Joint Committees, which was characterized by the presence of representatives of both chambers.

Table 11.7 provides an overview of the six attacks we were able to identify in the French case. Quite revealingly, none of these attacks

Table 11.7 *Attacks during the instances of dismissals in Germany*

	Gov.	BMAS	BA	CDU	FDP	Merkel	von der Leyen	Westerwelle	'Hartz IV parties'	SPD	Greens	Linke	Steinmeier	Attacks	Attacks/ pr. rel.
CDU										2	1	1		4	0.57
SPD	1						2							3	0.43
Greens	3				2									5	0.71
Linke	2			5	5	1	3	1	4	1			1	23	1.10
DGB	3													3	0.75
PW	4	1					1							6	0.33
KOS	1													1	0.33
ELF			1	3	2									6	1.00
	14	1	1	8	9	1	6	1	4	3	1	1	1	51	

Table 11.8 *Attacks during the debate on youth unemployment in France*

	Gov.	UMP	Sarkozy	'UMPS'	Unions	Attacks	Attacks/ pr. rel.
PS	1	1				2	0.67
FN			1	1	1	3	3
CFECGC			1			1	0.5
	1	1	2	1	1	6	

occurred in relation to the negotiations on youth unemployment. This confirms the 'peaceful' impression we gained from the major event that took place in France during our empirical investigation. Four out of the six reported attacks followed the expected direction (i.e., left and radical right as sender and the right as receiver). The remaining two attacks stemmed from the *Front national*. The far-right party attacked the labour unions in general as well as the two major parties by using a combined label for the ruling Conservatives and the Socialists ('UMPS').

With respect to Switzerland, the attacks made in the context of events of mass dismissals follow one clear pattern. As emerges from *Table 11.8*, the labour unions AS, Syna, and Unia turned out to be the only actors that relied on negative campaigning. A large share of their press releases contained one attack. Unia went negative by attacking the various firms which announced to fire employees (Alstom, Roche, Mayr-Melnhof, Clariant, Karl Meyer, and Suez-Cofely). Thus, our hypothesis can be confirmed for the Swiss case.

Conclusion

The objective of this chapter was to shed light on the strategic interplay between the political actors involved in public debates. In order to explore the inner workings of the interaction context, we relied on a content analysis of the press releases the selected labour-market elites published during our field period in the United Kingdom, Germany, France, and Switzerland. To begin with, we looked at how the labour-market elites dealt with the major debate-specific events. We found that the political decision-making arena and the importance of a given political decision influence the actors' decision to get involved. More specifically, our results suggest that political parties tend to dominate events related to the parliamentary arena. When the issue becomes important, the whole elites tend to go public.

Table 11.9 *Attacks during the instances of dismissals in Switzerland*

	Alstom	Roche	Mayr-Melnhof	Clariant	Karl Meyer	Cofely-Suez	Attacks	Attacks/pr. rel.
AS	5		1				6	0.75
Syna	7		1				8	0.89
Unia	5	4	2		1	1	13	0.72
	17	4	2	2	1	1	27	

Subsequently, we considered the actors' strategies in terms of positioning. Our empirical analysis has been able to show that oppositional forces tend to adopt adversarial strategies toward the major issue-specific decisions. The only exception concerns uncontroversial issue domains on which the most important actors take part in the decision-making process, as the case of the French negotiations on youth unemployment suggests.

In a second step, we focused on issue framing by examining the level of message convergence between actors from the left and those from the right. We have established that actors from different camps tend to put emphasis on different aspect. Higher levels of message convergence are observable on comparatively uncontroversial issue-specific debates.

Finally, we examined attack politics. We have been able to demonstrate that the left and the radical right tend to heavily rely on negative campaigning by attacking government actors. Only in rare instances do the latter revert to negative campaigning. The two cases which occurred in the parliamentary arena (Germany and United Kingdom) suggest that the government's main target is its main party competitor from the left.

Taken together, three main conclusions emerge from this chapter. First, the cleavage between left and right seems to be prevalent when it comes to the interaction context. Actors from the left have generally been shown to be more active in public. This can be attributed to the fact that the left enjoys some kind of 'issue ownership' in the labour-market domain. An alternative explanation refers to the actor configuration during our period of investigation, as the right dominated the national governments in all country cases under scrutiny. Thus, the left faced an incentive to go public in order to mobilize public opinion. The fact that the left found itself in opposition certainly helps explain why these actors rejected the discussed reform proposal and attacked their fellows from the right in most instances. Second, this section has highlighted the crucial role played by debate characteristics. Most notably, the importance of the decision-making arena regarding the types of actors who are likely to go public suggest that the inner workings of the interaction context can only be understood when taking into account the specific setting in which it takes place.

Third, we have been able to present some differences between the country-specific debates, which may be essential for the reading of the country studies. As a case in point, we have established that the intensity of the various debates was rather different from one country to the other, thus confirming the figures presented in Chapter 4. While the debate on austerity caused quite a stir among the British labour-market elites, the French negotiations on youth unemployment only attracted a small population of collective actors. Its narrow scope and the lack of controversy explain why the opposition between employers and labour unions was less pronounced and instances of negative campaigning did not occur. The German debate on Hartz IV turned out to be an intermediate case, which came much closer to the British case. Finally, Swiss elite behaviour is very interesting from a theoretical perspective. Labour unions tried to politicize instances of mass dismissals, but failed to do so, as the remaining actors did not react to these events. Hence, the Swiss case can be interpreted as a debate that failed to take off. In a nutshell, this chapter has highlighted the crucial role played by debate characteristics when it comes to explain patterns of actor interactions across country contexts.

12   Quality of Public Debates

Regula Hänggli and Richard van der Wurff

As introduced at the beginning of this book, public debates are the sum of all public communications related to an issue in a process of argument and counterargument (Helbling et al. 2012). These debates may differ in terms of inclusiveness (who participates), diversity (what views are heard), style (ranging from very populist name-calling to a rational exchange of ideas), location (in news media, online forums, or packed halls), and level of moderation. Building on a review of normative and empirical studies, we argue that it is useful to characterize public debates in terms of their style and diversity. We also propose that these character-istics are ultimately shaped by countries' political and media systems. We explore these ideas by investigating and comparing actor perceptions of these dimensions across the most important public debate in each country, i.e. across six of our eight debates.

Cornerstone of Democracy

Public debates are a defining characteristic of democracy. Many scholars would agree with statement. But views diverge immediately when we start to explore these public debates further. Normative democratic theories in particular present different ideas about who should participate (only elites? Or the public too?) and consequently what views should be expressed (all possible views or only those of important social groups?); how ideas should be presented (dispassionate and reasonable, or also emotional and offensive?); and what the aims of public debate are and should be (transparency for voters, careful consideration of options, mobilization of supporters, rapid closure and effective decision-making, empowerment and recognition of minority groups and views, or trans-cendence of self-interests and a higher level of rational decision-making) (Ferree et al. 2002, Strömbäck 2005). Deliberative theory in particular argues that public debates should be diverse, informed, rational, and civil (e.g., Wessler 2008). But empirical research on news media reporting suggests that coverage might rather emphasize one dominant view and

257

focus on strategic and sensationalist aspects. Likewise, actors may excel in populist rhetorics (Jagers & Walgrave 2007), discrediting opponents, rather than engage in the rational exchange of arguments that is advocated by deliberative theory. Based on these ideas, we propose the analysis of two important characteristics of public debates: (1) debate diversity; and (2) debate style.

Debate Diversity and Debate Style

Whether phrased according to the American notion of the "marketplace of ideas," the journalistic principle of "balanced reporting," or public broadcasters' missions to serve and bring together wide ranges of people, the diversity of ideas and opinions is an important indicator of media performance in modern Western democracies (see Müller 2014[1]). Scholars expect media content to reflect and express a range of views, and to confront audiences with dissenting beliefs. They consider political diversity to be an important condition for well-informed decision-making and an expression of a healthy democracy (McQuail 1992). Porto (2007) even identifies idea diversity as the most important factor enabling citizens to make real-life political choices.

Diversity of news media content encompasses at least two dimensions: diversity of *sources* cited, and diversity of *ideas* expressed. These two types of content diversity are generally considered to be related, although empirical research suggests that source diversity does not, in fact, guarantee idea diversity (Voakes et al. 1996). Content diversity, in turn, is considered to stimulate exposure diversity: the reception of diverse ideas by audiences (van der Wurff 2011). A further important distinction to be made is between *internal* and *external* diversity of media content (McQuail and van Cuilenburg 1983, Wessler 2008). A media outlet is internally diverse if it presents different ideas within its columns. Media outlets, by contrast, are externally diverse when each partisan outlet presents a different voice. Media outlets are then internally homogeneous, but together offer a range of views.

Internal diversity implies that audience members are inevitably exposed to diverse content options, even if they use but one media outlet. It contributes to the reception of antagonistic ideas and stimulates deliberations across political groups. External diversity rather implies that audiences can choose to receive only like-minded information.

---

[1] According to Müller, we are dealing with the horizontal function of democracy at the content level which requires the representation of diverse societal viewpoints in the news coverage.

It contributes to user choice, and enables societal groups to develop their own ideas and build internal cohesion. But external diversity also facilitates audience fragmentation. Especially with the rise of an abundance of partisan online information sources, some fear that external diversity contributes to the emergence of cyber-ghettos (Johnson et al. 2009). Yet, empirical findings suggest that audiences do not shy away from dissonant ideas and might even have some preference for diversity (van der Wurff 2011).

Debate Diversity and Opinion Quality

Several studies have shown empirically that audience exposure to diverse ideas can stimulate information processing and reduce the likelihood of manipulation (Zaller 1992). For example, citizens who are exposed to opposing arguments of an issue are more likely to choose the alternative that is consistent with their values and predispositions (Sniderman and Theriault 2004, Chong and Druckman 2007a). Moreover, individuals are more motivated to engage in conscious evaluation when they are exposed to opposing considerations (Chong and Druckman 2007b). However, the impact of diversity on the quality of the opinion depends on, among other things, the quality of the messages (Barabas 2004). While diversity motivates citizens to process information more intensely, it is the quality of arguments rather than superficial cues that count (Petty et al. 2009). This reminds us of the deliberative principle that different ideas should not only be stated in the media but also justified, and that counterclaims should be rebutted (Wessler 2008). Without this, diversity of ideas cannot lead to reasoned opinions but merely presents different lone voices crying in the wilderness.

Whether news media indeed regularly confront citizens with a diverse supply of justified ideas is a matter for empirical investigation. Generally speaking, available studies seem to suggest that representations of public debates in news media, in contradiction to normative expectations, tend to be dominated by elite sources and the dominant elite view, or at best two conflicting elite views (Tewksbury et al. 2000, Cottle and Rai 2006, Gamson and Modigliani 1987, Lee et al. 2008). There is relatively little room for alternative minority viewpoints (Bennett 1990b, Graber 2003, Bennett et al. 2004, Dimitrova and Strömbäck 2009). Recently, alternative views have found new outlets online, but overall, the reach of these outlets is small compared with mainstream media.

Based on these considerations, and following Bennett et al. (2004) and Wessler (2008), we define three indicators to assess diversity in mediated debates: whether different actors are involved; whether one or more viewpoints are presented; and whether these viewpoints are justified.

The second characteristic we propose is the style of debates. Deliberative models of democracy advocate a rational, information-rich and issue-oriented style. Deliberation – it is argued – requires mutual civility and respect for the opinions of others, as conditions that enable and support the exchange and justification of arguments (Habermas 1996, Wessler 2008, De Vries et al. 2010, Bächtiger et al. 2010b, Zhang et al. 2013). Such a style is substantive and not contest-oriented (Hänggli and Kriesi 2012). We call it a policy-oriented debate style.

In contrast to this policy-oriented debate style, we propose a media-oriented debate style. This style builds upon the idea that capturing and retaining audience interest is at least as important for the success of political actors as providing substantive arguments and information. It reflects the growing dominance of a commercial logic in media, the concomitant professionalization of political communication, and the related rise of populism – trends that have been extensively discussed in the political communication literature (Strömback 2008). Political actors and media increasingly follow a media logic in their communication activities rather than a journalistic or public logic. They build communication strategies around news values, dramatizing, personalizing, and emotionalizing the news. This results in the growth of strategic, horse race and news, the personalization of politics, and a shortening of sound bites (Hallin 1992, Blumer and Kavanagh 1999, Brants and van Praag 2006). Applying these trends to public debates, we propose that the media-oriented style relies on rhetoric and the strategic use of news values rather than substance, sound bites rather than lengthy arguments, and attempts to discredit opponents rather than uphold mutual respect. This media-oriented style is thus the opposite of the careful and rational approach advocated in the deliberative model of democracy.

Debate Style and Opinion Quality

Research suggests that the rise of media logic undermines the ability of news media to inform their customers about what is going on in today's society. For example, Iyengar et al. (2004) show that news media users are more interested in horse race and strategy news – focusing on the campaigning and communication strategies and tactics of politicians – than in substantive, issue-oriented coverage. However, the latter type of news is more informative to audiences than the former. Jamieson and Cappella (1997) likewise show that media coverage of political events and issues emphasizes the "game" of politics rather than its substance. In their view, this starts a "spiral of cynicism," which causes an erosion of citizen interest and, ultimately, citizen participation. Of course, the style of public debates will differ according to the country, time period and medium considered. Swiss direct-democratic campaigns, for example, are found to be quite substantive, whereas in US elections, campaigners rely heavily on negative or attack advertisements (Iyengar and McGrady 2007: 147ff.). Likewise, news media reporting on Dutch election campaigns is more substantive than US reporting (Brants and van Praag 2006).

Building on this literature, we propose to assess the style of mediated public debates in terms of three indicators: the extent to which the debate is civilized, the extent to which actors respect other views, and the extent to which the focus in the debate is on the substance itself. These differentiate a policy-oriented style – involving an issue-oriented, rational style of debating and substantive contributions that focus on the issue(s) at stake – from a media-oriented style – involving a disrespectful, emotional style of debating and non-substantive media contributions that highlight the contest per se: the horse race (who wins?) and the strategies and tactics (what are they doing to win?).

Types of Public Debate

The combination of the two dimensions gives us four types of public debates: Scandalous; Insider; Competitive; and Deliberative (see *Table 12.1*).

Scandalous debates are characterized by a media-oriented style and present only one dominant view. This term is based on the work of Kepplinger (2009), who defines publicistic conflicts as scandalous if there is only one legitimate position. In Switzerland, the campaign against pit bull terriers and other breeds of fighting dog in the winter of 2005/

Table 12.1 *Public debate types*

		Style	
		Media-oriented	Policy-oriented
Diversity	High	Competitive	Deliberative
	Low	Scandalous	Insider

2006 can be considered as an example of a scandalous public debate which was led by the media. The issue arose because several children had been attacked or even killed by such dogs. Since 2000, the major Swiss tabloid newspaper *Blick* has put the issue at the top of its agenda several times and supported the claim that these dogs should be banned. Another example is the media campaign against the plans of the incoming Liberal-Labour government in the Netherlands in 2012 to reform the health-care payment system. The key to this reform was the attempt to make health-care payment more dependent on income. Led by the right-wing newspaper *De Telegraaf*, and joined by the main public and commercial television news broadcasts, news media hyped the issue and created considerable citizen opposition and unrest. Thousands of people responded angrily on newspaper websites and to politicians, but only after news media published critical comments, major headlines and doubtful calculations about the implications of the reform for different income groups. Within two weeks, the plan was withdrawn by the government.

Insider debates are policy-oriented in style and dominated by one single view. Public debates in the follow-up to a crisis like the financial crisis or 9/11 would fit into this category when there is only one legitimate position (Kepplinger 2009). *Competitive debates* are media-oriented in style and tend to present a variety of views. Bächtiger et al. (2010a: 203) suggest that the most typical public debate is competitive. In addition to public debates, election campaigns are typically competitive debates too. They are characterized by argument contestation, and the style can be quite media-oriented during election campaigns. *Deliberative debates* are policy-oriented in terms of style and show a diversity of views. Deliberative debates do not necessarily meet the standards of deliberativeness. However, of the four types of debate distinguished in this chapter, this type comes closest – especially if the communication style becomes highly policy-oriented (Bächtiger et al. 2010a: 205). Swiss direct-democratic campaigns could be considered good examples of deliberative debates. Direct-democratic campaigns typically give rise to a confrontation between two opposing camps. This is a consequence of the binary choice: Direct-democratic campaigns force voters to choose either in favor of (pro) or against (con) an issue-specific proposition at stake. Generally, one camp claims the position of the government and the majority of Parliament, and the other argues in favor of the position of some challengers and the minority of Parliament. In addition, the communication style is relatively substantive (Hänggli 2018).

Determinants of Debate Diversity and Style

We focus here on actor perceptions of the diversity and the style of mediated public debates. We expect these two debate dimensions to vary across countries and debates, ultimately reflecting structural differences in political and media systems as well as policy-specific coalition dynamics (e.g., Esser 2008). In addition, we expect actor perceptions of these debate dimensions to depend on characteristics of those actors themselves, in particular their power, extremity of views, and type of organization (actor characteristics). We first discuss country and debate characteristics that influence debate diversity.

Country-level Influences on Debate Diversity – Structural Pluralism: Strength of State and Strength of Civil Society

Diversity in mediated public debates depends first of all on structural pluralism (Demers 1998), which refers to the number and variety of views that are present in society and the relative power position of actors supporting these views (also Bennett 1990b, Entman 2003). When diverging ideas are present in society and supported by equally strong actors, it is more likely that diverse ideas will be expressed in media content. On the other hand, when – for example, in case of war or terrorist attack – elite and public opinion rally behind the dominant national position (Schudson 2002), little media diversity can be expected. The same holds for (local) communities dominated by a single political-economic elite (Demers 1998).

We assess structural pluralism in the area of labor policy (the focus of our study) with two fundamental indicators: the strength of the state, and the strength of civil society. Strong states will dominate news reporting and contribute to lower diversity of debates. Esser (2008), for example, argues that the traditional strong position of the state in France has contributed to a non-interventionist political news culture in this country, where journalists follow the lead of government when reporting on policy issues. Strong social actors (and a strong parliament with strong opposition parties), on the other hand, can counterbalance the influence of the state and add different ideas to (mediated) public debates. In labor policy issues, relevant social actors include unions, businesses and industrial organizations, and experts or think tanks.[2]

---

[2] Another possible explanation links diversity to the role of media ownership. According to this line of reasoning, one could argue that newspapers' tendency to follow government when reporting news is linked to the amount of resources journalists have. In fact, press resources have dropped quite substantively in France. However, if one controls for resources it does not explain the outstanding position of France and does not contribute to explain the finding. Italy, for instance, has similarly reduced means and not such a low level of diversity.

Two countries in our sample – France and Denmark – are generally considered to have strong states, characterized by an autonomous relationship to its environment and a centrally organized internal structure (Badie and Birnbaum 1983). Social actors, in turn, are relatively strong in corporatist countries, defined as countries where centralized unions and employers play an important role in economic policy and management (Siaroff 1999: 177). Denmark, Germany, and Switzerland belong to this group of corporatist countries (Lijphart and Crepaz 1991, Siaroff 1999, Kriesi 2007: 286). These are, at the same time, consensus democracies where parliament and opposition parties have relatively strong positions and thus more impact on media reporting than in majoritarian democracies (Van Dalen 2012). France, Italy, and the UK on the other hand are characterized by a weakly organized and fragmented society (Lijphart and Crepaz 1991, Siaroff 1999, Kriesi 2007: 286) and by majoritarian political systems. Here we expect social actors and opposition parties to have less impact on the debate, which will lead to less debate diversity. We hypothesize:

HIA: Debate diversity will be lower in countries with stronger states (Denmark, France).

HIB: Debate diversity will be lower in countries with weaker civil societies (France, Italy, UK).

Strong social actors may counterbalance the influence of a strong state and contribute to concerted action in labor policy and a more diverse mediated debate. On the other hand, when a strong state coexists with a weak civil society – as in France – both effects may reinforce each other, resulting in "etatist intervention" (Kriesi 2007: 286) in the economy and a state-dominated debate. Thus, we expect:

HIC: Debate diversity will be especially low in countries with both a strong state and a weak civil society (i.e. France).

Characteristics of the Media system

In addition to structural pluralism, debate diversity also depends on characteristics of the media system; that is, on journalistic and media organizational forces that induce media to seek out existing alternative views and to give more equal access to relevant diverging ideas and actors (McQuail and Van Cuilenburg 1983). A relevant distinction here is the one made by Hallin and Mancini (2004) between democratic-corporatist, liberal and polarized-pluralist systems (see also Chapter 3). Journalism in polarized-pluralist systems is less professionalized than in democratic-corporatist and liberal systems, and news media are more closely aligned with political actors. Accordingly, in polarized-pluralist systems, news media are internally less diverse. Each news medium would primarily present its own political view. In democratic-corporatist and liberal systems, on the other hand, professional journalists are expected to provide relatively neutral, balanced and diverse media coverage. In our sample, Denmark, Germany, and Switzerland adhere to the corporatist-democratic model, the UK represents the liberal model, and France and Italy the polarized-pluralist model. Hence, we predict:

H2: The diversity of the debate is lower in countries with a polarized-pluralist media system (i.e. France, Italy) than in countries with democratic-corporatist or liberal media systems (Denmark, Germany, Switzerland, the UK).

Country-level Influences on Debate Style – Political Communication Systems

When explaining the style of debates, at the country level, the political communication system (i.e. the communication activities of relevant actors) as well as the media system (the way these activities are expressed and mediated by journalists) are theoretically relevant. In Chapter 3 we characterized the political communication system in terms of two dimensions: whether the distance between journalists and politicians is large or small, and whether communication activities (specifically, the writing of press releases) are guided by a media or political logic. Although both dimensions overlap in practice (at least for the countries investigated in this volume, see Chapter 3), we focus for theoretical reasons in particular on the latter dimension that characterizes the activities of the political and social actors in the debates that we investigate.

In Switzerland, Germany, and France, political communication systems are driven by substantive and political considerations (Chapter 3). Perhaps facilitated by and contributing to a larger distance between journalists and politicians in these countries, political actors' communication activities are dominated by a political logic. This contrasts with the populist communication systems of Italy, the UK and (surprisingly) also Denmark. In these countries, media considerations dominate the communication activities of political actors, and journalists and politicians have closer professional and personal contacts. We predict these characteristics of the political communication system to influence the style of mediated public debates:

H3: The style of public debates will be more media-oriented in countries with a populist political communication system (i.e. in Denmark, Italy and the UK) and more policy-oriented in countries where political communication activities are dominated by a political logic (i.e. France, Germany, and Switzerland).

Actor Characteristics on Debate Diversity and Style

Actor perceptions of the mediated public debates will depend not only on structural characteristics at the country level, but also on some characteristics of the actors themselves. Specifically, we expect the power, extremity, and type of actors to play a role.

Power and Debate Diversity

First, we predict that perceptions of the diversity of debates depend on the power of actors. The underlying intuition is that a lack of diversity is most easily grasped when one's own view is not represented in the media. In this respect, it is important that powerful actors tend to have preferential access to media coverage. Numerous studies have shown that media attention is biased toward these actors (e.g., Galtung and Ruge 1965, Gans 1979, Schulz 1997, Hänggli 2012b, see also Chapter 9); and content primarily represents the views of these elites. As Bennett argued in his indexing hypothesis, "[m]ass media news professionals (. . .) tend to 'index' the range of voices and viewpoints (. . .) according to the range of views expressed in mainstream government debate about a given topic" (Bennett 1990b: 106). Hence, it is unlikely that powerful actors will experience that their view is *not* covered in the public debate. This means that powerful actors are less likely to observe a lack of diversity than less powerful actors. Rephrased in positive terms, we hypothesize:

H4: More powerful actors are more likely to perceive diverse debates than less powerful actors.

Extremity and Debate Style

Second, we expect that more extreme actors – that is, actors, with more extreme views – will perceive the debate to be more media-oriented, because of their outsider status. After all, extreme actors tend to pursue a different goal than moderate actors. The latter might pursue the goal of influencing the issue at stake or winning the next election. By contrast, extreme actors aim rather at maintaining grassroots participation, limiting leadership control and harnessing public support. Harmel and Janda (1994: 275) call this the "intraparty democracy" goal. To reach this goal, extreme actors aim at strengthening the group identity. One way to strengthen this identity is to distinguish between in-group and out-group, and to denounce the others or to be less respectful. Extreme actors have indeed found to use more contest frames (Hänggli and Kriesi 2012). In addition, members of extreme organizations are found to use a different style of political engagement (McClosky and Chong 1985). They are more likely to attribute personal failings to those who are far from their own political ideals. This may focus the attention of extreme actors, consciously or unconsciously, on media-oriented aspects of the debate. Finally, extreme actors, because of their outsider status, will be covered less intensively and less substantively in news media than mainstream actors (e.g., Bennett et al. 2004). This will reinforce extreme actors' perception that the debate is media-oriented. Thus, we expect:

H5: Extreme actors are more likely to perceive public debates to be media-oriented rather than policy-oriented, in comparison to more moderate actors.

Actor Type and Debate Diversity and Style

In addition to power and extremity, actor perceptions of diversity and style of debates may vary with other characteristics. For example, parties in government and the administration tend to respond substantively to issues raised by the media (see also: Walgrave and van Aelst 2006). This reflects both the potential power of these actors to act substantively as well as the care they have to take to maintain intricate intra-coalition relationships. For non-governing actors it is relatively easy and safe to jump on the media bandwagon and demand "drastic measures"; much more than it is for coalition parties and the administration (if the administration becomes active at all). Accordingly, we assume that government parties and the administration, confronted with these media-oriented activities of the opposition, will consider the debate less substantive and diverse than they would prefer. To assess, we investigate:

H6: Actors belonging to the government parties or the administration perceive the debate as less substantive and policy-oriented than other actors.

Operationalization

We analyze six of the unemployment-related debates, one per country: The debate on youth unemployment in France, the labor dispute in Italy, the spending review debate in the UK, the government reform of unemployment policy in Denmark, the Hartz IV unemployment benefit reform in Germany, and the debate on mass dismissals in Switzerland (for more information, see Chapter 4).

Debate Diversity and Style

All actors involved in these debates were asked several questions about the quality of the debates. Three items asked about respondents' perceptions of the *diversity* of the debate. They were asked whether many different actors participated (participation), whether a wealth of different viewpoints was present (different views), and whether the actors gave lots of reasons and explanations for their views (justification). Three more questions covered the *communication style*. Respondents were asked how substantive, how respectful, and how civilized they perceived the debate to be. The exact wording of the questions can be found in Appendix 12.1. Response categories for all items range from strongly agree to strongly disagree on a 5-point Likert scale.

Table 12.2 shows the underlying factor analysis and demonstrates that these six items load onto two factors, as expected. Hence, the individual indicators are aggregated to the two dimensions. Cronbach's alpha is high: For diversity, it is 0.79, and for style it is 0.87. Both dimensions are standardized, i.e. have a mean of 0 and a standard deviation of 1. Style ranges from −2.1 to 2.0, while diversity ranges from −2.4 to 1.7.

Table 12.2 *Results of exploratory factor analysis*

	Factor 1	Factor 2
	Style	Diversity
Respectful	0.92	0.13
Civilized	0.88	0.03
Substantive	0.83	0.24
Participation	−0.03	0.88
Justified	0.22	0.82
Different views	0.31	0.76
Eigenvalue	3.04	1.52

The standardized mean of each factor (which equals 0) serves as the cut-off values for the respective dimension.

Determinants of Diversity and Style

To assess the impact of determinants on debate characteristics, we include a range of dummy variables. For debate diversity, these differentiate between countries with strong and weak states (Strong State = 1 for Denmark and France); countries with weak and strong social actors (Weak Corporatism =1 for France, Italy and the UK); and belonging to the polarized-pluralist media system or other media systems (Polarized-Pluralist = 1 for Italy and France). We also include an interaction term (strong state * weak corporatism = 1 for France) to assess the reinforcing impact of both determinants. For debate style, we include a dummy variable that distinguishes between countries in which political communication activities are dominated by a political or a media logic (populist political communication system = 1 for Denmark, Italy, and the UK. As an alternative, we also use country dummies.

The power of actors is operationalized by a reputational indicator as introduced in Chapter 5. It is measured at the organizational level and standardized. Extremity of actors is measured on a left–right polarity scale. We asked the political actors where they would position their organization on a scale from 0 to 10, with 0 being far left and 10 being far right. The distance from 5 is used as extremity measure.[3] Finally, all actors are classified as belonging to one of the following actor type categories: governing party, administration, non-governing party, union, business interest association, social movement organization, think tanks and charities. Actors not belonging to governing party or the administration are the reference category in the models.

Results

Table 12.3 investigates how the selected cases fit in the proposed typology. First, we focus on the diversity dimension. One-sample t-tests show that debate diversity, on average and in the perception of German actors, is significantly higher than the overall mean (0), whereas debate diversity in France is significantly lower ($p < 0.05$). Perceptions of debate diversity in

---

[3] We also used an alternative extremity measure: Positions between 3 and 8, and missing values were coded as being moderate. The remaining positions are coded as extreme. The results did not change.

Table 12.3 *Country means of factors*

Country	Mean	95% CI			
		Lower	Upper		
Diversity					
CH	0.12	−0.31	0.56		
D	0.42	0.13	0.70	*	F
DK	0.10	−0.23	0.43		
F	−0.70	−1.22	−0.18	°	D
I	0.08	−0.36	0.53		
UK	0.03	−0.77	0.82		
Style					
CH	0.40	0.11	0.70	*	UK, I
D	−0.26	−0.63	0.11		F
DK	−0.14	−0.50	0.22		F
F	1.06	0.66	1.45	**	D, DK, I, UK
I	−0.96	−1.43	−0.50	**	CH, F
UK	−0.51	−0.76	−0.25	*	CH, F

Superscripts in one but last column indicate that a one-sample
t-test shows that the mean score for a country differs significantly
from 0 at *** $p < 0.001$, ** $p < 0.01$, * $p < 0.05$.
Country indicators in last column indicates that a Games-Howell
post-hoc test shows the mean score for a country differs
significantly at $p < 0.05$ from mean scores of indicated other
countries.

the other four countries hover, on average, around the mean. In addition,
analysis of variance and Games-Howell post-hoc tests show that debate
diversity in Germany is significantly higher than in France ($p < 0.05$). But
differences between all other combinations of countries are not
significant.

The differences in style are larger. One-sample t-tests show that the
style in Switzerland and France is definitely on the policy-oriented side;
the style in Italy and the UK on the media-oriented side. The style in
Germany and Denmark is mixed (does not differ significantly from 0).
Likewise, analysis of variance and Games-Howell post-hoc tests confirm
that the debate style in France and Switzerland is more policy-oriented
than in Italy and the UK and – as far as France is concerned – also more
policy oriented than in Denmark and Germany.

Figure 12.1 shows a visual representation of the country means. In line
with the results above, we can see once more that the debate in Germany

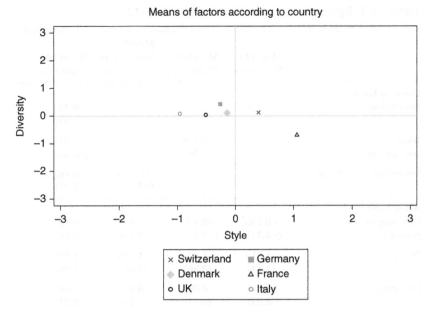

Figure 12.1 Mapping the public debates according to the two quality criteria

Note: The basis of this figure is provided in *Table 12.7.*

is relatively diverse compared with France. The debates in the other countries are very similar in terms of diversity of expressed ideas. We can also state that there are larger differences across countries in style than in diversity. The style is clearly more policy-oriented in Switzerland and France than in Italy and UK. In Germany and Denmark, the style is mixed, "in-between" media- and policy-oriented.

These descriptives indicate that our typology is to some extent useful to describe the differences in debates across different countries. In the next section, we set out to explain these differences. Since communication style varies more than diversity, the driving factors of style (and its hypothesis) also might explain more.

Determinants of Diversity and Style

We look first at factors that influence debate diversity. We present different regression models, testing the impact of different factors. Model 1a and 1c support the idea (as predicted in H1a and H1c) that the strength of state and the interaction between a strong state and weak social actors in France

Table 12.4 *Influence factors on diversity: Model 1a-1d*

	Model 1a: Strong state	Model 1b: Weak corp.	Model 1c: Strong state * weak corp.	Model 1d: Combination
Country level				
Strong state	-0.529^{**}			-0.253
	(-2.90)			(-0.95)
Weak corporatism		-0.288		-0.076
		(-1.59)		(-0.36)
Strong state * weak corp.			-0.726^{**}	-0.467
			(-3.32)	(-1.27)
Actor level				
Extremity of positions	-0.130^{*}	-0.127^{*}	-0.125^{*}	-0.127^{*}
	(-2.22)	(-2.11)	(-2.16)	(-2.18)
Power	1.813^{***}	1.570^{**}	1.505^{**}	1.598^{**}
	(3.54)	(2.96)	(2.96)	(3.05)
Gov. party	-0.010	0.034	-0.051	-0.067
	(-0.03)	(0.11)	(-0.18)	(-0.23)
Admin	0.202	0.254	0.271	0.211
	(0.64)	(0.78)	(0.88)	(0.66)
Constant	0.007	-0.000	0.019	0.083
	(0.04)	(-0.00)	(0.11)	(0.40)
Observations	111	111	111	111
Adjusted R^2	0.21	0.17	0.23	0.22

t statistics in parentheses.
$^{*} p < 0.05$, $^{**} p < 0.01$, $^{***} p < 0.001$.
Note: Strong state and weak corporatism correlate with 0.68.

Table 12.5 *Influence factors on diversity*

	Model 2: Country dummies
Country level	
France	-0.745^{**}
	(-2.68)
Denmark	-0.203
	(-0.67)

Table 12.5 *(cont.)*

	Model 2: Country dummies
UK	−0.146
	(−0.46)
Germany	0.114
	(0.41)
Italy	0.062
	(0.22)
Actor level	
Extremity of positions	−0.130[*]
	(−2.17)
Power	1.603[**]
	(3.01)
Gov. party	−0.066
	(−0.22)
Admin	0.194
	(0.60)
Constant	0.035
	(0.14)
Observations	111
Adjusted R^2	0.21

t statistics in parentheses.
[*] $p < 0.05$, [**] $p < 0.01$, [***] $p < 0.001$.

Table 12.6 *Influence factors on diversity: Model 3*

	Model 3: Pol.plur. media system
Country level	
Pol. plur. media system	−0.327
	(−1.74)
Actor level	
Extremity of positions	−0.119
	(−1.97)
Power	1.534[**]
	(2.89)

Table 12.6 *(cont.)*

	Model 3: Pol.plur. media system
Gov. party	0.042 (0.14)
Admin	0.304 (0.95)
Constant	−0.033 (−0.17)
Observations	111
Adjusted R^2	0.17

t statistics in parentheses.
* $p < 0.05$, ** $p < 0.01$, *** $p < 0.001$.

reduce the diversity of the debate. Corporatism, however, does not have a significant influence on its own (Model 1b, contradicting H1b). In the combined model (Model 1d), both the strong state and the interaction term become insignificant because they are highly correlated (0.68). We see, however, that the interaction term is stronger. In model 2 (*Table 12.5*), we use country dummies instead. This model shows that France stands out. Considering all findings presented so far, we conclude that that it is in particular the combination of strong state and weak corporatism, as seen in France that reduces diversity. In model 3 (see *Table 12.6*), we test the influence of the polarized pluralist media system and find that it does not matter. Thus, the media system is no driving factor of debate diversity.

Considering the actor characteristics, we find in all models that more powerful actors indeed perceive the debate to be more diverse (in line with H4). Actor type has no impact. We also included actor extremity as additional control in the regression, and found an effect in model 1 and 2. In model 3, the effect is close to be significant ($p < 0.06$). On the basis of these findings we conclude that powerful actors perceive debates to be more diverse whereas extreme actors tend to perceive it as less diverse. Actor type does not play a role.

Table 12.7 shows which factors influence the communication style. First, we see that the style of debates is definitely more media-oriented in populist political communication systems (in line with H3). Regarding actor characteristics, the findings show that actors with

Table 12.7 *Influence factors on communication style: Model 1 and 2*

	Model 1: Pop. pol. comm. system	Model 2: Country dummies
Country level		
Pop. pol. comm. system	−0.976*** (6.00)	
France		0.624** (2.92)
Denmark		−0.667** (−2.88)
UK		−1.037*** (−4.22)
Germany		−0.843*** (−3.96)
Italy		−1.314*** (−6.02)
Actor level		
Extremity of positions	−0.204*** (−3.71)	−0.214*** (−4.66)
Power	0.459 (0.96)	0.537 (1.31)
Gov. party	−0.440 (−1.64)	−0.296 (−1.31)
Admin	−0.176 (−0.59)	−0.214*** (−4.66)
Constant	−0.265 (−1.43)	0.730*** (3.80)
Observations	111	111
Adjusted R^2	0.31	0.53

t statistics in parentheses.
* $p < 0.05$, ** $p < 0.01$, *** $p < 0.001$.

extreme positions judge the debates as more media-oriented (H5), also when we control for power and actor type. These findings correspond to our expectations. Model 2 uses the country dummies. In line with the expectation, the actors from populist communication system countries

(Denmark, Italy, and UK) perceive the debate as more media-oriented than in Switzerland (reference category, a non-populist communication style country). Germany is less policy-oriented than Switzerland. This finding goes back to the rougher, less gentle tone in Germany in general.

Discussion

It should be noted that the statistical results presented here need to be considered as exploratory in nature. We studied six countries and one debate per country. In every specific debate, the impact of general political and media system characteristics will vary with contextual, issue- and debate-specific factors (see Chapter 3). The limited number of debates and countries included in our study prevents us from adopting a multilevel model that would be appropriate to differentiate between different levels of influences.

Classifying and Explaining Debates

In terms of our typology, our findings mean that only the debate in France can be straightforwardly classified as an "insider debate." The range of views is limited, and the style is policy-oriented. The debates in Italy and the UK, are definitively more media-oriented whereas the Swiss debate is more policy-oriented. In terms of diversity, they are at the borderline between high and low diversity. Based on our reading of the debate, we think the debates in Italy and in the UK best can be classified as competitive debates whereas Switzerland best can be put in the deliberative debate category. The debate in Germany is diverse but is at the borderline between media-oriented and policy-oriented communication style. We classify it most likely as a competitive debate. Finally, Denmark is at the borderline of both dimensions. We conceive it also as a competitive debate.

In line with the finding that debate diversity varies less than communication style, the explanatory power of the underlying causes is also weaker for this dimension. One reason might be that the structural pluralism of the investigated debates is relatively similar across cases. In retrospect, our analysis focused on debates with at least two main protagonists in all countries. This means that we found similar levels of diversity across most debates (so there is little variation to explain). Only France is an exception. Here the media representation of the debate is clearly less diverse. We attributed this lack of diversity in structural terms to the typical French combination of strong state and weak social actors. This state-centred tradition of French politics has been identified before as contributing to a less autonomous tradition in French journalism, where journalists give the government the upper hand in public mediated debates (Esser 2008). At a more specific level, as argued in Chapter 11, the political debate between social partners on youth unemployment in this country was even more consensual because of contextual factors (primarily the focus, at that time, of French politics on the governmental pension reform).

We did not find an impact of media systems on diversity either. This suggests that different media systems perform equally well in reporting public debates between two main protagonists. Van Dalen et al. (2012) came to a similar conclusion. They showed that the partisan alignment of news media with political actors is not reflected in news media content (12).

Differences in style are clearly related to differences in political communication systems. The typology introduced in Chapter 3, assessing the dominant logic of political communication activities in combination with the distance between journalists and politicians, was helpful.

Variation within Countries

The differences in perceptions between actors are at least as interesting as the differences between countries. The standard deviations of actor perceptions presented in *Table 12.8* show that actors' assessments of debate diversity and style vary considerably within countries. That is, different actors perceive the debates differently. The variation in actor perceptions of debate diversity is especially large in the UK, France and Switzerland (SD > 1.0), and relatively small in Germany and Denmark (SD < 0.7). Variation in the perception of the style, in contrast, is relatively small in Switzerland, Denmark and especially the UK (SD < 0.7), and moderate in other countries. Overall, actor perceptions of the debate converge to the greatest extent in Denmark. Our analysis suggests that power and extremity play a role here, but not actor type.

In *Figures 12.2 to 12.7*, we take a more detailed look at individual actor perceptions per country. Overall, these detailed findings are in alignment with our country-level assessment. This gives us confidence in our conclusions.

Table 12.8 *Mean position (and standard deviation) of political actors on the two quality dimensions for each country*

		Debate types					
		Insider		Competitive			Deliberative
		F	I	UK	DK	GER	CH
		youth	industrial	spending	activation	Hartz IV	mass
		unempl.	relation	review	policy	reform	dismissal
		(n=21)	(n=18)	(n=13)	(n=16)	(n=20)	(n=23)
Diversity	Mean	−0.70	0.08	0.03	0.10	0.42	0.12
	SD	1.14	0.89	1.32	0.63	0.61	1.01
Style	Mean	1.06	−0.96	−0.51	−0.14	−0.26	0.40
	SD	0.88	0.92	0.43	0.68	0.80	0.68

Note: Actor scores on the dimensions are standardized. They have a mean of 0 and a standard deviation of 1.

France

The French debate on youth unemployment is clearly an Insider Debate, also at the actor level (and also when we look at the underlying debate between social actors (see Chapter 11). Most actor positions are found in the fourth quadrant (bottom right). Only a few actors diverge. Two outsider parties (Lutte Ouvrière and Parti anticapitaliste) regard the style as media-oriented rather than policy-oriented. And three actors perceive diversity as rather high. These are the responsible minister (Ministère du Travail, de l'Emploi et de la Santé), the most important employers' association (MEDEF) and some other important economic interest groups (Confédération française de l'encadrement – Confédération générale des cadres, Confédération française des travailleurs chrétiens, Union professionnelle artisanale). This pattern clearly illustrates our prediction that powerful actors will perceive the range of views to be rather diverse, whereas more extreme actors will perceive the debate to be more media-oriented. We also note that the observed variation in the perception of the diversity of the debates is primarily variation within the lower-right quadrant, between actors that perceive no or a little diversity.

Germany

The debate in Germany on the Hartz IV reform tends to emerge as a competitive debate (located in the first quadrant at the top left) when

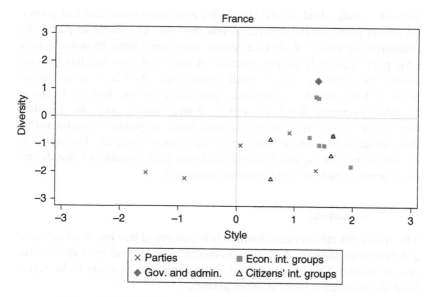

Figure 12.2 Positions of French political actors on the two quality dimensions according to actor types

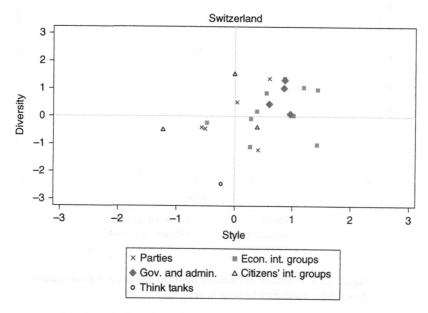

Figure 12.3 Positions of Swiss political actors on the two quality dimensions according to actor types

we look at individual actors' views. We note once more that less power-ful actors perceive the debate as less diverse. The NPD in particular evaluates the range of views as more dominated than all other actors. This party has little power, because it does not pass the five percent hurdle for entering the national parliament. And it is even further isolated because of its thematic proximity to the former National Socialist German Workers' Party. Some actors, like the German Greens, evaluate the communication style as policy-oriented rather than media-oriented. In line with our expectation, the Greens hold moderate positions; the *Erwerbslosenforum* that considered the debate most media-oriented hold extreme positions.

Switzerland

The Swiss debate on mass dismissals is perceived by almost all actors as a deliberative debate. A clearly diverging view is held by a think tank, Avenir Suisse. This less powerful actor considers diversity to be rather limited, in contrast to most other players.

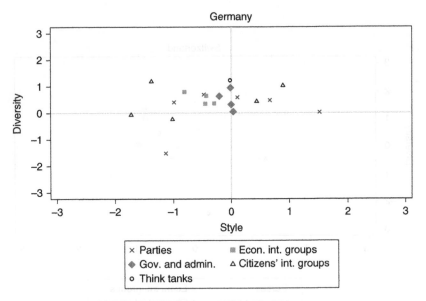

Figure 12.4 Positions of German political actors on the two quality dimensions according to actor types

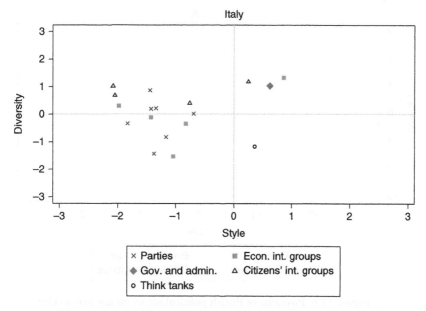

Figure 12.5 Positions of Italian political actors on the two quality dimensions according to actor types

Italy

The debate in Italy is more difficult to classify when we look at the position of individual actors. The actors disagree on the diversity of the debate. Like in other countries, the three actors that perceive the debate as most dominated are outsiders with relatively little power: Comitati di Base della Scuola, Istituto per lo Sviluppo della Formazione Professionale dei Lavoratori, and Partito dei Comunisti Italiani. By contrast, the actors agree that the style of the debate was rather media-oriented.

UK

In the spending review debate in the UK we observe likewise relatively disagreement on how diverse the debate was, and agreement on the media-oriented style of the debate. In this country, the Green Party and the Scottish Trades Union Congress perceive the diversity to be relatively low, whereas two citizens' interest groups (center for cities, and Tax

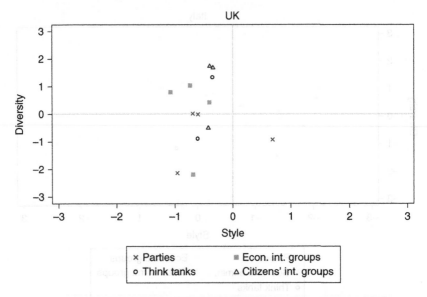

Figure 12.6 Positions of British political actors on the two quality dimensions according to actor types

Payers' Alliance) conceive the debate relatively diverse. According to our participants, the two citizen groups are powerful actors. Thus, these findings again confirm that powerful actors tend to be more convinced that the debate was diverse. The Scottish Trades Union Congress, on the other hand, is a clear exception. This powerful actor is relatively skeptical regarding diversity. The explanation can be found in another policy area. The Union attaches strong value to the independence for Scotland, a subject of ongoing debate that might not be properly reflected (in the Union's view) in the spending review debate. In addition, it should be noted that in the UK case, state actors did not respond to our questions. In general, state actors are powerful actors that consider debates to be relatively diverse. Participation of state actors in the study would there-fore most likely have put the UK case more firmly in the upper left quadrant.

Denmark

The Danish debate, finally, appears as relatively moderate from the individual actor perspective. There is little disagreement on diversity,

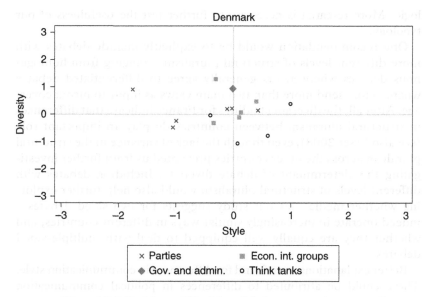

Figure 12.7 Positions of Danish political actors on the two quality dimensions according to actor types

more so on style. The Social Democrat party evaluates the communication style as media-oriented, whereas the Danish Economic Council sees the debate as policy-oriented. These differences do not really reflect differences in power or extremity, but may rather reflect how satisfied these actors were with the outcome of the debate.

Conclusion

The contribution of this chapter is to provide a tool that allows the public debates to be evaluated at the media content level. The quality of public debates can be assessed by at least two dimensions – diversity and style. Based on these two dimensions, the quality of a public debate can be defined as scandalous, insider, competitive, or deliberative. Recalling the limitations of our study – that included a sample of six debates in six countries – we note that our results suggest that *public* debates tend to be moderately diverse and media-oriented, which points to the competitive debate type as the most prevalent type. This would fit a long tradition of news media research that suggests that news media (at best) present two views and that news media coverage is increasingly shaped by a media logic. More research is necessary to further test the usefulness of our typology.

One recommendation would be to explicitly include debates with more different levels of structural pluralism – ranging from homogenous debates where actors generally agree to differentiated debates where actors send more than two main views as input to media coverage. After all, the diverging findings for France indicate that differences in structural pluralism between countries do play an important role (see also Esser 2008), even though the lack of variance in the structural pluralism across the other countries prevented us from further investigating this determinant of debate diversity. Including debates with different levels of structural pluralism would also help further exploring whether media – as our study suggests for two-sided debates – indeed operate in increasingly similar ways in different countries, and whether they are equally well equipped to deal with multiple-sided debates.

Better explanations were found for differences in communication style. These could be attributed to differences in political communication system.

Actor perceptions of debate characteristics vary with actors' power and extremity. More powerful actors perceive the debate to be more diverse, arguably because they are able to get their message across and are therefore not confronted with debates in which their view is missing. And more extreme actors perceive the debate to be more media-oriented, arguably because they are treated as outsiders and adopt a media-oriented communication style themselves. The review of individual actor positions supported these general findings, but also suggested another factor to be included in future research, namely the extent to which actors are satisfied with the outcome of debates. Remarkably, perceptions of debate diversity and style did not differ across actor types.

These are important issues to be explored further. We are aware of the importance of a diversity of views. From mass opinion formation and framing effects research, we know that only debates with at least two viewpoints have positive effects on public opinion formation and thus can be evaluated as good in a normative sense. In general, direct-democratic campaigns (Hänggli 2018) and election campaigns seem to meet this standard by offering a confrontation of views. As we saw in this chapter, one-sided situations are rare when we consider public debates. On the other hand, there still seems to be ample room to improve on the diversity included in these debates: the less powerful in particular feel that their perspective is not taken sufficiently into consideration. We need to know better under what conditions debate diversity occurs and how it can be improved.

Looking at the communication style, it is unclear whether a media-oriented or a policy-oriented style is better for the public opinion formation process. From research on direct-democratic campaigns, we know that at least some kind of biased processing is at work in deliberative debates (Colombo & Kriesi 2017). It is possible that biased processing can be reduced if the style is less policy-oriented. For instance, focusing on a very different type of debate – online discussions between citizens in the US on the 2004 presidential elections – Zhang et al. (2013) found that the exchange of more diverse arguments is associated with an increase in the use of impolite words. In such a case, people might get more involved because the communication style is more aggressive. Future research should therefore explicitly investigate which communication style leads to less biased or manipulated opinion formation processes.

Appendix 12.1   Questions on debate quality

[If there were participation in the debate] I will now read you several statements about the debate on... Could you please indicate on a scale of 1 to 5 to what degree your organization agrees with these statements? (1 = completely disagree, 5 = completely agree)
Range of Views:

The debate was characterized by....
–the participation of lots of different political actors (=participation)
–lots of reasons and explanations [well-grounded arguments, examples given] (=justification)

The debate....
–had a wealth of different viewpoints (=different views)
Communication style:

The debate....
–was respectful [there were no insulting comments about other political positions and opposing arguments.] (=respect)
–had content [emphasis was put on content and facts rather than creating conflict and news stories] (=substantive)
–was civilized [no "hot button" language]

Part IV

Conclusion

13 Conclusion

Laurent Bernhard

Back in the eighteenth century, Jean-Jacques Rousseau famously stated that the English mistakenly regard themselves as free. In the *Contrat Social*, Rousseau provocatively maintained that the English citizens are free only during elections. After Election Day, slavery takes over again. While certainly exaggerated, there seems to be a grain of truth to Rousseau's observation in contemporary democracies (Esaiasson & Narud 2013). Indeed, governments obviously enjoy a great deal of autonomy vis-à-vis citizens outside electoral contexts.

To confront this view, one may argue in line with Manin (1997) that the regularity of elections is the key mechanism that allows voters to influence the decisions of the rulers in modern democracies. It is because of the repetition of elections that the democratically elected representatives are forced to consider the voters' retrospective judgement about their policies in the next elections. Hence, elected representatives may be under an anticipatory pressure to account for the preferences of their voters. According to this line of reasoning, representative democracy is not the form of government that allows the people to govern, but it is the form of government, in which any decision is subject to the judgement of the public. In other words, under such a regime, the elected members of government face a strong incentive to be alert both to the opinion of the public and the dominant opinion emerging in the public sphere. In a similar vein, the theory of dynamic representation states that governments regularly react to public opinion, not just via election results, but over the election cycle (Stimson et al. 1995, Soroka & Wlezien 2010). Morris (1999: 75) has even famously claimed that every day is Election Day in modern democracies.

This book has analyzed policy-related public debates in everyday settings, i.e. between elections and outside referendum campaigns (Kriesi et al. 2012). In democracies, political actors are constantly engaged in debates with one another over a number of policy issues (Green-Pedersen & Mortensen 2010). So far, most empirical analyses about the political actors' mobilization and communication strategies have focused on elections. As a consequence, the state of the art in this field is mainly restricted to political parties (and the affiliated individual candidates) operating in extraordinary intense settings. To the extent that policy-related contributions exist, they are limited to the comparison of a few countries. We believe that the study of public debates presents two major analytical advantages over electoral campaign contexts. Public debates not only capture a more diverse population of actors but also everyday politics. As opposed to exclusive studies of electoral contests, examining public debates at least potentially allows for the analysis of the full range of political actors. At the level of political organizations, these actors include state actors, political parties, economic interest groups, citizen groups, think tanks, and research institutes. These actors may contribute to policy-specific public debates either by means of verbal claim-making or by various forms of action enabling them to cross the threshold of public attention and gain access to the media, which is of crucial importance in the framework of public debates. Second, while electoral campaigns stand for exceptional periods in politics including a tremendous intensification of political communication by parties, public debates much more represent "ordinary politics," which is both characterized by a high degree of routine behavior and varying degrees of public engagement. They tend to be much less institutionalized than electoral campaigns, which occur at more or less regular intervals and are subject to specific regulations. In other words, the examination of public debates may better be able to reflect the political actors' standard practice of everyday politics.

In this book, we have taken a supply-side perspective by examining the ways in which political actors tried to shape the public debates on the salient topic of unemployment in six Western European countries (Germany, France, Italy, the United Kingdom, Denmark, and Switzerland) in fall/winter 2010/11. The case selection was motivated by the objective to obtain a sample that captures the full range of labor-market regimes in Western Europe. According to the typologies elaborated by Hall & Soskice (2001) and further developed by Schmidt (2008), this analysis includes a liberal market economy (LME; United Kingdom), two state-influenced market economies (SME; France and Italy), as well as three coordinated market economies (CME). While France stands for the ideal-type of a SME, Italy represents a more compound case. The CMEs can be further distinguished by their type of interaction between labor and business: social corporatism (Denmark), sectoral corporatism (Germany), and liberal corporatism (Switzerland). Initially, it was our contention that the elites' strategies are decisively shaped by the national macro-contexts. This is why we devoted great deal of attention to contextual typologies in Chapter 3, notably to the political opportunity structure, the media opportunity structure, the so-called cultural models as well as the more specific policy context. With respect to the latter, we have elaborated some detailed concepts to characterize the labor-market policy context in each country. In drawing on the work of Thelen (2012), we have distinguished between flexicurity (Denmark, Switzerland), dualization (Germany, France, Italy), and deregulation countries (United Kingdom).

Drawing on first-hand accounts obtained in the framework of interviews conducted with representatives of the national labor-market elites, we have studied their communication and mobilization strategies in a comparative perspective. How did the political actors deal with the great preoccupation of the public with the economic consequences of the crisis on the labor market? What kind of policy measures did they offer to fight unemployment? And how did they attempt to shape the public debate in hard times?

We chose a particular period for the study of the policy-related public debates. Our study took place against the background of the current Great recession. Future historians will probably look back at the present years as a disastrous time for the Western world in economic terms. Due to the bankruptcy of the investment bank Lehman Brothers in September 2008, advanced democracies have been hit by a severe financial and economic crisis. The following recession has been the greatest economic downturn since the Great Depression in the 1930s. In its wake, economic issues such as the rescue of banks, the stabilization of financial markets, deteriorating public finances, and macroeconomic policies (e.g., the adoption of fiscal stimulus packages versus austerity programs) have become major preoccupations in Western democracies. Increasing levels of unemployment levels can be considered the most obvious and palpable manifestation of the current crisis in the citizens' perception. Indeed, the serious economic crisis has led to a considerable rise in unemployment that caused a great deal of pain and desperation among individuals. Despite the fact that encouraging signs of recovery surfaced at least in some countries, the problem of comparatively high levels of unemployment have generally persisted since then. In line with the serious economic consequences of the Great recession, at the time of our study European citizens of the six selected countries consistently identified unemployment as the politically most pressing issue (see Chapter 1). Considering the uniformity of the overall experience of the crisis, and the uniformity of the preoccupation with unemployment at this point in time, we set out to study how the issues related to unemployment were debated in the selected time period. In a world where the international economic and political context decisively shapes national economic policy-making, choosing a specific period for our study has the major advantage of holding this context constant.

The Missing Reforms

Given the obtrusiveness and salience of the problem of unemployment, we expected to find the issue of unemployment at the top of the policy-makers' agenda, inciting lively policy-specific public debates. We assumed that a uniform exogenous shock like the financial and economic crisis created a tremendous amount of popular discontent. These grievances constituted the conflict potential for mobilization in any one of the various political arenas. In line with the influential theory of economic voting, the empirical evidence has established that increasing levels of unemployment are a major reason for the voting out of incumbents in national elections (Lewis-Beck & Paldam 2000). Confirming this hypothesis, Kriesi (2014) has shown that those government parties, which have not been able to cope with the crisis has clearly tended to be defeated at the polls. Thus, governments should have faced a great incentive to implement policy measures aiming at reducing the number of jobless people or at least to improve their prospects.

During our period of investigation (fall and winter 2010/11), unemployment did not turn out to be a key issue on the political agenda, however. As has been elaborated in Chapter 4, limited policy adjustments prevailed over major reforms. As a consequence, questions on how to fight unemployment were not discussed in the first place. At first glance, the absence of major policy initiatives and related public debates is puzzling. Contrary to macroeconomic policy making, one could not argue that the hands of national governments were tied in the labor-market domain. This field is still largely a domain of national decision-makers. In the course of the last major recession during the 1970s, new labor laws were adopted and regulations were introduced that restricted the ability of employers to fire individual workers or engage in collective dismissals (Pontusson & Raess 2012).

Part of the explanation of this puzzle relates to the fact that the rescue of banks and the banking system, the sovereign debt problem and the stabilization of the international finance system turned out to be the most fundamental challenges for policy-makers in the current crisis in Western Europe. Policy-makers were rapidly forced to solve these urgent questions, thus leaving the issue of unemployment to one side. As an immediate reaction to the crisis, most governments relied on stimulus packages in fall/winter 2008/2009 (Armingeon 2012). This Keynesian response proved to be short-lived, however. One year later, when our study took place, decision-makers generally implemented austerity measures. This change in macroeconomic orientation was a direct consequence of soaring public debts and the insolvency of various banks. European governments focused on the stability of their national banking systems by adopting bank rescue packages. The huge costs of the bailout, and the looming danger of further banking failures, seriously threatened the viability of the debt situation of many countries. Amongst others, the European Central Bank (ECB) insisted that governments should return to sustainable patterns of spending. The debates were brought to a head with the Greek crisis which broke out in early 2010 and culminated in a first bailout of Greece in May 2010. The euro crisis exacerbated existing economic imbalances between European countries (Scharpf 2011, Lane 2012), with which the governments' policies were unable to cope. The subsequent ramifications of the sovereign debt crisis provided a strong set of rhetorical arguments for Germany, the European Central Bank, and other actors who advocated fiscal retrenchment (Farrell and Quiggin 2012: 36–7). The rhetorical claim that markets "wanted" fiscal austerity proved to be a compelling one. The governments of the weaker economies (especially those in Southern Europe) not only had to resort to austerity measures, in several cases, these measures did not even achieve their intended goal of reducing the public deficits. As a result, the economic imbalances were aggravated, leading to the so-called "euro crisis" whereas the European Monetary Union (EMU) governance structures revealed their weakness (Eichengreen 2012). The ensuing complex policies of crisis management involved hard bargaining between European governments, their domestic constituents, and supranational actors (such as the European Commission, the European Banking Authority, the ECB, and the International Monetary Fund).

Given that governments prioritized these vital economic issues, the key challenge of how to fight unemployment lost importance. The sovereign debt problem, the rescue of banks, and the stabilization of financial markets crowded out the unemployment issue from the top position of the policy-makers' agenda. As the fundamental stabilization we have just outlined above demanded many resources, introducing costly labor-market reforms was not a feasible option. This is partly why most governments refrained from engaging in major reforms on the labor market even in economic hard times. It is thus consistent to observe fine-tuning of ongoing programs (i.e. adaptive measures that allow for adjustments of existing policies to the requirements of the crisis) rather than fundamental changes. In the medium to long run, however, the deep structural problems of the labor market needed to be addressed. Yet, in the absence of urgency and money, politicians preferred muddling through as long as possible, not least because they are usually short of ready-made solutions for the structural problems. Given that there are existing programs for dealing with unemployment, other policies that may require reforms more urgently compete for the government's attention in the short run. Thus, unemployment in the Great Recession offers the opportunity to study a policy issue that, although highly salient to the general public, was not necessarily at the top of the agenda of macropolitics.

In line with these considerations, there were only minor reform attempts in five out of the six countries during our period of interest. As has been shown by means of mass media data in Chapter 1, the public debate on unemployment was in fact much larger than the policy-related public debate on unemployment. The public was confronted with a debate on the issue that does not necessarily involve political actors and reform proposals. Given that we were interested in studying the part of the debate that is shaped by political actors, we have devoted a great deal of attention to the policy-related aspects throughout the chapters of this book. Despite the fact that public debates are rather open in nature, the policy-specific parts of the debates were linked to specific problems and related to reform proposals in which some actors stuck to the *status quo* and others looked for a policy change.

In Germany and Denmark, the public debates revolved around the country-specific adjustments of the unemployment schemes – a reform of the so-called "Hartz IV" benefits in Germany, and a reorganization of the activation system in Denmark. As far as Italy is concerned, the long-lasting debate about making the labor market more flexible crystallized in the case of Pomigliano, a plant the carmaker FIAT threatened to delocalize, during our period of investigation. In France, social partners decided to take measures in order to combat high levels of youth unemployment. These negotiations occurred as a reaction to the impressive participation of students in the protest movement against the governmental pension reform in fall 2010. The Swiss case is exceptional in that it did not give rise to any policy-related debate at all. Admittedly, this was partly due to the fact that citizens had approved a minor adjustment of the unemployment insurance in the framework of a direct-democratic vote just some weeks before we went into the field.

The content of these debates illustrates that public debates are embedded in national policy-specific contexts (see Chapter 3). When it comes to reforms or adjustment, the policy legacy conditions the policy options to a large extent – even in hard economic times. Policy legacies constitute a crucial determinant for current policy adjustments, since they not only determine the policy-specific problem pressure, but also the possibilities of policy makers to deal with them. The various labor-market regimes cause specific problem pressures. Coping with these problem-pressures may prove very challenging, as they are inherent to the basic policy-specific institutional setting of a given country. The variability of these contexts is likely to explain why we have found such great differences in the substance of the national debates between the countries. More specifically, the cases at hand indicate that policy adjustments and related policy debates are driven by regime-specific challenges.

In the *flexicurity countries*, the major challenge in phases of recession is to cope with rising levels of expenditures of the key unemployment scheme. Due to the flexible labor markets, the number of unemployed tends to quickly increase when entering an economic crisis. As compensation to the individuals' risks of losing their jobs, unemployment benefits are particularly generous in flexicurity countries. When the number of recipients increases, the basic scheme is likely to go off the rails. In the case of Denmark, it is thus coherent that the policy debate pertained to the domain of activation, which forms the backbone of the often praised Danish model. During our period of analysis, cases of abuses at the local level which were made public by the media gave rise to a public debate. As a consequence of a media storm, the Parliament felt impelled to enact policy measures in order to improve the activation model. In Switzerland, policy-makers focused on the traditional unemployment insurance. This is also in line with our line of reasoning, as passive benefits are at the center of the successful Swiss approach towards fighting unemployment. In light of too optimistic expectations about the level of unemployment, citizens approved a reform hammered out in the federal parliament that contained some additional revenues as well as minor retrenchment measures.

With respect to the *dualization countries*, the crucial challenge concerns the question of lacking flexibility, which is commonly assumed to be responsible for the pronounced discrepancy between labor-market insiders and outsiders. It is thus no coincidence that policy reform proposals and related public debates focused on this crucial question in Germany, France, and Italy. Among the three countries of this regime studied here, Germany has certainly gone furthest when it comes to introducing flexibility into the labor market. The introduction of the Hartz IV reforms in 2005 has attracted a great deal of attention. Even though the reform was enacted under a so-called "red-green" government coalition under the leadership of Gerhard Schröder, the new scheme has remained highly contested among the left as well as in public. This is probably why a slight modification of the Hartz IV scheme that had been demanded by a ruling of the German Federal Court, caused quite a stir among political elites, thus nurturing a debate of medium intensity. In financial terms, parliament decided at the end of a long bargaining process to increase the standard rates (*Regelsätze*) by only 5 euros after all.

In France, the public debate pertained to the question of youth unemployment, which is a chronic problem of the dualized countries. Young people have become the primary victims of rigid and segmented labor markets. This manifests itself by a high level of youth unemployment and by the fact that most of those who have a job are employed in the framework of atypical contracts (as opposed to regular contracts of indefinite duration). As far as the French case is concerned, social partners negotiated on technical matters in order to improve the access of young people into the French labor market during our period of interest. This bipartite type of cooperation took place in response to a huge but unsuccessful protest mobilization against a pension reform decided by the government of Nicolas Sarkozy which overshadowed the remaining issues in fall 2010. Many students took to the streets, claiming that a higher retirement age would worsen their job opportunities in the French labor market.

Italy also suffers from the drawbacks of a notorious inflexible labor market. The public debate took place against the background of tensions in the industrial relations during the time period covered. Sergio Marchionne, the CEO of the carmaker FIAT threatened to delocalize two factories to Serbia. FIAT and labor unions struggled over the conditions under which this delocalization could be avoided. Given that FIAT has been the flagship of the Italian economy as well as a model in terms of industrial relations, this opposition gave rise to a very intensive public debate. Amongst other things, radical labor unions and far left parties jointly staged a series of protest events to combat a deterioration of workers' rights.

The only exception to the general pattern of policy adjustment occurred in the United Kingdom, our only representative of the *deregulation countries*. While we found path-dependent trajectories in the five Continental European countries, the British case resembles much more an exogenous shock. Therefore, the regime-specific challenges are not able to explain the substance of the radical reform proposals announced by the coalition government. During recessions, the liberal regime available in the United Kingdom tends to produce a high number of new jobless people. This is due to the flexible labor market which enables enterprises to easily fire their employees when demand falls for their goods and services. As unemployed people have difficulties to find a new job in economic hard times, the low level of protection in terms of benefits is likely to cause a serious problem of poverty. Unlike the United States, where the unemployment scheme has been temporarily expanded by means of a prolongation of the length of the claiming period, the audacious coalition government led by David Cameron took the decision to engage in a fundamental reorganization of the British welfare state. In fall 2010, Iain Duncan Smith announced the establishment of the so-called "Universal Credit," which was closely linked to the Comprehensive Spending Review. Amongst other things, this reform aimed at tightening the work-conditionality for recipients of unemployment benefits and at fostering the re-integration of jobseekers into the labor market by means of tougher sanctions.

From a theoretical perspective, the British case can be viewed through the lens of the punctuated equilibrium approach (Baumgartner & Jones 1993). Periods of policy stability and incremental adjustments were suddenly interrupted by instances of major policy changes. As far as the Universal Credit reform is concerned, this change took place because of an exogenous shock that occurred outside the labor-market subsystem. Soon after the general elections held in May 2010, Conservatives and Liberal Democrats ended a thirteen-year period of Labour government, corresponding to the party's longest uninterrupted time in power. The new partisan composition of the British government can be conceived of as a change of the dominant coalition that enjoyed a policy monopoly. The major policy reform came about since this powerful actor that pertains to the realm of macropolitics entered the labor-market subsystem. In the terminology of Baumgartner & Jones (2002), a serial shift occurred in this domain, thus attracting not only the attention of specialists but also that of a broader population of elite actors.

The Prevalence of Country Similarities

The overall research question of this book referred to the impact of the context by focusing on patterns of country-specific similarities and dis-similarities. Indeed, studying the unemployment-related policy debate comparatively is particularly interesting, since we are confronted with a paradoxical situation. On the one hand, as a result of the exogenous shock of the financial and economic crisis which hit West European countries, unemployment can be considered a common problem. On the other hand, given the importance of the path-dependency of this policy-domain, labor-market debates are carried out in decidedly coun-try-specific terms. The contrast between the similarity of the overall structure of labor-market conflicts, and the country-specific dissimilarities in the issues debated has preoccupied us throughout this study.

Regarding the question of contextual similarities and dissimilarities, the evidence tends to lend support to the convergence thesis. This is the main finding of this book. Despite the fact that the political actors were embedded in different kinds of general and policy-specific contexts, it is intriguing to observe that the selected countries did not vary in many respects. To begin with, the labor-market domain has been shown to be fundamentally structured by the classical divide between the left and the right. Based on the political actors positioning about issue-specific measures, the empirical analysis of the labor-market policy space in Chapter 6 has confirmed that this conflict is still rooted in the traditional state/market antagonism. The latter proves to be by far the key structuring dimension when it comes to the policy preferences of the labor-market elites. However, the most stimulating finding of Chapter 6 refers to the emergence of a second conflict dimension. This dimension revolves around activation-related measures and is strongly dependent on the labor-market context of a given country. More specifically, the meaning varies according to regime type. Even though future research should clarify this issue, it seems to be the case that the activation dimension refers to atypical and innovative reform proposals for each of the countries analyzed here. When these kinds of policy measures are discussed, political actors do not necessarily rely on the left–right heuristic. This may pave the way for new reform coalitions. The actors' configuration depicted in Chapter 6 at least suggests that the second dimension creates a division among the left. The third-way coalition which is composed of progressive actors seems to distinguish itself from the traditional left, thereby coming closer to the center and especially to the right coalition.

The classical antagonism between left and right has not only been shown to be importance to these objective coalitions based on policy preferences, but also when it comes to subjective coalitions. The analysis of coalition behavior presented in Chapter 7 has revealed that parties from the left tend to closely cooperate with labor unions, while right-wing parties join forces with employers' associations. However, there is one notable exception to this prevailing pattern. Deviations are observable in the presence of veto player on either side of the class divide. In such cases, we have been able to demonstrate close cooperation between the dominant coalition from the right and the veto players from the left. These cross-class coalitions suggest that political organizations display a high degree of strategic flexibility in order to bring about policy change.

Differences between the two sides of the class conflict also appeared with respect to the communicative interplay. In Chapter 11, which took a closer look at the interaction context, we have disclosed that actors from the left tended to more frequently address the public in the debates under scrutiny. This propensity to rely on outside strategies can be explained by the fact that the right was in power at that time. In order to prevent the governmental proposals from being realized, labor unions, left-wing parties, and sometimes citizens' groups tried to appeal to a broader public. Consistent with this view, the actors from the left have been shown to reject these proposals in public and to go negative by attacking powerful actors from the right. The latter largely refrained from retaliating. Regarding the main messages by the various protagonists, Chapter 11 we have concluded that the two opposing camps relied on very different kinds of rationales.

A closely related indication of the predominance of the left–right conflict across country cases has been made visible in Chapter 10. With respect to the former, the extensive examination of the main arguments used in the various public debates of interest reveals that these arguments are structured along the actors' core beliefs, which correspond to a large extent to the traditional state/market antagonism. This result is of primary importance for our study. Despite the impression that public debates on unemployment revolved around very heterogeneous topics from one country to another, the same ideological positions and general arguments are in fact available across Europe. Behind the surface of the "Babylonian confusion," public debates follow a very familiar logic. At a higher level of aggregation, we have established that the debates were basically waged in similar ways, as the conflict proved to be structured along the divide between the left and the right. In other words, the debates can be regarded as being functionally equivalent to a large extent. The activation dimension introduced in Chapter 6 played an important role only in the case of Denmark. This finding is insofar consistent, as this debate precisely dealt with the activation issue, which is moreover of major significance in this country.

Beyond the prevalence of the left–right conflict, the present study also consistently finds convergence regarding the aspect of the actors' power. In Chapter 5, we have established that the same kinds of organizations generally enjoy high levels of reputational power across the six countries studied here. This concerns the state actors (public administrations and governments), the parties in power as well as social partners (i.e. peak-level labor unions and employers' associations). This finding is appealing, since context properties (such as the labor-market regimes) do not affect the power levels of these crucial actors. The only notable exception concerns the extraordinary strength of the French state actors and the limited power of each of the five Swiss governing parties. Regarding the crucial question of the effect of power, the results presented in Chapter 9 turned out to be unequivocal. Indeed, we have been able to show that the actors' power exerts a tremendous impact on public debates. More specifically, by using the indicator elaborated in Chapter 5, we report that power is instrumental when it comes to message resonance. In other words, a given message turns out to be important in the framework of a debate when it has been aired by a powerful actor. Perhaps most tellingly, the most important message in the French debate about youth unemployment proved to be a phrase pronounced by President Nicolas Sarkozy about vocational training during an interview on TV.

By contrast, a domain in which we consistently found patterns of dissimilarities at the contextual level concerned the action repertoires used by the labor-market elites. According to the main results which have emerged from Chapter 8, we have shown that the scope of both outside and inside activities turned out to more narrow in Switzerland than in the remaining countries. In the next section, we will argue that this finding is consistent with the view that the organizations belonging to the Swiss labor-market domain found themselves in a remote mode during our period of investigation, a setting we will propose to label as "quiet politics." In terms of protest activities, Chapter 8 documents that British actors opposed to austerity measures expanded their moderate action repertoire in the context of the debate on austerity. This occasional radicalization of activities, which has been foremost used by labor unions, can be interpreted as a reaction to the planned Comprehensive Spending Review by the British government. Not least as a result of this choice to take to the streets, the debate on austerity displayed an extraordinary high level of public intensity. Therefore, we propose to call this case an ideal-typical example of "forum politics" (see below). British actors have also been found to rely much more on Web 2.0 applications (such as blogs, Twitter, and Facebook) than their peers in Continental Europe. This pattern of dissimilarity did not turn out to be debate-specific but rather general in nature, however.

Finally, another substantial pattern of divergence has been found in the French debate. Indeed, this case turns out to be exceptional in many respects. We have established that this debate has been less conflictive (Chapter 9, and Chapter 11), and of more respectful, civilized, and substantial in (Chapter 12). This result can be explained by advancing debate-specific considerations. It is consistent that the reported desirable outcomes are observable in this kind of relative confidentiality. However, Chapter 12 also concluded that the French debate performed poorly in terms of diversity, as actor participation, the inclusion of different points of view as well as public justifications turned out to be extraordinary low. Hence, when it comes to debate quality, a decent communication style may go hand in hand with low levels of diversity. As will be suggested below, the French case can be labeled as "committee politics." In such a setting, top officials engage in insider negotiations/bargaining without being under the pressure of the public.

Having assembled the empirical evidence of this book, we are now able to briefly summarize our main empirical results. Despite some context-specific differences, it generally appears that similarities across countries are stronger than dissimilarities in Western Europe. To the extent that country-level divergences are available, they are rather attributable to debate characteristics than to the standard typologies referring to the general and the policy-specific macro-contexts.

It's the Mobilization, Stupid!

This book has shown that the relationship between economic distress and policy responses turned out to be far less straightforward than initially expected. Intensive public debates could not be taken for granted. The topic of unemployment was no longer inescapable in the public during our period of interest. In the absence of a functional translation of the salient unemployment problem into public debates, the *mobilization* of the public by the political actors turned out to be of crucial importance. The latter cannot be assumed to always be willing to publically exploit existing socio-economical dissatisfaction to their advantage. In other words, agency is needed. The issue of unemployment rather became a matter of political maneuvering by strategic political actors.

This interpretation reminds us of Schattschneider's (1975 [1960]) famous notion of the scope of conflict and its crucial importance in politics. Some conflicts involve the participation of numerous public actors, while others are restricted to a small population of usually well-organized groups. According to Schattschneider (1975 [1960]: 3), the most important strategy of politics is concerned with altering the scope of conflict. In this view, political conflicts basically move in two directions – they can either be privatized or socialized. It is typically the weak actors who wish to transform a given conflict from the domain of "elite politics" to "mass politics." Given that these actors found themselves in a minority position, expanding a given conflict to a more public sphere constitutes the only possibility to shift the balance of forces to their favor. According to this line of reasoning, the mobilization by losers and

Table 13.1 *Four stages of conflict mobilization*

	Quiet politics	Committee politics	Plenum politics	Forum politics
Characteristic arena	administrative	"corporatist"	parliamentary	public
Participating actors	bureaucrats and vested interests	specialists (subsystem)	generalists (macropolitics)	wide variety (pluralism)
Public intensity	inexistent	low	medium	high
Country cases	Switzerland	France	Denmark, Germany	Italy, United Kingdom

outsiders determines the extent to which the public becomes involved in everyday politics. By contrast, strong actors prefer restricting the scope of conflict, as the confidentiality of the private sphere obviously plays into their hands. Indeed, if the scope of conflict is not expanded, conflicts are characterized by the prevalence of the dominant and established participants of each decision-making arena. As Schattschneider has observed long ago, the political system constitutes an uneven playing field. Each arena holds certain biases by favoring certain actors over others. Who is involved and who isn't thus greatly determines the balance of power of any political conflict.

Based on the country cases studied in this book, which suggest that political actors markedly diverged in their propensity to articulate and communicate the issue of unemployment, we propose the distinction between *four stages of conflict mobilization*. As shown in *Table 13.1*, we propose to label these stages "quiet politics," "committee politics," "plenum politics," and "forum politics." These categories are ordered according to increasing levels of mobilization, implying both increased public intensity and a larger number of participants (i.e. actor expansion).

While conflicts lie at the root of all politics, it is often overlooked that most conflicts fail to come to the fore (Mair 1997). However, most scholarly analyses have focused on the tip of the iceberg by studying the most intensive conflicts. In a similar vein, Culpepper (2011) observes that political scientists have largely ignored issues of low salience so far. "Quiet politics," a term we borrow from Culpepper (2011), constitutes our first category and is characterized by the absence of any mobilization by political actors. In such a setting, a given policy subsystem finds itself in its remote mode from a communicative point of view. This tends to be the case when a publically waged conflict has recently been settled or when uncontroversial and highly technical issues are at stake. As a consequence, these conflicts completely escape public attention. The scope of participating actors is most limited. Typically, political decisions are taken by members of the public administration who are responsible for the implementation of policies and benefit from a superior level of knowledge. In this kind of bureaucratic governance area, lobbying activities by specialized interest groups are particularly effective. "Quiet politics" can be conceived of as the domain of pressure politics, where – in the absence of mobilized challengers – vested interests (such as those held by business groups) often succeed in achieving their desired policy outcomes (Culpepper 2011).

In the framework this study, the Swiss case displays the hallmark of "quiet politics." The federal labor-market elites were concerned with the implementation of the ordinance of the unemployment insurance, which had to be revised as a consequence of the adoption of a popular vote in September 2010. Considering the Swiss policy cycle and the outstanding performance of the labor market in terms of joblessness, it seems consistent that the issue of unemployment was characterized by the absence of elite mobilization at that time. However, we need to highlight that Switzerland stands for a case of successful diversion, according to our reading. Despite three major events of mass dismissals and the steadily appreciation of the Swiss franc against the euro, which threatened to undermine the international competitiveness of the Swiss economy and to lead to a severe loss of jobs, the topic of unemployment did not enter the public agenda. As has been shown in Chapter 11, this was primarily due to the fact that only the labor unions put much emphasis on this issue, while the remaining collective actors did not address it. The powerful business associations, the public administrations as well as the parties from the right succeeded in preventing the unemployment theme from entering the political arena. Because of the privatization of the conflict, the issue of unemployment became invisible in Switzerland. This case highlights the fact that public attention needs to be regarded as a scarce resource, as a large number of social problems compete for being taken into consideration. Given the finite carrying capacity of the media, only a very limited number of issues attract the public's attention (Hilgartner & Bosk 1988). In Schattschneider's words (1975 [1960]: 69), "some issues are organized into politics while others are organized out." As there are only a few very successful problems to achieve widespread "celebrity" status and attention under highly competitive conditions, political actors may try to avoid certain issues altogether.

"Committee politics" is the domain in which specialized elite actors of a given policy subsystem negotiate with each other to make policy decisions. In terms of actor types, participation is restricted to those who benefit from a direct access to the various decision-making arenas, thus leading to a pronounced upper-class bias. These powerful actors try to prevent competitors from achieving full entry into the decision-making arena (Gamson 1968). Hence, the conflicts are played out in narrow scope. Typical examples include deputies engaged in parliamentary committees, or representatives of organized interest groups involved in the framework wage bargaining. As these negotiations take place behind closed doors, political decision-makers are generally able to maintain a high degree of confidentiality. In other words, the various decision-making arenas are shielded from the public's view. Except for some far-reaching decisions, the public at large does not take note of these negotiations. Thus, the decision-making process basically takes place without the influence of the public at large. This is attributable to the fact that mass media usually do not extensively cover such negotiations as they are usually not interested in the technical content of the issues at stake and often do not get the most newsworthy information pertaining to the negotiations. Only quality newspapers will typically publish some articles dealing with the actors, the stakes, and the policy options. Thus, the level of public intensity usually turns out to be rather low in the area of "committee politics."

Among the cases studied here, only the French negotiations on youth unemployment qualify for an instance of "committee politics." The bipartite meetings involved the representatives of the country's eight most important peak associations – three organizations on the side of the employers and five labor unions. The content analysis of press releases in Chapter 11 has indeed shown that social partners were the only actors to address this issue in public. Consistent with our theoretical expectation, the remaining actor categories largely refrained from going public. Furthermore, the public debate on these negotiations proved to be of very low intensity, since they did not attract a lot of media attention. Only quality and business newspapers reported on these rather technical and uncontroversial matters. In Chapter 1, we have established that social partners excelled in terms of media standing. The French case suggests that, when faced with valence issues of high complexity, conditions are ripe for policy-making by power elites, characterized by an obvious disinterest in the public sphere.

In "plenum politics," the locus of a given conflict moves from the smoke-filled back rooms to the front stage, thus becoming visible to a larger public. This stage of mobilization basically refers to what Culpepper (2011) labels "partisan contestation," i.e. traditional policy decision-making based on the principles of representative government. Parliaments can thus be considered the paradigmatic arena of "plenum politics." The central actors are political parties, which struggle with each other to publically distinguish themselves and to achieve the passage of desired laws. The hostility between government and opposition lies at the heart of "plenum politics." As for "committee" politics, this stage is dominated by established actors. Yet, specialists tend to be replaced by generalists who belong to the domain to macropolitics, including prominent figures such as members of government and party leaders. Given that these newsworthy actors come into play, the debate at stake generally attracts a considerable degree of media attention. As a consequence of the mass media's news coverage, politically interested citizens will take note of the issues being discussed by the political elites. Thus, the debate takes place in front of a large audience. As is the case in a stage production, the citizen public takes a passive role, however.

According to our reading of the various debates, the German and the Danish case stand for examples of "plenum politics." Indeed, the adjustment of the Hartz IV scheme as well as the reform of the activation policy predominantly occurred in the parliamentary arena.[1] Based on media data reported in Chapter 1, we have been able to show that political parties were the most crucial actors in these two countries during our period of interest. In both cases, the debated issues gave rise to rather high levels of public intensity. This is consistent with the view that the mass media heavily report on conflicts which are brought into the stage of "committee politics." It is quite revealing that we are dealing with two emotionally charged issues here. Both the Hartz IV scheme in Germany and the activation policies in Denmark refer to highly contested reforms packages which were adopted in a recent past. The evidence presented in this study suggests that even small adjustments of these policies can cause quite a stir among the elites and in public when highly symbolic topics are at stake. It is important to observe that the two cases vary with regard to the logic of mobilization. Whereas the adjustment of Hartz IV was institutional in nature, as it originated from a ruling by the Federal Constitutional Court, the reform of the Danish activation scheme came

---

[1] In the German case, we need to mention that the final stage of the decision-making process moved back to the level of "committee politics." Since both Chambers were not able to come to an agreement, parliamentary bargaining took place in the framework of joint committees (*Vermittlungsausschüsse*).

about as a reaction to a non-institutionalized "media storm" launched by one of the country's most important newspapers. This case confirms that the media are from time to time able to dictate the political decision-makers as public concern seriously began to rise (Walgrave & Massens 2000). Thus, in the latter case, the debate moved from the public sphere into the political sphere, while the opposite direction applied to the German case. In other words, the political agenda preceded the public agenda in Germany and the public agenda determined the political agenda in Denmark (Cobb & Elder 1972).

Finally, "forum politics" distinguishes itself by a high level of competitiveness. On this stage, political actors mobilize citizens in the public sphere. The strategy of going public can happen either inside (elections, or direct democratic votes) or outside the electoral arena (protest politics, or non-institutionalized political campaigns). While citizens have the final say with respect to the former, the minority tries to mobilize public opinion in order to force decision-makers to adopt their demands in the latter. Compared to the previously discussed types of mobilization, the scope of actors expands into "mass politics," as it typically includes not only the established actors, but also a wide range of irregular participants. Fundamentally, "forum politics" is open to all kind of collective and individual actors and can be conceived as the most pluralistic form of elite mobilization. Particularly worth of emphasis are social movement organizations (SMOs), which face a strong incentive to seek a public trial, as they usually lack direct access to the decision-making arenas. Participating actors seek to mobilize public opinion for their respective policy positions. Public debates become more intensive, mostly because mass media extensively report on the issue(s) at stake. As a consequence, citizens are confronted with clear policy alternatives, are likely to be more knowledgeable about the political choices, and will possibly even actively take part in politics. This host of promising effects on individuals is attributable on the vigorously public-oriented engagement by the political elites in general and especially by the losers and outsiders. This mechanism offers the "semi-sovereign people" their best chance for exerting a role in the decision-making process. It is precisely for this reason that mobilization is key. Or put the other way round: as long as political conflicts remain behind closed doors, the people are powerless.

Among the country cases studied here, the debates on the flexibilization of the Italian labor market as well the debate on austerity in the United Kingdom have come closest to the notion of "forum politics." In both cases, the entire labor-market elites participated in the debates. In other words, public involvement was not limited to the dominant actors of the respective decision-making arenas, as was the case in France, Germany, and Denmark. As we have been able to show in Chapter 11, the British debate on austerity displayed a more pluralistic pattern of elite participation in the public sphere, partly because actors from the left tried to actively avoid the Comprehensive Spending Review from being implemented. The British case revealed the crucial role played by state actors during a competitive debate. Members of the government frequently went public (Kernell 1997) before the official announcements of the Comprehensive Spending Review and the Universal Credit in order to impose their points of view about the radical austerity measures in the political struggle. Whereas the British case rather corresponds to an institutionalized kind of debate, as the date of the announcement of the austerity plans were known long in front of these events, the conflict in Italy obviously followed a non-institutional logic. Opposed labor unions and parties from the left brought the conflict about the planned flexibilization at the FIAT factory of Pomigliano from the political to the public sphere by making use of the action repertoire of the domain of protest politics. This case thus very much resembles a mobilization effort of social movement organizations, which triggered a public debate about workers' conditions. In line with the mechanism posited by Schattschneider, actors from the minority tried to mobilize public opinion in order to prevent the adoption of an undesired decision, that was expected to create significant spillover effects in the realm of Italian industrial relations. Ultimately, the challengers did not succeed in imposing their positions the two cases at hand. We should bear in mind that in the absence of any conflict mobilization, these actors would have lost anyway, however.

This book invites the conclusion that representative democracy is to a large degree directed from above. Established elite actors tend to dominate policy-related debates and authoritarian decision-making is pervasive. There is no doubt that Jean-Jacques Rousseau had a point in his provoking critique of representative government. Yet, elected decision-makers will be responsive to the demands of citizens under some specific circumstances. From a realistic perspective, this is likely to be the case when a given issue becomes salient as a result of an extraordinary high level of conflict mobilization, thus leading to the participation of a large number of actors and giving rise to intensive policy-related public debates.

References

Altheide, David L. and Robert P. Snow (1979). *Media Logic*. Beverly Hills: Sage.

Anastasia, Bruno, Letizia Bertazzon, Massimo Disarò, Gianluca Emireni and Maurizio Rasera (2011). *Chi percepisce l'indennità di disoccupazione? Tassi di copertura e selettività dei requisiti richiesti*. Veneto: Working Paper.

Ansell, Chris, Sarah Reckhow and Andrew Kelly (2009). 'How to Reform a Reform Coalition: Outreach, Agenda Expansion, and Brokerage in Urban School Reform'. *Policy Studies Journal*, 37(4), 717–743.

Ansolabehere, Stephen, Shanto Iyengar, Adam Simon and Nicholas Valentino (1994). 'Does Attack Advertisement Demobilize the Electorate?' *American Political Science Review*, 88(4), 829–838.

Anstead, Nick and Andrew Chadwick (2009). 'Parties, Election Campaigning, and the Internet: Toward a Comparative Institutional Approach'. In Andrew Chadwick and Philip N. Howard (eds.): *Handbook of Internet Politics*. New York: Routledge, pp. 56–71.

Arcenaux, Kevin (2006). 'Do Campaigns Help Voters Learn? A Cross-national Analysis'. *British Journal of Political Science*, 36(1), 159–173.

Armingeon, Klaus (1997). 'Swiss Corporatism in Comparative Perspective'. *West European Politics*, 20(4), 164–179.

Armingeon, Klaus (2012). 'The Politics of Fiscal Responses to the Crisis 2008–2009'. *Governance*, 25(4), 543–565.

Baccaro, Lucio and Marco Simoni (2008). 'Policy Concertation in Europe: Explaining Government's Choice'. *Comparative Political Studies*, 41(1), 1323–1348.

Bächtiger, André, Seraina Pedrini and Mirjam Ryser (2010a). 'Prozessanalyse Politischer Entscheidungen: Diskurstypen und Sequenzialisierung'. In Joachim Behnke, Thomas Bräuninger and Susumu Shikano (eds.): *Jahrbuch für Handlungs- und Entscheidungstheorie. Band 6: Schwerpunkt Neuere Entwicklungen des Konzepts der Rationalität und ihre Anwendungen*. Wiesbaden: VS Verlag für Sozialwissenschaften, pp. 193–226.

Bächtiger, André, Simon Niemeyer, Simon Neblo, Marco R. Steenbergen and Jürg Steiner (2010b). 'Disentangling Diversity in Deliberative Democracy: Competing Theories, Their Blind-spots, and Complementarities'. *Journal of Political Philosophy*, 18(1), 32–63.

Badie, Bertrand and Pierre Birnbaum (1983). *The Sociology in the State*. Chicago: University of Chicago Press.

Baglioni, Simone, Donatella Della Porta and Paolo Graziano (2008). 'The Contentious Politics of Unemployment: The Italian Case in Comparative Perspective'. *European Journal of Political Research*, 47(6), 827–851.

Barabas, Jason (2004). 'How Deliberation Affects Policy Opinions'. *American Political Science Review*, 98(4), 687–701.

Barbier, Jean-Claude and Valeria Fargion (2004) 'Continental Invonsistencies on the Path to Activation: Consequences for Social Citizenship in Italy and France'. *European Societies*, 6(4): 437–460.

Barbier, Jean-Claude and Wolfgang Ludwig-Mayerhofer (2004). 'Introduction: The Many Worlds of Activation'. *European Societies*, 6(4), 424–436.

Bardi, Luciano (2007). 'Electoral Change and Its Impact on the Party System in Italy'. *West European Politics*, 30(4), 711–732.

Bartolini, Stefano (2000). *The Political Mobilization of the European Left, 1860–1980: The Class Cleavage*. Cambridge: Cambridge University Press.

Bartolini, Stefano, Alessandro Chiaramonte and Roberto D'Alimonte (2004). 'The Italian Party System Between Parties and Coalitions'. *West European Politics*, 27(1), 1–19.

Baumgartner, Frank R. and Brian D. Jones (2002). *Policy Dynamics*. Chicago: University of Chicago Press.

Baumgartner, Frank R. and Beth L. Leech (1998). *Basic Interests: The Importance of Groups in Politics and in Political Science*. Princeton: Princeton University Press.

Béland, Daniel (2001). 'Does Labor Matter? Institutions, Labor Unions, and Pension Reform in France and the United States'. *Journal of Public Policy*, 21(2), 153–172.

Bennett, W. Lance (1990a). 'Taking the Public by Storm: Information, Cuing, and the Democratic Process in the Gulf Conflict'. *Political Communication*, 10(4), 331–351.

Bennett, W. Lance (1990b). 'Toward a Theory of Press-state Relations in the United Stats'. *Journal of Communication*, 40(2), 103–125.

Bennett, W. Lance, Viktor W. Pickard and David P. Iozzi (2004). 'Managing the Public Sphere: Journalistic Construction of the Great Globalization Debate'. *Journal of Communication*, 54(3), 437–455.

Benson, Rodney (2014). *Shaping Immigration News: A French-american Comparison*. Cambridge: Cambridge University Press.

Berinsky, Adam J. and Donald R. Kinder (2006). 'Making Sense of Issues Through Media Frames: Understanding the Kosovo Crisis'. *Journal of Politics*, 68(3), 640–656.

Bernhard, Laurent (2012). *Campaign Strategy in Direct Democracy*. Basingstoke: Palgrave Macmillan.

Bernhard, Laurent (2015). 'Going Negative in Direct-democratic Campaigns'. In Alessandro Nai and Annemarie Walter (eds.): *New Perspectives on Negative Campaigning: Why Attack Politics Matters*. Colchester: ECPR Press, pp. 147–164.

Berton, Fabio, Matteo Richiardi and Stefano Sacchi (2009). 'Flessibilità del lavoro e precarietà dei lavoratori in Italia'. *Rivista Italiana di Politiche Pubbliche*, 1, 33–70.

Bertozzi, Fabio and Giuliano Bonoli (2002). 'Verso una convergenza delle politiche nazionali per l'occupazione? La costruzione di un modello europeo attraverso il metodo di coordinamento aperto'. *Rivista Italiana di Politiche Pubbliche* 3, 31–57.

Beyers, Jan (2004). 'Voice and Access: Political Practices of European Interest Associations'. *European Union Politics*, 5(2), 211–240.

Blumler, Jay G. and Michael Gurevitch (1995). *The Crisis of Public Communication*. London: Routledge.

Blyth, Mark (2002). *Great Transformations: Economic Ideas and Institutional Change in the Twentieth Century*. Cambridge: Cambridge University Press.

Boczkowski, Pablo J., Eugenia Mitchelstein and Marin, Walter (2011). 'Convergence Across Divergence: Understanding the Gap in the Online News Choices of Journalists and Consumers in Western Europe and Latin America'. *Communication Research*, 38(3), 376–396.

Boeri, Tito, Gordon H. Hanson and Barry McCormick (2002). *Immigration Policy and the Welfare System*. Oxford: Oxford University Press.

Bohl, Marian (2016). *Explaining the Choice for Personalization as a Campaign Strategy*. Dissertation, manuscript, University of Zurich.

Bonoli, Giuliano (2000). *The Politics of Pension Reform: Institutions and Policy Change in Western Europe*. Cambridge: Cambridge University Press.

Bonoli, Giuliano (2005). 'The Politics of the New Social Policies: Providing Coverage Against New Social Risks in Mature Welfare States'. *Policy and Politics*, 33(3), 431–449.

Bonoli, Giuliano (2006). 'New Social Risks and the Politics of Post-industrial Social Policies'. In Klaus Armingeon and Giuliano Bonoli (eds.): *The Politics of Post-industrial Welfare States*. London: Routledge, pp. 3–26.

Bonoli, Giuliano (2007). 'Too Narrow and Too Wide at Once: The "Welfare State" as a Dependent Variable in Policy Analysis'. In Jochen Clasen and Nico A. Siege (eds.): *Investigating Welfare State Change: The "Dependent Variable Problem" in Comparative Analysis*. Northampton: Edward Elgar, pp. 24–39.

Bonoli, Giuliano (2010). 'The Political Economy of Active Labour Market Policy'. *Politics and Society*, 38(4), 435–457.

Bonoli, Giuliano (2013) *The Origins of Active Social Policy: Labour Market and Childcare Policies in a Comparative Perspective*. Oxford: Oxford University Press.

Bonoli, Giuliano (2012). 'Active Labour Market Policy and Social Investment: A Changing Relationship'. In Nathalie Morel, Bruno Palier and Joakim Palme (eds.): *Towards a Social Investment Welfare State? Ideas, Policies and Challenges*. Bristol: The Policy Press, pp. 181–204.

Bonoli, Giuliano and Patrick Emmenegger (2010). 'State-society Relationships, Social Trust and the Development of Labour Market Policies in Italy and Sweden'. *West European Politics*, 33(4), 830–850.

Bonoli, Giuliano and André Mach (2001). 'The New Swiss Employment Puzzle'. *Swiss Political Science Review*, 7(2), 81–94.

Bonoli, Giuliano and David Natali (2012). *The Politics of the New Welfare States: Analysing Reforms in Western Europe*. Oxford: Oxford University Press.

Boorstin, Daniel Joseph (1977). *The Image: A Guide to Pseudo-events in America*. New York: Atheneum.

Boydstun, Amber, Anne Hardy and Stefaan Walgrave (2014). 'Two Faces of Media Attention: Media Storm Versus Non-storm Coverage', *Political Communication*, 31(4), 501–531.

Bradley, David, Evelyne Huber, Stephanie Moller, François Nielsen and John D. Stephens (2003). 'Distribution and Redistribution in Postindustrial Democracies', *World Politics*, 55(2), 193–228.

Brants, Kees and Philip van Praag (2006). 'Signs of Media Logic: Half a Century of Political Communication in the Netherlands'. *Javnos – The Public*, 13(1), 25–40.

Bredgaard, Thomas, Flemming Larsen and Per Krogshøj Madsen (2006). 'Opportunities and Challenges for Flexicurity – The Danish Example'. *Transfer*, 12(1), 61–82.

Budge, Ian and Dennis Farlie (1983). 'Party Competition – Selective Emphasis or Direct Confrontation? An Alternative View with Data'. In Hans Daalder and Peter Mair (eds.): *Western European Party Systems: Continuity and Change.* Beverly Hills: Sage, pp. 267–305.

Burstein, Paul (1998). *Discrimination, Jobs, and Politics: The Struggle for Equal Employment Opportunity in the United States Since the New Deal.* Chicago: University of Chicago Press.

Carragee, Kevin M. and Wim Roefs (2004). 'The Neglect of Power in Recent Framing Research'. *The Journal of Communication*, 54(2), 214–233.

Casey, Bernard H. (2004). 'The OECD Jobs Strategy and the European Employment Strategy: Two Views of the Labour Market and the Welfare State'. *European Journal of Industrial Relations*, 10 (3), 329–352.

Champion, Cyrielle (2011). 'Switzerland: A Latecomer Catching Up?'. In Jochen Clasen and Daniel Clegg (eds.): *Regulating the Risk of Unemployment. National Adaptations to Post-industrial Labour Markets in Europe.* Oxford: Oxford University Press, pp. 121–139.

Chong, Dennis and James N. Druckman (2007a). 'Framing Public Opinion in Competitive Democracies'. *American Political Science Review*, 101(4), 637–656.

Chong, Dennis and James N. Druckman (2007b). 'A Theory of Framing and Opinion Formation in Competitive Elite Environments'. *Journal of Communication*, 57(1), 99–118.

Chong, Dennis and James N. Druckman (2007c). 'Framing Theory'. *Annual Review of Political Science*, 10, 103–126.

Claassen, Ryan (2011). 'Political Awareness and Electoral Campaigns: Maximum Effects for Minimum Citizens?' *Political Behavior*, 33(2), 203–223.

Clasen, Jochen (2011). 'The United Kingdom: Towards a Single Working-age Benefit System'. In Jochen Clasen and Daniel Clegg (eds.): *Regulating the Risk of Unemployment. National Adaptations to Post-industrial Labour Markets in Europe.* Oxford: Oxford University Press, pp. 15–33.

Clasen, Jochen and Daniel Clegg (2011). *Regulating the Risk of Unemployment: National Adaptations to Post-industrial Labour Markets in Europe.* Oxford: Oxford University Press.

Clasen, Jochen, Daniel Clegg and Jon Kvist (2012). *European Labour Market Policies in (the) Crisis.* Brussels: EUI aisbl (Working Paper).

Cobb, Roger and Charles D. Elder (1972). *Participation in American Politics: The Dynamics of Agenda Building.* Boston: Allyn and Bacon.

Colombo, Céline and Hanspeter Kriesi (2017). 'Party, Policy – or Both? Partisan-biased Processing of Policy Arguments in Direct Democracy'. *Journal of Elections, Public Opinion and Parties*, 27(3), 235–253.

Cottle, Simon and Mugdha Rai (2006). 'Between Display and Deliberation: Analyzing TV News as Communicative Architecture'. *Media Culture and Society*, 28(2), 163–189.

Couldry, Nich and Andreas Hepp (2012). 'Comparing Media Cultures'. In Frank Esser and Thomas Hanitzsch (eds.): *Handbook of Comparative Communication Research*. London: Routledge, pp. 249–261.

Culpepper, Pepper D. (2002). 'Power, Puzzling, and Pacting: The informational Logic of Negotiated Reforms'. *Journal of European Public Policy*, 9(5), 774–790.

Culpepper, Pepper D. (2011). *Quiet Politics and Business Power: Corporate Control in Europe and Japan*. Cambridge: Cambridge University Press.

Czada, Roland (2005). 'Social Policy: Crisis and Transformation'. In Simon Greene and William Paterson (eds.): *Governance in Modern Germany: The Semisovereign State Revisited*. Cambridge: Cambridge University Press, pp. 165–189.

Daguerre, Anne (2007). *Active Labour Market Policies and Welfare Reform. Europe and the US in Comparative Perspective*. Houndmills: Palgrave Macmillan.

Daguerre, Anne and Peter Taylor-Gooby (2004). 'Neglecting Europe: Explaining the Predominance of American Ideas in New Labour's Welfare Policies Since 1997'. *Journal of European Social Policy*, 14(1), 25–39.

Dahl, Robert A. (1961). *Who Governs? Democracy and Power in an American City*. New Haven: Yale University Press.

Danielian, Lucig H. and Benjamin I. Page (1994). 'The Heavenly Chorus: Interest Group Voices on TV News'. *American Journal of Political Science*, 38 (4), 1056–1078.

Dares (2010). *Les apprentis sortis du système scolaire en 2004: 86% des jeunes en emploi trois ans après la fin du contrat d'apprentissage*. Paris.

Deacon, Alan (2000). 'Learning from the US? The Influence of American Ideas Upon "New Labour" Thinking on Welfare Reform'. *Policy and Politics*, 28(1), 5–18.

Demers, David K. (1998). 'Structural Pluralism, Corporate Newspaper Structure, and News Source Perceptions: Another Test of the Editorial Vigor Hypothesis'. *Journalism and Masse Communication Quarterly*, 75(3), 572–592.

de Vries, Raymond, Aimee Stanczyk, Ian F. Wall, Rebecca Uhlmann, Laura J. Damschroder and Scott Y. Kim (2010). 'Assessing the Quality of Democratic Deliberation: A Case Study of Public Deliberation on the Ethis of Surrogate Consent for Research'. *Social Science and Medicine*, 70(12), 1896–1903.

Diani, Mario (2003). 'Leaders or Brokers? Position and Influence in Social Movements Networks'. In Mario Diani and Doug McAdam (eds.): *Social Movements and Networks: Relational Approaches to Collective Action*. Oxford: Oxford University Press, pp. 105–122.

Dimitrova, Daniela V. and Jesper Strömbäck (2009). 'Look Who's Talking'. *Journalism Practice*, 3(1), 75–91.

Dingledey, Irene (2010). 'Agenda 2010: Dualisierung der Arbeitsmarktpolitik'. *Aus Politik und Zeitgeschichte*, 48(10), 18–25.

Dingledey, Irene (2011). 'Germany: Moving Towards Integration whilst Maintaining Segmentation'. In Jochen Clasen and Daniel Clegg (eds.): *Regulating the Risk of Unemployment. National Adaptations to Post-industrial Labour Markets in Europe*. Oxford: Oxford University Press, pp. 55–74.

Disch, Lisa (2012). 'The Impurity of Representation and the Vitality of Democracy'. *Cultural Studies*, 26(1), 207–222.

Downs, Anthony (1972). 'Up and Down with Ecology: The "Issue Attention Cycle"'. *Public Interest*, 28(1), 28–50.

Druckman, James N. (2001). 'On the Limits of Framing Effects: Who Can Frame?'. *Journal of Politics*, 63(4), 1041–1066.

Druckman, James N., Erik Peterson and Rune Slothuus (2013). 'How Elite Partisan Polarization Affects Public Opinion Formation'. *American Political Science Review*, 107(1), 57–79.

DWP (Department for Work and Pensions) (2010). *Universal Credit: Welfare That Works*. London.

Eagly, Alice H. and Shelly Chaiken (1993). *The Psychology of Attitudes*. New York: Harcourt Brace Jovanovich College Publishers.

Ebbinghaus, Bernhard (2006). *Reforming Early Retirement in Europe, Japan and the USA*. Oxford: Oxford University Press.

Ebbinghaus, Bernhard (2010). 'Reforming Bismarckian Corporatism: The Changing Role of Social Partnership in Continental Europe'. In Bruno Palier (ed.): *A Long Goodbye to Bismarck? The Politics of Welfare State Reform in Continental Europe*. Amsterdam: Amsterdam University Press, pp. 255–278.

Eichengreen, Barry (2012). 'European Monetary Integration with Benefit of Hindsight'. *Common Market Studies*, 50(1), 123–136.

Elster, Jon (1976). 'Some Conceptual Problems in Political Theory'. In Brian Berry (ed.): *Power and Political Theory: Some European Perspectives*. London: Wiley, pp. 245–270.

Emmenegger, Patrick (2009). 'Barriers to Entry: Insider/Outsider Politics and the Political Determinants of Job Security Regulations'. *Journal of European Social Policy*, 19(2): 131–146.

Emmenegger, Patrick (2010a). 'The Long Road to Flexicurity: The Development of Job Security Regulations in Denmark and Sweden'. *Scandinavian Political Studies*, 33(3), 271–294.

Emmenegger, Patrick (2010b). 'Low Statism in Coordinated Market Economies: The Development of Job Security Regulations in Switzerland'. *International Political Science Review*, 31(2), 187–205.

Entman, Robert M. (1993). 'Framing: Toward Clarification of a Fractured Paradigm'. *Journal of Communication*, 43(4), 51–58.

Entman, Robert M. (2003). 'Cascading Activation: Contesting the White House's Frame After 9/11'. *Political Communication*, 20(4), 415–432.

Entman, Robert M. (2004). *Projections of Power Framing News, Public Opinion, and U.S. Foreign Policy*. Chicago: University of Chicago Press.

Esaiasson, Peter and Hanne Marthe Narud (2013). *Between-election Democracy: The Representative Relationships After Election Day*. Colchester: ECPR Press.

Esping-Andersen, Gøsta (1990). *Three Worlds of Welfare State Capitalism*. Princeton: Princeton University Press.

Esping-Andersen, Gøsta (1996). 'Welfare States Without Work: The Impasse of Labour Sheddling and Familiarism in Continental European Social Policy'. In Gøsta Esping-Andersen (ed.): *Welfare States in Transition: National Adaptions in Global Economies*. London: Sage, pp. 66–87.

Esping-Andersen, Gøsta (2009). *The Incomplete Revolution: Adapting to Women's New Roles*. Cambridge: Polity Press.

Esser, Frank (1999). 'Tabloidization of News: A Comparative Analysis of Anglo-American and German Press Journalism'. *European Journal of Communication*, 14(3), 291–324.

Esser, Frank (2008). 'Dimensions of Political News Cultures: Sound Bite and Image Bite News in France, Germany, Great Britain, and the United States'. *International Journal of Press/Politics*, 13(4), 401–428.

Esser, Frank (2013). 'Mediatization as a Challenge: Media Logic versus Political Logic' In Hanspeter Kriesi, Sandra Lavenex, Frank Esser, Jörg Matthes, Marc Bühlmann and Daniel Bochsler (eds.): *Democracy in the Age of Globalization and Mediatization*. Basingstoke: Palgrave Macmillan, pp. 155–176.

Esser, Frank, Claes H. de Vreese, Jesper Strömbäck, Peter van Aelst, Toril Aalberg, James Stanyer, Günther Lengauer, Rosa Berganza, Guido Legnante, Stylianos Papathanassopoulos, Susana Salgado, Tamir Sheafer and Carsten Reinemann (2012). 'Political Information Opportunities in Europe. A Longitudinal and Comparative Study of Thirteen Television Systems'. *The International Journal of Press/Politics*, 17(3), 247–274.

Esser, Frank and Thomas Hanitzsch (eds.) (2013). *The Handbook of Comparative Communication Research*. London: Routledge.

Esser, Frank and Jörg Matthes (2013). 'Mediatization Effects on Political News, Political Actors, Political Decisions and Political Audiences'. In Hanspeter Kriesi, Sandra Lavenex, Frank Esser, Jörg Matthes, Marc Bühlmann and Daniel Bochsler (eds.): *Democracy in the Age of Globalization and Mediatization*. Basingstoke: Palgrave Macmillan, pp. 177–201.

Esser, Frank and Jesper Strömbäck (2012a). 'Comparing Election Campaign Communication'. In Frank Esser and Thomas Hanitzsch (eds.): *Handbook of Comparative Communication Research*. London: Routledge, pp. 289–307.

Esser, Frank and Jesper Strömbäck (2012b). 'Comparing News on Elections'. In Frank Esser and Thomas Hanitzsch (eds.): *Handbook of Comparative Communication Research*. London: Routledge, pp. 308–327.

Estevez-Abe, Margarita, Torben Iversen and David Soskice (2001). 'Social Protection and the Formation of Skills'. In Peter A. Hall and David Soskice (eds.): *Varieties of Capitalism*. Oxford: Oxford University Press, pp. 145–183.

Farrell, Henry and John Quiggin (2012): *Consensus, Dissensus and Economic Ideas: The Rise and Fall of Keynesianism During the Economic Crisis*.

Ferree, Myra Marx, William A. Gamson, Jürgen Gerhards and Dieter Rucht (2002). *Shaping Abortion Discourse. Democracy and the Public Sphere in Germany and the United States*. Cambridge: Cambridge University Press.

Ferrera, Maurizio (1996). 'The "Southern Model" of Welfare in Social Europe'. *Journal of European Social Policy*, 8(1), 17–37.

Ferrera, Maurizio (2012). Ideological Change and Social Policy in Europe: Towards a Liberal Neo-Welfarism. Florence: EUI (Working Paper).

Ferrera, Maurizio and Elisabetta Gualmini (2004). *Rescued by Europe? Social and Labour Market Reforms in Italy from Maastricht to Berlusconi.* Amsterdam: Amsterdam University Press.

Fillieule, Olivier and Danielle Tartakowsky (2008). *La manifestation.* Paris: Presses de Sciences Po.

Finkel, Steven E. (1993). 'Re-examining the "Minimal Effects" Model in Recent Presidential Campaigns'. *Journal of Politics*, 55(1), 1–21.

Fischer, Manuel, Alex Fischer and Pascal Sciarini (2009). 'Power and Conflict in the Swiss Political Elite: An Aggregation of Existing Network Analyses'. *Swiss Political Science Review*, 15(1), 31–62.

Fiske, Susan T. and Shelley E. Taylor (1991). *Social Cognition.* New York: McGraw-Hill (2nd edition).

Fleckenstein, Timo (2008). 'Restructuring Welfare for the Unemployed: The Hartz Legislation in Germany'. *Journal of European Social Policy*, 18(2), 177–188.

Fournier, Patrick, Fred Cutler, Stuart Soroka and Greg Lyle (2004). *Who Responds to Elections Campaigns? The Two-mediator Model Revisited.* University of Montréal (Working Paper).

Fossati, Flavia (2017a) 'How Regimes Shape Preferences. A Study of Political Actors' Labour Market Policy Preferences in Flexicurity and Dualizing Countries', *Socio-economic Review* 16(3): 523–544. https://doi.org/10.1093/ser/mwx040.

Fossati, Flavia (2017b) 'Who Wants Demanding Active Labour Market Policies? Public Attitudes Towards Policies That Put Pressure on the Unemployed'. *Journal of Social Policy*, 47(1): 77–97 https://doi.org/10.1017/S0047279417000216.

Gallie, Ducan and Serge Paugam (2000). 'The Experience of Unemployment in Europe: The Debate'. In Duncan Gallie and Serge Paugam (eds.): *Welfare Regimes and the Experience of Unemployment in Europe.* Oxford: Oxford University Press, pp. 1–22.

Galtung, Johan and Marie H. Ruge (1965). 'The Structure of Foreign News'. *Journal of Peace Research*, 2(1), 64–91.

Gamson, William A. (1968). *Power and Discontent.* Homewood: Dorsey Press.

Gamson, William A. (1992). *Talking Politics.* Cambridge: Cambridge University Press.

Gamson, William A. and David S. Meyer (1996). 'Framing Political Opportunity'. In John D. McCarthy, John D. Zald and Mayer N. Zald (eds.): *Comparative Perspectives on Social Movements.* Cambridge: Cambridge University Press, pp. 275–290.

Gamson, William A. and Andre Modigliani (1987). 'The Changing Culture of Affirmative Action'. *Research in Political Sociology*, 3(1), 137–177.

Gans, Herbert J. (1979). *Deciding What's News: A Study of CBS Evening News, NBC Nightly News, Newsweek, and Time.* New York: Pantheon Books.

Gelman, Andrew, David Park, Boris Shor, Joseph Bafumi and Jeronimo Cortina (2008). *Red State, Blue State, Rich State, Poor State. Why American Vote the Way They Do.* Princeton: Princeton University Press.

Gelman, Andrew and Gary King (1993). 'Why Are American Presidential Election Campaign Polls So Variable When Votes Are So Predictable?'. *British Journal of Political Science*, 23(4), 409–451.

Gibson, Rachel and Andrea Römmele (2008). 'Political Communication'. In Daniele Caramani (ed.): *Comparative Politics*. Oxford: Oxford University Press, pp. 473–491.

Giddens, Anthony (2000). *The Third Way: The Renewal of Social Democracy.* Cambridge: Polity Press.

Gilbert, Neil (2002). *Transformation of the Welfare State: The Silent Surrender of Public Responsibility.* Oxford: Oxford University Press.

Gingrich, Jane and Ben Ansell (2011). *The Dynamics of Social Investment: Human Capital, Activation, and Care.* Working Paper.

Giugni, Marco (2010). *The Contentious Politics of Unemployment in Europe: Welfare State and Political Opportunities.* Basingstoke: Palgrave Macmillan.

Glyn, Andrew (2006). *Capitalism Unleashed: Finance Globalization and Welfare.* Oxford: Oxford University Press.

Gourevitch, Peter (1984). 'Breaking with Orthodoxy: The Politics of Economic Policy Responses to the Depression of the 1930s'. *International Organization*, 38(1), 95–129.

Gourevitch, Peter (1986). *Politics in Hard Times: Comparative Responses to International Economic Crisis.* Cornell: Cornell University Press.

Graber, Doris (2003). 'The Media and Democracy: Beyond Myths and Stereotypes'. *Annual Review of Political Science*, 6(1), 139–160.

Graziano, Paolo (2007). 'Adapting to the European Employment Strategy? Recent Developments in Italian Employment Policy'. *The International Journal of Comparative Labour Law and Industrial Relations*, 23(4), 543–565.

Green-Pedersen, Christoffer (2010). 'The Dependent Variable Problem Within the Study of Welfare State Retrenchment: Defining the Problem and Looking for Solutions'. *Comparative Policy Analysis: Research and Practice*, 6(1), 3–14.

Green-Pedersen, Christoffer and Peter B. Mortensen (2004). Who Sets the Agenda and Who Responds to It in the Danish Parliament? A New Model of Issue Competition and Agenda-setting. *European Journal of Political Research*, 49(2), 257–281.

Gurevitch, Michael and Jay G. Blumler (2004). 'State of the Art of Comparative Political Communication Research: Posed for Maturity?'. In Frank Esser and Barbara Pfetsch (eds.): *Comparing Political Communication. Theories, Cases, and Challenges.* Cambridge: Cambridge University Press, pp. 325–343.

Habermas, Jürgen (1981). *Theorie kommunikativen Handelns.* Frankfurt am Main: Suhrkamp.

Habermas, Jürgen (1991). *Erläuterungen zur Diskursethik.* Frankfurt am Main: Suhrkamp

Haberman, Jürgen (1992). *Faktizität und Geltung: Beiträge zur Diskurstheorie des Rechts und des demokratischen Rechtsstaaates.* Frankfurt am Main: Suhrkamp

Habermas, Jürgen (1996). *Between Facts and Norms: Contributions to a Discourse Theory of Law and Democracy.* New Baskerville: MIT Press.

Hackett, Robert A. (1985). 'A Hierarchy of Access: Aspects of Source Bias on Canadian TV News'. *Journalism Quarterly*, 62(2), 256–265.

Hall, Peter A. (1990). 'Pluralism and Pressure Politics'. In Peter A. Hall, Jack Hayward and Howard Machin (eds.): *Developments in French Politics.* London: Macmillan, pp. 77–92.

Hall, Peter A. (1993). 'Policy Paradigms, Social Learning, and the State: The Case of Economic Policymaking in Britain'. *Comparative Politics*, 25(3), 275–296.

Hall, Peter A. (1997). 'The Role of Interests, Institutions and Ideas in the Comparative Political Economy of the Industrialized Nations'. In Mark I. Lichbach and Alan S. Zuckerman (eds.): *Comparative Politics: Rationality, Culture, and Structure*. Cambridge: Cambridge University Press, pp. 174–207.

Hall, Peter A. (2005). 'Preference Formation as a Political Process: The Case of Monetary Union in Europe'. In Ira Katznelson and Barry R. Weingast (eds.): *Preferences and Situations: Points of Intersection Between Historical and Rational Choice Institutionalism*. New York: Russell Sage Foundation, pp. 129–160.

Hall, Peter A. and Daniel Gingerich (2009). 'Varieties of Capitalism and Institutional Complementarities in the Political Economy'. *British Journal of Political Science*, 39(3), 449–482.

Hall, Peter A. and David Soskice (2001). *Varieties of Capitalism*. Oxford: Oxford University Press.

Hallin, Daniel C. (1992). 'Sound Bit News: Television Coverage of Elections, 1968-1988'. *Journal of Communication*, 42(2), 5–24.

Hallin, Daniel C. and Paolo Mancini (2004). *Comparing Media Systems: Three Models of Media and Politics*. Cambridge: Cambridge University Press.

Hamann, Kerstin and John Kelly (2004). 'Unions as Political Actors: Revitalization?'. In Carola M. Frege and John Kelly (eds.): *Varieties of Unionism: Strategies for Union Revitalization in a Globalizing Economy*. Oxford: Oxford University Press, pp. 93–116.

Handler, Joel F. (2003). 'Social Citizenship and Workfare in the US and Western Europe: from Status to Contract'. *Journal of European Social Policy*, 13(3), 229–243.

Handler, Joel F. (2004). *Social Citizenship and Workfare in the United States and Western Europe: The Paradox of Inclusion*. Cambridge: Cambridge University Press.

Hänggli, Regula (2012a). 'Key Factors in Frame Building: How Strategic Political Actors Shape News Media Coverage'. *American Behavioral Scientist*, 56(3), 300–317.

Hänggli, Regula (2012b). 'Key factors in Frame Building'. In Hanspeter Kriesi (ed.): *Political Communication in Direct Democratic Campaigns. Enlightening or Manipulating?* Basingstoke: Palgrave Macmillan, pp. 125–142.

Hänggli, Regula (2018). The Origin of Dialogue in the News Media University of Fribourg (Book manuscript).

Hänggli, Regula and Hanspeter Kriesi (2010). 'Political Framing Strategies and Their Impact on Media Framing in a Swiss Direct-democratic Campaign'. *Political Communication*, 27(2): 141–157.

Hänggli, Regula and Hanspeter Kriesi (2012). 'Frame Construction and Frame Promotion (Strategic Framing Choices)'. *American Behavioral Scientist*, 56(3), 260–278.

Harmel, Robert and Kenneth Janda (1994). 'An Integrated Theory of Party Goals and Party Change'. *Journal of Theoretical Politics*, 6(3), 259–287.

Hassel, Anke (2003). 'The Politics of Social Pacts'. *British Journal of Industrial Relations*, 41(4), 707–726.

Hassel, Anke (2006). *Wage Setting, Social Pacts and the Euro: A New Role for the State*. Amsterdam: Amsterdam University Press.

Hassel, Anke and Hugh Williamson (2004). *The Evolution of the German Model: How to Judge Reforms in Europe's Largest Economy*. Working Paper.

Häusermann, Silja (2006). 'Changing Coalitions in Social Policy Reforms: The Politics of New Social Needs and Demands'. *Journal of European Social Policy*, 16(1): 5–21.

Häusermann, Silja (2010). *The Politics of Welfare State Reform in Continental Europe: Modernization in Hard Times*. Cambridge: Cambridge University Press.

Häusermann, Silja and Bruno Palier (2008). 'The Politics of Employment-friendly Welfare Reforms in Post-industrial Economies', *Socio-Economic Review* 6: 559–586.

Häusermann, Silja, Georg Picot and Dominik Geering (2013). Review Article: Rethinking Party Politics and the Welfare State – Recent Advances in the Literature, *British Journal of Political Science*, 43(1): 221–240.

Helbling, Marc, Dominic Höglinger and Bruno Wüest (2010). 'How Political Parties Frame European Integration'. *European Journal of Political Research*, 49(4), 495–521.

Helbling, Marc, Dominic Höglinger and Bruno Wüest (2012). 'The Impact of Arenas in Public Debates over Globalization'. In Hanspeter Kriesi, Edgar Grande, Martin Dolezal, Marc Helbling, Dominic Höglinger, Swen Hutter and Bruno Wüest (eds.): *Political Conflict in Western Europe*. Cambridge: Cambridge University Press, pp. 207–228.

Hemerijck, Anton and Werner Eichhorst (2010). 'Whatever Happened to the Bismarckian Welfare State? From Labor-shedding to Employment-friendly Reforms'. In Bruno Palier (ed.): *A Long Goodbye to Bismarck? The Politics of Welfare Reform in Continental Europe*. Amsterdam: Amsterdam University Press, pp. 301–331.

Hilgartner, Stephen and Charles L. Bosk (1988). 'The Rise and Fall of Social Problems: A Public Arenas Model'. *American Journal of Sociology*, 94(1): 53–78.

Hillygus, Sunshine (2010). 'Campaign Effects on Vote Choice'. In Jan Leighly and George C. Edwards III (eds.): *Oxford Handbook on Elections and Political Behavior*. Oxford: Oxford University Press, pp. 326–345.

Hinrichs, Karl and Olli Kangas (2003). 'When Is a Change Big Enough to Be a System Shift? Small System-shifting Changes in German and Finnish Pension Policies'. *Social Policy and Administration*, 37(6), 573–591.

Hirschman, Albert O. (1991). *The Rhetoric of Reaction*. Cambridge: Belknap Press of Harvard University Press.

HM Treasury (2010). *Spending Review Framework*. London.

Howell, Chris (2006). *Trade Unions and the State*. Princeton: Princeton University Press.

Huber, Evelyne and John D. Stephens (2001). *Development and Crisis of the Welfare State: Parties and Policies in Global Markets*. Chicago: University of Chicago Press.

Immergut, Ellen M. (1990). 'Institutions, Veto Points, and Policy Results: A Comparative Analysis of Health Care'. *Journal of Public Policy*, 10(4), 391–416.

Ingold, Karin and Frédéric Varone (2011). 'Treating Policy Brokers Seriously: Evidence from Climate Policy'. *Journal of Public Administration Research and Theory*, 22(2), 319–346.

Iversen, Torben (1999). *Contested Economic Institutions: The Politics of Macroeconomics and Wage Bargaining in Advanced Democracies*. Cambridge: Cambridge University Press.

Iversen, Torben and Anne Wren (1998). 'Equality, Employment, and Budgetary Restraint: The Trilemma of the Service Economy'. *World Politics*, 50(4), 507–546.

Iyengar, Shanto and Jennifer A. McGrady (2007). *Media Politics: A Citizen's Guide*. New York: W. W. Norton and Company.

Iyengar, Shanto, Helmut Norpoth and Kyu S. Hahn (2004). 'Consumer Demand for Election News: The Horserace Sells'. *Journal of Politics*, 66(1), 157–175.

Iyengar, Shanto and Adam F. Simon (2000). 'New Perspectives and Evidence on Political Communication and Campaign Effects'. Annual Review of Psychology, 31, 149–169.

Jagers, Jan and Stefaan Walgrave (2007). 'Populism as Political Communication Style: An Empirical Study of Political Parties' Discourse in Belgium'. *European Journal of Political Research*, 46(3), 319–345.

Jamieson, Kathleen Hall and Joseph N. Cappella (1997). *Echo Chamber: Rush Limaugh and the Conservative Media Establishment*. Oxford: Oxford University Press.

Jarren, Otfried (2000). 'Gesellschaftliche Integration durch Medien? Zur Begründung normativer Anforderungen an Medien'. *Medien und Kommunikationswissenschaft*, 48(1), 22–41.

Jarren, Otfried and Patrick Donges (2002). *Politische Kommunikation in der Mediengesellschaft. Bd. 2: Akteure, Prozesse und Inhalte*. Wiesbaden: Westdeutscher Verlag.

Jasper, James M. (2004). 'A Strategic Approach to Collective Action: Looking for Agency in Social Movement Choices'. *Mobilization*, 9(1), 1–16.

Jasper, James M. (2006). *Getting Your Way: Strategic Dilemmas in the Real World*. Chicago: The University of Chicago Press.

Jegen, Maya (2003). *Energiepolitische Vernetzung in der Schweiz: Analyse der Kooperationsneztwerke und Ideensysteme der energiepolitischen Entscheidungsträger*. Basel: Helbing and Lichtenhahn.

Jenkins, J. Craig (1981). 'Sociopolitical Movements'. In Samuel L. Long (ed.): *Handbook of Political Behaviour*. Vol. 4. New York: Plenum Publishers, pp. 81–154.

Jenkins-Smith, Hank C. (1990). *Democratic Politics and Policy Analysis*. Pacific Grove: Brooks and Cole.

Jerit, Jennifer (2004). 'Survival of the Fittest: Rhetoric During the Course of an Election Campaign'. *Political Psychology*, 25(4), 563–575.

Jessop, Bob (1993). 'Towards a Schumpeterian Workfare State? Preliminary Remarks on Post-fordist Political Economy'. *Studies in Political Economy*, 40, 7–40.

Jessoula, Matteo and Tiziana Alti (2010). 'Italy: An Uncompleted Departure from Bismarck'. In Bruno Palier (ed.): *A Long Goodbye to Bismarck?*

The Politics of Welfare Reform in Continental Europe. Amsterdam: Amsterdam University Press, pp. 157–182.

Jessoula, Matteo, Paolo R. Graziano and Ilaria Madama (2010). 'Selective Flexicurity in Segmented Labour Markets: The Case of Italian Mid-Siders'. *Journal of Social Policy*, 39(4), 561–583.

Johnson, Thomas J., Shannon L. Bichard and Weiwu Zhang (2009). 'Communication Communities or 'Cyberghettos'?: A Path Analysis Model Examining Factors that Explain Selective Exposure to Blogs'. *Journal of Computer-mediated Communication*, 15(1), 60–82.

Jones, Bryan D. (1994). *Reconceiving Decision-making in Democratic Politics: Attention, Choice, and Public Policy.* Chicago: University of Chicago Press.

Jørgensen, Henning and Michaela Schulze (2012). 'A Double Farewell to a Former Model? Danish Unions and Activation Policy'. *Local Economy*, 27(5–6), 637–644.

Karvonen, Lauri (2010). The Personalisation of Politics: A Study of Parliamentary Demoracies. Colchester: ECPR Press.

Kaplan, Noah, David K. Park and Travis N. Ridout (2006). 'Dialogue in American Campaigns? An Examination of Issue Convergence in Candidate Television Advertising'. *American Journal of Political Science*, 50(3), 724–736.

Katzenstein, Peter (1985). *Small States in World Markets.* Ithaca/New York: Cornell University Press.

Keck, Margaret E. and Kathryn Sikkink (1998). 'Transnational Advocacy Networks in the Movement Society'. In David S. Meyer and Sidney Tarrow (eds.): *The Social Movement Society: Contentious Politics for a New Century.* Boulder: Rowman and Littlefield, pp. 217–238.

Kemmerling, Achim and Oliver Bruttel (2006). 'New Politics in German Labour Market Policy? The Implications of the Recent Hartz Reforms for the German Welfare State'. *West European Politics*, 29(1): 90–112.

Kepplinger, Hans Matthias (2009). *Publizistische Konflikte und Skandale.* Wiesbaden: VS Verlag für Sozialwissenschaften.

Kernell, Samuel (1997). *Going Public: New Strategies of Presidential Leadership.* Washington: Congressional Quarterly Press.

King, Desmond and Mark Wickham-Jones (1999). 'From Clinton to Blair: The Democratic (Party) Orignis of Welfare to Work'. *The Political Quarterly*, 79(1), 62–74.

Kiousis, Spiro, Michael Mitrook, Xu Wu and Trent Seltzer (2006). 'First- und Second-Level Agenda-Buildung and Agenda-Setting Effects: Exploring the Linkages Among Candidate News Releases, Media Coverage, and Public Opinion During the 2002 Florida Gubernatorial Election'. *Journal of Public Relations Research*, 18(3), 265–285.

Kitschelt, Herbert (1994). *The Transformation of European Social Democracy.* Cambridge: Cambridge University Press.

Klar, Samar, Joshua Robison and James N. Druckman (2013). 'Political Dynamics of Framing'. In Travis N. Ridout (ed.): *New Direction in Media and Politics.* New York: Routledge, pp. 173–192.

Kluver, Randolph, Nicholas W. Jankowski, Kristen A. Foot and Steven M. Schneider (2007). *The Internet and National Elections: A Comparative Study of Web Campaigning*. London: Routledge.

Knoke, David, Franz U. Pappi, Jeff Broadbent and Yutaka Tsujinaka (1996). *Comparing Policy Networks: Labor Politics in the U.S., Germany, and Japan*. Cambridge: Cambridge University Press.

Koistinen, Pertti and Pascual A. Serrano (2009). 'Introduction'. In Pertti Koistinen, Lilja Mósesdóttir and Amparo Serrano Pascual (eds.): *Emerging Systems of Work and Welfare*. Bruxelles: Peter Lang, pp. 95–114.

Kollman, Ken (1998). *Outside Lobbying. Public Opinion and Interest Group Strategies*. Princeton: Princeton University Press.

Koopmans, Ruud (2004). 'Movements and Media: Selection Processes and Evolutionary Dynamics in the Public Sphere'. *Theory and Society*, 33(3/4), 367–391.

Koopmans, Ruud and Paul Statham (1999). 'Ethnic and Civic Conceptions of Nationhood and the Differential Success of the Extreme Right in Germany and Italy'. In Marco Giugni, Doug McAdam and Charles Tilly (eds.): *How Social Movements Matter*. Minneapolis: University of Minnesota Press, pp. 225–252.

Korpi, Walter (1980). 'Social Policy and Distributional Conflict in the Capitalist Democracies. A Preliminary Comparative Framework'. *West European Politics*, 3(3), 296–316.

Korpi, Walter (1983). *The Democratic Class Struggle*. London: Routledge and Kegan Paul.

Kriesi, Hanspeter (1980). *Entscheidungsstrukturen und Entscheidungsprozesse in der Schweiz*. Frankfurt am Main: Campus.

Kriesi, Hanspeter (1998). 'The Transformation of Cleavage Politics: The 1997 Stein Rokkan Lecture'. *European Journal of Political Research*, 33(2), 165–185.

Kriesi, Hanspeter (2004). 'Political Context and Opportunity'. In David H. Snow, Sarah A. Soule and Hanspeter Kriesi (eds.): *The Blackwell Companion to Social Movements*. Oxford: Blackwell Publishing, pp. 67–90.

Kriesi, Hanspeter (2007). *Vergleichende Politikwissenschaft, Teil I: Grundlagen*. Baden-Baden: Nomos.

Kriesi, Hanspeter (2011). 'Personalization of National Election Campaigns'. *Party Politics*, 23(1), 1–20.

Kriesi, Hanspeter (2014). 'The Political Consequences of the Economic Crisis in Europe: Electoral Punishment and Popular Protest'. In Nancy Bermeo and Larry M. Bartels (eds.): *Mass Politics in Tough Times: Opinions, Votes, and Protest in the Great Recession*. Oxford: Oxford University Press, pp. 297–333.

Kriesi, Hanspeter, Silke Adam and Margit Jochum (2006). 'Comparative Analysis of Policy Networks in Western Europe'. *Journal of European Public Policy*, 13(3), 341–361.

Kriesi, Hanspeter, Laurent Bernhard, Céline Colombo, Regula Hänggli, Christian Schemer and Marco Steenbergen (2012b). *Campaign Effects: Voters' Information Processing in Swiss Direct Democratic Campaigns*. Zurich: Working Paper.

322   References

Kriesi, Hanspeter and Daniel Bochsler (2013). 'Varieties of Democracy'. In Hanspeter Kriesi, Sandra Lavenex, Frank Esser, Jörg Matthes, Marc Bühlmann and Daniel Bochsler (eds.): *Democracy in the Age of Globalization and Mediatization*. Basingstoke: Palgrave Macmillan, pp. 69–102.

Kriesi, Hanspeter, Edgar Grande, Martin Dolezal, Marc Helbling, Dominic Höglinger, Swen Hutter and Bruno Wüest (2012): *Political Conflict in Western Europe*. Cambridge: Cambridge University Press.

Kriesi, Hanspeter, Edgar Grande, Romain Lachat, Martin Dolezal, Simon Bornschier and Timotheos Frey (2008). *West European Politics in the Age of Globalization*. Cambridge: Cambridge University Press.

Kriesi, Hanspeter and Maja Jegen (2001). 'The Swiss Energy Policy Elite: The Actor Constellation of a Policy Domain in Transition'. *European Journal of Political Research*, 39(2), 251–287.

Kriesi, Hanspeter, Ruud Kopmans, Jan W. Duyvendak and Marco R. Giugni (1995). *New Social Movements in Western Europe: A Comparative analysis*. Minneapolis: University of Minnesota Press.

Kriesi, Hanspeter and Alex Trechsel (2008). *The Politics of Switzerland. Continuity and Change in a Consensus Democracy*. Cambridge: Cambridge University Press.

Kriesi, Hanspeter, Anke Tresch and Margit Jochum (2007). 'Going Public in the European Union: Action Repertoires of Western European Collective Political Actors'. *European Journal of Political Research*, 40(1), 48–73.

Kriesi, Hanspeter, Laurent Benrhard and Regula Hänggli (2009). The Politics of Campaigning – Dimensions of Strategic Action. In Frank Marcinkowski and Barbara Pfetsch (eds.): *Politik in der Mediendemokratie*. Wiesbaden: VS, pp. 345–365.

Kübler, Daniel (2001). 'Understanding Policy Change with the Advocacy Coalition Framework: An Application to Swiss Drug Policy'. *Journal of European Public Policy*, 8(4), 623–641.

Kuklinksi, James H. and Gary M. Segura (1995). 'Endogeneity, Exogeneity, Time, and Space in Political Representation'. *Legislative Studies Quarterly*, 20(1), 3–21.

Labbé, Dominique (1996). *Syndicats et syndiqués en France depuis 1945*. Paris: L'Harmattan.

Lahusen, Christian (2009). 'The Hidden Hand of the European Union and the Silent Europeanization of Public Debates on Unemployment: The Case of the European Employment Strategy'. In Marco Giugni (ed.): *The Politics of Unemployment in Europe. Policy Responses and Collective Action*. Farnham/ Burlington: Ashgate, pp. 151–172.

Lane, Philip R. (2012). 'The European Sovereign Debt Crisis', *Journal of Economic Perspectives*, 26(3), 49–68.

Laumann, Edward O. and Franz U. Pappi (1976). *Networks of Collective Action: A Perspective on Community Influence Systems*. New York: Academic Press.

Lawrence, Regina (2000). *The Politics of Force: Media and the Construction of Police Brutality*. Berkeley: University of California Press.

Lee, Nam-Jin, Douglas M. Mc Leod and Dhavan V. Shah (2008). 'Framing Policy Debates, Issue Dualism, Journalistic Frames, and Opinions on Controversial Policy Issues'. *Communication Research*, 35(5), 695–718.

Lehmbruch, Gerhard (1976). *Parteienwettbewerb im Bundesstaat.* Stuttgart: Kohlhammer.

Lehmbruch, Gerhard (1979). 'Liberal Corporatism and Party Government'. In Philippe C. Schmitter and Gerhard Lehmbruch (eds.): *Trends Toward Corporatist Intermediation.* London: Sage, pp. 147–183.

Levy, Jonah D (1999). 'Vice into Virtue? Progressive Politics and Welfare Reform in Continental Europe'. *Politics and Society*, 27(2), 239–273.

Lewis-Beck, Michael S. and Martin Paldam (2000). Economic Voting: An Introduction. *Electoral Studies*, 19(2), 113–121.

Lijphart, Arend (1999). Patterns of Democracy. Government Forms and Performance in Thirty-six Countries. New Haven: Yale University Press.

Lijphart, Arend and Markus M. L. Crepaz (1991). 'Corporatism and Consensus Democracy in Eighteen Countries: Conceptual and Empirical Linkages'. *British Journal of Political Science*, 21(2), 235–246.

Lilleker, Darren G., Karolina Koc-Michalska, Eva Johanna Schweitzer, Michal Jacunski, Nigel Jackson and Thierry Vedel (2011). 'Informing, Engaging, Mobilizing and Interacting: Searching for a European Model of Web Campaigning'. *European Journal of Communication*, 26(3), 195–213.

Lipset, Seymour and Stein Rokkan (1985 [1967]). 'Cleavage Structures, Party Systems and Voter Alignments'. In Seymour Lipset (ed.): *Consensus and Conflict. Essays in Political Sociology* . New Brunswick: Transation Books, pp. 1–64.

Livingston, Steven and W. Lance Bennett (2003). 'Gatekeeping, Indexing, and Live-event News: Is Technology Altering the Construction of News?'. *Political Communication*, 20(4), 363–380.

Lødemel, Ivar (2004). 'The Development of Workfare Within Social Activation Policies'. In Duncan Gallie (ed.): *Resisting Marginalization. Unemployment Experience and Social Policy in the European Union.* Oxford: Oxford University Press, pp. 197–222.

Lødemel, Ivar and Heather Trickey (2001). *An Offer You Can't Refuse. Workfare in International Perspective.* Bristol: The Policy Press.

Mahoney, Christine (2007). 'Networking vs. Allying: The Decision of Interest Groups to Join Coalition in the U.S. and the EU. *Journal of European Public Policy*, 14(2), 366–383.

Mair, Peter (1997). 'EE Schattschneider's the Semisovereign People'. *Political Studies*, 45(5), 947–954.

Marcus, George E., Russell W. Neuman and Michael MacKuen (2000). Affective Intelligence and Political Judgments. Chicago: University of Chicago Press.

Manin, Bernard (1997). *The Principles of Representative Government.* Cambridge: Cambridge University Press.

Mancini, Paolo (1997). 'Professioneller Journalismus in Italien zwischen traditionellen Wurzeln und Anforderungen des Marktes: Eine Übersicht über wesentliche Charakteristika'. In Gert G. Kpper and Paolo Mancini: *Kulturen des Journalismus und politische Systeme.* Dortmund: Vistas, pp. 93–108.

Martin, Cathie J. (2004). 'Reinventing Welfare Regimes: Employers and the Implementation of Active Social Policy'. *World Politics*, 57(1), 39–69.

Martin, Cathie J. and Kathleen Thelen (2007). 'The State and Coordinated Capitalism: Contributions of the Public Sector to Social Solidarity in Postindustrial Societies'. *World Politics*, 60(1), 1–36.

Mazzoleni, Gianpietro (2008). 'Populism and the Media'. In Daniele Albertazzi and Duncan McDonnel (eds.): *Twenty-first Century Populism. The Spectre of Western European Democracy*. Basingstoke: Palgrave, pp. 49–64.

McAdam, Doug, Sidney Tarrow and Charles Tilly (2001). *Dynamics of Contention*. Cambridge: Cambridge University Press.

McClosky, Herbert and Dennis Chong (1985). 'Similarities and Differences Between Left-wing and Right-wing Radicals'. *British Journal of Political Science*, 15(3), 329–363.

McQuail, Dennis (1992). *Media Performance: Mass Communication and the Public Interest*. London: Sage.

McQuail, Dennis and Jan J. Cuilenburg (1983). 'Diversity as a Media Policy Goal'. *Gazette*, 31(3), 145–162.

Mearsheimer, John J. (2001). *The Tragedy of Great Power Politics*. New York: Norton.

Meguid, Bonnie M. (2005). 'Competition Between Unequals: The Role of Mainstream Party Strategy in Niche Party Success'. *American Political Science Review*, 99(3), 347–359.

Morel, Nathalie, Bruno Palier and Joakim Palme (2012). Towards a Social Investment Welfare State? Ideas, Policies, and Challenges. Bristol: Chicago Policy Press.

Morris, Dick (1999). *The New Prince: Machiavelli Update for the Twenty-first Century*. Los Angeles: Renaissance Boooks.

Müller, Lisa (2014). *Comparing Mass Media in Established Democracies: Patterns of Media Performance*. Basingstoke: Palgrage Macmillan.

Myles, J. and J. Quadagno (2002). 'Political Theories of the Welfare State'. *Social Service Review*, 76 (1), 34–57.

Nadeau, Rihard, Neil Nevitte, Elisabeth Gidengil and André Blais (2008). 'Election Campaigns as Information Campaigns: Who Learns What and Does it Matter?' *Political Communication*, 25(3), 229–248.

Nai, Alessandro (2013). 'What Really Matters is Which Camp Goes Dirty: Differential Effects of Negative Campaigning on Turnout During Swiss Federal Ballots'. *European Journal of Political Research*, 52(1), 44–70.

Nelson, Thomas E., Zoe M. Oxley and Rosalee A. Clawson (1997). Toward a Psychology of Framing Effects. *Political Behavior*, 19(3), 221–246.

Neuman, W. Russell (1990). 'The Threshold of Public Attention'. *Public Opinion Quarterly*, 54(2), 159–176.

Nowlin, Matthew C. (2011). 'Theories of the Policy Process: State of the Research and Emerging Trends'. *The Policy Studies Journal*, 39(1), 41–60.

Oesch, Daniel (2006). *Redrawing the Class Map. Stratification and Institutions in Britain, Germany, Sweden and Switzerland*. Basingstoke: Palgrave Macmillan.

Oesch, Daniel (2007). 'Weniger Koordination, mehr Markt? Kollektive Arbeitsbeziehungen und Neokorporatismus in der Schweiz seit 1990'. *Swiss Political Science Review*, 13(3), 337–368.

Opedal, Ståle, Hilmar Rommetvedt and Karsten Vrangbæk (2012). 'Organised Interests, Authority Structures and Political Influence: Danish and Norwegian Patient Groups Compared'. *Scandinavian Political Studies*, 35(1), 1–21.

O'Reilly, Tim (2005). *What is Web 2.0? Design Patterns and Business Models for the Next Generation of Software*. http://www.oreillynet.com/lpt/a/6228.

OECD (Organization for Economic Co-operation and Development) (2006). *OECD Employment Outlook: Boosting Jobs and Incomes*. Paris.

Ossipow, William (1994). 'Le système politique Suisse ou l'art de la compensation'. In Yannis Papadopoulos (ed.): *Elites politiques et peuple en Suisse : Analyse des votations fédérales (1970–1987.)* Lausanne: Réalités sociales, pp. 9–56.

Palier, Bruno (2010). 'The Dualization of the French Welfare State'. In Bruno Palier (ed.): *A Long Goodbye to Bismarck?* Amsterdam: Amsterdam University Press, pp. 73–99.

Palier, Bruno and Kathleen Thelen (2010). 'Dualization and Institutional Complementarities. Industrial Relations, Labor Market, and Welfare State Changes in France and Germany'. In Patrick Emmenegger, Silja Häusermann, Bruno Palier and Martin Seeleib-Kaiser (eds.): *The Age of Dualization*. Oxford: Oxford University Press, pp. 201–225.

Petrocik, John R. (1996). 'Issue Ownership in Presidential Elections with a 1980 Case Study'. *American Journal of Political Science*, 40(3), 825–850.

Petty, R E., P. Briñol and J. R. Prieser (2009). 'Mass Media Attitude Change: Implications of the Elaboration Likelihood Model of Persuasion'. In J. Bryant and M. B. Oliver (eds.): *Media Effects: Advanves in Theory and Research*. New York: Routledge, pp. 125–164.

Pfetsch, Barbara (2003). *Politische Kommunikationskultur, Politische Sprecher und Journalisten in der Bundesrepublik und den USA im Vergleich*. Wiesbaden: Westdeutscher Verlag.

Pfetsch, Barbara (2004). 'From Political Culture to Political Communications Culture: A Theoretical Approach to Comparative Analysis'. In Frank Esser and Barbara Pfetsch (eds.): *Comparing Political Communication. Theories, Cases, and Challenges*. Cambridge: Cambridge University Press, pp. 344–366.

Pfetsch, Barbara (ed.) (2014). *Political Communication Cultures in Europe: Attitudes of Political Actors and Journalists in Nine Countries*. Basingstoke: Palgrave Macmillan.

Pierson, Paul (1994). *Dismantling the Welfare State: Reagan, Thatcher, and the Politics of Retrenchment*. Cambridge: Cambridge University Press.

Pierson, Paul (1996). 'The New Politics of the Welfare State'. *World Politics*, 48(2), 143–179.

Pontusson, Jonas and Damian Raess (2012). 'How (and Why) Is This Time Different? The Politics of Economic Crisis in Western Europe and the United States'. *Annual Review of Political Science*, 15(1), 13–33.

Porto, Mauro P. (2007). 'Frame Diversity and Citizen Competence: Towards a Critical Approach to News Quality'. *Critical Studies in Media Communication*, 24(4), 303–321.

Regini, Marino (2000). 'Between Deregulation and Social Pacts: The Responses of European Economies to Globalization'. *Politics and Society*, 28(1), 5–33.

Rhodes, Martin (2001). 'The Political Economy of Social Pacts: Competitive Corporatism and European Welfare Reform'. In Paul Pierson (ed.): *The New Politics of the Welfare State*. Oxford: Oxford University Press, pp. 165–194.

Rietig, Katharina (2014). '"Neutral" Experts? How Input of Scientific Expertise Matters in International Environmental Negotiations'. *Policy Sciences*, 47(2), 141–160.

Riker, William H. (1996). *The Strategy of Rhetoric for the American Constitution*. New Heaven: Yale University Press.

Rueda, David (2005). 'Insider–outsider Politics in Industrialized Democracies: The Challenge to Social Democratic Parties'. *American Political Science Review*, 99(1), 61–74.

Rueda, David (2006). 'Social Democracy and Active Labour-Market Policies: Insiders, Outsiders and the Politics of Employment Promotion'. *British Journal of Political Science*, 36(3), 385–406.

Rueda, David (2007). *Social Democracy Inside Out: Government Partisanship, Insiders, and Outsiders in Industrialized Democracies*. Oxford: Oxford University Press.

Sabatier, Paul A. (1987). 'Knowledge, Policy-oriented Learning, and Policy Change: An Advocacy Coalition Framework'. *Science Communication*, 8(4), 649–692.

Sabatier, Paul A. (1988). 'An Advocacy Coalition Framework of Policy Change and the Role of Policy-oriented Learning Therein'. *Policy Sciences*, 21(2), 129–168.

Sabatier, Paul A. and Hank C. Jenkins-Smith (1988). 'Special Issue: Policy Change and Policy-oriented Learning: Exploring an Advocacy Coalition Framework'. *Policy Sciences*, 21(2), 123–278.

Sabatier, Paul A. and Hank C. Jenkins-Smith (1993). *Policy Change and Learning: An Advocacy Coalition Approach*. Boulder: Westview.

Sabatier, Paul A. and Hank C. Jenkins-Smith (1999). 'The Advocacy Coalition Framework: An Assessment'. In Paul A. Sabatier (ed.): *Theories of the Policy Process*. Boulder: Westview, pp. 117–166.

Sabatier, Paul A. and Christopher M. Weible (2007). 'The Advocacy Coalition Framework: Innovations and Clarifications'. In Paul A. Sabatier (ed.): Theories of the Policy Process. Boulder: Westview (2nd edition), pp. 189–220.

Sacchi, Stefano, Stefano Pancaldi and Claudia Arisi (2011). 'The Economic Crisis as a Trigger of Convergence? Short-time Work in Italy, Germany and Austria'. *Social Policy and Administration*, 45(4), 465–487.

Scharpf, Fritz (1981). The Political Economy of Inflation and Unemployment in Western Europe: An Outline. Berlin: WZB.

Scharpf, Fritz (1984). 'Economic and Institutional Constraints of Full Employment Strategies: Sweden, Austria, and West Germany, 1973–1982'. In John H. Goldthorpe (ed.): *Order and Conflict in Contemporary Capitalism: Studies in the Political Economy of Western European Nations*. Oxford: Oxford University Press, pp. 257–290.

Scharpf, Fritz W. (1997). *Games Real Actors Play. Actor-centered Institutionalism in Policy Research*. Oxford: Westview Press.

Scharpf, Fritz W. (2011). 'Monetary Union, Fiscal Crisis and the Preemption of Democracy'. Cologne, *MPIfG Discussion Paper* 11/11.

Schattschneider, Elmer E. (1975 [1960]). *The Semisovereign People: A Realists' View of Democracy in America*. New York: Wadsworth Thomson Learning.

Schlager, Edella (1995). 'Policy Making and Collective Action: Defining Coalitions Within the Advocacy Coalition Framework'. *Policy Sciences*, 28(3), 243–270.

Schmidt, Vivien A. (2008). 'European Political Economy: Labor Out, State Back in, Firm to the Fore'. *West European Politics*, 31(1–2), 302–320.

Schmidt, Vivien A. (2009). 'Putting the Political Back into Political Economy by Bringing the State Back in Yet Again'. *World Politics* 61, 3: 516–546.

Schmitt-Beck, Rüdiger and David M. Farrell (2002). Studying Political Campaigns and Their Effects. In David M. Farrell and Rüdiger Beck-Schmitt (eds.): *Do Political Campaigns Matter? Campaign Effects in Elections and Referendums*. London: Routledge, pp. 1–21.

Schmitter, Philippe C. (1982). 'Reflections on Where the Theory of Corporatism Has Gone and Where the Praxis of Neo-corporatism May Be Going'. In Gerhard Lehmbruch and Philippe C. Schmitter (eds.): *Patterns of Corporatist Policy-making*. London: Sage, pp. 259–290.

Schmitter Philippe C. and Gerhard Lehmbruch (eds.) (1979). *Trends Toward Corporatist Intermediation*. London: Sage.

Schneider, Martin R. and Mihai Paunescu (2012). Changing Varieties of Capitalism and Revealed Comparative Advantages from 1990 to 2005: A Test of the Hall and Soskice Claims, *Socio-economic Review* 10(4): 731–753.

Schudson, Michael (2002). 'The News Media as Political Institutions'. *Annual Review of Political Science*, 5, 249–269.

Schulz, Winfried (1976). *Die Konstruktion von Realität in den Nachrichtenmedien*. Freiburg/München: Verlag Karl Alber.

Schulz, Winfried (1997). *Politische Kommunikation: Theoretische Ansätze und Ergebnisse empirischer Forschung zur Rolle der Massenmedien in der Politik*. Opladen: Westdeutscher Verlag.

Schwander, Hanna (2012). *Social Democratic Parties as Insider-parties? Counter-Evidence from France, Germany, and Great Britain*. Paper prepared for the annual *Congress of Swiss Political Science Association* in Lucerne, Switzerland, 2–3 February 2012.

Seco (2010). *Faktenblatt: Warum das Gesetz über die Arbeitslosenversicherung revidiert wird*. Bern.

Seco (2011). *Wirtschaftliche Lagebeurteilung im Licht des Schweizer Frankens*. Bern: Press release published on 14 January 2011.

Seeleib-Kaiser, Martin and Timo Fleckenstein (2006). *Discourse, Learning and Welfare State Change. The Case of German Labour Market Reforms*. Working Paper.

Shoemaker, Pamela J. and Stephen D. Reese (1996). *Mediating the Message. Theories of Influences on Mass Media Content*. White Plains: Longman Publisher (2nd edition).

Siaroff, Alan (1999). 'Corporatism on 24 Industrial Democracies: Meaning and Measurement'. *European Journal of Political Research*, 36(2), 175–205.

Sides, John, Daron Shaw, Matt Grossmann and Keena Lipsitz (2015). *Campaigns and Elections: Rules, Reality, Strategy, Choice.* New York. W. W. Norton (2nd edition).

Slothuus, Rune (2008). 'More Than Weighting Cognitive Importance: A Dual Process Model of Issue Framing Effects'. *Political Psychology*, 29(1), 1–28.

Slothuus, Rune (2010). 'When Can Political Parties Lead Public Opinion? Evidence from a Natural Experiment'. *Political Communication*, 27(2), 158–177.

Smith, Duncan I. (2010). *Universal Credit: Welfare that Works.* London.

Sniderman, Paul M. and Sean M. Theriault (2004). 'The Structure of Political Argument and the Logic of Issue Framing'. In Paul M. Sniderman and Sean M. Theriault (eds.): *Studies in Public Opinion: Attitudes, Nonattitudes, Measurement Error and Change.* Princeton: Princeton University Press, pp. 133–165.

Soroka, Stuar N. and Christopher Wlezien (2010). *Degrees of Democracy: Politics, Public Opinion, and Policy.* Cambridge: Cambridge University Press.

Stiller, Sabina and Minna van Gerven (2012). 'The European Employment Strategy and National Core Executives: Impacts on Activation Reforms in the Netherlands and Germany'. *Journal of European Social Policy*, 22(2), 118–132.

Stimson, James A. (2015). Tides of Consent: How Public Opinion Shapes American Politics. Cambridge: Cambridge University Press (2nd edition).

Stimson, James A, Michael B. Mackuen and Robert S. Erikson (1995). 'Dynamic Representation'. *American Political Science Review*, 89(3), 543–565.

Streeck, Wolfgang (2009). *Re-forming Capitalism: Institutional Change in the German Political Economy.* Oxford: Oxford University Press.

Stroebe, Wolfgang (2007). 'Strategies of Attitude and Behavior Change'. In Klaus Jonas, Wolfgang Stroebe and Miles Hewstone (eds.): *Sozialpsychologie.* Berlin: Springer, pp. 225–264.

Strömbäck, Jesper (2005). 'In Search of a Standard: Four Models of Democracy and Their Normative Implications for Journalism'. *Journalism Studies*, 6(3), 331–345.

Strömbäck, Jesper (2008). 'Four Phases of Mediatization: An Analysis of the Mediatization of Politics'. *The International Journal of Press/Politics*, 3(13), 228–246.

Strömbäck, Jesper and Lars Nord (2006). 'Do Politicians Lead the Tango?' *European Journal of Communication*, 21(2), 147–164.

Swanson, David L. and Paolo Mancini (1996). *Politics, Media, and Modern Democracy. An International Study of Innovations in Electoral Campaigning and Their Consequences.* London: Praeger.

Swenson, Peter (1991). 'Bringing Capital Back in, or Social Democracy Reconsidered: Employer Power, Cross Class Alliances and Centralization of Industrial Relations in Denmark and Sweden'. *World Politics*, 43(3), 513–544.

Szarka, Joseph (2010). 'Bringing Interests Back in: Using Coalition Theories to Explain European Wind Power Policies'. *Journal of European Public Policy*, 17(6), 836–852.

Tarrow, Sidney (2008). 'Charles Tilly and the Practice of Contentious Politics'. *Social Movement Studies*, 7(3), 225–246.

Taylor-Gooby, Peter (2005). 'New Risks and Social Change'. In Peter Taylor-Gooby (ed): *New Risks, New Welfare. The Transformation of the European Welfare State*. Oxford: Oxford University Press, pp. 1–28.

Taylor-Gooby, Peter and Trine P. Larsen (2005). 'The UK – A Test Case for the Liberal Welfare State?'. In Peter Taylor-Gooby (ed): *New Risks, New Welfare. The Transformation of the European Welfare State*. Oxford: Oxford University Press, pp. 57–82.

Taylor-Gooby, Peter and Gerry Stoker (2011). 'The Coalition Programme: A New Vision for Britain or Politics as Usual?'. *The Political Quarterly*, 82(1), 4–15.

Taylor-Gooby, Peter (2012). 'Root and Branch Restructuring to Achieve Major Cuts: The Social Policy Programme of the 2010 UK Coalition Government'. *Social Policy and Administration*, 46(1), 61–82.

Tewksbury, David, Jennifer Jones, Matthew W. Peske, Ashlea Raymond and William Vig (2000). 'The Interaction of News and Advocate Frames: Manipulating Audience Perceptions of a Local Public Policy Issue'. *Journalism and Mass Communication Quarterly*, 77(4), 804–829.

Thelen, Kathleen (2001). 'Varieties of Labor Politics in the Developed Democracies'. In Peter A. Hall and David Soskice (eds): *Varieties of Capitalism: The Institutional Foundations of Comparative Advantage*. Oxford: Oxford University Press.

Thelen, Kathleen (2012). 'Varieties of Capitalism: Trajectories of Liberalization and the New Politics of Social Solidarity'. *Annual Review of Political Science*, 15, 2.1–2.23.

Thelen, Kathleen and Christa van Wijnbergen (2003). 'The Paradox of Globalization: Labor Relations in Germany and Beyond'. *Comparative Political Studies*, 36(8), 859–880.

Therborn, Göran (1986). *Why Some Peoples Are More Unemployed Than Others*. London: Verso.

Tilly, Charles (1978). *From Mobilization to Revolution*. Indianapolis: Addison-wesley

Tilly, Charles (1995). *Popular Contention in Great Britain, 1758–1834*. Cambridge: Harvard University Press.

Tilly, Charles (2008). *Contentious Performances*. Cambridge: Cambridge University Press.

Torfing, Jacob (1999). 'Towards a Schumpeterian Workfare Post National Regime: Path-shaping and Path-dependency in Danish Welfare State Reform'. *Economy and Society*, 28(3), 369–402.

Treu, Tiziano (1994). 'Procedures and Institutions of Incomes Policy in Italy'. In Ronald Dore, Robert Boyer and Zoe Mars (eds.): *The Return of Income Policy*. London: Printer, pp. 161–174.

Trickey, Heather and Robert Walker (2001). 'Steps to Compulsion Within British Labour Market Policies'. In Ivar Lødemel and Heather Trickey (eds.): *'An Offer You Can't Refuse'. Workfare in International Perspective*. Bristol: The Policy Press, pp. 181–213.

True, James L., Bryan D. Jones and Frank R. Baumgartner (2007). 'Punctuated-Equilibrium Theory: Explaining Stability and Change in Public Policymaking'. In Paul A. Sabatier (ed.): *Theories of the Policy Process*. Boulder: Westview (2nd edition), pp. 155–187.

Tsebelis, George (2002). *Veto Players: How Political Institutions Work*. Princeton: Princeton University Press.

Valkenburg, Patti M., Holli A. Semetko and Claes H. de Vreese (1999). 'The Effects of News Frames on Readers Thoughts and Recall'. *Communication Research*, 26(5), 550–569.

Vergeer, Maurice, Liesbeth Hermans and Steven Sams (2011). 'Online Social Networks and Micro-blogging in Political Campaigning: The Exploration of a New Campaign Tool and a New Campaign Style'. *Party Politics*, 30(1), 1–25.

van Dalen, Arjen (2012). 'Structural Bias in Cross-national Perspective: How Political Systems and Journalism Cultures Influence Government Dominance in the News'. *International Journal of Press/Politics*, 17(1), 32–55.

van Dalen, Arjen, Claes de Vreese and Erik Albæk (2012). 'Different Roles, Different Content? A Four-country Comparison of the Conceptions and Reporting Style of Political Journalists'. *Journalism*, 13(7), 901–920.

van der Meer, Tom W. G., Annemarie Walter and Peter van Aelst (2016). 'The Contingency of Voter Learning: How Election Debates Influenced Voters' Ability and Accuracy to Position Parties in the 2010 Dutch Election Campaign'. *Political Communication*, 33(1), 136–157.

van der Wurff, Richard (2011). 'Do Audiences Receive Diverse Ideas From News Media? Exposure to a Variety of News Media and Personal Characteristics as Determinants of Diversity as Received'. *European Journal of Communication*, 26(4), 328–342.

Vliegenthart, Rens and Liesbet van Zoonen (2011). 'Power to the Frame: Bringing Sociology Back to Frame Analysis'. *European Journal of Communication*, 26(1), 101–115.

Voakes, Paul S., Jack Kapfer, David Kurpius and David Shano-Yeon Chern (1996). 'Diversity in the News: A Conceptual and Methodological Framework'. *Journalism and Mass Communication Quarterly*, 73 (3), 582–593.

Walgrave, Stefan and Jan Manssens (2000). The Making of the White March: The Mass Media as a Mobilizing Alternative to Movement Organizations, *Mobilization* 5(2), 217–39.

Walgrave, Stefaan and Peter van Aelst (2006). 'The Contingency of the Mass Media's Political Agenda Setting Power: Toward a Preliminary Theory'. *Journalism of Communication*, 56(1), 88–109.

Ward, Stephen and Rachel Gibson (2009). 'European Political Organizations and the Internet: Mobilization, Participation, and Change'. In Andrew Chadwick and Philip N. Howard (eds.): *Handbook of Internet Politics*. New York: Routledge, pp. 25–39.

Wassermann, Stanley and Katherine Faust (1994). *Social Network Analysis: Methods and Applications*. Cambridge: Cambridge University Press.

Watson, Roland (2010). 'Benefits: Three Strikes and You're Out'. *The Times*. 11th November.

Wessler, Hartumt (2008). 'Investigating Deliberativeness Comparatively'. *Political Communication*, 25(1), 1–22.

Wien, Charlotte and Christian Elmelund-Præstekær (2009). 'An Anatomy of Media-Hypes: Developing a Model for the Dynamics and Structure of

Intense Media Coverage of Single Issues'. *European Journal of Communication*, 24(2), 183–201.

Woldendorp, Jaap (2011). *Corporatism in Small North-West European Countries 1970–2006: Business as Usual, Decline, or a New Phenomenon*. Amsterdam: Working Paper.

Wolfsfeld, Gadi (1997). *Media and Political Conflict. News from the Middle East*. Cambridge: Cambridge University Press.

Wolfsfeld, Gadi and Tamir Scheafer (2006). 'Competing Actors and the Construction of Political News: The Contest over Waves in Israel'. *Political Communication*, 23(3), 333–354.

Zaller, John R. 1992). *The Nature and Origin of Public Opinion*. Cambridge: Cambridge University Press.

Zhang, Weiyu, Xiaoxia Cao and Minh Ngok Tram (2013). 'The Structural Features and the Deliberative Quality of Online Discussions'. *Telematic and Informatics*, 30(2), 74–86.

Index

in Denmark, 138–42, 160, 164–65, 171
in deregulated labor market regimes,
   145–47
in dualized labor market regimes, 142–45
in flexicurity labor market regimes,
   138–42
in France, 142–45, 160, 165–67, 171
in Germany, 142–45, 160, 162–63, 170
in Italy, 142–45, 160, 166–67, 172
in Switzerland, 138–42, 160, 172
in the United Kingdom, 138–39, 145–47,
   160, 163–64, 170–71
objective versus subjective type of, 121,
   169–70
role of reform project in formation of, 157
role of reform projects in, 154
role of veto players in, 154, 157–60, 298
third-way type of, 137
traditional class-based, 139–42
typology of, 135–36, 138
labor market conditions. *See also*
   unemployment; long-term
   unemployment; youth
   unemployment
labor market conflict
as multidimensional, 28, 121–23,
   127–28, 131, 132, 148–50, 298–99
cross-national variation in, 123–26,
   129–35
recent activation axis of, 27, 120–21,
   127–28, 132, 135, 148–50, 298–99
scholarly debates over, 119–21
traditional socioeconomic axis of, 28,
   120–21, 127–28, 131, 135, 148–50,
   157, 237, 298–99
labor market policy
influence of policy legacies on, 15
labor market actors views on, 216–18
limited supranationalization of, 109, 114,
   156, 292
reform of
   scholarly debate, 119–20
labor market regimes, 55
and problem pressures, 295
definition of, 40, 55–58
four-fold typology of, 57–58
influence on policy debates of, 40
legacies of, 123
labor unions
organizational strength of, 52
relative labor market power of, 100–2
Labour Party (United Kingdom), 111, 139,
   146–47, 150, 159, 163–64, 170–71,
   240–42, 247, 251
Lega Nord, 105, 111, 113, 142–44, 166–67

Liberal Alliance (Danish political party), 79
Liberal Democrats (United Kingdom),
   105, 111, 113, 146–47, 163–64,
   240–41
liberal media systems, 263–69
Local Government Denmark (KL), 78, 80
Lutte ouvrière (French political party),
   142–44, 165–66, 245–46, 278

Marchionne, Sergio, 89, 92, 296
Mayr-Melnhof (Swiss industrial group),
   235, 243, 252–54
MEDEF (French employers' association),
   88, 110, 113, 142–44, 165–66,
   245–46, 278
media systems
'media logic' versus 'political logic',
   45–47, 49, 260
democratic corporatist type of, 5
influence on policy debates, 31
liberal type of, 5
polarized pluralist type of, 5
varieties of, 47–50, 263–69
Merkel, Angela, 251–52
mini-jobs (Germany), 62
Ministry of Finance (Denmark), 110, 112
Ministry of Finance (Italy), 111, 112
Ministry of Labor (Denmark), 164–65
Ministry of Labor (France), 112, 142–44,
   165–67, 245–46
Ministry of Labor (Italy), 111, 142–45, 161,
   166–67
MNCP (French NGO), 142–44, 165–66,
   181, 245–46
Movimento Associazione Lavoratori
   Vittime del Precariato (Italian
   NGO), 142–44, 161, 166–67

National Bank of Switzerland (SNB), 27,
   83, 84, 85, 208
National Democratic Party of Germany
   (NPD), 142–44, 161, 242–43,
   280
National Labor Market Authority of
   Denmark (NLMA), 110, 139–42
National Youth Agency (British interest
   group), 146–47, 163–64, 170–71,
   240–41
NCCR-Democracy, 8
negative campaigning, 234, 250–56
in France, 251
in Germany, 250–52
in Switzerland, 250–51
in the United Kingdom, 250–51
neoliberalism, 101, 102, 124, 137

338   Index